THE BASIC THEORY O

The Forms and Substance

*Also by Makoto Itoh*

VALUE AND CRISIS
THE VALUE CONTROVERSY (*with Ian Steedman, Paul Sweezy and others*)

*In Japanese*
CONTEMPORARY CAPITALISM
MARXIAN ECONOMICS TODAY
(*and other works*)

# The Basic Theory of Capitalism

## The Forms and Substance of the Capitalist Economy

Makoto Itoh

*Professor of Economics*
*University of Tokyo*

M

MACMILLAN
PRESS

First published 1988
Reprinted 1988

Published by
THE MACMILLAN PRESS LTD
Houndmills, Basingstoke, Hampshire RG21 2XS
and London
Companies and representatives
throughout the world

Printed in Hong Kong

British Library Cataloguing in Publication Data
Itoh, Makoto
The basic theory of capitalism: the forms
and substance of the capitalist economy.
1. Capitalism
I. Title
330.12′2 HB501
ISBN 0-333-37284-0 (hardcover)
ISBN 0-333-37285-9 (paperback)

# Contents

# Preface

We are living in a peculiar and uncertain age – a *fin de siècle*. After a century in which the historical evolution of capitalism increasingly strengthened the economic role of the state, the capitalist world seems suddenly to have lost any sense of progress as it experiences the great depression which began in 1973. There has spread an overall disillusion with views that state policies of either a Keynesian or Monetarist sort can prevent or mitigate economic instability and distress. Indeed, it is asked whether they are not rather aggravating the disasters. Such serious doubt and disillusion are combined in economic theory with the damage to the analytical foundation of neoclassical price theory given by both the so-called capital controversy and recent Marxian critiques, and thus present a deep crisis for orthodox marginalist economic theories. This constitutes an important element of the general crisis and distrust in the conventional social sciences, within the framework of bourgeois ideology, which regards the capitalist social order as natural. As a result, an irrational nationalism and militarism has tended to gain ground, often alongside a general indifference to substantial socio-economic problems even among young students.

It is ironic to see that despite all this, in the very process of the great depression in our age, capitalism seems to be strongly reasserting the workings of its intrinsic and violent law of motion rather than weakening itself. What has been weakened is rather the social position of workers and their trade-union organisations. The economic position of the 'third world' countries has also generally been worsened. The actions of capitalist firms to increase the efficiency of the valorisation process through 'rationalisation' and restructuring are so much facilitated. 'The social structure of accumulation' of capitals seems to be under reconstruction in full scale throughout the capitalist world.

In spite of the actual deep crisis in the capitalist economy, as well as in bourgeois social thought, the socialist movement is not gaining, but rather suffering with the weakening social position of workers. Moreover, added to it, there have been problematic situations in the existing socialist countries, including international conflicts – even wars and military invasion – among them. The process of the cultural revolution in China, the weak social position of workers expressed in the Polish solidarity movement and the role of orthodox Marxian theories which tend uncritically to legitimise the status quo in those countries are some of these issues. The gap between the ideal and the reality of socialism generally seems great. Socialism, including Marxism, as an alternative to capitalism is thus also in crisis. This element was not present in the preceding historical crises during the great depressions in the late nineteenth century and in 1930s. The feeling of proceeding along the blind alley of the capitalist world at the end of our century must thus be heavier. We have to recognise that human history as a whole, across the West and the East, as well as the North and the South, is on serious trial.

What can we do for the future? Even if it may seem roundabout, one of the surest ways intellectually to overcome the sense of the impasse of human history at this time, must be in our attempt non-dogmatically to revive the potential of Marxian theory as a sounder social science. It is indispensable not merely for a proper and systematic understanding of the workings of capitalism, which is actually being restrengthened, but also for our re-examination of what socialism can do as an alternative to capitalism. The revival of the Western Marxian economic school since the 1970s must incorporate this intention. Let us co-operate internationally and strive further to push forward in this direction.

Due to the basic character of a capitalist economy itself, as we shall discuss in this volume, our analytical understanding of its working cannot be satisfactory as fragments and separated theories. Marx's *Capital*, if with not a few incompletenesses, convinces us among others of the necessity for a systematic and consistent method of treating the working of the capitalist economy. Through fervent controversies on, and studies of, Marxian theories of value, skilled labour, joint products, the transformation problem, business cycles and crises – which are still vividly proceeding – we have to reconsider from time to time both the implications and the location of each topic concerned in the light of the whole conceivable system of the basic theory of capitalism. We may lose a sound sense of our orientation without such reflection. After so many years of theoretical *Sturm und Drang* in the process of the recent revival and growth of the Western Marxian school in political economy it must be high time for us to attempt to materialise such a total theoretical system anew. While lecturing and giving seminars in various universities in Europe and North America from 1974, I began to be convinced of such a necessity. *Capital* or P. Sweezy's *The Theory of Capitalist Development* (1942), for example, would no longer suffice, though they must surely serve as classical foundations.

I also intended, in preparing this book, to explore my possible contributions to the basic theory of capitalism by attempting systematically to solve a series of recent controversial problems in the West from the view of Japanese Uno theory. As I described in my previous book, *Value and Crisis* (1980), there is a rich tradition in Marxian economic thought in Japan, dating back to the First World War. Upon such a historical basis, K. Uno's works of the post-Second World War period were distinguished and influenced our generation to form the Uno School. The separation of the task of Marxian social science from the role of ideological thought; the methodological distinction of the levels of research in Marxian political economy into the basic principles, the stages theory of capitalist development and the empirical analyses of the current situation; and the extensive study of Marx's *Capital* as the principles of political economy are the main characteristics of the Uno School. In the area of the basic principles the importance of the forms of value and commodity economy for capitalism to organise its substantial socio-economic activity, based on the labour process, is much emphasised as a kernel of Marx's original theory clarifying the historical specificity of capitalism.

As we shall see in Part I of this book, these viewpoints are all very relevant to the clarification of the fundamental orientation and tasks of Marxian political economy against the long historical development of various other economic schools. The basic theoretical meanings of current controversies and conflicts between neo-classical, neo-Ricardian and Marxian schools, or among Marxians themselves, as we shall discuss in Part II and III, then become more consistently and easily understandable. Especially a deeper and sharper analytical concern about the form and substance of the capitalist economy is essential for our proper understanding of the basic character and working of capitalism, as well as for the solution of the recent controversies.

While dealing with the recent Western theoretical debates and complications I had naturally to re-examine and extend my own positions as a Uno theorist. I also felt it rather fortunate to have an opportunity to reconsider systematically such topics as the importance of the development of economic theories along the lines of neo-Ricardians and its impact on Marxian theories; the contents of the law of value including the elasticity in the distribution of surplus labour; the perplexed issues on skilled labour, joint production and the transformation from values to prices of production: the basic theory of regular business cycles and long waves; and some theoretical implications for conceivable socialism which are deducible from our basic theory of capitalism. Since ready-made answers for these were either not given or remained unsatisfactory, I had to strike out from Uno's own theoretical treatments, often consciously as Japanese readers might well and easily notice. Just as Uno did to Marx, I tried to think by myself what Marx and Uno would argue on these issues today.

It must be left to the reader's judgement how far the author has successfully achieved the initial intentions stated above. I shall look forward to critiques and comments for the further development of our common theories. I can just hope that this book is properly oriented and of some use for the further theoretical growth of Marxian political economy as a sound social science, which would at least enable us intellectually to surmount irrational reaction and conscious or unconscious nihilism towards human social progress.

It happens to be exactly twenty years since I began continuously to give lecture courses and seminars on the principles of political economy in our Department of Economics, at the University of Tokyo. I have been fortunate in having excellent forerunners, colleagues and good students here in Japan, to whom my debts are obvious. In particular, communications and discussions with Nabuo Okiskio, Tsuyoshi Sakurai, Shigekatsu Yamaguchi and Michiaki Obata among others have been encouraging and helpful in the writing this book. Since my previous book, *Value and Crisis*, served as a good preparation for this volume, my acknowledgements stated in its Preface to comradely friends in the West should remain, though I will not repeat all of their names again. Among them, Andrew Glyn and Bob Rowthorn read the whole manuscript of this book, and continuously provided useful advice. By happy chance both of them separately visited me here in Tokyo recently, and directly discussed with me portions of the manuscript. Though I could not follow some of their advice, this book is deeply indebted to them. Let me also state my thanks for arranging my visits to, and my teaching at, the New School for Social Research in 1978 to Anwar Shaikh; at New York University in 1978 to Jim Becker; at Cambridge University and Queen Mary College in the University of London in 1980 to Bob Rowthorn,

Simon Mohun and Sue Himmelweit; and at the University of Manitoba in 1985 to John Loxley and Cy Gonick.

All these opportunities were most helpful to me in preparing and writing this book. Last but not least, my gratitude to Paul Bullock who with his thorough understanding of the issues discussed, and a firm grasp of my arguments carefully and perseveringly edited my English and prepared the index.

Though I am certainly responsible for whatever imperfections this book may contain, I feel with some satisfaction that it incorporates not just my individual views but the broader associated achievements in the subject in the recent decades, both in Japan and in the West effecting in its contents, as in the process of its birth, international co-operation and communication in the field of Marxian political economy.

MAKOTO ITOH

## EDITOR'S NOTE

In correcting the manuscript of this book I have endeavoured to ensure that the arguments of the author are presented as he intends. Our friendship over thirteen years, and our own understanding of the differences between us on the issues discussed, have helped me in this task.

PAUL BULLOCK

# Part I
# Economic Schools and Ideologies

Capitalism is a special social formation where both the selling and buying of commodities organised by capital dominate human economic activities. As capitalism began to develop in Western Europe, from about the sixteenth century, economic theories also began to evolve as a specific field of social sciences. It was not a mere coincidence nor simply part of a new tendency for modern sciences to grow separately from a comprehensive system of theology or philosophy. On the one hand, capitalism broadened and complicated social relations in production, distribution and consumption. The social mechanism of economic life, which was now carried on through commodities, money and capital, not only became more and more important for society but it was also impossible to fully understand it merely by daily common sense. On the other hand, economic activities based on commodity transactions, unlike those in various precapitalist societies, basically tended to be self-operating and became independent of extra-economic, religious and political forces. Consequently political economy grew as an independent and basic social science alongside the development of capitalism.

In its process of growth and development, the study of the capitalist economy gave rise to various schools. The distinctions among major schools are apparently linked with the different frameworks of ideologies. Ideology can roughly be defined here as a more or less total system of social thought, or 'a co-ordinated set of beliefs and ideas' which is historically relative and apt to be related with a certain political position.[1] A new school of economic theory often arises in order to support a new political perspective, and this school may then become popular as a logical basis for such an ideology, reflecting the direction of social change and developing social interests. In most cases the new social thought and its theoretical expression asserted their universal objectivity and truth, and criticised the older or the other as being partial, distorted and one-sided, or totally wrong.

However, the successive changes of dominant schools of economic theories cannot be regarded simply as a continuous progress toward objective truth. For one thing it is difficult to compare the absolute degree of objectivity or truth between various schools when their main aims of researches do not have identical frameworks. The relations between each major school of economic theory and its guiding ideology also differ. The positive roles and negative limitations of ideological views are often inseparable from their theoretical content, and tend to be completely dismissed in the minds of supporters of some schools so long as their own ideologies are believed to be both universal and natural.

With this in mind, it may seem inevitable that we should take a relativist position, because each school of economic theory and its ideological framework seems to have its own justification and cannot be totally dismissed by other schools as wrong. We should be able to discuss the degree of internal consistency and actual relevance of a theoretical system, or analyse the objective rationality of certain means and aims, while personal value judgement or a selection of conflicting ideologies would better be put outside of the scope of objective social sciences, as Max Weber emphasised.[2]

A defect of these relativist positions, including Weber's, is that they tend to treat ideologies merely as personal views because they neglect the social bases of major ideological currents. Besides, if totally separated from social thought, economic theories must become too formal and technical to be socially meaningful. In many cases complete separation of economic theories from ideologies is also difficult. Seemingly objective formal theories often contain unconsciously, or even consciously, ideological preoccupations in their premises. Attempts to pursue purely objective science in economic research are sometimes deceptive and even thoroughly ideological in their hidden (or apparent) presuppositions.

Contrariwise it also happens that ideological views and frameworks restrict and distort the theoretical observations of the real character and the total mechanism of a capitalist economy. How can we pass between these dangerous Scylla and Charybdis and reach a more solid ground for the basic theory of capitalism? Let us briefly examine the development of major schools of economic theory and consider especially how their contributions and limitations correspond to their ideological and political stances.

# 1 The Birth of the Theoretical System of Capitalism

## 1.1 MERCANTILISM

The first major school of economic theories was mercantilism. It grew for two and a half centuries following the explosive expansion of world trade with the discovery of the new continent and worldwide sea routes up until the middle of the eighteenth century. It was also a period of the formation of rival modern nation states in Western Europe through a continuous process of civil and international wars. In order to strengthen the fiscal basis of nation states by various custom duties and levies on monopoly traders, mercantilist policies were called for. The systematic development of such policies had been unnecessary in the preceding feudal period. Mercantilist theoretical observations more or less expressed the interests of an expanding merchant class and the state protection necessary for them.

Until the beginning of the seventeenth century mercantilism appeared as bullionism, where silver and gold were esteemed as absolute treasure. The growth of wealth was to be achieved by accumulating these precious metals which served as money. A typical policy was the 'balance of bargain system' which compelled British traders to bring back a portion of hard money obtained by each export trade. T. Gresham (1519–79), who observed in 1558 'Bad money drives out good,' and J. de Malynes (fl. 1586–1641) were among representative bullionists.

The main stream of mercantilism later turned to the 'balance-of-trade system,' where the total national balance of trade rather than the balance of each individual bargain was underlined. This position was expressed by E. Misselden (fl. 1608–54) and T. Mun (1571–1641) among others. They defended a certain type of trade by the East India Company against the bullionists and asserted that the outflow of monetary treasure for imports is both necessary and desirable in order to increase both exports and the national balance of trade. Though T. Mun and his co-theorists began to recognise the importance of manufacturing industries, they believed that it was fostered by, and the basis of, foreign trade, and that foreign trade was *the* source of national wealth and treasure. Their argument, especially Mun's, was so influential in supporting mercantilist policies up until the middle of the eighteenth century, that according to A. Smith 'the title of Mun's book, *England's Treasure by Foreign Trade* [1664], became a fundamental maxim in the political economy, not of England only, but of all other commercial countries'.[1]

James D. Steuart (1712–80) systematised the mercantilist theories in *An Inquiry into the Principles of Political Economy* (1767). Although it was unduly neglected by A. Smith and generations of his followers, it was a remarkable and great work in the following sense. First, it presented a whole range of political economy. It begins from a systematic description of a commercial society, analyses the functions of money and credit and discusses the role and the appropriate usage of public debt and taxes. In its description, various forms in a commodity economy such as prices, costs, profits, money, credit, interest, demand and supply are more or less organically studied as principles of a commercial society, in particular from the view of circulation and trade. Money, for instance, is no longer treated as an absolute treasure as with bullionism, but observed in various forms and functions including money of account, the measure of value, bank money, coins as the means of circulation and the bullion as universal money. This treatment of money is clearly wider than that of the classical school where money is regarded only as the conventional means of circulation. Together with his critique of D. Hume's quantity theory of money where the level of prices is mechanically determined by a rise or a fall of the quantity of money, Steuart's monetary theory obviously contributed to part of Marx's later theoretical system, although it was not then based upon the labour theory of value.

Second, in describing a commercial society which is driven by self-love to pursue trade, Steuart does not believe in the assurance of equilibrium between demand and supply or between jobs and population. Rather, he emphasised a possible crisis of disequilibrium which is often worsened by foreign trade. Hence he argues for the necessity of mercantile protectionist policies or even fiscal policy to restore the balance. In this respect he can be regarded as an important forerunner of T. R. Malthus and further J. M. Keynes. Third, Steuart is conscious of the historical character of a commercial society in comparison with serfdom or feudal society, on the basis of his observation of different societies on the Continent during his seventeen years of refugee life. This point of view, which is mostly lost in the classical school, anticipates the later historical school and the Marxist as well.

Fourth, in spite of these remarkable views Steuart's theoretical framework remained 'the rational expression of the Monetary and Mercantile systems',[2] in so far as it thoroughly stresses the central role of trade and commerce. In particular Steuart believed that profit upon alienation, being determined by the degree of demand, always enters into the prices of goods together with real value or prime costs. In his concept of 'positive profit' which 'results from an augmentation of labour, industry or ingenuity',[3] Steuart seems to be already taking off from a mere mercantilist view where profit is always observed as an increment of real wealth to be obtained in commerce. However, so far as 'Steuart makes no attempt to explain' how positive profit arises from such productive activity,[4] he cannot go beyond a theoretical limitation of mercantilist theory of value and profit.

Such a theoretical limitation reflects the basic character of capitalism in the mercantilist period. Capitalist accumulation in this period had not yet established its own industrial basis in the form of the modern factory system. The development of woollen manufacture, which organised a subtle division of labour in factories under capitalist management, was an important key industry for the expansion of global trade. But capitalist manufacture could not defeat small-scale domestic woollen industry so long as it was based on handwork technology. As a result the main source of capitalist profit and the augmentation of social wealth seemed to originate from merchant activity particularly in a large-scale foreign trade. The expansion and penetration of the commodity economy carried out by merchant activity in this period powerfully transformed the European societies and wove every country into a Euro-centred world market. Throughout the central and peripheral societies the capitalist expansion of the commodity economy was not just a peaceful idyllic process. As Marx made clear, the so-called 'primitive accumulation' which preceded and prepared industrial capitalist accumulation, was full of violence and state intervention. 'The exploitation of the agricultural producer, of the peasant, from the soil, was the basis of the whole process' (I, p. 876)[5] to create wage-labourers for capitalist production, as was classically shown in the British enclosure movement. The colonial system, the slave trade and the system of trade protection also worked in the great transformation process of society from the feudal or semi-feudal to the fully capitalist society. It is striking to see how violent means and state power served as the midwife for the birth of a seemingly peaceful commercial capitalist society. Unawareness of the role of violence in dissolving small farms and peasant holdings through enclosure movements in the British and other European societies, and in subordinating or enslaving peripheral societies, is another limitation of the mercantilists' view.

The mercantilists argument for protectionist policies and their central concept of profit upon alienation, obtained in circulation, were closely tied to the unstable transitory and immature character of the capitalist economy of their age. Since the transitory period contained both residual and incipient social characteristics and elements, other types of theory such as physiocracy and the classical school also began to grow. It is remarkable, however, to see how the monetary and the mercantile systems were overwhelmingly influential before the industrial revolution. At the same time the contributions of mercantilist theories concerning the various forms found in the circulation process of a commodity economy should not be neglected or despised, as was often the case in historical reviews of economic theories, especially from the Ricardo–Marxian School.[6] Certainly, the mercantilists did not develop the labour theory of value or of surplus-value. But their theoretical categories for analysing the commodity economy were no less important, and sometimes richer than those of the classical school's. It also well suits the basic character of capitalism to have mercantilists as the first major school of observers, since capitalism is nothing but a unique social formation to be fully penetrated and organised by the forms of commodity economy. Just as the expansion of commodity circulation both in foreign trades and domestic market initiated the growth of capitalism, the theoretical self-recognition of capitalism had to begin with the mercantilist observation of trade and circulation.

## 1.2 PHYSIOCRACY

The second major school of economic theory was physiocracy. It appeared in France in the eighteenth century and played an important intermediary role in the transition from mercantilism to the classical school. In particular, it converted the theoretical concern about the origin of surplus-value from circulation to production. It simultaneously shifted the policy stance from protectionist interventionism to free trade.

Its background and historical character were not simple. In the preceding period there had been a growing failure of the French absolutist economic policies. At the zenith of French absolutism, Louis XIV (1643–1715) and his Minister of Treasury, Colbert, pushed forward a French type of mercantilism. In comparison with British mercantilism which made much of foreign trade, the French type attached importance to establishing privileged royal manufacturers producing luxury goods alongside patented trading companies. The development of the French capitalist economy lagged tendentially behind the British, and could not provide a broad national bases for such a policy. The king's wars and ruling-class luxury, like the building of the Versailles Palace, put a heavy burden on agriculture, which was still definitely the biggest industry of the country. The prohibition and restriction on the export of agricultural products, in order to keep their prices lower so as to help domestic manufacturers, was also damaging agriculture. The failure of John Law's operation to handle the state debt and the resultant financial crisis in 1720 added to the difficulties of French commercial and manufacturing capitalists. In agriculture, capitalist large-farm management was also still limited, in spite of its potential growth, and was only partly being introduced in northern France. For the more part agriculture was carried out by small tenant peasants suffering from low productivity and high rents. As a whole, the French economy in the transitional period from feudalism to capitalism was more domestic, more dependent on agriculture and less dependent on foreign trade than the British economy.

Against this background there appeared with the Enlightenment a group of economists who asserted the importance of agriculture for restructuring the French economy. P. Boisguillebert (1646–1714), S. Vauban (1633–1707) and R. Cantillion (1680–1734) anticipated the tendency, and then F. Quesnay (1694–1744) with his able followers such as A. Turgot (1727–81) established physiocracy as a distinguished school. Springing from the Enlightenment the Physiocrats believed in a deistic natural law. They believed that mercantilist policies were harmful for the realisation of such natural law in socio-economic life. How, then could a natural social economic order work continuously to reproduce and distribute social wealth and revenue?

Quesnay summarised an ideal economic order in his *Tableau Économique* (*Economic Table*, 1758). The main points of his 'Analysis of the Arithmetical Formula of the Tableau Économique' (1766) with a simplified Tableau, are as follows:[7] 'The nation is reduced to three classes of citizens: the productive class, the class of proprietors, and the sterile class.' The productive class advances the expenditures for agricultural labour and cultivation, and reproducccs national wealth including the net product to be paid to the class of proprietors. The class of proprietors contains the sovereign, the owners of land and the tithe-owners. This class subsists on the revenue or the net product paid by the productive class. The sterile class is composed of all the citizens who are engaged in works or services other than agriculture. For instance, in a kingdom of about 30 million population, the productive class owns 10 milliards (livres) primitive advance, of which 1 milliard is yearly depreciation (which is confusedly called interest for the primitive advance) and also expends 2 milliards yearly advance. Three milliards advance in total brings about 5 milliards yearly agricultural products including 2 milliards net products. The productive class owns also 2 milliards (livres) money which is equivalent to the net product and pays it to the class of proprietors. Of 5 milliards (livres) agricultural products 1 milliard is to be consumed by the class of proprietors, 1 milliard (as foods) and another 1 milliard (as raw material) are to be used by the sterile class, and the remaining 2 milliards is reserved in kind as the yearly advance for the next year's cultivation. The sterile class does not produce any net products (surplus-value). It reproduces the same 2 milliards (livres) just as it consumes both 1 milliard raw material by yearly advance and another milliard for means of consumption. One-half of its (manufactured) products is sold to the proprietors and the other half is to the productive class. Then Quesnay's simplified tableau (Figure 1.1) shows the total transaction as follows:

While each milliard of products of the productive and the sterile class moves along the lines in the opposite direction to arrows, 2 milliards (livres) of money flows back directly and indirectly via the sterile class to the productive class which originally pays that money to the class of proprietors, and the advanced money of 1 milliard from each side is also regained for the next year.

Quesnay's table was the first original attempt to observe the total material relations of social reproduction and clearly preceded Marx's reproduction schema and Leontieff's later inter-industry relations table. Quesnay's theoretical analyses of the table and its implications also provided a remarkable advance in the theory of capitalist production. In contrast with the mercantilist theory of profit upon alienation the source of surplus-value is now found in the sphere of production. In particular, surplus-value as the net product is seen as obtainable from capitalist advances, and is the surplus product over and above the necessaries of life and the means of production used

*Figure* 1.1 FORMULA OF THE *TABLEAU ECONOMIQUE*
*Total reproduction: Five milliards*

(Arrow-heads added by Itoh)

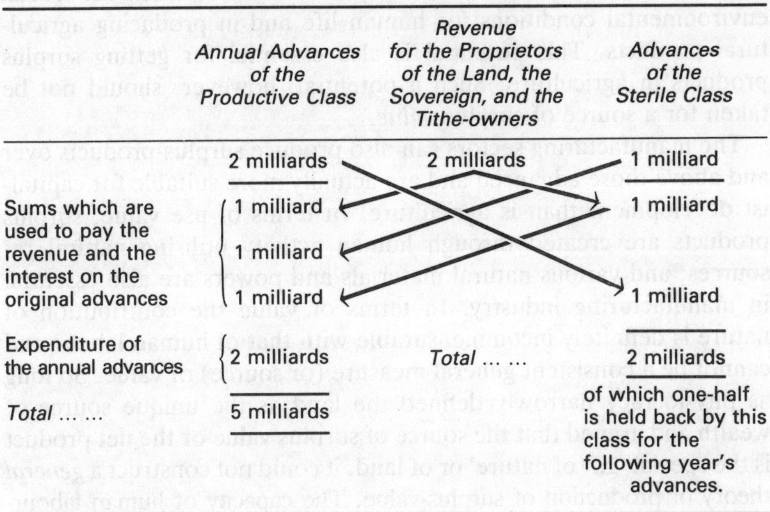


up. The theory of the capitalist production of surplus-value is thus virtually explored in the work of Quesnay. Such a theory of capitalist production was still far from being actually realised in the French economy in general. The Physiocrats described rather an ideal process of social reproduction in accordance with a conceived natural law deduced from the partial development of capitalist farming. Interestingly, the theoretical attempt to see a natural economic order which was realisable by abolishing mercantile interventionist policies had to presuppose a capitalist commodity economy even in the physiocratic writings. It reflects the special character or ability of the commodity economy to mould a modern individualistic society in an increasingly capitalist manner, basically through private self-reliant transactions independent of religious or political power. Such an economic order could easily be taken for a natural economic law from the standpoint of Enlightenment individualism. In this regard, physiocracy overlaps and foreshadows the basic view of the classical school.

Nevertheless there are various limitations and a narrowness in physiocratic theories in comparison with the later classical school. In particular, the theoretical analysis of the source of surplus-value is consciously limited to the agricultural sector. The manufacturing sectors are regarded as being incapable of producing surplus-value and are therefore unable to accommodate capitalist production. The recent ecologists are quite correct in asserting that we should not neglect the special potential of the soil both in maintaining the crucial environmental conditions for human life and in producing agricultural products. This potential is also essential for getting surplus products in agriculture. Such a potential, however, should not be taken for a source of surplus-*value*.

The manufacturing sectors can also produce surplus-products over and above those advanced and are actually more suitable for capitalist development than is agriculture. In terms of use value, surplus products are created through human activity utilising natural resources; and various natural materials and powers are also essential in manufacturing industry. In terms of value the contribution of nature is definitely incommensurable with that of human labour and cannot be a consistent general measure (or source) of value. So long as physiocracy narrowly defined the land as the unique source of wealth and argued that the source of surplus value or the net product is the special 'gift of nature' or of land, it could not construct a *general* theory of production of surplus-value. The capacity of human labour-power to produce surplus-products, and its capitalist utilisation in the form of wage-labour to produce surplus-value were not yet clarified. Symbolically the three major classes in Quesnay's table did not signify the distinction between the capitalist and the labourer class, although Turgot later introduced such a division into both the productive and the sterile class.

Corresponding to the lack of generality in its theory of surplus-value, the value theory of physiocracy could not establish a common productive basis for values. Quesnay asserted that a stable 'bon prix' (proper price) was desirable and realisable under a natural order of economy, set free from the artificial distortions of mercantilism. His definition of a 'bon prix' was a sort of factor cost-price theory generating constant equilibrium prices as the prices which would guarantee normal reproduction for agriculture. The common social substance of commodity values was not yet investigated and was left out of consideration.

These theoretical limitations are clearly related to the characteristic view of the physiocrats that the development of productive capitalism is conceivable only in agriculture. From the view of capitalist development in manufacture and trade, such an idea might even seem reactionary, favouring the feudalistic *ancien régime*. An acquisition of the total surplus-product by the proprietor class also seems feudalistic in its social content. So far the theoretical treatment of capitalist production in physiocracy had to remain incomplete, and could hardly be a generalised theory of value and surplus-value. Clearly, physiocracy presented a theoretical analysis neither of a feudal economy *per se*, nor of an entirely capitalist economy. Though it attempted to show an ideal economy to be achieved in a capitalist direction, its theoretical presentation had to reflect the complex transitional and immature character of the French society of its age.

## 1.3 THE CLASSICAL SCHOOL

### Its Formation

The classical school investigated the inner relations of the capitalist economy more or less along with the formation of the labour theory of value.[8] Ideologically it is closely related to the modern social concept of natural law and a juridical view of the private property title, basically founded upon private labour. It also became increasingly linked with *laissez-faire* liberalism. As both agriculture and manufacturing industries were gradually involved in a commodity economy, it was in a sense natural that the productive basis of the value of commodities was inquired into even in the mercantilist period.

We see, for instance, an important initiator of the labour theory of value in W. Petty (1623–87). He wrote *A Treatise of Taxes and Contributions* (1662) and discussed how to promote the national wealth and fair taxes considering the problem of restructuring the UK budget just after the Restoration (1660). While discussing the practical devices of public finance, Petty occasionally refers to the theories of value, money, rent, interest, etc. His labour theory of value was fragmented and immature, and was mixed with a mercantilist view defining the final result of national wealth as gold and silver; and also with the partly physiocratic view that 'labour is the father and active principle of wealth, as lands are the mother',[9] or that 'all things ought to be valued by two natural denominations, which is land and labour'.[10] Nevertheless he obviously initiates the labour theory of value by asking what is to be the natural standard and measure of values. He is not satisfied with the ordinary measurement using gold and silver because the prices of gold and silver themselves fluctuate. According to him the basis of the equalisation and the balancing of the values of various goods is the expenditure of the same amount of labour. Remarkably he avoids the complication of treating the values of the means of production by simply taking up the values of neat proceeds or net products of the same amount of labour in different industries.

B. Franklin (1706–90) was also among the early theorists of labour value. Discussing a practical issue in *A Modest Enquiry into the Nature and Necessity of a Papercurrency* (1729) he states that trade is generally nothing but the exchange of labour. In the New World where the restriction of land was still relatively unimportant the contribution of human labour to economic wealth could more easily be emphasised.

A series of social and political philosophers like J. Locke (1632–1704) and D. Hume (1711–76) were also important for the formation of the social thought of the classical school. Against the feudalistic notion of the divine rights of kings, they asserted fundamental human rights in which the private ownership or the property title based on labour was contained. The ideas of individual rights suitable for a capitalist economy were being systematically formulated and were regarded as essential for the realisation of a natural social order of human liberty. The ideological framework of the classical school was thus already prepared in the mercantilist period before A. Smith. Hume was evidently opposed to mercantilism, and argued for free trade by presenting the quantity theory of money.

However, in this early period the labour theory of value and classical social thought had not yet developed into a theoretical system of the capitalist economy. They were presented in a more or less fragmentary way in the discourses of practical policy issues or as parts of political philosophy. In most cases the labour theory of value was presented by presupposing commodity exchanges between independent producers working by themselves. The theory was not really extended to the study of the inner structure of capitalist production.

### Adam Smith

*An Inquiry into the Nature and Causes of the Wealth of Nations* (1776) by A. Smith (1723–90) was epoch-making in formulating a theoretical system of a capitalist economy as a study of its inner economic structure. In the first two Parts especially, before the three parts treating economic history, previous systems of political economy and public finance, the book describes theoretically the nature and the construction of a fully capitalist economy. The basic theories of value and distribution in a bourgeois society were comprehensively presented separately from (but together with) the other major fields of economics. Although the apparent scope of Smith's work is not very different from that of Steuart's *Principles*, the ideological and theoretical bases are radically altered.

Smith, unlike Steuart believed that in principle individualistic behaviour guided by self-interest, would realise a prescribed harmony and an economic system of natural liberty guided by an invisible hand. In Smith's view the best policy to achieve such a social order was *laissez-faire*, free trade and the removal of artificial mercantile protectionism so as to require the smallest possible state supervision. It is clear that he was deeply influenced by the deistic social ideas of natural law and individualism, and also by physiocracy in its opposition to mercantilism.

In order to show the relevance of *laissez-faire* liberalism, Smith inquires how a commercial society autonomously sustains itself, by producing and distributing yearly output among the major classes. In this inquiry, the productive basis of value and surplus value is universalised through the labour theory of value, and the major classes are converted into the capitalists, the landowners and the wage-labourers, in contrast with Quesnay's physiocratic analysis.

Beginning from the effect of the division of labour on productivity, Smith describes a commercial society as a society based upon a comprehensive social division of labour and the exchange of products as commodities. In his analysis, unlike mercantilist theory, money is only a conventional instrument of exchange and commerce, not the absolute measure of wealth. Therefore nominal prices, as measured by money, cannot be a satisfactory measurement for a study of commodity exchange and national wealth. He asks what the real measure of exchange values can be, or what is the real price behind the nominal price? The answer is labour, because labour is always 'the original purchase-money that was paid for all things',[11] and also because 'equal quantities of labour, at all times and places, may be said to be of equal value to the labourer',[12] as being the same amount of 'toil and trouble'.[13] Accordingly, labour is 'the real standard by which the value of all commodities can at all times and places be estimated and compared. It is their real price, money is their nominal price only'.[14]

The labour theory of value is thus adopted more decisively than in the case of earlier theorists like Petty. As is well known however, Smith's value theory is not consistent. It comprises three different theories of value, namely the embodied labour theory of value, the commanded labour theory of value and a sort of factor costs theory. The labour commanded theory of value defines the value of a commodity as the labour which can be obtained in exchange with the commodity, and not as the labour embodied in it. This complexity of value theories relates fundamentally to an ideological stance regarding commercial society and the process of exchange as being a natural order of production. Smith especially constantly mixes up and makes analogies between the labour and production process and exchanges in the market and vice versa. Notwithstanding the fact that human labour used to produce useful goods from nature is an economic basis for any society, regardless of the existence or non existence of commodity exchanges, labour is defined by Smith as the original purchase money to be used in exchanges between man and nature. Thus the amount of labour which is obtainable through the exchange of a commodity with others is viewed as a substitute for such original purchase money paid to nature. The amount of labour embodied in a commodity is regarded as generally to be equal to the amount of labour commanded through exchange. Both amounts are conceived to be equal as the measure of exchange values. This position can hold so far as every producer works by himself and exchanges his products with others according to the same amount of labour in a simple commodity producers society, or in Smith's 'early and rude state of society'.[15] Certainly both the amounts of labour embodied and commanded can also diverge even in a simple commodity society when the balance of demand and supply is lost. While the embodied labour theory does not accord with the demand and supply theory of value, the labour commanded theory can do. But when separated from the former, the latter theory can not be a theory determining the exchange-ratios by itself. Such divergence in Smith's labour theories of value, however, might be regarded as accidental or exceptional cases in the exchanges of simple commodity producers.

When 'stock has accumulated in the hands of particular persons'[16] and all the land has become private property, Smith's dual-labour theories hardly turn out to be consistent in matters of principle. The total products of labour and the value produced can no longer belong solely to the labourers. The value which is added to raw materials by labour must now be decomposed into three parts. Labourers obtain just a part, as wages. Another part is acquired as profit by the capitalist who employs the labourers, and a third part as rent by the landowner who rents his land to the capitalist. This is the deduction theory of value which in fact attributes the surplus value (profit and rent) to the surplus labour of wage-labourers. This theory is nothing but an extension of the labour embodied theory.

However, Smith is inclined to see labour as an exchange process and thereby tends to slip off to the other theory of value. So long as labour is observed just in the exchange process it seems to be the means of exchange to obtain necessary consumption goods to live on, no longer from nature, but now from the capitalist. The amount of labour which a labourer offers to a capitalist in exchange for the necessary means of consumption must be exactly the same amount of labour obtainable by these means if these are used as capital to employ wage-labourers. Thus the equal amounts of labour seem to be exchanged between a labourer and a capitalist from the viewpoint of the labour commanded theory of value. If a wage-labourer can get the same amount of labour as he expends, then the source of surplus value, i.e. profit and rent, cannot be in his labour. Here appears a deep division in Smith's dual-labour theories, and further, a switch to a sort of factor costs theory of value or an adding-up theory of value in which wages, profit and rent are defined as original independent sources of exchange values. It is not too hard to recognise here some residues of the mercantilist and physiocratic views of revenues.

There remained many problems in Smith's complex theories of value. It may not be much of an exaggeration to say that all the later studies of value relate in one way or the other to these problems. Presently let us reconfirm just the discrepancy (with related points) between the deduction theory of value and the adding-up theory of value. It is clear that these theories directly contradict each other for instance in the case of a rise of wages. When wages rise, other circumstances being equal, according to the deduction theory, the other components, i.e. profit and rent, must be reduced within the same amount of value being defined by the embodied labour time in a commodity. On the contrary, according to the adding-up theory, the exchange value of a commodity must rise so long as an independent decline of profit or rent does not happen to cancel the rise of wages. Interestingly even in the recent debates about inflation the basic views of these opposite positions have repeatedly appeared. Smith might not have been very conscious or concerned about the discrepancy in his theories. However, while he conventionally operated and used different theories, he could not consistently extend the labour theory of value to more precise studies of the inner relations between wages, profit and rent. There was plenty of room for such an extention through the embodied labour theory, even excepting for the moment a further sophisticated attempt to consolidate this sort of value theory with the other adding-up theory, which is seemingly more easily accepted in the common sense of daily life.

**David Ricardo**

D. Ricardo (1772–1823) clarified Smith's complex value theory and completed the classical school in his main work, *On the Principles of Political Economy and Taxation* (1817). One of the biggest political issues in his age was the corn law. As industrial capitalists grew stronger through the industrial revolution, various mercantilist policies were one by one being removed, and free trade was pushed forward. But the law restricting the importation of corn remained and became more and more protective of the interest of a relatively small number of aristocratic landowners by keeping the corn price higher. T. R. Malthus, for instance, argued, in defence of the corn law, that the higher price of corn maintained higher rents, and also made possible higher profits for manufacturing industries and agriculture by increasing the effective demand for their products. Against such arguments and the corn law itself Ricardo asserted that a lower price of corn would increase profit by lowering wages and encouraging capital accumulation. His assertion was initially based on a theory defining the rate of profit and the wage-rate in terms of corn.[17] Then in order to generalise the assertion he shifted the theoretical basis from the physical corn rate theory of profit and wages to the labour theory of value in his *Principles*.

Ideologically Ricardo believed in J. Bentham's utilitarianism and a more rational liberalism in comparison with Smith's belief in an 'invisible hand'. His opposition to the corn law was certainly a part of his broader political position in support of the *laissez-faire* liberalism following Smith. However, compared with Smith, Ricardo attempted theoretically to show in a more consistent way how an economic law works to distribute annual production among the three major classes (i.e. the landowners, the capitalists and the labourers) in a society. This task in his work was clearly declared in the Preface to the *Principles* and understandably was well oriented to the corn law issue as well. Beginning from the chapter on value, the first six chapters of the *Principles*, deductively investigates the internal relations among wages, profit and rent and the natural course of their motion in the process of capital accumulation. Obviously the basic theory of a capitalist economy is systematically investigated here as a theory of a naturally autonomous social order. Following chapters on foreign trade, taxes, and controversial problems are clearly distinct in their nature from the basic theory in the first six chapters and are mostly applicatory in character, except two supplementary chapters 'On currency and banks' (ch. 27) and 'On machinery' (ch. 31).

Ricardo begins the chapter on value with the distinction between value in use and value in exchange, quoting Smith. Although value in use or utility of a commodity is essential to its exchange value, the magnitude of value in exchange is not determined by the degree of usefulness. Some things which have the greatest value in use have frequently little or no value in exchanges as we see in the case of water or air. What then does determine the magnitude of values in exchange of commodities? Ricardo deliberately refers to certain sorts of commodities such as antiques or wines of peculiar quality whose exchange values depend on their scarcity in comparison with the wealth and inclinations of those who want them, and he excludes those commodities because they form only a very small part of the mass of commodities exchanged daily in the market. Then he takes into consideration just those commodities being produced by human industry without any restriction on competition. As for these commodities he believes that the amounts of labour bestowed on them are the foundation of their exchangeable value.

From beginning to end Ricardo concentrates only on the capitalist economy and treats it as if it were an eternal natural order. For example he recognises the necessity of capital even in an early and rude state of society, on the ground that 'without some weapon, neither the beaver nor the deer could be destoroyed'. While Smith initially showed the embodied labour theory of value as applied to an earlier society without capital stock being accumulated; Ricardo applied the clarified labour theory of value to commodity production under capital throughout. Criticising Smith's complex duality of value concept, Ricardo emphasises that a rise or a fall of wages does not affect (absolute) values of commodity products but has an inversely affect on the level of profit. This tense rival relation between wages and profit within the values of commodities determined by embodied labour is a focus of Ricardo's complete theoretical system.

In this treatment, Ricardo is not concerned with the historical specificity of a capitalist economy, and does not ask why and how the surplus labour of wage-labourers is taken up by capitalists as profit. A capitalist social order is already given and for him the quantitative distribution of yearly products to its major classes is the main concern. Therefore how to explain the source of profit (and rent) starting from the value of labour being paid to wage workers remained as an unsolved or rather untouched problem after Smith.

A second problem left in Ricardo's value theory concerns heterogenous labour. Ricardo referred to the problem of how to compare the quantities of different qualities of labour, but he did not explore the point beyond stating that 'As the inquiry to which I wish to draw the reader's attention, relates to the effect of the variations in the relative value of commodities, and not in their absolute value, it will be of little importance to examine into the comparative degree of estimation in which the different kinds of human labour are held. We may fairly conclude that, whatever the ingenuity there might originally have been in them, whatever the ingenuity, skill, . . . it continues nearly the same from one generation to another; or at least, that the variation is very inconsiderable from year to year, and therefore can have little effect, for short period, on the relative value of commodities.' [18]

A third problem is most consciously investigated and the content is called 'Ricardo's exceptional revision of the labour theory of value'. His basic position was that a rise or a fall of wages did not affect commodity values. However, he noticed that the position must be revised on certain occasions in view of the equalisation of profit rates across various industries. It is because there are different proportions between circulating capital invested in wages and fixed capital in machinery and buildings, and also different speeds in turnover of capital across industries. A rise of wages must affect more the costs of such industries having a higher proportion of circulating capital for wages or a lower speed of turnover. Therefore such industries must suffer from a greater decline of profit rates than others so far as the exchange values of their products remain constant in spite of a rise of wages. Or, exchange values must alter so as to equalise the rates of profit in accordance with the new level of wages. Needless to say the effect of decline of wages is similar, but in a contrary direction. This is the problem of how theoretically to relate the law of the equalisation of profit rates to the labour theory of value. It cannot be a problem of an exceptional case, as the different compositions of capital and the various speed of turnover of capital exist rather generally across industries. Ricardo pointed to the problem, but did not solve it. He could not help but insist on the basic correctness of the labour theory of value either by assuming that the necessary revision was quantitatively insignificant,[19] or by defining rather general phenomena as exceptional, or conversely by directly revising the basic labour theory in such 'exceptional' cases.[20]

In relation to this, Ricardo raised a fourth problem of how to find an invariable measure of value. If relative exchange values have to change according to a rise or a fall in wages, is it possible for us to have a commodity which can serve as an invariable standard of value against which the labour time embodied as values in other commodities could be read off by comparing the price of a commodity with that of the standard? Ricardo suggested in his *Principles* that the composition of capital in gold production might be regarded as about near a social average, so as to let gold be used as the conventional standard of value. Apparently he was unsatisfied with this treatment, since the labour value embodied in a unit of gold would change, and also since the composition of capital producing it would not be stable with a change in distribution. He pursued the problem, not very successfully, until his final essay 'On the invariable measure of value.'[20]

These are remarkably lasting problems which have been repeatedly inquired into and discussed from various angles. Through the contributions of, Marx and then Sraffa's among others, these problems have especially gained a new theoretical interest, and can be seen as an important origin of the subject in the value controversy since the 1970s. We shall have many opportunities in this volume to come back to these points.

Ricardo's theory of ground rent was designed, to explain consistently the determination and the nature of ground rent from his labour theory of value. Assuming the law of diminishing returns for the extension of cultivation, Ricardo defines the value of a unit of the product of land, say corn, as the necessary amount of labour to produce it on the least productive land socially required to satisfy the demand. So far as capital investment on such land gains a socially average rate of profit, capital invested in more fertile land obtains more crops and extra profit (beyond the average rate of profit) to be paid as rent to the landowners. The effect of the law of diminishing return for units of capital being invested in the same land causes similar extra profit to be paid as rent. This theory of differential rent thus clearly explains ground rent not as a causal factor to determine exchange values (as in Smith's adding-up theory of value) but as a consistent result of the determination of the labour value of products of the land.

Closely linked with this theory of rent Ricardo formulated the natural course of capital accumulation in the law of falling rate of profit. As capital accumulation proceeds and the labouring population grows, the natural price or the value of labour, which is determined by the value of foodstaffs and other necessaries to maintain the wage labourer's life with his family, must rise as a result of extension of cultivation accompanied by the law of diminishing returns. Along with such a rise in the value of labour, the rate of profit must fall in the long run while ground rent increases. Through such a process, capital accumulation will finally die out by losing its driving stimulus in profit. Evidently this argument serves as a basis for the free traders opposition to the corn law. Although a restriction on capital accumulation is clearly implied as a result of the falling rate of profit, the basis of the restriction is here attributed not to the internal contradiction of capital, but to the external natural limitation. As was drastically shown twice in the oil crisis in the 1970s, capital accumulation might actually be restricted by the limited fertility of land. Such limitation should not, however, be viewed as an unavoidable absolute fate for capital accumulation because it is generally linked with a given set of technologies which can be changed.

Apart from the long-range view of the absolutely falling rate of profit, Ricardo basically did not present a theory of economic crisis or of general overproduction. He referred to economic distress caused by sudden changes in channels of trade, but he believed that the oversupply in such a case was just temporary, partial and solved by the equalisation process of the rates of profit across industries. Another possible case of disturbance which is referred to in his *Principles* (in ch. 21) is a rise of wages due to too rapid increase of the fund for the maintenance of labour in comparison with population. According to Ricardo this case is reduced to a partial oversupply of necessaries, and can easily be overcome by the increase of population which is prompted by a rise of wages. Ricardo's exposition here is highly unpersuasive, since the shortage of labouring population due to an over-accumulation of capital cannot be identical with a partial oversupply of necessaries, and hardly guarantees a rapid increase of population. In ch. 31 'on Machinery', which was added in the third edition of *Principles*, Ricardo also recognised the possibility of rendering labourers redundant and distressed as a result of introducing machinery. Until the second edition Ricardo believed that the number of workers thrown out of jobs by the introduction of more productive machinery would certainly be able to get new jobs in other industries, such as producing such machinery. But he found by the third edition that this balance between the reduction and the increase in employment cannot be guaranteed and may create an unfavourable effect on workers.

These references about the possible imbalances and disturbances in the process of capital accumulation show well Ricardo's theoretical sincerity. However, they were still too fragmented to make up a theoretical system of economic crisis, and tended just to be treated as partial or exceptional cases. In this regard we must acknowledge that Ricardo's ideological belief in the natural character of a capitalist economy restricted both his theory of value and his theoretical studies on the dynamism of capital accumulation. The theoretical inconsistencies and insufficiencies in Ricardo's *Principles* which remained at the peak of the classical school provoked the dissolution of the school and a diversification in the direction of economic studies.

# 2 The Dissolution of the Classical School and the Diversification of Schools

## 2.1 THE DISSOLUTION

### Anti-classical Theories

Various anti-classical theories had already sprung up from critiques of the limitations and weaknesses of the classical school, even in Ricardo's lifetime. In particular the ideological belief in a prescribed harmony in a capitalist economy and the resultant theoretical inconsistencies in the value theory of the classical school were a source of critiques and deviations.

A representative anti-Ricardian theorist at that time was T. R. Malthus (1766–1834). Although he was an intimate friend of Ricardo he opposed him and championed landed interests and the corn law. In *An Essay on the Principles of Population* (1798) Malthus warned of the inevitability of excessive population and poverty on the grounds of the natural gap between the geometric increase of population, and the arithmetic progression of the production of foodstuffs. Moral restrictions on increasing the population were recommended by him as a remedy. The necessity of birth-control has been emphasised by his followers, called neo-Malthusians, from the end of nineteenth century. A similar position tends repeatedly to appear in our age, associated with the restriction of natural resources and economic crises, especially in the third world. Though Malthus's law of population was a counter to the classically prescribed harmony, it was also based on a sort of naturalism and was far from appropriate so far as it attributed the excessive population and poverty to natural law. Marx pointed out these defects sharply and in addition underlined Malthus's theoretical plagiarism from his forerunners such as J. Townsend and J. Anderson.[1]

In the value theory Malthus seemingly follows Smith, but he actually abandons the embodied labour theory. In contrast to nominal value in exchange, or price which is estimated in the precious metals as money, Malthus defines intrinsic value in exchange as the power of purchasing determined by the state of supply compared with demand, and ordinarily by the elementary costs of production.[2] He thus succeeds Smith's 'labour commanded' theory of value and argues for the contribution of demand to the values of commodities. This view is closely related to his theory of overproduction.

According to Malthus the conversion of revenue into capital when pushed beyond a certain point must cause a relative shortage in effective demand for products, and this causes overproduction and a depression of wealth.[3] The effective demand of the labourers employed is insufficient in comparison with the supply of their products. As a palliative or a solution the role of expenditures by an unproductive class including landlords, clergymen, statesmen, etc., is very much emphasised.[4] The corn law is defended as a means of securing the revenue and the unproductive expenditure of the landlords.

In comparison with Ricardo, Malthus was not theoretically consistent and did not clarify the internal source and relations of the incomes of major classes. For instance, he explains that the primary cause of ground-rent is 'the gift of nature to man'[5] after the fashion of physiocracy. The common internal basis of the various revenues, and the possible balance between demand and supply, both on the grounds of labour expenditure in the classical view, are disregarded. It must be noted, however, that Malthus pointed to the unharmonious character of the capitalist economy and a tendency towards overproduction, and he thus also heralded Keynesianism more than Stuart by emphasising the role of unproductive effective demand.

Interestingly, disregarding the embodied labour theory of value did not necessarily lead to the theory of overproduction. J.-B. Say (1765–1832) for instance attempted to represent A. Smith on the Continent and asserted the "*théorie des débuchés*" or Say's law, which stated that 'supply creates its own demand'.[6] This view was linked with a conversion of Smith's complex value theory into a superficial utility theory of value. Though Say's negation of general overproduction was common to the classical school, his basic theory of value was not. The recent restoration of Say's law by the supply-side economists against Keynesianism does not imply a return to the classical theory.

In the classical school, the basic theory of embodied labour value was internally related to the view of the balance between the total supply and demand. Dissolution of the embodied labour theory of value could be related either to Say's law or with the opposite. J. C. L. Simonde de Sismondi (1773–1842) also took over Smith's adding-up theory of value, but was decisively opposed to Say and Ricardo on the Continent. He emphasised the inevitability of superabundance of production which surpassed consumption more sharply than Malthus, and stated especially that capital accumulation reduced consumers demand by substituting machinery for labourers and pauperising peasants on the one hand, and, on the other, increasing the supply of products regardless of the level of consumer demand.[7] Compared with Malthus Sismondi ascribed the cause of overpopulation and poverty not to natural law, but to the increasing introduction of machinery into the process of capital accumulation. In this regard his under-consumption theory was more influential than Malthus's in later forming an aspect of Marxian crisis theory. His proposed solution was different from those of Malthus and Marx. It argued for a return to a patriarchal peasant farming system where an ideal natural balance between production, income and population seemed easily tenable. Sismondi thus initiated a stream of romanticism in economics and anticipated Russian *narodniki* ideas among others.[8]

## Utopian Socialism

Against the prescribed harmonious view of a capitalist economy in the classical school, a series of early socialists such as C. H. de R. Saint-Simon (1760–1825), F. M. C. Fourier (1772–1837) and R. Owen (1771–1858) criticised the increasing anarchical disorder and poverty of the masses in the process of industrialisation, and they argued for the construction of a more associational society. They were the intellectual heirs of the Enlightenment and were born out of the shocks of both the French Revolution and the Industrial Revolution.

Saint-Simon proposed that 'all men are brothers' and drew up an ideal in a co-operation between scientific scholars and industrialists on the basis of the equal duties of labour and distribution according to abilities.[9] Fourier described a more precise and sytematic plan for a harmonious future society.[10] A unit of a co-operative society was called a *phalanx*, where a population of 1600-1700 would live together in a palace called a *phalanstere*. Mechanised agriculture and manufacturing would be combined, and four-twelfth of social income would go to capital, five-twelfth to labour and three-twelfth to talents, though the proportion to labour would increase along with the growth of social wealth. Even detailed daily time-tables for a person in the *phalanstere* were planned. In June for instance the inhabitants would get up as early as 3:30 in the morning, work for $13\frac{1}{2}$ hours in the garden, field, forest and factory, and go to bed at 10:00 in the evening. Fourier waited in vain for a charitable benefactor who would appreciate his blueprint for the best social system.

R. Owen also believed that reason and education could remove the disastrous social effect of the Industrial Revolution and lead to a rational social system. He was, however, more practical than Saint-Simon and Fourier. As a joint manager of a cotton-spinning factory at Lanarkshire in south Scotland, he attempted to build up an experimental ideal factory system in the first quarter of nineteenth century. His factory shortened working hours from generally 14–16 hours, to 10 hour, provided a public nursery, a school and a mutual-aid association shop, and could still raise profit. On the basis of this experience Owen stated his views and ideas for a new harmonious society[11] and further initiated a co-operative movement and a trade-union movement. Among his followers T. Hodgskin[12] (1787–1869) and W. Thompson[13] (1775–1833) asserted labour's claim to whole returns, utilising Ricardo's labour theory of value. As Ricardo could not by his value theory show theoretically why capitalists can obtain surplus-value while by paying the 'value of labour' to workers, it was in a sense natural for his radical successors to assert labour's claim to all the net labour products as a sort of fair payment to workers for their labour, relying upon the same labour theory of value – essentially a Utopian assertion to abolish capitalist exploitation by keeping the commodity form of labour-power and the transactions or the relations of production between capitalists and workers.

Critiques of capitalism, especially concerning its devastating effects on labour in the process of the Industrial Revolution were sharply presented by these Utopian socialists. Their critiques, however, were not based upon any theoretically objective understanding of the workings and the mechanism of a capitalist economy. So far as the object of the socialist movement, or what should be changed, was not scientifically clarified, their solutions tended to be reformist and partial, and appeared rather as a secular counterpart of salvationist attitudes in religious ages. The potentiality of wage-labourers to liberate themselves as the driving subjective social force was not much counted upon. In contrast the opportunities for enlightened capitalists, managers or rich benefactors to undertake progressive measures were clearly overestimated. Detailed Utopian ideas for a future society were drawn up in order to persuade such ruling persons. Though plenty of important insights into human nature and its potential for a future society were penned, the theories of these early socialists did not offer theoretical solutions to the difficulties left by the classical school. Socialism had to be shifted by Marx from such an early Utopian, to a scientific basis, as Engels later claimed. Marx did this by clarifying the mechanisms of a capitalist economy beyond the limitations of the classical school, and thereby discovering the potential role of working-class movement.[14]

## The Revisionist Succession to Classical Theory

The attempts to succeed classical theory could not be made objectively and effectively without more or less seceding from the purely Ricardian labour theory of value, and also from a simple naturalist view of capitalism. Among a series of theorists who made such attempts J. S. Mill (1806–73) was most eminent. His father James Mill (1773–1836) was a close friend of D. Ricardo. While propagating Ricardo's theory James Mill distinguished four aspects to economic laws, namely production, distribution, exchange and consumption.[15] Ricardo's coherent theoretical system, based on the labour-value concept, tended to be weakened by such a mechanical distinction. The labour-value concept itself was also stretched, as James Mill noted that the increment of the price of wine in a period of necessary maturity was to be regarded as a result of so much indirect labour expenditure. J. R. McCulloch (1789–1864) pushed this way of revising value theory more openly, by asserting that the means of production, such as machinery, etc., also laboured. [16]

J. S. Mill learned economic theory from his father in his childhood. He followed the idea of treating production, distribution, exchange and consumption separately, and added the distinction between static and dynamic theory. What was characteristic of his work was the contrast between the theory of production and that of distribution. According to him 'the laws and conditions of the production of wealth partake of the character of physical truth', whereas the distribution of wealth is 'a matter of human institution solely'.[17] These contrasting treatments reflect his sympathy with co-operative socialism and a sense of the historical limits of a capitalist economy. Theoretically his position was really eclectic, because he characterised capital together with labour and nature as eternal physical factors of production by following classical naturalism in the theory of production on the one hand, while, on the other, he believed in the possibility of altering the laws and institutions of distribution, along a socialist path. Here is a theoretical source of reformist socialism.

J. S. Mill was an eclectic in value theory as well. He seemed to follow Ricardo's value theory in stating that the source of profit was in the fact that labour produces more than what is necessary for its maintainance, and that 'the value of commodities . . . depends principally . . . on the quantity of labour required for their production'.[18] But he simultaneously explained profit as reward for restraining from consuming capital, and further used the cost of production theory of value. As a result the labour theory of value in J. S. Mill appeared in the extremely restricted sense that wages usually made up the principal part of money costs of production for the capitalist.

Thus, in spite of their subjective intention of keeping Ricardo's theory, these theorists were in fact revising and gradually dissolving the substantial basis of classical economics. A more decisive farewell to the classical tradition, taking the form of the marginalist revolution, was already being prepared. At the same time the classicists' neglect of the historical character of the capitalist economy was being criticised ideologically by the early socialists, and eclectically in J. S. Mill's theory of distribution. R. Jones (1790–1855) stepped forward in this direction and compared various social forms especially the forms of ground-rent in different societies with the capitalist forms in England.[19] The dissolution of the classical school, in the form of the historical school, was able to find its antecedents in these ideological and theoretical critiques and Jones' method of positivist comparative observation.

## 2.2 THE HISTORICAL SCHOOL

A more decisive critique of the classical school and an initiating work for the German historical school was made by F. List (1789–1846). In his view the classical school over-generalised the particular interest of the advanced British economy in asserting the *laissez-faire* liberal policy as if it were cosmopolitan natural justice. For a less-advanced and developing country like Germany, national protectionist policies enabling a rise in productive power were both necessary and justifiable in the process of catching up. List formulated five stages for the development of national economies; 'original barbarism, pastoral condition, agricultural condition, agricultural-manufacturing condition, and agricultural-manufacturing-commercial condition'.[20] He believed it necessary to protect the domestic market from the advanced competitive country especially when the less-advanced country was shifting, under the pressure of international competition, from the fourth to the final fifth stage. He also believed in the effect of national political unification, as well as the influence of individual mental and physical powers, social institutions, natural resources, and the balance between agriculture and industry, on the growth of national productivity.

Thus List critically asserted that Manchesterism in the classical school could not be an universal political stance, but a specific representation of British interests as the most advanced country. He also argued for certain necessary conditions and economic policies required to strengthen the national productive power of a less-advanced country, like Germany, confronting the competition of an advanced country. Along with such criticisms and assertions List disregarded general economic theories and tended to replace them with concrete studies of history and politics. His historicism contained a passionate German nationalism emphasising the importance of national unification.

W. Roscher (1817–94), B. Hildebrand (1812–78) and K. Knies (1821–98) among others established the German historical school, by extending the path which List had indicated. They maintained that national economies were always formed in close relation with a historical development of laws, the state and culture, and thus appeared as concretely historical phenomena.[21] Therefore comparative studies and historical approaches would be essential for understanding the nature and cultural stages of each national economy. Basic general theories were apparently discarded and detailed descriptive studies of specific concrete historical phenomena were generally pursued and absorbed in historical material.

When German capitalism actually began to grow rapidly after the victory in the Franco-Prussian War (1870–1) the German workers movement also grew and became increasingly guided by Marxism. Against this Marxian influence G. Schmoller (1838–1917), L. Brentano (1844–1931), A. Wagner (1835–1917) and others organised *Verein für sozial Politik* in 1873 and formed the younger German historical school. This school tried to combine political economy or economic history with social ethics, and was called Katheder (lecture-desk) socialism by their liberal and Marxist opponents. For example, Schmoller asserted that social policies to support and to increase the middle class were necessary in order to dissolve class confrontation.[22] Brentano emphasised the necessity of stabilising the workers economic life by their own union efforts,[23] and Wagner laid stress on national-socialistic reformism and protectionism for the same purpose.[24]

The younger German historical school obtained decisive authority among German academia and produced certain achievements in its historical studies. However, the school could not establish a firm methodological and theoretical basis, and tended to mix personal or directly political judgements with scientific studies. The methodological debate in the 1880s was between Schmoller and K. Menger, who criticised the historical school by asserting the need for theoretical economics as a precise science,[25] which was rejected and neglected by Schmoller and his school at that time. Later, at the beginning of twentieth century, M. Weber (1864–1920) attempted to amend some weaknesses in the historical school as its successor. As I mentioned at the beginning of this part, he distinguished political or personal value judgements from scientifically objective recognition. In his opinion, freedom from value judgements was both possible and necessary for scientific researches. Weber adopted an approach of building up ideal types (*Idealtypen*) to study human behaviour in social life especially concerning motivation. *The Protestant Ethic and the Spirit of Capitalism*[26] (1904–5) was a product of such an approach.

The development of the German historical school influenced and echoed among similar tendencies with more or less different colours in other countries. In England a series of historical studies by J. K. Ingram (1823–1907), W. J. Ashley (1860–1927) and A. Toynbee (1852–1883), or the concrete institutional studies like *Lombard Street* (1873) by W. Bagehot (1826–77),[27] and *Imperialism* (1902) by J. A. Hobson (1858–1940)[28] represented such tendencies. In USA, the institutional school was originated by T. B. Veblen (1857–1922)[29] and was followed by W. C. Mitchell (1874–1948), J. R. Commons (1862–1945) and J. M. Clark (1884–1963). Further we see more recently this tradition in the works presented by J. K. Galbraith (1908–),[30] or even by some US radical economists. K. Polanyi[31] (1886–1964), who came from Hungary and worked in Austria, Britain and then the USA since 1946, was also a sort of successor to the historical school. There was also a strong influence from the German historical school, especially the younger, among the founders of Japanese academia in economics since the end of the nineteenth century. This influence has remained particularly among economic historians in Japan, overlapping with thc influence of the views of Marxian economics, as I have referred to elsewhere.[32]

Anyway, the historical school and its various successors as a whole tended to be more or less critical of the universal claims and relevancies of the classical school, and further of the neo-classical and the Marxian theories as well. They attached importance to the concrete factors of socio-economic development which were often neglected by the theoretical studies in economics. The typological studies of human motivation, social institutions and ethics were pushed forward and they shed light on the different concrete situations of economic development. Thus starting from studies of economic policies for the less-advanced capitalist countries like Germany the historical school contributed quite a lot from various angles to the concrete observation of other national economies. Whenever dominant orthodox economics reaches a deadlock in its theoretical relevance, as we are again witnessing, the approach of the historical school has a good chance of being revived. Socio-economic difficulties within the third world countries in particular might provoke such an approach.

However, so long as the main stream of the historical school has opposed Marxism as well as the classical and the neo-classical schools, it has often been reformistic and technocratic, easily combined with varieties of ideologies including extreme nationalism or Nazism. At the same time with its inclination to stick to the national concrete features of economic development, the historical school could not or intentionally did not present theoretically systematic studies of the capitalist economy and thereby overcome the theoretical defects of the classical school.

## 2.3 THE NEO-CLASSICAL SCHOOL

The birth and the growth of the neo-classical school was another reaction to the deadlock and dissolution of the classical school.[33] This school has attempted to formulate universal theories in sharp contrast to the historical school, and has become dominant among Anglo-American academia, and then extended throughout the capitalist world in the period after the Second World War. We follow here the concept of the neo-classical school in its broadest sense, including Keynesianism. As is well known the mariginal revolution led by C. Menger (1835–1921), M. E. L. Walras (1834–1910) and W. S. Jevons (1835–82) initiated the school at the beginning of 1870s.[34]

As a whole this school switched the theoretical focus to circulation and shifted back the determination of profit from profit-on-production to profit-on-alienation, although its expressions became mathematically sophisticated.

C. Menger among the initiators, and his followers like E. von Böhm-Bawerk (1851–1914) and F. von Wieser (1851–1926) formed the marginal utility school or Austrian school based in Vienna. They assumed the measurability of the individuals subjective utility for various goods, and a law of diminishing utility for each additional unit of the same good consumed. Upon such assumptions the maximum satisfaction of consumers would be a situation where the marginal utility of a commodity to be purchased by a unit of income becomes equal for every different commodity. This is the law of equal marginal utilities. As the physical units of various goods are not directly comparable the maximum satisfaction of consumers households would be obtained when the proportions of the marginal utility to the price of each sort of commodity become equalised.

Thus the price theory of the Austrian School, shifted its basis from production to the personal psychological selection of consumers. It clearly assumed consumers sovereignty and treated goods simply as given materials in the market for the subjective judgements of consumers. Although it seemed to present a new and consistent explanation of equilibrium prices, it also contained some basic difficulties. For instance, is individuals subjective utility really measurable and comparable between different goods and individuals? Or, is the law of diminishing marginal utility applicable to money? (So far as the value of money was explained separately by the quantity theory of money, the value theory of the Austrian School was not very consistent.) Further, how can the value of producers' goods and the source of profit be explained? Since producer goods or means of production do not have utility for consumers Wieser imputes these prices from the prices of consumers' goods. This theory of imputation, however, cannot explain profit or interest obtained within prices other than costs of production.

Böhm-Bawerk presented his agio theory in order to show the rationality of profit or interest in the framework of the Austrian school.[35] He asserted that interest for capital arose from the different utilities acknowledged between present consumption and the future consumption of goods. Men and women as consumers would supposedly acknowledge greater utility from the present goods, because the future goods are to be assessed in a less certain and distant perspective. The marginal utility of the means of production, which is imputed from the marginal utility of future consumption goods (yet to be produced), will grow gradually as the perceived future goods become the actual present goods through production in the process of time. This growth of the marginal utility of means of production is defined as the source of capital interest by Böhm-Bawerk. Apparently this explanation may not hold in a stable economy with a constant scale of reproduction, not to mention the more extreme case where quantities of future products could supposedly be reduced so as to increase their marginal utility above that of the present goods. Avoiding these cases, Böhm-Bawerk assumes the effect of roundabout production which enables more consumption goods to be obtained in the future by utilising the present goods for production, and makes an additional explanation of the source of capital interest out of this effect.

Böhm-Bawerk's theory of capital interest is one of the rare serious attempts to explain the source of profit or interest, consciously substituting it for the classical or Marxian theory of profit on the basis of the labour theory of value. However it does not seem very persuasive. Besides the difficulty in the case of a stable or shrinking economy mentioned above, the additional explanation about the effect of roundabout production is not merely remote from marginal utility theory, but also lacks of logical proof as why the increased physical quantities of products should constitute increased amounts of value as a whole. More fundamentally from the Marxian view, the effect of roundabout production, as well as the psychological attitude about present and future goods in Böhm-Bawerk's treatment could in a sense be regarded as common to any social formation, and could not therefore be a sufficient basis from which to explain surplus value as specifically generated in a capitalist society. On the other hand, the universal human ability to perform surplus labour as a basis of bringing about surplus products by 'round-about' production in any society was completely dismissed from a narrowly limited view of the market from a marginalist framework . Thus, by a naturalist view of profit-upon-alienation, Böhm-Bawerk failed theoretically to clarify what was the basis of the economic surplus really common to all the societies and what made it appear in the forms of profit and interest specific to the commodity economy. The seemingly universal psychological attitude about present and future goods may represent human motivation, as promoted by a capitalist economic order, and may not really exist independently of the existence of interest.

L. Walras presented a general equilibrium theory and initiated the Lausanne School. Assuming the law of the maximisation of the utility of commodities by individuals (just like the law of equal marginal utilities), and the equality of income and expenditure of each commodity owner, Walras showed that a general equilibrium condition can be defined and reached between prices, and in the demand and supply of all commodities in a market, by solving a series of simultaneous equations. The same approach was extended to the determination of equilibrium prices of productive services in a market, and further also to capital stock, securities and money. Though Walras treated the measurability of utility as a sort of necessary logical assumption, his follower, V. Pareto [36] (1843–1923), replaced it by the theory of choice as represented in indifference curves.

General equilibrium theory found widespread and powerful supporters outside of Lausanne University where Walras and Pareto worked, like J. A. Schumpeter[37] (1883–1950) and J. R. Hicks [38] (1904–). While it seems consistent in itself, it is definitely a formal theory of equilibrium prices, without analysing the substantial values and surplus values behind them, and is even more superficial than marginal utility theory, not to mention classical price theory. It is also essentially a static equilibrium theory and cannot be extended to a fully dynamic theory in a coherent way.

A. Marshall (1824–1924), who founded the Cambridge School (or the neo-classical school in the narrowest sense), attempted to combine static micro-price theory and dynamic macro-theory. In his *Principles of Economics*[39] Marshall inherited the marginal utility theory from Jevons and also the production costs theory from J. S. Mill. He distinguished short-term normal prices and long-term normal prices, and asserted that marginal utility theory is more relevant to short-term prices, while the production costs theory is more relevant to long-term prices. He believed in a biological and evolutionary approach to long-term economic growth. Though ideologically he tended to represent the interests of industrial capital he also maintained that the trade-union movement would be viable and effective in raising workers' incomes in the process of increasing productivity. While wages and profit oppose each other in the short run they could grow harmoniously in the long run in Marshall's view.

Marshall was clearly eclectic in combining the marginal utility theory and the production costs theory, or short-term equilibrium theory and long-term dynamic growth theory. His long-term theory in particular handed down a practical character in the observation of the social economic relations between workers and capitalists from the traditionally British views of political economy. A. C. Pigou (1877–1959) extended such social concerns into welfare economics and asserted, for instance, that national economic welfare usually increased with the increase of the share of national income going to poorer people.[40] Including such welfare economics as well as the more basic marginal micro theory of prices, general equilibrium theory, and dynamic macro growth theory, the neo-classical school has formed an eclectic but comprehensive ensemble of partial theories, and became a general name for all the theoretical economics following the marginalist revolution, not only confined to Anglo-American economic academia.

The neo-classical theories typically represented by Marshall and Pigou had various limitations. Among others there were at least two serious theoretical problems even from the marginalist point of view. First, the working of a market mechanism to adjust the supply and demand of commodities in a harmonious equilibrium was one-sidedly presumed, as well as the operation of Say's law. Involuntary unemployment was theoretically regarded as impossible in a freely competitive market, and full employment would always be achieved in an equilibrium market. This neo-classical view of a harmonious market economy was untenable in regard to the historical fact that capitalism was accompanied by many economic crises and depressions, and especially with the experience of 1930s. Second, there was an inconsistency between the theory of price determination, and the quantity theory of the value of money as has been mentioned already in the case of the Austrian School.

J. M. Keynes (1883–1946) attempted to overcome the limitations of the neo-classical school. In *The General Theory of Employment, Interest and Money*[41] he introduced the concept of liquidity preference into the theory of money and interest so as to restore consistency with the theory of prices of other commodities. He intended also to generalise marginalists economic theory by negating Say's law and showing the possibility of equilibrium with underemployment. According to Keynes the increase in the effective demand of consumers must be less than the posssible increase in national income so far as the marginal propensity to consume is less than one. Without sufficient investment demand to fill the gap, the total effective demand must be less than necessary to realise full employment. Thus it is by no means accidental for an economy to be in equilibrium, with various levels of involuntary unemployment, when incentive or opportunities for capitalist investment are insufficient. As this sort of economic situation tends to appear and continue in matured individualistic capitalism, state policies to control effective demand have to be legitimised in order to solve the difficulty. Policies to increase the propensity to consume by mitigating the existing imbalance of income distribution, does not suffice. An easy-money policy to stimulate new investment by pulling the rate of interest down to the marginal efficiency (or the marginal rate of profit) of capital, and a fiscal spending policy to add to the effective demand through state public expenditures, must therefore be operated in combination in order to realise and maintain full employment. Such economic policies can work elastically only when the controlled currency system is adopted by abolishing the gold-standard system.

A theoretical model similar to Keynes's was also presented by M. Kalecki[42] independently and rather earlier (though the English translation from the Polish appeared after *The General Theory*). This stressed the strategic importance of the level of capitalist investment in determining the macro-economic levels of national income and employment. In contract with Keynes Kalecki emphasised more the role of the degree of monopoly and the level of gross profit in determining the amount of investment. Keynesian theory became influential in the capitalist world after the Second World War and up until the beginning of the 1970s. US Keynesians like A. Hansen (1887–1975) or P. Samuelson (1915– ) gained prestige, as Keynesian policy operations in the USA seemed successful in maintaining the continuous economic growth of the world capitalism in this period. A combination of neo-classical micro-price theories and Keynesian macro theory was called the 'neo-classical synthesis' or 'mainstream economics,' and tended to prevail in most capitalist countries. Although Keynesian theory opposes some propositions of the previous neo-classical school, it has in fact a basic approach common to the neo-classical micro price theories. For instance, personal preference and the decisive role of demand are commonly taken as the launching bases for theoretical analyses, and price determination in a market by the marginalist approach is taken for the unconditional framework.

Keynes as well as the preceding neo-classicists observed the capitalist economy not as a class society, but as a free society of commodity owners. In the neo-classical tradition including Keynesians, economic theories thus tend in effect to legitimate the existing capitalist social order. The theoretical equality, for example, between the marginal productivity, the subjective rate of preference over time and the rate of interest is generally understood to mean that interest or profit is a reward for the sacrifice of postponing consumption, being proportional to the marginal contribution of capital to production. Such a view is combined with a similar concept that wages and ground rent are rewards for sacrificing leisure time and use of land, each being paid in proportion to the marginal contribution of labour and land to production. It works as a theory justifying a social relation in which owners of capital can obtain interest or profit, irrespective of the personal intention or motivation of those learn or teach the neo-classical economics. As B. Rowthorn clearly points out, 'neo-classical economics constitutes an "epistemological obstacle" whose significant effect on a scientific plane is simply to inhibit the development of an authentic science of modes of production'.[43] In these regards neo-classical economics must belong to what Marx called 'vulgar economy'.[44]

As we have seen, the source and the essence of profit and interest are not properly explained, and the capitalist system which acquires surplus labour in particular social forms is totally dismissed by the neo-classical school. It also dismisses the fact that there are various societies where abstinence from present consumption, or the contribution of means of production to productivity, or their combination does not generate any profit or interest. A capitalist economy is regarded as so natural. The distribution of the initial endowments of factors of production and services for individuals is assumed to be given; and the social process and the mechanism which determines the distribution of these endowments is theoretically unquestioned in neo-classical theory, even though this distribution is decisive for the pattern of income distribution settled in a market.

Further, theoretically, neo-classical theory contains an internal inconsistency. Historically it abandoned, via J. S. Mill, the objective labour theory of value, and formed a theory defining wages and the rate of profit (or the rate of interest) as well as prices of goods on the conceptual basis of the marginal preference of consumers and marginal productivity of factors of production. The marginal productivity of capital determining the rate of profit then logically presupposes a homogeneous value of capital across various means of production. But there is a vicious circle so long as values of capital goods can not be determined independently from the rate of interest. A similar logical inconsistency is shown effectively by P. Sraffa (1898–1983) on the 'reswitching problem.'[45] According to the neo-classical marginal theory the aggregate production function must be selected monotonously from more to less capital intensive technology as wages continuously decline and the rate of profit, conversely, goes up. But Sraffa showed that a certain type of technology with a higher capital intensive production function can possibly reappear when wages come down. In sum, what Sraffa proved was that it was impossible to equate profits with some notion of 'marginal productivity' of capital advanced. This demonstration was a considerable blow to the neo-classical distribution theory of wages and profit based on the concept of the aggregate production function, as well as to the marginalist theory of capital value.

The marginal revolution which initiated the neo-classical school, originally seemed able to resolve or rather avoid the logical deadlock of the classical school in explaining prices, including the equalised rate of profit across various industrial technologies, from the basic labour theory of value. It is striking to see that a similar deadlock reappeared from a different angle nearly a century later, again for neo-classical theory in its inability to resolve capital values and the reswitching problem consistently in relation to the determination of the rate of profit. The neo-Ricardian school after Sraffa, effectively criticised this logical difficulty for the neo-classical school, and showed that prices and the general rate of profit could be determined on the basis of physical data concerning technological processes of production and a wage goods bundle. Since the amounts of labour embodied in products are apparently also calculable from the physical data of production, neo-Ricardian price theory naturally revived interest in the objective labour theory of value, especially that of Marx. Interestingly, so far as Marxian theory initially assumes prices proportional to labour values, the transformation problem of how to reconcile values with the prices of production, including the equalisation of the rate of profit, remains as we shall see later, substantially in the same logical spot where both classical value theory and neo-classical theory with an aggregate production function have come into deadlock.

In comparison with the neo-classical school, the neo-Ricardians explicitly analyse the opposing economic interests of the capitalists and the labouring class. However, the class relation is observed concerning just the division of the physical outputs and is not related to social surplus-labour or with the production process. In this regard the neo-Ricardians, unlike Marxians, do not inherit the classical labour theory of value, and do not attempt substantially to solve its difficulty. In a sense the neo-Ricardian school is still trapped by the neo-classical view that the determination of prices in a market is absolutely the major problem for economic theories, and as a price theory, the Sraffa model cannot really negate the consistency of the general equilibrium type of demand – supply theory. As we shall see later, the Marxian theory is free from such a narrow view of a market economy and may overcome the theoretical limitations not only of the classical school, but also of the neo-classical and the neo-Ricardian school from a broader point of view, by restoring the substantial social content of the value theory.

We must not overlook the fact that Keynesian theory contains serious insights into the conflicting and unstable nature of a capitalist economy in spite of its many theoretical limitations, held in common with the preceding neo-classical theories. However, as we have seen, the Keynesians are concerned exclusively with the shortage of total effective demand as the cause of involuntary unemployment, and also believe in the effectiveness of state policies to realise full employment. Their analyses cannot go further than the framework of a market economy, into the deeper inner contradictions of the capitalist production and accumulation process which under certain circumstances finally annul Keynesian policies as we witness today. Supply-side economics and monetarist economics has become the theoretical basis for Thatcherism and Reaganomics after the collapse in prestige of Keynesianism. They represent a reactionary return to the older neo-classicist beliefs in Say's law and the harmonious working of a market economy. They are thus further removed from studying the roots of the self-contradictions of a capitalist economy with its historically specific character. The weaknesses and limitations of Keynesian theory, as well as of the monetarist, may also be overcome by a fundamentally different development of the economic theory of capitalism in the framework of the Marxian school.

# 3 The Marxian Theory of Capitalism

## 3.1 HISTORICAL MATERIALISM AND MARX'S ECONOMICS

### Hegel, Feuerbach and Marx

The Marxian school which was founded by K. Marx (1818–1883) also arose out of the theoretical limits and deadlocks of the classical school. Marx's renovation of economics was, however, quite different from the directions of other contemporary economic schools. Unlike the historical school or the neo-classical school, Marx did not discard the essential theoretical contents and achievements of the classical school which was based on the labour theory of value, but fully attempted to inherit them by criticising and solving the deadlocks in the classical theories from within. In such an attempt Marx consciously and systematically clarified the historical character of a capitalist economy.

Indeed Marx's innovation in economics is in the reformulation and extension of the major tasks of economics itself. He initiated systematic and theoretical studies of the capitalist economy with its historically limited character. *Both* the ahistorical views of the classical and the neo-classical school, *and* the non-theoretical studies of economic history in the historical school, could in effect be criticised as narrowly one-sided by Marx and his followers. How did Marx originally reach such a new approach to economic theories?

As is well known, Marx studied history and philosophy, especially Hegel's works, while he was a student of law in the University of Berlin from 1836. Though Hegel had died in 1831 his philosophy was still prestigious and attractive. It formed a zenith of German idealist philosophy and was really a grand and erudite system of philosophy which explained dialectically all the phenomena of the human spirit, of external nature, and social structures as a logical development of contradictions in the process of the self-revelation of the absolute spirit. The absolute spirit in Hegel was a driving and creative subject, like a rationalised Christian god, in his dialectical system, moving repeatedly through thesis, anti-thesis and synthesis. The dialectic, which was extensively mobilised by Hegel, was not concervative in its essence. In a rational form, as Marx reflects later, it can be radically progressive 'because it includes in its positive understanding of what exists a simultaneous recognition of its negation, its inevitable destruction; because it regards every historically developed form as being in a fluid state, in motion, and therefore grasps its transient aspect as well' (I, p. 103). In Hegel, however, dialectic took a msytified form so long as the absolute spirit or the *Idea* was taken for the creator of the real world. The existing society in Prussia could then interpreted as a completed realisation of the rational *Idea*, and actually tended to be conservatively glorified by Hegel's famous *double entendre* proposition 'What is rational, that is actual, and what is actual, that is rational.'[1]

However, there appeared a radical left wing among Hegelians. Critiques of religion especially of Christianity which was still dominant in German societies were the major concern of left Hegelians. They represented in a German fashion the progressive contemporary European spirit of liberating human activities from the older feudal social order. In contrast with the economic Industrial Revolution in England and the French political Revolution, the German radical movement had yet to remain in the ideological field. A leader of left Hegelians in Berlin was B. Bauer (1809–82), who denied the godhood of Jesus Christ. Marx as a student joined Bauer's group and wrote a doctoral dissertation on 'The Difference in Natural Philosophy between Demokritos and Epikuros' emphasising the essential freedom of human will from the point of view of a left Hegelian in 1841. Although he had been invited by Bauer to take a teaching job at the University of Bonn, the invitation was not realised because Bauer himself had to leave the university with the change of the political tide in Prussia. Thus Marx took a more practical job as an editorial writer of a newspaper, the *Rheinische Zeitung* , in 1842 and began to write and think more about real social problems.

A most distinguished philosopher who pushed forward the left Hegelian critique of religion at that time was L. A. Feuerbach (1804–72). His main work *The Essence of Christianity*[2] appeared in 1841 and created a profound affect among the younger progressive generation including Marx and F. Engels. It emphasised that the human being was not a creation of god but of a natural existence. Simultaneously it asserted that the Christian god was nothing but an idealisation of common supreme human feelings such as fraternity or love. God is not then a creator, but a creation of the human mind, being a sort of fantasy. Human life in this world should be liberated from such religious fetishism. Feuerbach thus came to oppose idealism and the theological implications of Hegels work, and asserted a humanistic materialism. It would seem that Feuerbach prepared an important clue to Marx to invert Hegel's dialectic, which was 'standing on its head', or an idealism. However, the inversion of the dialectical method from idealism to materialism by Feuerbach was not sufficient. Albeit powerful and influential, it was limited to a philosophical critique of religion and concentrated only on the spiritual activities of mankind. In other words, human life in this world was still observed abstractly without considering the social or historical concreteness of practical activity. Nor was the liberation of human life related to social concrete activity.[3]

Marx felt such insufficiencies in Feuerbach, while writing editorial articles for the *Rheinische Zeitung* concerning actual social issues. For instance there were issues about the strengthening censorship; the law on the theft of wood prohibiting the traditional communal right of Rhineland peasants to utilise the forest; free trade or protectionist trade duties; and French socialist or communist thought. Although Marx could discuss censorship fairly well in the light of humanistic materialism, he realised that he was not yet fully qualified to handle economic issues. While he was against the immature socialism or communism from France, he felt that the topic must also be studied further. When the progressive tone of the newspaper became difficult to maintain under the strengthened censorship, he thus resigned the job at the *Rheinische Zeitung* and moved to Paris to study anew in 1843.

In Paris Marx began seriously to study classical and anti-classical political economy, and wrote what have become known as his 'Economic and Philosophical Manuscripts' in 1844, where he began to use the concept 'alienated labour' as a key to criticise both classical economics and Hegelian philosophy. In the same year F. Engels (1820–95) visited Paris, meeting Marx and starting a lifelong fraternal co-operation. The next year, 1845, Marx was exiled from France and moved to Brussels. He worked with Engels to write *The Holy Family* (1845, in *MECW*, vol. 4, pp. 5 ff.) and *The German Ideology* (1845–6, in *MECW*, vol. 5, pp. 19 ff.), and began to create his own new materialism or historical materialism through criticising and clearing up his previous standpoint along with the whole of German philosophy after Hegel. The contents of historical materialism was published first in a controversial style in *The Poverty of Philosophy*

(1847, in *MECW*, vol. 6, pp. 105 ff.), and then briefly formulated later in the Preface to *A Critique of Political Economy* (1859). Once obtained as the general result of the critical review of Hegelian philosophy along with the investigation of political economy, historical materialism 'served as a guiding thread',[4] for Marx's further studies which were more and more concentrated on the basic economic theory of capitalism. Its main points can be summarised as follows.[5]

A social superstructure and ideologies like politics, law, religion and social consciousness do not move independently. They are not created nor moved by the heavenly *Idea* or the absolute spirit. They are formed and conditioned by the economic structure, the real foundation of each society. The economic social structure mainly consists of the material productive forces and the relations of production, and develops historically through the dialectical motion between the productive forces and the relations of production. An epoch of social revolution begins when the relations of production turn from being the appropriate forms for the forces of production into fetters on the development of those forces. The changes in the economic foundation lead sooner or later to the transformation of the whole immense superstructure; and men become conscious of this social basic conflict and fight it out in various ideological forms. 'In broad outline, the asiatic, ancient, feudal, and modern bourgeois modes of production may be designated as epochs marking progress in the economic development of society'. The bourgeois mode of production is the last antagonistic form of the social process of production. The prehistory of human society ends, therefore, with this social formation.

In view of this historical materialism, not only Hegel's idealism but also Feuerbach's spiritual liberation from the medieval Christian fetter through humanistic materialism is obviously far from being sufficient. Really total human liberation is realisable only in the true history, or the history of human society which begins after abolishing the final class relations of production as developed in a capitalist society. The driving subject of the dialectic was thus turned from Hegel's absolute spirit or the *Idea* via Feuerbach's natural human being to the productive forces of Marx's new world view. The productive forces are the degree of development of productivity based upon technological changes. With the inevitable progress in the productive forces, the nature of the relations of production, which represent the social system organising the direct workers under the ruling class in class societies, must change sooner or later. This view of the dialectic between the forces of production and the relations of production by Marx also enabled him to overcome the weaknesses in early socialism, particularly the romantic tendency to admire past societies. It is now clear that Marx's original reframing of the basic economic theory of capitalism is guided by his new world view, i.e. historical materialism.

### The Role of Historical Materialism

Marx's pithy materialist concept of history is an indispensable 'guiding thread' for Marxian socialism and economics. Accordingly its role and contents are worth careful consideration. Serious damage might occur from its misuse.

For instance, in a conventional explanation of Marxism, historical materialism tends to be treated as an absolute truth which is formed by the application of the materialistic dialectic to human history prior to economic studies. Marxian economics is then an application of historical materialism to the economic process of a bourgeois society. The reversal of the Hegelian idealistic dialectic into the materialist dialectic is fundamental to this view. The process and grounds of such a reversal often seem metaphysical or remain unexplained in this type of explanation.

Engels later attempted to write *Dialectics of Natures*[6] in 1873–86, but left it unfinished. Judging from the structure of his *Anti-Dühring*[7] (1877-8), Engels had seemingly it in mind to base a materialist dialectic firstly on natural philosophy and the natural sciences. A materialist concept of history might then be obtainable on the basis of a materialist dialectical method prior to and independently from economic studies. Such a view seems to be implied when Engels declares that 'These two great discoveries, the materialistic concept of history and the revelation of the secret of capitalistic production through surplus-value, we owe to Marx. With these discoveries Socialism became a science.'[8]

There may be many cases where a materialist dialectic can be a useful guiding thread for researches in the natural sciences. However, the characters of various natural phenomena from almost infinitely divisible material elements to the vast macrocosmos are so diverse that any unified logic covering all of them seems almost impossible. In fact Engel's attempt to show a materialist dialectic in natural phenomena is not only unfinished but also appears to be a collection of examples suitable to his position. His atempt to establish a materialist dialectic, firstly in the realm of nature, could not be very successful in spite of his encyclopedic knowledge at that time. Historical materialism could not find a very solid basis in such an approach.

The formation of historical materialism by Marx was actually performed not through merely abstract philosophical thinking or through general reflection on the natural sciences. Marx's reversal of the Hegelian idealist dialectic was achieved by way of Feuerbach's humanistic materialism and then by overcoming Feuerbach on the basis of critical studies of the classical school. Marx's concern about the actual conditions of human existence especially in a capitalist economic order, which was being analysed by economic theory, was a decisive factor for him in forming the materialist dialectical method and historical materialism simultaneously. In view of such a formation process, historical materialism in Marx could not be separated from his economic studies, and should not be regarded as an absolute external premise for the social sciences.

It is also indispensable for historical materialism to receive support from theoretical studies of a capitalist economy. For instance, it would be difficult to show clearly and at a stroke the autonomous motion of the economic substructure separately from the superstructure of a society for every social formation throughout the whole of human history. The relations of production in precapitalist societies were usually intermingled with political and religious orders, and seemed to be dominated by and maintained through such superstructures. Whereas in the historical development of capitalism, social reproduction which was organised in a commodity economy, revealed more and more clearly its own autonomous economic mechanism of motion separate from political or juridical superstructures. The classical school was, to a certain extent, identifying such a character in the capitalist economy and Marx confronted its achievements with a critique of its naturalism. In particular therefore a strong argument for historical materialism could be given through theoretical researches into a capitalist economy. K. Uno (1897–1977), who was a non-dogmatic creative Marxian theorist initiating the Uno school in post-Second World War Japan, methodologically emphasised this point. He stated that 'the characteristic of Marx's method could be found in the fact that Marx established historical materialism in the process of studying political economy and also attempted scientifically to corroborate it by economic researches'.[9]

Whereas both must thus be closely related, the difference between the task of historical materialism and that of political economy should not be confused. Historical materialism is a more or less ideological and hypothetical view of total human history. It cannot be a fully objective scientific recognition. In contrast Marx attempted to show, in his economic theory, the objectively recognisable law of motion of a capitalist economy particularly in his main work *Capital*. Certainly the role of historical materialism as a guide to Marxian economics towards broader problems, which are usually hidden in the economic theories confined by bourgeois ideology, can never be denied. However, the contents of economic research by Marx and his followers should be regarded not as mere ideological reproaches, but as objective and scientific studies of a capitalist economy. The results of Marxian economic research must be judged and revised according to theoretical logic and historical facts just as in any other social sciences.

It is actually easier for Marxian theorists than those of other schools, consciously to distinguish the role of ideology and that of economic research, because they can broadly be concerned with the historical changes in ideological superstructures and the economic substructure. By clarifying the historically specific forms and mechanisms of a capitalist economy, Marxian economic theory reveals the source and the social functions of fetishised common sense concerning commodity, money and capital in our bourgeois society. Marxian socialist ideology is formed only when such fetish bourgeois common sense is critically overcome. Marxian economics thus offers a theoretical ground from which to criticise bourgeois ideology and to assert a socialist ideological view of history. As we shall gradually see later in this volume, the Marxian economic theory of capitalism also reveals the basically autonomous character of capitalism's economic substructure, the dynamism between its productive forces and its relations of production, as well as the general material basis common to all societies, and those common to all *class* societies. Among others these points in the Marxian theory of capitalism can undoubtedly serve as the basis upon which to clarify concepts for historical materialism.

By confining its direct object of study to a historically limited social formation, i.e. capitalism, Marxian economic theory can define its starting-points, logical sequences and the system of basic principles, and thus objectively reflects the character of its object. Historical materialism is a useful guiding thread for orienting economic study to such an object from a historical point of view, but it cannot directly assure the scientifically objective correctness of economic studies, or cannot by itself be the explanatory concepts of a capitalist economy. It must be stressed, however, that historical materialism unlike other ideological views of history can be established through scientific economic studies of a capitalist economy. As Uno emphasised against conventional Marxism, Marxian economics must serve as a scientific basis of historical materialism, and not vice versa. The materialist dialectical method might also be more properly grounded by Marxian social sciences on the basis of economics rather than the natural sciences.

From the viewpoint of Marxism as a scientific argument and movement for socialism, the economic theory can show the *possibility* of transforming capitalism into socialism by objectively defining the historical specificity and limitations of a capitalist economy. But Marxian economics remains as an objective recognition of a possibly revolutionisable economic order, and cannot be a directly positive assertion of socialism. In this sense Marxian economics is certainly not sufficient for a completed Marxism. Historical materialism practically summarises the whole of human history in a formula which is at least partly supported by theoretical research on the nature of the substructure of a capitalist society. It is thus indispensable for Marxists in asserting the end of the history of class societies with the end of capitalism, and in building up a communal society of freely associated individuals. A dialectical, mutual relation between Marxian economics and historical materialism is therefore necessary to support Marxism from different aspects and levels.

Since it has obscured and weakened the sound scientific ground of Marxism to treat historical materialism as an absolutely proved theorem given prior to economic researches, we should not avoid handling the contents of historical materialism as a hypothetical theorem to be confirmed and amended through the development of both history itself and social scientific studies. For instance, Marx's formulation of historical materialism defined the productive forces as a most basic driving subject for the dialectical process of history by substituting these forces for the absolute spirit in Hegel's dialectic or the natural human being in Feuerbach's. The development of productive forces, however, must not be taken for an independent neutral process against the relations of production, that is, human social relations. In fact, the pace as well as the directions of the growth of productive forces under capitalism is apparently guided by the interests in the valorisation of capitals, and determined in the process of capital accumulation, and thus cannot be neutral or independent of the motion of capitals. As we shall discuss later in detail, the logical inevitability of cyclical crises in the process of capital accumulation should be clarified as an expression of the inner contradiction between the growth of productive forces determined by the motion of capitals and the relations of production of capital. Neither can the transformation of capitalism into socialism be a process of mechanical inevitability driven by a neutral development of productive forces. Social revolutions are necessary both consciously to establish communal orders and the development of production processes under autonomous workers control through the dissolution of the capitalist relations of production. These revolutions may make possible the reorientation of the contents of the development of productive forces so as to be more suitable for such co-operative communal associations.

There seems to have been an unfortunate mechanical interpretation of historical materialism in the post-revolutionary soviet type of society, where the growth of productive forces in central key industries through larger and larger scale of mechanisation has been believed to be the absolute basis for solving all the social problems. Distorted statism and economism have consequently been seriously conspicuous there.[10] The relation between the formulation of historical materialism and the contents of political economy has thus been not merely closely related in the process of their formation but also need to be reconsidered repeatedly with consequent political implications.

## Political Economy in the *Manifesto*

Soon after creating historical materialism Marx wrote with Engels the *Manifesto of the Communist Party* and published it in February 1848 by request of The Communist League. This *League* had been formed in June 1847 by linking up the main centres of communist activities in Paris, London, Brussels and Cologne. This pamphlet has been one of the most popular and influential among the massive volume of works by Marx and Engels, and presents prototypes of some of Marx's theories of capitalism. Those theories were clearly made up at that time by applying historical materialism more directly than in Marx's later writings like *Capital*. There are four sections in the *Manifesto of the Communist Party*[11] namely 'Bourgeois and Proletarians', 'Proletarians and Communists', 'Socialist and Communist Literature' and 'Position of the Communists in relation to the Various Existing Opposition Parties'. Marx and Engels's positive analyses and assertions are mainly in the first two sections. From the view of political economy the first section is particularly important.

The section begins with an impressive statement that 'The history of all hitherto existing society is the history of class struggles'. And then it describes the inevitable process of birth, growth and decline of the modern bourgeois society from the historical materialist view of class struggles. According to the authors the modern bourgeois society that sprouted from the ruins of feudal society has decomposed various lower middle classes into the proletariat, and has increasingly simplified class struggles into the social antagonism between the bourgeoisie and the proletariat. Such a modern society was born when the feudal relations of property were no longer compatible with the developing productive forces and were consequently broken down. With the growth of modern society the productive forces developed by capital began to revolt against the modern bourgeois properly relations. The revolt is manifested in the commercial crises that by their periodical return put on trial, each time more threateningly, the existence of the entire bourgeois society. Along with the periodical crises as well as the severe competition among bourgeois, and with the development of large-scale modern industry, property is concentrated more and more into a fewer hands, and the proletariat becomes concentrated into greater masses with increasing instability and poverty in their life and work.

'Thereupon the workers begin to form combinations (trades unions) against the bourgeois; they club together in order to keep up the rate of wages. . . . Here and there the contest breaks out into riots. Now and then the workers are victorious, but only for a time. The real fruit of their battles lies, not in the immediate result, but in the ever-expanding union of the workers.' Though in substance an international struggle, in form it is at first a national struggle of proletariat against the bourgeoisie in each country. With the development of modern industry the bourgeoisie produces 'its own grave-diggers'. 'Its fall and the victory of the proletariat are equally inevitable.'

The second section then describes the position of communists within the proletarian class, the measures to be taken by the victorious proletariat and the nature of the comunist society to be realised. For instance, the communists do not set up any sectarian principles of their own, by which to mould the proletarian movement. They always represent the interest of the proletarian movement as a whole. In order to do this, they must maintain and develop a theoretical understanding of the conditions, the line of march, and the general results of the proletarian movement. The first step in the revolution by the working class is to raise the proletariat to the position of ruling class, to win the battle of democracy. 'The proletariat will use its political supremacy to wrest, by degree, all capital from the bourgeoisie, to centralize all instruments of production in the hands of the state, i.e. of the proletariat organized as the ruling class; and to increase the total of productive forces as rapidly as possible.' In such a course of development, class distinctions will disappear and the public power will lose its political character. Then in place of the old bourgeois class society, we shall have an association, 'in which the free development of each is the condition for the free development of all'.

In the third section Marx and Engels criticise other preceding types of socialism such as reactionary, bourgeois, and Utopian. In the fourth section they propose communist strategies towards other opposition parties and conclude with an famous appeal that 'The proletarians have nothing to lose but their chains. They have a world to win. Working men of all countries, unite.'

The logical process of development of modern bourgeois society from its birth to decline in this *Manifesto* clearly depends on historical materialism. The development of productive forces is treated as a driving power breaking down the feudal social relations, intensifying commercial crises, and making inescapable the decline of the bourgeoisie through fostering poverty, combinations and revolutionary unions of workers. On the other hand, the growth of the productive forces is *not* viewed here one-sidedly as an independent neutral variable, determining the nature and the motion of the relations of production.

In accord with its class struggle view of history, the *Manifesto* recognises the different features of the growth of productive forces corresponding to the nature of the ruling class in each society. It says, for example, that 'conservation of the old modes of production in unaltered form, was . . . the first condition of existence for all earlier industrial classes'. On the contrary, 'the bourgeoisie, during its rule of scarcely one hundred years, has created more massive and more colossal productive forces than have all preceding generations together'. And further, the proletariat when organised as the ruling class will use its political supremacy 'to centralize all instruments of production in the hands of the State', and 'to increase the total of productive forces as rapidly as possible'.

Later in *Capital* the bourgeoisie is defined more concretely as 'capital personified' (e.g. I, p. 739), and the development of productive forces is analysed as a function of the motion of capital. Therefore in the process of reversing Hegel's idealistic dialcctic, Marx seems to have switched the subject of the rational materialist dialectic in three steps from the development of productive forces, via the changing ruling class, to capital itself. Though this switch certainly coincides with the shift of topics and may not immediately be inconsistent, it suggests that the path of growth of productive forces should not be regarded as a bare natural necessity. This is a point for us to reconsider and may enable us to deepen the formulation of historical materialism.

Another point is the concept of the relations of production, which tends to be identified in the *Manifesto* with the social relations of ownership of the instruments of production. The development of the relations of production, corresponding to the growth of productive forces, was conceptualised mainly as the historical changes in the form and the scale of ownership of means of production. Bourgeois society was formed when the instruments of production were centralised as the private property of the bourgeoisie organised as modern manufacturing forces of production. As bourgeois society develops, the degree of the centralisation of the means of production into the hands of a smaller number of bourgeoisie is intensified, being coupled with the increasing number and misery of the proletariat. Hence the polarisation of society into smaller number of richer bourgeoisie and the increasing number of poorer proletariat will proceed. Finally, bourgeois society will end when the means of production are taken back from the bourgeoisie and centralised in the hands of the state through the organised revolutionary struggle of the proletariat.

These theoretical views of a capitalist economy in the *Manifesto*, which were obtained by the inferential application of historical materialism, very much affected some parts of the formation of Marx's own economic theory as well as the development of Marxism after Marx, which we shall come back to occasionally. Although Marx attempted later, particularly in the light of the Paris Commune, to modify his view in the *Manifesto* concerning the proletariat's appropriation of the state as a ready-made apparatus, a distorted statism in a post-revolutionary society could well be legitimised by the theoretical overestimation of both the changes and centralisation of ownership of the means of production as well as by a deterministic (and in a sense too optimistic) belief in the effect of the growth of productive forces for socialism. On the other side the theory of the polarisation of a bourgeois society and the increasing misery of proletariat has been a source of confusion and continuous controversy about the relevancy of Marx's economic theory for the development of capitalism.

The *Manifesto* has served as a guiding star for workers' socialist movements and socialist revolutions all over the world. Its political role and influence have been so great that its theoretical contents have tended either to be literally believed by majority of orthodox Marxians or to be totally distrusted by non-Marxians. However, so far as it contains not merely political assertions, but also theoretical views of the economic development of bourgeois society, we must try to check the correctness or incorrectness of such views repeatedly from the standpoint of objective social science. At least Marx himself was not satisfied with his political economy in the *Manifesto*. He seemed to be aware that his socialist ideology did not assure by itself fully correct theories of a capitalist economy, and also that scientific endeavour for a more complete theoretical understanding of capitalism was indispensable in order to ground his socialist assertions more solidly. Therefore Marx resumed his critical studies of political economy. He devoted the latter half of his life mainly to working out a new system of the basic theory of capitalism, when exiled to London expelled again from his mother country Prussia, as well as from France and Belgium in 1849, after the revolutionary activities in the previous year.

## 3.2 THE SCOPE OF THE THEORETICAL SYSTEM OF *CAPITAL*

### The Formation and Structure of *Capital*

Marx studied carefully and critically a wide range of economic literature in the reading room of the British Museum during the 1850s, and began to write his life-work in 1857. He wrote systematic drafts of his main work three times over again before writing the first volume of *Capital* in 1866–7. (i) The first draft was written in 1857–8 mainly in seven notebooks and was entitled *Grundrisse*.[12] Then, *A Contribution to the Critique of Political Economy* (1859) was written in 1858–9. Besides the famous preface, where as we have seen historical materialism was briefly formulated, this *Critique* published only two introductory chapters on Commodities and Money, which were later revised and summarised in the first Part of the first volume of *Capital*. (ii) The second draft in twenty-three notebooks is *The Critique of Political Economy* (Manuscript 1861–3),[13] which begins with 'The Transformation of Money into Capital' following the contents of *The Critique*. About one-half in the middle of this draft has been separately published as *Theories of Surplus-Value*. (iii) The third draft, entitled *Capital* for the first time, was written in 1863–5. Its last part served as the sole material for Engels to edit and publish the third volume of *Capital* (1894). Only after preparing these three massive drafts, Marx wrote and published the first volume of *Capital* (1867). Its second volume (1885) was edited by Engels from Marx's drafts, mainly in the 1870s.

What Marx attempted to work out in *Capital* through such extensive studies and writing was clearly not a mere reproach to capitalism from the standpoint of his socialist ideology, nor a simple application of historical materialism to capitalism. The economic theory in *Capital*, unlike that of Sismondi or Malthus, does not negate the autonomous growth of a capitalist economy in spite of the logical necessity of (periodic) overproduction. Nor does it plans in detail a social order of reason and justice in order to realise socialism from above by enlightenment, to reform workers conditions like Fourier, Owen and other Utopian socialists did. Conversely it systematically clarifies the law of motion of an autonomous capitalist economy with its historical specificities and limitations. It thereby attempts to show wage-workers in basic principles the social mechanism and conditions which restrict their economic situation, and the object to be changed through their social movements in order to liberate themselves as really free human beings. Thus the economic theory of *Capital* intends to establish the basic principle of political economy as a critical social science, by absorbing the preceding theoretical achievements and systematically solving the problems left by the classical school.

In the first two Parts of the first volume of *Capital*, the basic forms of a commodity economy, i.e. commodities, money and capital are theoretically investigated through their logical relations. Marx inherited the labour theory of value from the classical school, but he dualised the value concept into the substance and the forms of value, which was essential in order to overcome naturalism in classical value theory. He discovered the wage-labourers in a modern society sold their commodity labour-power, and not directly labour itself, to capital under historically specific conditions. In the following three Parts, from the third to the fifth, Marx showed how capital could utilise the use-value of labour-power to produce surplus-value after paying its commodity value, and how capital could increase the efficiency of producing surplus-value. These Parts obvioulsy solved one of basic difficulties for the classical school, to explain the source of surplus-value on the basis of the labour theory of value. Decisive in this was the distinction between a full days labour obtainable for capitalists as the use-value of the commodity labour-power, and the portion of necessary labour time in it returned to workers as the value substance of the same commodity labour-power, obtained by the workers through the exchange between that commodity and the necessary means of consumption. Then the sixth Part, 'Wages', shows how the wage form conceals the secret of the production of surplus-value by the common-sense view of time-wages and piece-wages as full payment for all the labour performed, not to the value of the commodity labour-power. The seventh Part considers the influence of capital accumulation on the working class. The eighth Part reviews the historical process of the formation of a capitalist society typically in England, through the so-called primitive accumulation which is actually a violent process of creating a proletariat on a social scale.

Following the first volume 'The Process of Production of Capital', the second volume *Capital* investigates 'The Process of Circulation of Capital' in three Parts. In the first Part, three forms of the circuit of capital are investigated, and in the second the turnover of capital with its elements is studied. In these Parts there are original theoretical insights about the nature of capital in its incessant circuit of motion through circulation and production over time, and also about the restriction as well as the necessity of circulation for the capitalist production of surplus-value. Then in the third Part, 'Reproduction and Circulation of Total Social Capital', Marx presents his *tableaux économique* in the reproduction schemes.

The third volume of *Capital*, 'The Process of Capitalist Production as a Whole', contains seven Parts. The famous transformation procedure from values into prices of production or from surplus-value into average profit through competition of capitals is in the initial two Parts, and it forms another solution to a basic problem left by the classical school. The third Part discusses 'The Law of the Tendency of the Rate of Profit to Fall' and the exposition of the internal contradictions in the process of capital accumulation. The fourth, fifth and sixth Parts present the basic theories of the secondary distribution of surplus-value from industrial capitals to commercial capital, interest-bearing or money capital, and landowners in the forms of commercial profit, interest and ground-rent. These concrete forms of surplus-value and capital systematically work simultaneously as the social mechanisms carrying through the law of value in the concrete process of the competitive equalisation of profit and the extension of production, though they may occasionally play a converse and destructive role in the process of causing periodical crises. The seventh and final Part is a very incomplete draft, but it roughly summarises, with a critique of vulgar economic theories, how major forms of revenue in a capitalist society, i.e. wages, profit or interest and ground-rent, seem from an ordinary view to spring independently from labour, capital and land so covering the real social class-relations of production. It also presents some of Marx's insights on socialism upon the basis of his theory of value and surplus-value.

The basic theory of a capitalist economy contained in the three volumes of *Capital*, unlike the neo-classical theory, substantially succeeded the labour theory of value of the classical school, though with some important transformations and developments. It was indeed impossible for Marx to succeed classical value theory simply by making it quantitatively more precise in the same dimension. Marx had to innovate with the whole theoretical system so as to remedy the defects of classical theory. For instance, the creation of the theory of forms of value, the theoretical distinction between use-value and value of the commodity labour-power, discovery of the concept of prices of production, and the attempt to complete a crises theory in conjuncture with the labour theory of value were conspicuous theoretical innovations by Marx beyond the limitations of the classical theory. At first sight these innovations may seem mutually independent and to deduce them directly from a single point, one by one, rather hard. It is obvious, however, that all of them relate theoretically to the historical specificities of a capitalist economy based upon commodity relations. The theory of forms of value fundamentally clarifies the specific forms of social relations appearing within a commodity economy. The theoretical analysis of the commodity labour-power directly shows a logically specific precondition for capitalist production. The prices of production are a uniquely capitalistic economic form for distributing social surplus-labour. The crisis theory shows an economic dynamism which is also specific to a capitalist society. Since these historical characters of a capitalist economy were completely neglected within the naturalist ideology of the classical school as well as of the neo-classical school, we can easily assume that Marx in the field of economic theory renovated the 'paradigm' in T. Kuhn's sense,[14] by following the guiding thread of historical materialism. However, it should be emphasised here again that historical materialism as a guiding thread (at a meta-level so to say) could not immediately assure completely renovated scientific theories. That is why Marx had to attempt repeatedly and so seriously to work out his own theoretical system, and also why Marx could not thoroughly solve but still left various theoretical incompletenesses, as we shall see later.

**Marx's Initial Plan and the Scope of *Capital***

When Marx began to write the first draft of his lifework toward the end of the 1850s he drew several plans for the whole conceivable work.[15] These plans contain differences in length and details, but they are in a similar framework which can briefly summarised as follows:

I. Capital
  (a) Capital in general
    (1) Production process of capital
    (2) Circulation process of capital
    (3) Unity of both processes, or profit and interest of capital
  (b) Competition
  (c) Credit
  (d) Joint-stock capital
II. Landed property
III. Wage labour
IV. State
V. Foreign trade
VI. World market

What items in this original plan did *Capital* cover? Is *Capital* a systematically complete work, or only a part of a more extensive work to be realised according to the original plan? Or was the plan changed in effect in the process of writing *Capital*? These points have formed the so-called 'plan problem', which is methodologically of some importance concerning how to extend our work after Marx.

(Since this 'plan problem' is so little known to most Western readers, this subsection might seem too specialised. The reader can initially skip over it, and go directly to the next subsection if this is felt to be easier.)

For instance, since Marx entitled the sixth and final book 'World Market and Crisis' in some plans, the crisis theory seems to be beyond the scope of *Capital* so far as *Capital* covers just an initial part of the original plan. After publishing very briefly his plan of work at the beginning of the Preface to *A Contribution to the Critique of Political Economy*, Marx did not refer to any alteration of the plan at least in published materials. Moreover, there are some sentences in *Capital* which can easily be interpreted as restricting the scope of *Capital* within the range of Capital in general in the original plan. For example, Marx states in *Capital* that the 'special study of wage-labour' (I, p. 683), 'the further analyses of industrial cycles' (III, p. 482), 'a detailed analysis of the credit system' (III, p. 525), or 'the analysis of landed property in its various historical forms' (III, p. 751), fall beyond the scope of his present work.[16] He also suggests that he does not yet treat 'the actual movement of competition' but 'presents only the internal organisation of the capitalist mode of production, in its ideal average, as it were' (III, p. 970).

Therefore, it is not strange to read repeatedly the interpretation that *Capital* covers just the part of 'Capital in general' in the original unaltered plan, treating capital generally or as a whole, without covering the items after competition among individual capitals. R. Wilbrandt argued that the first volume of *Capital* was a 'torso' in a twofold sense, for it was not only the first of a few volumes on Capital, but also the first part of the first book among the six books planned[17] (i.e. Capital, Landed Property, Wage Labour, State, Foreign Trade and World Market, as indicated in the Preface to *A Contribution to the Critique of Political Economy*). Though Wilbrandt did not refer to the inner items within Capital, K. Kuruma intended to be more precise. He asserted that *Capital* dealt with only 'capital in general' in the initial plan, by emphasising Marx's phrases to restrict the scope of his present work in *Capital* as well as the fact that we could not find any written evidence in Marx to note a fundamental change in his original plan.[18] He then argued that Marx's crisis theory, together with the whole system of the critique of political economy, must remain incomplete in *Capital*. The orthodox view in the USSR coincides with this line of argument in emphasising a strong continuity between the structure of *Capital* and 'capital in general' of the initial plan, although it admits some extention of the framework of 'capital in general'.[19]

Contrariwise there is another interpretation that Marx changed the original plan and intended to make *Capital* a complete work.

For instance, H. Grossmann (1881–1950), opposing Wilbrandt, asserted that *Capital* was not at all a 'torso' but an intentionally completed result of 'the change of the original 1859 plan'.[20] Marx's creation of the reproduction scheme and his letter of 15 August 1863 to Engels were pointed out as evidence by Grossmann. The reproduction scheme surely shows that a capitalist economy can in principle be self-reliant without depending on foreign trade or world market.[21] However, the reproduction scheme has not any direct relation to theories of 'competition', 'credit' or 'landed property' and 'wage-labour', and therefore it cannot be a sufficient and positive proof to judge if these items' originally being outside of 'capital in general' were logically to be included in *Capital* or not. Grossmann could not read and examine the actual theoretical contents of 'capital in general' of *Grundrisse* when he discussed the problem in 1929. Besides, his other evidence does not seem very powerful. In his interpretation Marx's statement that 'I've had to demolish everything' (*alles unschmeissen*) in a letter of 15 August 1863 referred to the alteration of the original plan. However, it may possibly mean that Marx had to demolish not his plan, but every theoretical matter in the classical school. F. Behrens followed Grossmann's interpretation of that letter of Marx and asserted a similar explanation about the plan problem, although he criticised Grossmann's 'external-mechanistic' method.[22]

R. Rosdolsky (1898–1967) could later fully utilise the theoretical structure of *Grundrisse* to handle the problem more in detail. It is clear that the theoretical system of *Grundrisse* is strictly confined within 'capital in general' of the original plan. By comparing the contents of *Grundrisse* with *Capital* Rosdolsky found that 'what was initially useful and necessary eventually had to turn out to be a superfluous and obstructive limitation, . . . The blueprint had served its purpose and could therefore be dropped in the further stages of the analysis.'[23] The alteration from the initial plan into a theoretical system of *Capital* is summarised by Rosdolsky in Figure 3.1 as follows:[24]

*Figure* 3.1

| THE ORIGINAL PLAN (6 books) | THE CHANGED PLAN |
|---|---|
| I. ON CAPITAL | 'CAPITAL' (3 volumes): |
| a) Capital in general | |
| 1) Production process | I. Production process of capital (Sections): |
| | 1) Commodity and money |
| | 2) Transformation of money into capital |
| | 3–5) Absolute and relative surplus-value |
| | 6) Wage |
| | 7) Accumulation process |
| | II. Circulation process of capital |
| 2) Circulation process | III. Process of capitalist production as a whole. |
| 3) Profit and interest | 1–3) Profit and profit rate |
| b) Competition | 4) Merchant capital |
| c) Credit system | 5) Interest and credit |
| d) Share-Capital | |
| II. ON LANDED PROPERTY | 6) Ground-Rent |
| | 7) Revenues. |
| III. ON WAGE LABOUR | |
| IV. STATE | |
| V. FOREIGN TRADE | |
| VI. WORLD MARKET | |

Unbroken lines: changes within the first three books
Dotted lines: changes within the *Book on Capital.*

Rosdolsky's treatment shown in Figure 3.1 is clear and definitely more persuasive than his opponents. However, he still compares rather superficially the items of Marx's initial plan incorporated in the *Grundrisse* with the parts of *Capital*. He is a *Grundrisse* fundamentalist,[25] and tends to neglect Marx's theoretical difficulties and development after writing the *Grundrisse*. He believes, for instance, that Marx's theory of transforming values into prices and the theory of crisis were already basically presented in the *Grundrisse*. As a result, Marx's effort through the second draft including *Theories of Surplus-Value* to work up the theory of ground-rent in relation to the theory of prices of production, on the basis of competition among many capitals, or the extension of the theory of crisis in relation to the theory of accumulation and credit is not much taken into consideration. In contrast to Rosdolsky's chart the theory of competition among many capitals is not confined to the first three Parts of the third volume of *Capital*, but organically developed through all the Parts of that volume. The theory on wage labour is not limited to the sixth Part on wages in the first volume, but extended from various angles throughout all the volumes from the second Part of the first volume, being increasingly linked with the dynamics of capitalism through the process of accumulation and the motion of profit and interest.

In its contents the theoretical study of the law of value as the law of motion of a capitalist economy could not be complete without dealing with the concrete forms of surplus-value through competition and credit. And the basic theory of wage-labour and landed property cannot be separated from the theory of motion of capital. Conversely the basic theory of a capitalist economy necessarily requires studies of not only the total capital as 'capital in general', but also the basic mechanisms of motion of capital through competition and credit. The studies of the basic position of wage-labour and landed property should also be included there. In spite of Marx's own restrictive statements concerning the scope of *Capital* it seems that the essential character of a capitalist economy forced him to extend his theoretical studies much beyond the original framework of 'capital in general' toward a complete principles of motion of a capitalist economy. Though Rosdolsky as well as other discussants did not reflect much on this point, it thus also relates to the problem of why the theoretical system of *Capital* could be separated from studies of the role of state, foreign trade and world market.

The problem can no longer be properly handled within mere interpretative considerations of Marx's initial plan. A wider methodological view concerning all economic studies including the theories of imperialism and more contemporary capitalism on the basis of *Capital* must now be discussed.

### How to Locate and Complete *Capital*

Opposing Kuruma's interpretation of the plan problem K. Uno asserted that the basic theories of wage-labour and landed property in a capitalist society were already present in *Capital*.[26] Regardless of what Marx initially meant by 'landed property' and 'wage-labour' in his plan, the theoretical system of *Capital* could not bc complete without the theories of wages and ground rent which define the basic social positions of workers and landowners in a capitalist society. The basic position of a capitalist form of landed property, not to mention that of wage-labour, cannot be a factor external to the economic motion of capital, unlike state power. At the same time Uno disagreed with Kuruma's merely interpretative adherence to Marx's original plan which excluded the crisis theory from the system of *Capital*. Although Marx's crisis theory actually remained incomplete, we should attempt by clarifying Marx's theoretical difficulties to complete it as a basic principle within a framework of the basic theory of capitalism. Without having such a basic theory of crisis a capitalist economy must be regarded abstractly as one-sidely harmonious, and the economic crises may not be defined theoretically as a phenomena specific to and unavoidable for capitalism.

Uno did not discuss the plan problem in detail by following the formation of Marx's manuscripts from the *Grundrisse*, but treated it from the theoretically wider view of how to locate and complete *Capital* as the system of basic principles for all of Marxian economics. Uno maintained that the whole of Marxian economics should be systematically broken down into three levels of research. The first and fundamental level is that of the basic principles of political economy; the stages theory of world capitalist development must be constructed at the second level; and further, the empirical analysis of the actual state of capitalism in the world or in each individual country must be carried out at the third most concrete level.[27] The major changes of the role of the state in the world market from mercantilism to liberalism, and then to imperialism, and the transformations of the economic positions of wage-labour and landed property must be clarified through the stages theory of world capitalist development, and further in the empirical analyses of individual countries. These studies, which relate to the corresponding items in Marx's initial plan, are to be at different, more concrete levels than the basic principles. They must be combined with studies of historically concrete changes of the typical leading capital and its industrial bases.

In view of this methodological distinction of research levels we can locate *Capital* as providing the basic principles of political economy, where basic theories of wage-labour, competition among capitals, credit, joint-stock capital and landed property in a capitalist economy should systematically be included, without discounting the importance of more concrete studies of these items outside of *Capital*. Although capitalist development always utilises and decomposes external non-capitalist modes of production within its own boundaries and in the peripheral world the basic principles do not treat this external aspect of capitalism nor the role of state which very often relates to this aspect. In this regard Uno emphasises that the basic principles must presuppose a purely capitalist society made up of the three major classes of capitalists, workers and landowners, on the basis of the actual historical tendency of British society to realise an increasingly purer capitalism up to Marx's own age.[28]

So far as Uno excludes the period after the end of nineteenth century from the historical basis of abstracting the basic theory of capitalism, his method leaves some difficulties. On the one hand, the basic principles might be regarded as a specific theory of *laissez-faire* capitalism. On the other, the concrete studies of capitalist development in the imperialist stage might stress only historically particular features which are different from the basic principles. The basic principles of political economy which are deducible from *Capital* must easily be recognisable and applicable even after the end of nineteenth century. Apparently, the relatively independent motion of a capitalist economy based on the exchange of commodities has *fundamentally* continued in spite of the increased role of the state, except during massive military mobilisations in periods of World War, and the process of decomposing non-capitalist modes of production in each major capitalist country has also been continuing.

It is certainly to be noted that capitalism passed through a period of *laissez-faire* liberalism, in order to understand clearly the basic autonomous character of the capitalist economy. Some realms of basic principles, for instance the theories of the working of the credit system and cyclical crises, can be clarified by abstracting from the liberalist stage of capitalism. However, some others might require a broader basis of abstraction. The basic theories of the forms of the commodity, money and capital might more clearly be understood if we observe the birth and growth of capitalism in the mercantilist stage, and also the existence of these forms from very ancient periods. Contrastingly the principles of joint-stock capital must be fully developed only when the historical experience of the imperialist stage is considered as the basis of abstraction. Thus I believe with some Uno theorists[29] that the basis of abstraction of the basic principles must be broadened to cover the whole history of capitalism, though I agree with Uno's distinction of research levels between the basic principles and the more concrete studies.

Anyway, the so-called plan problem must substantially be solved and the scope of *Capital* could be thus clarified through a methodological differentiation of the levels of research in Marxian economics.

## 3.3. THE TASKS OF MARXIAN STUDIES AFTER *CAPITAL*

### The Controversies on Revisionism and Imperialism

The development of Marxian economics after *Capital* was in fact performed at various levels of research. However, unawareness or the mixture of the different levels of research has often caused unnecessary confusion and difficulties. The theoretical basis of Marxism was not a little endangered on that account. Misunderstandings of Marx's economic theory and some incompleteness in *Capital* were other sources of confusion.

For instance, E. Bernstein (1850–1932), who was once regarded as one of most promising Marxian theorists after Engels, opened up a way for revisionism by negating the relevance of Marx's economic theories to late nineteenth century capitalism.[30] In particular the actual development of capitalism in Bernstein's view no longer accorded with Marx's theories in the *Manifesto of the Communist Party* and *Capital*, on the basis of which the *Erfurt Programme* (1891) of the German Social Democratic Party was constructed. According to Bernstein, contrary to the theoretical position of this Programme, the growth of joint-stock companies counteracted the centralisation of properties. Small producers and firms obstinately tended to remain and even increased in various sectors, especially in agriculture. The development of the means of transportation and communication, as well as the growth of credit and cartel systems, strengthened the adaptability of the capitalist economy in preventing acute economic crises. Therefore, said Bernstein, a capitalist economy was *no longer* polarising society into a smaller number of richer capitalists and a larger number of workers who were supposed to be more and more impoverished and revolutionised through increasingly severer crises. Since the first half of *Erfurt Programme* thus lost its basis, as did Marx's doctrine, the German Social Democratic Party should abandon these and should confine its tasks to the latter half of the *Programme* simply for democratic and gradual reforms.

Bernstein represents the first and typical position of revisionism which has been repeated at various times and places since then. There were two major sources of confusion. First, he accused Marx's basic theories of outdatedness by comparing them too hastily with the actual features of capitalism in late nineteenth century Germany, instead of systematically clarifying those new features on the basis of Marx's theory. Second, he narrowly interpreted the major line of Marx's economic theories as the theory of polarisation of capitalist society combined with the law of the impoverishment of workers just as in the *Manifesto*, and either he could not understand or he neglected the richer theoretical contents in *Capital*.

A most comprehensive counter-critique of Bernstein's revisionism at that time was presented by K. Kautsky (1854–1938).[31] Although Kautsky was successful in criticising Bernstein's superficial misunderstanding of Marx's basic theories, he could not overcome methodologically and theoretically the deeper sources of confusion. He attempted only to show that the tendential polarisation of society fully held through the various new features of German capitalist development. Even though he initiated an important Marxian field of study in *The Agricultural Problem*,[32] he was apt to emphasise just the *de facto* proletarianisation of peasant farmers, and could not clarify the economic ground for socialist alliance of the working class and the peasantry in lately developing countries such as Germany at that time. So long as only the relevance of Marx's basic theory was emphasised, the concrete new features of capitalist development in the late nineteenth century were not systematically studied, and therefore the actual roots for Bernstein's type of revisionism remained theoretically uncriticised. This methodological defect eventually caused another confusion among Marxians when imperialism became a serious issue toward the First World War.

Kautsky made light of the historical necessity and the political importance of imperialism, and defined imperialism as just one of the favourite policies for industrial capital or finance capital to expand trade with the agricultural areas. Even a peaceful ultraimperialism, a sort of Holy Alliance among the capitalist great powers, was supposed to be possible. As a result he could not present a theoretical basis for socialists and workers to resist and revolutionise the crisis of the imperialist World War, and he did not prevent the collapse of the second international (1889–1914) in voting for the war budget in the name of defending workers' fatherlands. It is tragic to see that Kautsky was never intentionally a 'renegade,' though objectively he became one as accused by Lenin.[33] In a sense his excessive adherence to Marx's basic theories of the driving force of historical materialism and of the polarisation of a society into bourgeoisie and proletariat prevented him to study concretely the crisis of imperialism. Certainly it was by no means a proper way of making the best of Marxian theories.

Against Kautsky, R. Luxemburg (1870–1919) attempted to show the logical inevitability of imperialism in *The Accumulation of Capital*.[34] In order to show it however, she demanded a serious revision in Marx's basic theory of reproduction. By observing the reproduction schema from the view of a circuit of money capital ($M - C \ldots P \ldots C' - M'$), she found that capitalism could not realise surplus-value internally by obtaining more money ($M'$) than advanced ($M$). Imperialism was then defined as a historically inevitable stage for capitalist great powers to struggle against each other to acquire increasingly scarce non-capitalist external market areas for the realisation of surplus-value. This theory of imperialism was not well founded. As Marx's reproduction schema shows, if properly studied from the view of a circuit of commodity capital ($C' - M' \cdot M - C \ldots P \ldots C'$), capitalism can in principle realise surplus-value internally and can expand by itself. Money to realise surplus-value can be supplied mutually by capitalists as a part of means of circulation. Besides, it remained unclear why capitalism became imperialistic especially since the end of nineteenth century, so for as Luxemburg sought the cause of imperialism in a very general logic of capitalist development. Though capitalism certainly utilised the peripheral countries throughout its development, the economic relation between the capitalist centre and the periphery cannot be confined only to a supplementary market for surplus-value, and must be clarified concretely with its historical changes at a research level which is different from the general principles of capitalist economy.

R. Hilferding (1877–1941) and V. I. Lenin (1870–1924) presented in fact a new method of constructing a Marxian theory of imperialism. On the one hand, Hilferding begins his *Finance Capital*[35] with abstract studies of Marx's theories of money and credit, and unfolds the logical formation of finance capital, which is defined as bank capital actually being 'transformed into industrial capital.'[36] This is done on the basis of the functions of joint-stock capital, as if it were an extension of the basic principles of political economy especially concerning the concentration and centralisation of capital along with the tendential polarisation of a capitalist society. On the other hand, he discusses, at a definitely more concrete level, the economic policies of finance capital in the fifth and final Part of the book. He attempts there to clarify the different features of British and German capitalists formation of finance capital, which demands larger and larger imperialist territories for the export of capital, sharply increasing the nationalistic rivalries in the world market as well as the danger of world war.

Lenin in his *Imperialism, The Highest Stage of Capitalism*[37] systematically studied with more decisively concrete considerations, 'a composite picture of the world capitalist system.'[38] Lenin followed Hilferding's concept of finance capital, supplementing to it a factor of monopoly. However, Lenin's *Imperialism*, in contrast with *Finance Capital*, directly begins with the historical economic process in the major heavy industries and the financial institutions of main capitalist countries. At the same time, it is confirmed that 'not in every branch of industry are there large-scale enterprise'.[39] Then, the export of capital which is characteristic of the monopolistic stage of capitalism, the division of the world among the groups of finance capitalists, the division and redivision of colonial territories among capitalist great powers, and the historical inevitability of imperialist World War, all these related matters are described with concrete historical facts or statistical data. Lenin could sharply criticise the view of the main line in the second international which defined the war as the war to defend the fatherland, and he presented the ground for his stategy to convert the imperialist war (viewed from whichever side) into a revolutionary civil war. Simultaneously, his study in *Imperialism* clearly shows how Marxian economics should investigate the historical metamorphoses of capitalism with the role of states in the world market. It can be regarded as a methodological solution of a series of debates concerning revisionism and imperialism.

### The Tasks of the Basic Theory

The basic principles of a capitalist economy in *Capital* should not easily be negated or revised by the new features of capitalist development after Marx. But a mere adherence to the basic principles does not suffice. Having the basic principles in *Capital* as the standard for researches, a comprehensive logical study of historical facts in particular stage of capitalist development, where finance capital became dominant leading capital, had to be performed at a different level of research. Even though many historical facts are also referred to in

*Capital*, they are basically illustrations for general theories of political economy, and can be omitted in studying the basic principles. In contrast, the historical facts often with proper nouns of firms, industries, and countries in a particular period are indispensable for *Imperialism*. Following Uno's methodology we may locate *Imperialism* as a initiating model of the stages theory of capitalist development at a more concrete upper level of research than the more basic level of *Capital*.

Marxian economics then, must extend the stages theory so as to include the studies of capitalist stages of mercantilism and liberalism as well as imperialism. The growth of productive power through changing key industries, the forms of leading capital, the social positions of workers, as well as the economic policies and the structure of the world market in each stage should be clarified. Having both such a stages theory of world capitalism and the basic theory as dual systematic frames of reference, we are offered the possibility of performing the empirical analyses of individual countries elastically and organically. As we saw in the controversy over Japanese capitalism,[40] the specific features of individual countries such as the existence of a mass of poor peasant farmers in rural areas may be defined mechanically as either heterogeneous non-capitalist and basically feudal components, or as simply decomposing elements within a capitalist society, so far as only the basic theory in *Capital* is contrasted to them. Anyway it must be clear by now that Marxian economics faces a very much wider range of researches outside the theoretical system of *Capital*, at both the level of the stages theory and at a more actual level of empirical analyses.

When the task of Marxian studies to develop the stages theory, and actual empirical analyses at the upper and more concrete levels of research are thus confirmed, then the task of the basic theory of capitalism becomes distinct and much clearer.

By mixing up the levels of research the theoretical system in *Capital* is sometimes defined as the theoretical model of an old competitive capitalism which must be replaced by a newer theoretical model of monopolistic capitalism,[41] or further, more recent state monopoly capitalism. Massive Marxian studies of the whole parts of *Capital* might then be regarded as being irrelevant to the actual issues of our age, being more or less of merely bibliographical curiosities. From what we have discussed, such an interpretation is by no means correct.

Being distinguished from the more concrete levels of research, the theoretical system of *Capital* must clearly be located and completed as the basic principles of capitalist economy. The task of such principles is dual. First, by showing the historical character of capitalist economy in a general theoretical system, such principles can serve as the most fundamental scientific ground for historical materialism and the socialist view of breaking down the capitalist economic system. The fundamental aims of the revolutionary socialist movement, which are usually expressed in the basic programmes, must be grounded on the basic principles of a capitalist economy, whereas the more concrete strategies and tactics must utilise the more concrete studies of world capitalism and individual countries at the levels of stages theory and of empirical analyses. Even the most abstract theory of value in *Capital* closely relates to such a task. This explains at least partly why so many critiques have been fervently repeated by non-Marxians of various types. Second, the basic theoretical system in *Capital* must serve as the standard frame of reference for the stages theory and the actual empirical analyses. Without having such a fundamental standard of research the concrete studies of world capitalism and individual countries might become fragmented, lacking focus, arbitrary and easily too eclectic.

When the location and the task of the theoretical system in *Capital* are thus confirmed, we are able to investigate its contents less dogmatically and more systematically. We can and must attempt to complete the basic theories of capitalism by studying *Capital* in view of their fundamental location and tasks. So far as *Capital* still contains concrete historical observations which are suitable for the stages theory or the empirical analyses, we have to separate them out, to purify the basic principles. Abstract inferences, deduced too directly from the formula of historical materialism, for instance in concluding the inevitable end of capitalism through the dialectical 'negation of the negation' (I, p. 929) of private property, have also to be excluded from the basic economic theory of capitalism, so far as they cannot be logically provable. Wherever Marx's theories are incorrect or incomplete we should not hesitate to do our best to overcome the defects. Even critiques from non-Marxian, to say nothing of the debates among Marxian writers, have often raised important theoretical problems to be solved scientifically. As in the theories of value and crisis the residues of immature theories of the classical and the anti-classical school are often sources of defects in *Capital*, and have to be carefully purified. As in the theory of joint-stock capital among others, the logic of capitalist development after Marx sometimes has to be taken into consideration in completing the basic theoretical system of the capitalist economy.

In the following chapters of this volume the basic economic theory of capitalism will be investigated through its major problematic issues in the light of these tasks and methodological interests.

# Part II
# Value, Labour and Capital

Since economic activities under capitalism are all carried on through the market mechanism of commodity transactions, all the major schools of economic theory which have appeared during the development of capitalism have naturally been concerned with the nature and determinants of the exchange of commodities as a fundamental problem. Value theories, in a broadest sense, comprise various logical investigations into this problem. However, the tasks and contents of the various types of value theory have differed according to the major concerns of the total theoretical system of each school. The differences in the theories of value have also been closely related to varying theories of surplus-value or profit.

For instance, the neo-classical theories concentrate on the determination of prices within a market on the basis of subjective and individual preference. Distribution of the social product between workers, capitalists and landowners is treated as a corollary of price theory applied to wages, profit and ground-rent. Alternatively, the neo-Ricardian theories show that equilibrium prices are determinable on the basis of objective physical data of the methods of production and real wages, leaving room for any changes in distribution between workers and capitalists to be treated as an independent variable determined prior to the prices of commodity products. In spite of their opposite positions concerning the determinants of prices however, both neo-classicists and neo-Ricardians believe that the determination of prices is the basic and central task of an economic theory, both also assuming that the market system is a given natural order for human economic activity. Capitalism may then be viewed as a natural society, not as a historically specific economy.

So far as both the question of equilibrium prices and the quantitative relation between wages and profit in a market are the major concern, the labour theory of value in the classical and the Marxian schools must be accused of being at best redundant. Both P. Samuelson, as a representative neo-classicist, and I. Steedman, as a neo-Ricardian, concur in this critique of the labour theory of value.[1] Both Samuelson and Steedman recognize that the necessary labour-time to produce commodities can be determined from the physical data of production processes under certain conditions. They repudiate however the labour theory of value on the grounds that the same physical data can directly and more consistently determine prices and profit in a market. In their eyes, prices, wages and profit in a market are the central economic issues to be studied theoretically. What are lost in such neo-classical and the neo-Ricardian types of theories are, among other things, the theoretical concerns about human social activity in the labour process, and the source of surplus-value. At the other extreme, by emphasising the material basis of class relations in the exploitation of labour, some Marxians have tended to believe that the price-form in a market is simply a fetish veil which only needs to be put aside in order to reveal the hidden relations of production. From this standpoint, theoretical concern with the price form in a market, as well as the neo-classical or neo-Ricardian price theories, would be regarded simply as very superficial and fetishised. At the same time the labour theory of value may become similar to the classical Ricardian type, or to a theory which demonstrates the social basis of class societies in general and not only capitalism.

In contrast, Marx's own value theory in *Capital* does not treat the market just as an intermediary veil hiding reality, but consciously elucidates the forms of a market economy as indispensable organising mechanisms of capitalist reproduction. This is because Marx's theoretical concern is in revealing the historically specific character of capitalism, where the social labour process is actually encompassed and driven on by the forms of the market economy. The distinction and relation between prices in a market and the underlying quantities of labour become essential. Marx dualised the notion of value into the forms and the substance of value in this regard. Whereas the substance of value is defined as the embodied labour in commodities, the forms of value refer to the nature of social relations specific to a commodity economy, shaping the economic relations between commodities, money and capital in a market. Quantitatively the forms of value become expressed and measured in terms of prices. As an analogy, the forms of value in a market could be seen as an image of a vessel constructed of mosaic, which can stand alone, independent of its content, but can be filled with a liquied, i.e. social labour substance in the case of capitalism[2]. Theoretical interest in only the substance or only the price forms of value in other schools can thus be criticised as narrowly one-sided and unhistorical. The theory of the forms of value itself, though it certainly investigates prices, must no longer remain a merely quantitative analysis of the determinants of prices. The historically specific character of social relations in the form of value initially requires more a qualitative elucidation. For instance, why must ordinary commodities always be exchanged through money or under the price form? And why does money monopolise the direct exchangeability with all other commodities? How are value forms logically related together and developed from commodity into money and capital? These problems were originally presented and studied in Marx's *Capital*.

However, the theoretical potential of Marx's dual notion of value and his original theory of the forms of value have not yet been fully utilised and extended, especially insofar as Marx's value theory has been discussed merely as if it were a revised version of Ricardo's by concentrating only on quantitative problems. Since there is some Ricardian residue in Marx's own theory, such a tendency among both critics of Marx and orthodox doctrinal Marxians is perhaps understandable. However, firstly we have to clarify the theoretical implications and potential of Marx's dual notion of value, by attempting to remove the residue of classical value theory. Then we may be better qualified to handle the theoretical confusions or difficulties in the recent value controversy from a different angle in the latter chapters of Part II.

# 4 The Forms of Value – Commodity, Money and Capital

## 4.1 COMMODITIES AND THE MYSTERY OF THE PRICE-FORM

### The Forms and the Substance of Value

Although Marx titles the first volume of *Capital* 'The Process of Production of Capital', he does not immediately investigate the substantital content of a capitalist mode of production. In the first two Parts of the volume, beginning from the analysis of the commodity as the elementary form, he elucidates the systematic relations between commodities, money and capital as the development of the forms of value. Both historically and spatially these forms appear as the basic components of commodity economy in general in much wider periods and the places than capitalist production. On the basis of the development of commodity economy, the free worker 'in the double sense that as a free individual he can dispose of his labour-power as his own commodity, and that . . . he is free of all the objects needed for the realisation [*Verwirklichung*] of his labour-power' (I, pp. 272–3) must be given for the birth and maintenance of capitalist production in a social scale.

Then, subsequently at the beginning of the third Part of the volume, where the investigation of the inner mechanism of capitalist production begins, *Capital* defines 'the labour process' as 'the universal condition for the metabolic interaction [*Stoffwechsel*] between man and nature, . . . common to all forms of society' (I, p. 290). For the first time in the long history of human societies this labour process becomes thoroughly embraced and treated by the forms of commodity economy. The forms of value in a commodity economy must then be firmly grounded in the social labour process. Or, conversely, the labour process common to all forms of society is turned into the source of value in a capitalist commodity economy.

Thus in the construction of its first three Parts, *Capital* theoretically distinguishes the three different historical characters of the forms of a commodity economy, the labour process and the capitalist economy. The distinction is original to Marx and unavailable in any other school. In clarifying the distinction Marx's value theory could not remain as a mere labour theory of value in the classical school, and it did not begin with the conception of the labour process. The social substance of values in a capitalist economy on the basis of the labour process is revealed in *Capital* through and behind the notion of the forms of value, which was left undiscovered by the classical school.[1]

At first sight there seems to be a gap between the subject of the initial two Parts and that of the other Parts of *Capital*. For the forms of value in commodity economy, which are studied in the first two Parts, have actually existed previous to, and more extensively than the capitalist mode of production. However, they also become the basic forms of economic order of a capitalist society, and give a very special character to the society.

As Marx points out, the 'the exchange of commodities begins where communities have their boundaries, at their points of contact with other communities, or with members of the latter' (I, p. 182), the commodity economy originally springs out as inter-social economic relations. Corresponding to this the commodity economy tended to grow always relatively independently of political regulations within each communal societies, and transferred inter-socially various products indifferent to the nature of modes of production behind them. The capitalist mode of production was founded when such a commodity economy came to be an internal social order subject to the motion of capital on the basis of the commodity form of labour-power. As capitalism develops as a thorough commodity economy, producing commodities by means of commodities, its economic process shows autonomy independent of political and legal superstructures. At the same time the autonomous motion of a capitalist economy is not qualitatively impeded by commodity transactions with other societies in the world market, unlike any other social formations. In this historically specific autonomy of a capitalist economy based on an anarchic market system, there is presented the grounds for the division by historical materialism of the superstructure and substructure of societies.

Thus, the historical character of a capitalist economy is essentially related to the character of commodity economy in general. The specifically anarchic autonomy of the economic process in capitalism is founded upon the forms of commodity economy, which, originating in an extra-social economic order, has been converted into the intra-social principles of production. Therefore, exactly in order to clarify the historical characteristics of the law of motion of a capitalist economy, we have to study first the forms of commodity economy which is not confined within capitalist society, just as Marx properly ordered his study in the first two Parts of *Capital*.

Although Marx's originality is thus clear in the major theoretical construction of the first three Parts of *Capital*, revealing the social substance of value in a capitalist economy after and behind the notion of the forms of value in commodity economy, his method of examining the substance behind the forms of value is not always made the best of, especially in the first chapter of *Capital* 'The Commodity'. Interestingly the topics of the first three sections of the first chapter are rather contrary to the major construction of the first three Parts. The first two sections 'The Two Factors of a Commodity: Use-Value and Value (Substance of Value, Magnitude of Value)' and 'The Dual Character of the Labour Embodied in Commodities' mainly concern the substance of value before, not after the analysis of 'The Value-Form, or Exchange-Value' in the third section. However, when separated from Marx's original notion of the forms of value, his notion of value had to remain not far from Ricardo's ahistorical concept of value with all its difficulties. Let us examine the contents of the first section.

Marx, unlike Ricardo, is certainly concerned with the historical character of the subject of his study from the beginning. At the very start of the first chapter of *Capital*, we read: 'The wealth of societies in which the capitalist mode of production prevails appears as an "immense collection of commodities"; the individual commodity appears as its elementary form. Our investigation therefore begins with the analysis of the commodity.' (I, p. 125) Marx explicitly refers to the capitalist mode of production from the first sentence as his major subject, and takes up the commodity as its elementary form. Also unlike the classical school, Marx notices that the use-values of commodities are common to all external objects of human needs, whatever the form of society, but that 'in the form of society to be considered here they are also the material bearers [*Trager*] of – exchange-value'. (I, p. 126). And then he defines that 'exchange-value appears first of all as the quantitative relation, the proportion, in which use-values of one kind exchange for use-values of another kind' (I, p. 126), before searching for a substantial common factor in commodities behind the appearance of exchange-values.

In this context Marx does not begin directly from the substance or the magnitude of value, but with careful attention from exchange-value as a form of value, in spite of the order of the titles of the first and the third sections. However, the logical relation between the form and the substance of value is somewhat mechanically cut off and neglected, in the subsequent process of abstracting the latter from the former.

After defining exchange-value Marx continues to inquire what is common to the exchange-values of commodities. So far as two commodities with different use-value, say corn and iron, are equated as exchange-value, there must be a third common something. In order to find out this third element, Marx abstracts from the use-value, saying, 'the exchange relation of commodities is characterised precisely by its abstraction from their use-values. Within the exchange relation, one use-value is worth just as much as another, provided only that it is present in the appropriate quantity'. (I, p. 127). With this abstraction from use-value, the common property in commodities is reduced to that being products of human labour in the abstract, regardless of its concrete forms. 'As crystals of this social substance, which is common to them all, they are values – commodity values.' (I, p. 128).

In this logical reduction to the notion of commodity values, Marx leaves out of consideration use-values and their exchange relations or the form of value in exchange. As a result Marx's notion of commodity values is boiled down here to the property of commodities as crystals of abstract labour, which must be common to labour products not confined to commodities. This notion does not include in itself any historical specificity of commodities and so far does not seem very different from Ricardo's notion of value. Certainly Marx knows that 'A thing can be useful, and a product of human labour, without being a commodity. He who satisfies his own need with the product of his own labour admittedly creates use-values, but not commodities. In order to produce the latter he must not only produce use-values, but use-values for others, social use-values.' (I, p. 131). This is not yet sufficient, however, as Engels points out, by referring to a corn-rent for the feudal lord as a counter-evidence, that 'in order to become a commodity, the product must be transferred to the other person, for whom it serves as a use-value, through the medium of exchange.' (I, p. 131). In this regard, commodity values must not be abstracted from exchange relations or the form of value. The property of labour products and the quantities of abstract labour embodied in them become the substance of value, only when they are handled through the form of exchange-value.

Thus, crystals of abstract labour cannot be the substance of value without being located behind the forms of value. The forms of value must therefore be indispensable for the concept of commodity values. In spite of Marx's ordering of the first and the third sections of the first chapter of *Capital*, the substance of value cannot, then, properly be defined prior to the notion of value-forms. How about the forms of value in commodity circulation? Can they theoretically be defined and developed prior to the notion of the substance of value?

This is an initiating issue of the extended discussion on value theory among Japanese Marxian economists inspired by the works of K. Uno. Uno discovered that the forms of value of commodities, money and capital were separable from social relations existing in labour time. He reformulated Marx's theories in the first two Parts of *Capital* as the theories of pure forms of circulation without referring to the substance of value.[2] This reformulation is well suited to Marx's original recognition that the commodity economy arose and developed through inter-social economic relations which remained external to the inner social labour processes in all precapitalist formations of society. It also serves to solve the basic difficulties in proving the labour theory of value in the theory of simple commodities.

The difficulties in demonstrating the labour theory of value in the theory of commodities are for both qualitative and quantitative reasons as follows. Qualitatively; whereas Marxians unlike Ricardians must consider the historical and social basis for a theory of value, it is extremely difficult to define the social conditions which definitely create value in commodities only in terms of commodities and labour. As Marx properly recognised, neither the labour process in general or the social division of labour was a sufficient condition for a commodity economy, in contrast to Smith's simplistic view, and as exemplified by the caste system (cf. I, p. 132). Even Marx's own definition that 'only the products of mutually independent acts of labour, preformed in isolation, can confront each other as commodities' (I, p. 132) is not exhaustive. The commodity products in precapitalist ages were often the surplus of combined labour in communal societies and were certainly not confined to the products of independent small commodity producers. The work in a capitalist factory producing commodities cannot be 'independent acts of labour,' and not a few non-labour products such as labour-power and land take the commodity form in a capitalist society. Thus, it is impossible to specify the social conditions by which commodity values are produced or given in the initial analysis only of commodities. In contrast, when we come to analyse the capitalist process of production after the theory of forms of value, then we can be sure to show the historically definite conditions where the substance of commodity values must be yielded by labour expenditure with *social necessity*.

So far as the qualitative social link between labour and commodity values is not assured for certain in the theory of mere commodities, it is also difficult quantitatively to prove the labour theory of value with a solid social basis at this level. Since the notion of capitalist production is not yet presented, the social basis for the labour theory of value in the initial analysis of commodities is usually assumed to be in precapitalist commodity production. In various precapitalist social formations, however, the main part of the labour process and reproduction is not maintained through commodity exchanges. While only some portion of (mostly surplus) products is commoditised, the law of value will not regulate exchanges with any real social necessity on the basis of labour expenditure. Actually, merchants would often repeatedly purchase from either peasants or the ruling landowners, at much cheaper prices than the labour values without destroying the existing mode of reproduction. A traditional interpretation of the labour theory of value, therefore, depends on the assumption of a society of simple commodity production in which social reproduction is effected entirely by small, independent commodity producers.[3] This interpretation, however, has to presuppose an imaginary classless society of commodity producers prior to a capitalist society, and cannot demonstrate the validity of the labour theory of value as the law of motion of capitalist production. With all these difficulties, Marx's labour theory of value in the initial analysis of commodities has been a source of incessant confusions and debates, including that of the 'transformation problem' from values into prices of production.

If, therefore, we can avoid discussing the labour theory of value prior to the notion of capitalist production, by purifying Marx's original theory of forms of value, we can dissipate the basic source of difficulties and confusions concerning Marx's value theory, and can expect later to demonstrate the labour theory of value with a much more solid social basis.

## The Value-form of Commodities

In the third section of the first chapter of *Capital*, Marx analyses the value-form of commodities, and investigates the mystery of money, or why commodities cannot be directly exchangeable, giving the monopolistic position of direct exchangeability to only the money commodity in their price-form. Although this section has not yet attracted sufficient attention in the recent Western value controversy as compared with the other sections of the same chapter, it contains the essential foundation for Marxian value-form theory, as well as some interesting problems. The logical development of the value-form of commodities is studied here from the simple form of value between two commodities, via the expanded and the general form of value, to reach the money form or the price-form.

In the analysis of the first, simple form of value of commodities, i.e. 20 yards of linen = 1 coat, or 20 yards of linen are worth 1 coat, Marx carries on an attractive dialogue with Aristotle. According to Marx, Aristotle already states that the money-form of the commodity is only a more developed aspect of the simple form of value. For he says that 5 beds = 1 house is indistinguishable from 5 beds = a certain amount of money. He further shows a genius in attempting to discover a relation of equality in the value-expression of commodities, by saying that 'there can be not exchange without equality, and no equality without commensurability'. However, Aristotle falters here and abandons a further analysis of the form of value, by stating that it is impossible in reality to find out qualitative equality or commensurability between such different things. The form of equation must therefore only be 'a makeshift for practical purposes'. In Marx's view what is left undiscovered by Aristotle as the commensurable homogeneous element in commodities is human labour as the common substance of value. In spite of Aristotle's genius the historical limitation of the society in which he lived prevented him from finding it out. 'Greek society was founded on the labour of slaves, hence had as its natural basis the inequality of men and of their labour-powers. The secret of the expression of value, namely the equality and equivalence of all kinds of labour, . . . could not be deciphered until the concept of human equality had already acquired the permanence of a fixed popular opinion. This, however, becomes possible only in a society where the commodity-form is the universal form of the product of labour.' (I, pp. 151–2).

Marx is very correct in pointing out that the common substance of value could be deciphered as homogeneous human labour only in a fully developed commodity society on the basis of general concept of human equality. However, Marx's critique of Aristotle here is somewhat one-sided, and does not lead fully to the point. For Aristotle does not clarify the logical development of the value-form from the simple form to the money-form, by stating that 5 beds = 1 house is directly indistinguishable from 5 beds = a certain amount of money. Although the form of value equation is in a sense something foreign to the true nature of things as use-values, it is by no means a mere tentative 'makeshift' but forms an endogenous logical order for commodities. Marx does not point to the lack of analysis of the inner logic of the equation, for Aristotle's attempt, to develop the value-forms, but just puts emphasis on the lack of the concept of the substance of value. If only the labour theory of value matters, the classical school prior to Marx already discovered it.

Nevertheless the labour theory of value in the classical school did not guarantee a way forward for the study of value-forms. As we quoted in note 1 of this chapter, Marx was well aware that the task of clarifying the value-form in this section of *Capital* had never been pursued by the classical school. The failure of the classical school to discover the form of value was due to the mistake of treating capitalist production and commodity economy as the eternal natural form of economy. In this regard the neo-classical and the neo-Ricardian school also are not immune from the same failure.

As is exemplified in his dialogue with Aristotle, Marx attempts to confirm the character of the substance of value, as well as the historical basis that enables us to recognise abstract human labour as the value substance through his theoretical analysis of the form of value. As an actual fact in the history of economic theory, Marx's theory of the forms of value could not have been obtained without superceding the classical labour theory of value and social reproduction. The mercantilist theories of circulation had to remain fragmental, and could not lead directly to systematic studies of the forms of value from a broader and deeper historical view like that of Marx's. *Capital* demonstrates a deepening process of 'a critique of political economy' by developing dialectically the theories of the forms and the substance of value. Thus Marx's critique of Aristotle in the theory of the value-form went dialectically to the historical basis of the abstraction of the substance of value.

A similar dialectical combination of the studies of the forms and the substance of value is observable in many places other than that of the dialogue with Aristotle. Although it is educative and interesting to read them as the formation of theories and critiques, the theory of the forms of value itself can and must be separated from the critical investigation into the substance of value, with a view to having a more fully completed and clearcut theoretical system. By such a separation and purification of the theory of value-forms, we can at least avoid a possible misunderstanding that the value-forms in commodity economy spring out of the substantial human relations in labour.

Can we then really trace the development of the value-forms from the simplest, to the money and the capital form without referring to the substance of value in a pure theory of the forms of value? A problem must here lie in the concept of value itself. How shall we define value when we separate it from its substance?

As we noticed, Marx did not define the concept of value immediately after analysing use-values in the first section of the first chapter of *Capital*. He took up *exchange-values* and inferred, from various quantitative equations between use-values in exchange, that 'As use-values, commodities differ above all in quality, while as exchange-values they can only differ in quantity, and therefore do not contain an atom of use-value'. (I, p. 128). Marx deduces immediately from this inference that the only one common property of commodities is that of being products of labour. The deduction is, however, incomplete and theoretically too hasty. For, as we have discussed, the common character of commodities is not limited to the property of being product of labour. Or the property of being product of labour is not a necessary and sufficient condition for commodities. What is more essential for commodities is that they have to be exchanged with other commodities. The property of requesting exchange is basically common to commodities and it must also call for a common quantitative comparability and some standard exchange ratios. This property of commodities can be initially conceived of as value separated from its substance in a purified theory of the forms of a commodity economy.

In the third section of the first chapter of *Capital* Marx notices: 'Everyone knows, if nothing else, that commodities have a common value-form which contrasts in the most striking manner with the motley natural forms of their use-values. I refer to the money-form.' (I, p. 139). From the view of the established money-form or the price-form, the quantitative homogeneity in the exchange-values of commodities is clearly not necessarily identical with the homogeneity of being the product of labour. We can pursue the origin of the price-form from the simplest expression of value, by depending, not upon the value substance as embodied labour, but upon the concept of value in form as the common property of commodities requiring exchange, calling for quantitative comparability and standard exchange ratios.[4] Marx does not clarify such a basic concept of value in form prior to the analysis of the value-form in the third section. Nor does he deduce the development of the expression of value directly from the concept of the substance of value as crystals of abstract labour, although he attempts to confirm the nature of the substance repeatedly through the development of value-forms. As a result the origin and the development of the value-form of commodities in the third section remain occasionally somewhat mechanically analytical, and it is difficult to follow the internal logic in it in spite of all its originality.

Marx begins the theory of the value-form from the simple form of value;

20 yards of linen = 1 coat, or: 20 yards of linen are worth 1 coat.

As Marx clarifies, the first commodity, linen, plays an active role in expressing its value in the coat taking the position of the relative form of value. The second commodity, the coat, is passively given the position of the equivalent form, and is so far directly exchangeable with the linen. In Marx's clarification, however, it does not seem fully clear what the expression of value means, and how it results in the direct exchangeability of the coat in the equivalent form. Marx tends to investigate the meaning of the value expression from the viewpoint of reducing different kinds of labour to human labour in abstract, and not so much in terms of the concept of value in its form.

If we remember that the concept of value is basically the property of commodities requiring them to exchange, the logic in the value-form can be more properly explained as follows. The expression of the value of the commodity linen in terms of coats means nothing but the request to exchange linen for a coat. The use-value of a coat is chosen by the owner of linen as a desirable object in which to realise the value of linen by exchange.[5] The request to exchange linen for the coat by placing linen in the position of the relative form of value is not certain to be realised, since the owner of a coat which is passively chosen as the equivalent, may not want linen. The specificity of the use-value of linen restricts the realisation of its value. Two commodities at the two poles of the expression of value are thus not generally convertible. So far as a coat is wanted as the equivalent of linen, the owner of a coat can directly exchange his commodity with linen if ever he wishes. The direct exchangeability given to the equivalent form can thus be understood easily from the basic nature of the value expression as the request for exchange.

There seems to be a methodological difficulty here of how to abstract the simple form of value between two commodities from a capitalist economy, where the exchange of commodities is already generally carried on through the use of money. If exchange-value is treated in the form of direct exchange as in the first section, the difficulty would be a real one and insoluble without assuming very primitive commodity exchanges.[6] In my view of the value-form, the property of commodities of requiring exchange with other commodities, can well be abstracted from beneath the price-form, and it leads to the simple form of value which represents the most basic motivation of commodity owners. An owner of a commodity, say linen, generally wants to obtain some other commodity, say a coat in exchange, even though his motivation is actually buried under the price-form in a fully developed commodity economy. The theoretical abstraction of such motivation becomes unrealistic when it is treated in the form of direct exchange as if it were generally realisable.

Insofar as we explore the basic motivation of commodity exchange in a simple form, the expression of the quantity of value cannot immediately be socially objective. In the expression that 20 yards of linen is offered in order to obtain 1 coat in exchange, the magnitude of value of linen is stated relatively in terms of a coat from the view of its owner. Since the owner of a coat may reject the requested ratio, the owner of linen cannot require too favourable terms of exchange, and has to take account of a social standard in his subjective expression. The quantities of embodied labour in commodities, together with technical conditions of production, do regulate the social standard of exchange-values from behind, but not so directly and strictly as Marx tends to describe the value-forms. The expression of value of each commodity is fundamentally rather anarchical and individualistic, not noticing the socially objective regulation even in the completed price-form.

As the request for the exchange of the commodity linen with another commodity cannot be confined to the request for a single kind of commodity, 'the simple form of value automatically passes over into' the expanded form of value[7] (I, p. 154)

20 yards of linen = 1 coat
10 yards of linen = 5 lb. tea
40 yards of linen = 2 quarter of corn
10 yards of linen = 1 ounces of gold
etc.

In this form the value of linen is expressed in terms of the various use-values of other commodities. Linen stands in a social relation more or less with the world of commodities and wishes to be a citizen of that world. Though the simple form of value remains as each component of this expanded form of value, the use-values of commodities which are requested by the linen in the expanded relative form stand for 'the particular equivalent form' (I, p. 156), as they are now in the position to be compared to each other in their specificity. By relating to each particular equivalent form in a series, the value of linen in an expanded relative expression then appears also indifferent to any specific use-value. In this regard, the nature of value is shown more distinctly from that of use-value. The quantity of value of linen, which is relatively expressed in the requested ratios of exchange with other commodities, must still be more or less subjectively and individualistically stated by its owners. But wider social relations of exchange-values must come to be taken into consideration here in comparison with the case of the simple form of value.

As Marx points out, certain defects are contained in the expanded form of value. The relative expression of value of a commodity cannot be complete, since the lines of equation can be added without a definite limitation. It is also 'a motley mosaic of disparate and unconnected expressions of value' (I, p. 156). These defects are reflected in the corresponding equivalent form. Each equivalent must be a limited and particular equivalent form among others, and each of the equivalent forms may exclude all the others in the actual process of exchange. Nor is there a unified form of expression of value. How can these defects be overcome?

Marx simply reverses the expanded form of value to get the third, general form of value, by saying: 'when a person exchanges his linen for many other commodities, and thus expresses its value in a series of other commodities, it necessarily follows that the other owners of commodities exchange them for the linen, and therefore express the values of their various commodities in one and the same third commodity, the linen' (I, p. 157). This logic contradicts the essence of Marx's own theory of forms of value. From the first, simple form of value, Marx emphasised the polarity of, and the different roles of, the relative form of value and the equivalent form. The relative expression of the value of linen in terms of a coat is not identical with the actual exchange between them, and does not necessarily imply the reverse request of an exchange from a coat into linen. The direct exchangeability is given only to the coat in the equivalent form, and not to the linen in the relative form of value. Therefore, the expanded form of value cannot simply be reversible. Marx thus left unsolved the question of how to overcome the defects in the expanded form of value, and how to pass over to the general form of value.

It is apparent that all the commodities do express each of their values in the simple, and then in the expanded relative form of value, just as the linen does. At first sight the defects in the expanded form of value of linen do not seem soluble in relation to the similar expressions of value of other commodities, but sink rather into a chaos which is composed of an unlimited number of different expressions of the values of various commodities.[8] In a chaotic series of parallel expressions of values however, some commodities must be found among the motley equivalents which are common at least for a certain number of commodities taking the relative form of value. Then this commodity, say tea, which is common among the equivalents for a certain range of commodities, comes to be required not only for its special use-value, say to drink, but also for its 'formal use-value' (I, p. 184), i.e. the direct exhangeability with other commodities. Under such circumstances the owners of commodities generally wish to obtain tea in exchange, and values of commodities become jointly expressed in terms of tea. The third, general form of value thus appears:

$$\left\{\begin{array}{l} \text{20 yards of linen} = \text{10 lb. of tea} \\ \text{2 coats} = \text{20 lb. of tea} \\ \text{1/2 quarter of corn} = \text{5 lb. of tea} \\ \text{etc.} \end{array}\right.$$

Insofar as commodities require to be exchanged with tea in this form, their form of value is simple, unified and common to all, 'hence general' (I, p. 157). The defects in the previous expanded form of value are so far overcome here. The general relative form of value of commodities imposes the character of general equivalent on the commodity tea, and entitles tea to take a monopolistic position of direct exchangeability with all other commodities. The values of commodities in this general relative form are now expressed not only in qualitatively equal term, but also in quantitatively comparable magnitude. The social correlations as quantified values must be more clearly considered, even though the expressions of value must be made, still more or less subjectively.

The range of commodities which have tea in common as their equivalent may not be comprehensive or universal. The other groups of commodities would each have a different general equivalent. The groups of commodities may overlap each other and can hardly be fixed for ever. Therefore, the general form of value cannot yet be solid nor universal. As long as plural equivalents coexist, the expression of value in the whole world of commodities cannot yet be completely unified. Thus, just as in the case of the transition from the expanded to the general form of value, the overlapping groups of commodities must further exclude weaker or less appropriate commodities (especially in terms of their 'formal use-value') from the position of the common and general equivalent. 'Only when this exclusion becomes finally restricted to a specific kind of commodity does the uniform relative form of value of the world of commodities attain objective fixedness and general social validity.' (I, p. 162). Through such exclusion and selection, silver and then gold was selected as the universal equivalent, because its physical durability, divisibility and purity in nature, as well as its external use-value for basic production and consumption are all well suited to the function of the universal equivalent. When silver and gold are fixed in the position of the universal equivalent, the money-form of value or the price-form solidly appears;

A yard of linen = 1/10 ounce of gold, or 7s. 9d.
1 coat = 2 ounces of gold, or £7. 15s. 9d.
A pound of tea = 1/5 ounce of gold, or 15s. 6d.
etc.

(When Marx wrote, an ounce of gold used to be coined as £3. 17s. 10½d.; £1 being 20 shillings and one shilling being 12 pence.)

The mystery of money, why gold as the money commodity monopolises direct exchangeability, or why all other commodities have to request an exchange with the money commodity, is no longer difficult to explain. As Marx summarises, 'the only difficulty in the concept of the money-form is that of grasping the universal equivalent form, and hence the general form of value as such'. By working further backwards the general form of value can be reduced to the expanded form of value, and its constitutive element is the simple form of value. 'The simple commodity form is therefore the germ of the money-form.' (I, p. 163). Thus, the endogenous character of commodity value, i.e. that it requires exchange with other commodities, being restricted as for realisation by the specificity of its use value, logically develops the value-form from the simple via the expanded and the general, into the money form, and then dualises the whole world of commodities into commodities and money. Money is therefore a commodity of some sort in its origin, and Marx is historically correct in his period in saying 'although gold and silver are not by nature money, money is by nature gold and silver' (I, p. 183). However, in its 'formal use-value' money can be separated from its gold basis under certain historical conditions, and with political devices as in major war periods, as well as in our own age. Although we cannot treat the concrete conditions and devices as well as the influences in substituting inconvertible state notes or bank notes for gold money within the framework of the basic theory of capitalist economy, it is worth noting that possibility of such substitution already exists in the 'formal use-value' of money.[9]

## 4.2 MONEY AND THE CIRCULATION OF COMMODITIES

In the third chapter of the first volume of *Capital* Marx analyses the basic forms of the functions of money. In the classical school as well as in the neo-classical school (before Keynes), money tends to be treated just as a conventional means of exchange. In contrast, Marx systematically puts in order the rich forms of the function of money, namely the measure of value, the means of circulation, and money as the absolute form of value which further comprises the forms of hoarding, means of payment and world money. Marx absorbed and made use of observations of the forms of money by the mercantilists like James Stuart. At the same time Marx's original analysis of the commodity form which clarifies the unique position of money in the world of commodities, enabled him theoretically to distinguish especially the function of money as the absolute form of value from that as the means of circulation. The analysis of the means of circulation itself also became richer than that of the classical school. In the light of the theory of the value-form, however, there are still some problems in Marx's theory of money, in particular concerning the measure of values in the first section of the third chapter.

### The Measure of Value

Marx defines the measure of values as the function of money in supplying commodities with the material for the expression of their values on the one hand, and, on the other, as the necessary form of appearance of the more substantial measure of value, i.e. labour-time. In Marx's words: 'The first main function of gold is to supply commodities with the material for the expression of their values, or to represent their values as magnitudes of the same denomination, qualitatively equal and quantitatively comparable. It thus acts as a universal measure of value, and only through performing this function does gold, the specific equivalent commodity, become money.' 'Money as a measure of value is the necessary form of appearance of the measure of value which is immanent in commodities, namely labour-time.' (I, p. 188). Apparently these definitions largely repeat and overlap the preceding definition of the money-form or the price-form which is given as the final result of the development of the value-form of commodities. Gold is shown there already at the position of universal equivalent which serves as the material for the common expression of commodity values in commensurable magnitudes. Such repetition occurred probably because the theory of value-form was completed and inserted later in its present place as we saw in note 5.

Another difficulty is in the theoretical relation between the function of money as the measure of value and the quantities of labour-time embodied in commodities. Marx defines here the first as the form of appearance of the second which is the more immanent, substantial measure of values of commodities. Though labour-time serves as the measure of the substance of values, the expressions of values in prices cannot directly nor exactly reflect the substance of values. They are performed without knowing the substantial quantities of labour-time embodied in commodities, and cannot be a deterministic form of appearance of labour-time. The expressions of values in terms of money must always be given more or less subjectively, individualistically and anarchically. As Marx himself perceptively notices, 'every owner of commodities knows that he is nowhere near turning them into gold when he has given their value the form of a price or of imaginary gold' (I, p. 190). 'The possibility, therefore, of a quantitative incongruity between price and magnitude of value, i.e. the possibility that the price may diverge from the magnitude of value, is inherent in the price-form itself. This is not a defect, but, on the contrary, it makes this form the adequate one for a mode of production whose laws can only assert themselves as blindly operating averages between constant irregularities.' (I, p. 196).

If the form of price is still subjectively equated to 'imaginary gold' by the individual owner of a commodity, and may often 'diverge from the magnitude of value', a function of money as the measure of value cannot simply be 'to supply commodities with the material for the expression of their value' just as already shown in the notion of the price form itself, but must somehow be to examine and measure the appropriateness and objectivity of individual pricing. This must be true, even when the notion of value is not yet related to embodied labour as the substance of value in commodities, but conceived of as the property of commodities requiring exchange, calling for standard exchange ratios. Despite his recognition of the subjective, imaginary and divergent character of individual pricing, Marx did not examine how money would function to measure and to objectify such prices. The presupposition of the labour substance of value probably induced Marx to define the measure of value just formally as a function of money, exactly expressing the immanent values in commodities.

As a part of restructuring Marx's theory of forms of value, Uno emphasised that the function of money as a means of purchase is a basic form in measuring and objectifying subjective individual prices. Indeed, when money is used repeatedly as a means of purchase, it serves as the measure of value in the circulation form in three senses. First, a price as a subjective expression of the value of a commodity requiring exchange with other commodities, has to be tested as to whether it is actually ever realisable or not by the action of purchase with money. When a purchase with money realises a price of a commodity, its value as request for exchange with other commodities becomes socially and qualitatively admitted. Second, subjective differences in pricing the same kind of commodity tend quantitatively to be equalised objectively in a market, making up a single price for a commodity, through repeated purchases with money. The unified price of a commodity would not remain static in accord with the value as the standard price of a commodity, and must rather incessantly fluctuate 'between constant irregularities' of anarchical demand and supply in the market. Third, however, the function of money repeatedly to purchase commodities in a market would generally reveal the standard price for each kind of commodity as a gravitational centre for the fluctuation of price, in so far as the commodity is competitively reproducible behind the market. In Uno's word the value of a commodity 'is confirmed only when, in recurrent transactions at prices fluctuating in response to the forces of demand and supply, a central price emerges at which normal trade takes place. . . .

Money, in the meantime, intermediates exchanges at prices gravitating towards value, thus measuring the value of all commodities. This process, therefore, enables commodities to regulate their supply [price] in response to the prevailing social demand.'[10]

The concept of value to be measured by recurrent purchase with money in this context, excludes the exchange-value of the commodity 'which is determined by their scarcity alone'[11], such as the price of non-reproducible curios, or the price of some imports whose supply cannot easily be adjusted in response to the fluctuation of demand in a market. There must be a social process of an adjusting supply of commodities in response to demand in a market, so that money may function as the measure of value in this regard. Although the working of the law of value cannot yet be analysed by explicitly referring to the labour theory of value in the pure theory of forms of value, the character of the value-forms which are well compatible with the working of the law of value based upon the social process of reproduction behind the market, must be observed through the function of money to be used in recurrent transactions. The notion of value even in its circulation form cannot thus be identical with fluctuating prices in general, or with a mere formal equilibrium price in a market, but must designate the gravitational centre of prices. The standard gravitational centre for prices cannot be immobile, but moves due to changes in the values of either general commodities or the money commodity. The function of money as the measure of value must thus be performed through the process of changes in the measure itself.

In comparison with the categorical scope of the theory of the value-form of commodities, resulting in the universal money-form in the world of commodities, the scope for money to function effectively as the measure of value must be relatively limited in a social market, where the supply of commodities can respond to demand. In its actual feature, the money commodity gold appears as the universal equivalent throughout the world market, whereas the function of money as the measure of value appears directly within each national or more local spheres of commodity circulation. Through the function of money to be used in recurrent transactions, the system of prices in each circulation market is unified and standardised on the one side, but on the other side the difference between the spheres of circulation with different systems of prices, reflecting the divergent social conditions of production behind them, becomes apparent. The difference between the spheres of circulation thus formulated would be an important premise for the concept of world money, and further, for the theory of transformation of money into capital as we shall discuss a little later. Before discussing these topics we have to examine other functions of money structurally forming each sphere of commodity circulation or a commodity market.

### The Means of Circulation

The second function of money is as the means of circulation. Within a market which is theoretically distinguished from the universal world of commodities by the function of money as the measure of value, money serves as the intermediary in carrying through the circulation of commodities. From the view of an individual owner of commodities, money which is expended in purchasing a commodity is usually obtained by selling his commodity in advance, and thus functions as the means of exchange of one commodity for another. Let us designate a type of commodity, say linen, $C_1$ and another, say a bible, $C_2$. If the owner of linen sells 20 yards of it at £2 and then buys a family bible of the same price the form of his transaction is formulated as follows:

$$C_1 - M - C_2$$

The first transaction $C_1 - M$ is the sale or 'the commodity's *salto mortale* [the mortal leap of commodity]' (I, p. 200), and not always guaranteed to be realised, whereas the second transaction $M - C_2$ is the purchase, and always easy to perform because of the position of money as the universal equivalent. As far as the material content of these transactions is concerned from the view of the initial owner of linen, the result of process seems to be reduced to $C_1 - C_2$, or the exchange of linen for a bible. Money seems just a means of exchange between $C_1$ and $C_2$.

In its essence, however, the exchange of commodities through money $C_1 - M - C_2$ quite differs from the direct exchange of them $C_1 - C_2$ as Marx noticed (cf. I, p. 207). When the weaver exchanges his linen for a bible through a sale and a purchase, the bible-pusher usually does not buy linen in return but buys a third commodity, $C_3$, say a bottle of brandy. And a sale of linen is realised by a purchaser who is usually different from the bible-pusher. Thus the transactions make up a continuous chain network in a form as follows:

*Figure* 4.1

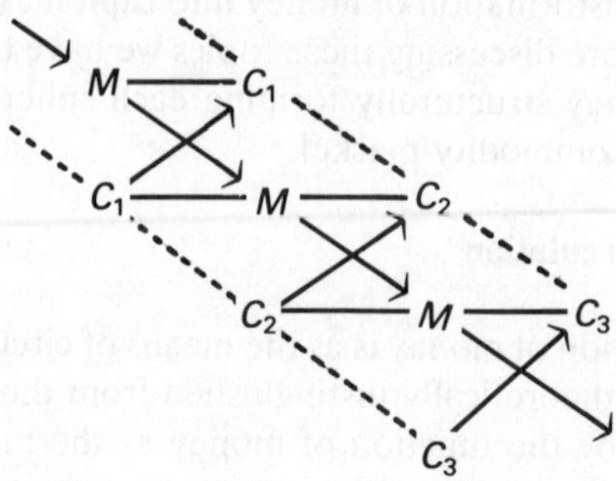


We see here 'how the exchange of commodities breaks through all the individual and local limitations of the direct exchange of products' (I, p. 207), and develops the broad interrelations between mutually unknown commodity-owners. The circulation of commodities, which pass the network from the lower left-hand side to the upper-right-hand side in Figure 4.1, is maintained by the current motion of money which flows from the upper left to the lower right remaining within the market as *currency*.

The means of exchange or circulation was the only form of the function of money for the classical school. Various other functions of money on the basis of its position as the universal equivalent were disregarded. Money was then treated just as a conventional means of exchange between basically harmonious commodities. *Say's law* originates in such a view of money. According to the law, the circulation of commodities necessarily implies an equilibrium between sales and purchases because every sale is a purchase, and every purchase a sale. Hence it is assumed that supply always creates its own demand. As Marx criticises (I, pp. 208–9), such a position is boiled down to a flat tautology to say that 'the number of actual sales accomplished is equal to the number of purchases', or it neglects the mutually independent and antithetical relation between sale and purchase. 'No one can sell unless someone else purchase. But no one directly needs to purchase because he has just sold.' A commodity becomes useless if it cannot be bought by the owner of money. The impossibility of selling a commodity may cause a similar difficulty for another commodity in a chain reaction, breaking the network of circulation of commodities. Therefore, contrary to Say's law, these forms of sale and purchase 'imply the possibility of crises, though no more than the possibility'. (I, p. 209).

The quantity theory of money in the classical school and further in the neo-classical school originates also in observing the function of money only as the means of circulation. Since other forms of money outside of the circulation like hoards or deposits, are neglected, all money is supposed to act as the means of purchase within a market. Every increase (or decrease) in the quantity of money must then result in a proportional increase (or decrease) of purchasing demand, and hence rise (or fall) of the level of prices of commodities. In short, prices are determined by the quantity of money in a country. If we designate the total quantity of transactions of commodities in a certain period $T$, the level of prices $P$, the quantity of existing money M, and the velocity of circulation of money $V$, then the quantity theory of money is formulated in I. Fisher's (1867–1947) equation of exchange:

$$MV = PT, \text{ or } P = M\frac{V}{T}$$

In this equation or rather identity $P$ is determined proportionally by $M$ in so far as other circumstances including $V$ and $T$ are unaltered.

Against the quantity theory of money Marx argues that the level of prices is determined not by the quantity of money, but basically by the substantial values of commodities and the value of gold (the money material). At the same time he takes into consideration that the quantity of money as the means of circulation is adjusted according to the needs of commodity circulation by having the convertible relation with other forms of money. Under the gold standard monetary system of his time the excessive quantity of money over that necessary for the circulating medium is pushed out into hoards or deposits, as he illustrates by the evidence that 'one has only to throw a given quantity of £1 notes into circulation in order to extract the same number of sovereign from it. This trick is well known to all bankers'. (I, p. 216). Thus, according to Marx, 'for a given interval of time during the process of circulation, we have the following equation: the quantity of money functioning as the circulating medium = the sum of the prices of the commodities divided by the number of times coins of the same denomination turn over'. (I, p. 216). Or symbolically:

$$M = \frac{PT}{V}$$

The equation signifies here that the quantity of money as the means of circulation or $M$ at the left-hand side is determined by the factors at the right-hand side.

From the point of view of the purified theory of the forms of value the level of prices or $P$ cannot yet be explicitly related to the value substance of commodities and gold as in Marx's argument. In fact $P$ also fluctuates in a market along with the changing balance between demand and supply. However, contrary to the quantity theory of money, the total demand is determined not by the quantity of money but by deeper and wider social factors behind the circulation such as the situation of capital accumulation. Besides, the repetition of the function of money as the means of purchase induces an adjustment in supply in reaction to the motion of demand and prices, as we have seen. Marx's position on the determination of the quantity of currency in use, combined with his consideration of the other forms of money, is thus largely maintained even in the purified theory of circulation, especially in so far as the gold money system is assumed. What happens then in the inconvertible paper money system?

Marx refers to the problem in the context of a series of possibilities of replacing bullion with coins and further with their symbol beginning from small change made of less precious metal like copper to end up with inconvertible paper money. Such possibilities spring from the function of money as the circulating medium, in which money is used as an intermediary means of exchange and not as an absolute form of value. Although Marx concretely observes *national* spheres of commodity circulation within which *national* uniforms are given to coins and their symbols, it is theoretically difficult here to conceive different actual *nations*. However, plural and different spheres of circulation with different systems of prices are theoretically conceivable and separable, as we have argued, through the function of money as the measure of value. As for money functioning as the means of circulation inside each of such spheres, it is not just possible but also technically and conventionally desirable to replace bullion with coins and small change, especially in the retail circulation. Even though the state usually coins and issues such small change up to a certain necessary amount, the state acts so far passively reflecting the technical necessity of commodity circulation. In basic, abstract theory, even a private individual with social reputation of wealth like a banker *may* do the same instead of the state. In the case of inconvertible paper money however, the political power of the state is necessary to force the circulation of paper money beyond its mere possibility or its technical convenience in commodity circulation. When the state has to depend on issuing paper money for budgetary needs, the state generally tends to overissue it.

As Marx noticed, if the amount of paper money exceeds the limit of the amount in gold coins of the same denomination which could have been in circulation, then the quantity of gold represented by each sheet of paper money has to diminish. For instance, if the quantity of paper money becomes twice as much as the limit, 'then in practice £1 will be the money-name not of 1/4 of an ounce of gold, but 1/8 of an ounce. . . . The value previously expressed by the price of £1 would now be expressed by the price of £2.' (I, p. 225). We see a simple basic case of inflation here. The quantity theory of money takes such a case for the general principle of determination of prices, or at least it cannot distinguish the law of monetary circulation for gold currency and that for paper money. At a very abstract level the contemporary inflation is basically understandable from the logic of motion of prices in the case of overissue of paper money. Hence there is a certain abstract relevancy in monetarism's desire to restrict the supply of money in order to calm down inflation. However, in comparison with simple paper money issued by the state, the inconvertible bank notes which now prevail together with various other sorts of credit-money have far more complex functions and influence on the level of prices, which must be investigated at the more concrete level of research. For instance, they are issued not merely to meet the state budget, and function more widely than the mere means of circulation. These complexities basically relate to the difficulty of *monetarism* in defining and effectively controlling the quantity of money in our age.

### Money as the Absolute Form of Value

So far as the quantity of currency is to be adjusted to the amount required by commodities to be circulated in a market, there must be other forms of money standing outside of the sphere of circulation. Outside of its function as the medium of circulation, money appears as the absolute form of value, or 'the sole form of value', or 'the only adequate form of existence of exchange value'. (I, p. 227). Marx calls such form simply 'money' (I, p. 227) or 'money as money'[12] and defines further three forms of function in it, namely 'hoarding', 'means of payment', and 'world money'.

Since money is the absolute form of value in the monopolistic position of direct exchangeability with other commodities, it tends to be saved and stored as mercantile wealth, generally by restricting purchase ($M - C_2$) as far as possible after selling ($C_1 - M$). 'The necessity and the passionate desire to hold fast to the product of the first metamorphosis' ($C_1 - M$) develop in a commodity economy. When money is saved as an end itself it is in a form of hoard. As money is qualitatively independent of all limits and quantitatively always limited in amount, 'the hoarding drive is boundless in its nature'. (I, p. 230). Hoards serve as reserve funds for the necessary fluctuations in the quantity of currency in the sphere of commodity circulation. On its basis, individual purchase and sale can be more elastically performed by utilising another function of money as means of payment.

A commodity can be traded for a promise to pay, when a purchaser cannot afford the necessary amount of money and the seller can await payment for a certain period on the basis of his reserve funds. After the transaction, the purchaser has to earn and save money by selling his own commodity, and has to pay by all means when due. Money which is paid on a due date functions as the means of payment. In this function money can be spared when a chain of debtor–creditor relationships contain mutual cancellations. But when actual payments have to be made, money functions not as a circulating medium, but as an absolute form of value. If the credit system is paralysed in a phase of acute crises, money as the means of payment in this absolute form is generally and massively wanted, and 'the antithesis between commodities and their value-form, money, is raised to the level of an absolute contradiction'.[13] (I, p. 236). In a normal condition of circulation, certificates of debts like bills of exchange are utilised as credit-money transferring debts to others on the ground of the function of money as means of payment. With the development of a commodity economy, hoarding must grow to serve more and more as reserve funds for the means of payment, and money in this function as the means of payment becomes also 'the universal material of contracts' (I, p. 238), as in payment of rent, taxes, reparation and so forth.

Money which is thus extracted and placed outside of a sphere of commodity circulation as an absolute form of value need not always serve for the same sphere of circulation, but can function also as world money moving across various spheres of circulation. Although Marx defines this function of money in relation with world trade concretely between nation-states, world money can be defined theoretically as universal money above a certain amount in the world of commodities, which is able to function between the plural spheres of commodity circulation, which are to be separated in basic theory through the function of money as the measure of value as we have argued. Given the different spheres of commodity circulation with different systems of prices, money can indeed theoretically serve across different spheres of circulation as the universal means of purchase, or as the universal means of payment, and thus as the universal wealth of the whole world of commodities. Historically, world money used to take the shape of bullion as Marx noticed (I, p. 240). However, it must be noted that coins and credit-money such as bills of exchange of the dominant sphere of circulation have also become increasingly used as world money with the development of the world market. On the basis of such a tendency, and under the floating exchange-rate system of international currencies since 1973, inconvertible dollar notes and dollar bills of exchange have come to function rather more extensively as world money at the cost of the previous stability in both money supply and the value of money under the gold standard systems. The historical necessity and the meaning of such changes in the international monetary system must be investigated together with the problems of inflation or stagflation again at a more concrete level of research outside of the scope of this volume.

## 4.3. THE TRANSFORMATION OF MONEY INTO CAPITAL

### How can Money be Transformed into Capital?

Money especially in the form of world money of some considerable quantity can easily be transformed into capital. World money is in a position from which different levels of values between plural spheres of commodity circulation are comparable. Therefore, it can be used to buy a commodity relatively cheaper in one sphere of circulation in order to sell it dearer in another. Money as the absolute universal form of value is thus increased in the form of circulation $M - C - M'$, where $M' = M + \triangle M$, i.e. the original sum advanced plus an increment. Marx calls this increment in money-form 'surplus-value' (I, p. 251), and continues to state that the motion of value to obtain such a surplus-value or to be valorised, 'converts it into capital'. (I, p. 252).

'As the conscious bearer of this movement, the possessor of money becomes a capitalist.' 'The ceaseless augmentation of value, which the miser seeks to attain by saving his money from circulation, is achieved by the more acute capitalist by means of throwing his money again and again into circulation.' Therefore, 'while the miser is merely a capitalist gone mad, the capitalist is a rational miser'. (I, pp. 254–5). In the circulation $M - C - M'$ possessed by a capitalist, the money and the commodity are no longer antithetical, but function as a different mode of existence of the value-form of capital. Thus capital appears as a special usage of money for valorisation, and forms the self-augmentative motion of value.

Once money is transformed into capital by utilising the different levels of values or the different systems of prices between different spheres of circulation, the fluctuation of prices above or below the gravitational standard prices is certainly made use of as far as possible both across and within the spheres of circulation. In this aspect capital moves always more or less speculatively since the direction and the range of fluctuation of prices according to the changing balance between demand and supply in a market, are not predictable for a certainty. Nor are values in form as the standard prices themselves immobile, but vary, depending on unforeseeable and imperceptible changes in the relative conditions of production of commodities and gold. Capitalists also utilise their position as the possessers of reserve funds of money in purchasing cheaper from persons who for various reasons need to sell their commodities urgently. Given the polar positions between money as the universal equivalent and general commodities, the owners of commodities have to await purchase after pricing and cannot positively instigate exchange for money. Therefore, they tend to make a special concession in prices to the purchasers who offer in one go to take from their shoulders the burden of realisation in quantity. Various non-capitalist producers are often apt to be expropriated by such transactions, while industrial capitalists can rather increase their efficiency of valorisation by the same method as we shall see later in Chapter 8, Section 8.1.

The form of the circulation of value, buying in order to sell dearer, $M - C - M'$ is nothing but the form of merchants' capital. However, industrial capital also appears as money which has been changed into commodities, and reconverted into more money by the sale of commodities. In this regard, $M - C - M'$ can be defined as 'the general formula for capital' (I, p. 257). So far as the aim of this formula of capital is augmentation of money through circulation, the efficiency of valorisation is not merely measured and compared by the ratio of surplus-value $\Delta M$ against the amount of money $M$

advanced to each particular transaction of a commodity, as the rate of profit for each transaction or turnover of capital. For sure it must be compared also in terms of the yearly rate of profit for the whole investment which includes various costs of merchants' business not confined to the purchasing costs of commodities to sell. Anyway, surplus-value $\triangle M$ is conceived as profit, when it is set against the amount of money advanced in order to obtain it. So far as capitalists compete each other for higher efficiency of valorisation, the yearly rate of profit (not the rate of profit for each turnover of capital in longer or shorter periods of time), which is usually called just 'the rate of profit' for the sake of simplification, matters more. In so far as capitals compete freely as the homogeneous motion of value augmenting itself in the form of money, their move to commodity transactions with perspectively higher rates of profit would eliminate any fixed difference in the rate of profit. However competition among merchants' capitals still lacks a solid basis for the equalisation of the rate of profit, although the equalisation of the profit rate is in a sense requested by the essentially homogeneous character of competitive capitals. Indeed, merchants' capitals do not have a common inner basis for valorisation themselves, but depends on the external chances to buy cheap and sell dear between and within the fluctuating markets. Anarchical speculation, full of accidental gains and losses, always characterises the activity of merchants' capital.

As the individual merchant capital has thus to strive to make the best of any rosy chance as quickly as possible, it extends trade by borrowing. Money as a reserve fund, being idle outside of circulation, can be mobilised for loans. A part of the increased profit of the merchant made possible by the use of credit is paid to the lender as interest. Money is thus also transformed into interest-bearing capital $M....M'$ theoretically on the basis of merchants' capital. This form of capital increases itself just by getting interest for loans and without any intermediary circulation of commodities.[14] As an external-form, interest-bearing capital broadly appears as being indifferent to its social ground. Its form is common to loan capital working in the capitalist credit system (to be analysed later in the second section of Chapter 8), as well as to older moneylender's or usurer's capital. Although a rational basis for interest from the view of capitalists is given in a part of profit increased by means of credit, the form of interest-bearing capital may expropriate borrowers in their economic difficulties through high rates of interest. We see such a function of this form of capital not merely in the precapitalist usurer's practice, but also in periods of modern economic crises or in the contemporary problem of the cumulative debt of the 'third world' countries.

The form of interest-bearing capital, unlike merchants' capital, does not include any different use-values in each of its motions. It obtains surplus-value $\Delta M$ simply as the rental price of money for a certain period. Surplus-value obtained as interest appears here in the form of pure self-proliferation of money in each period. In such a form, interest-bearing capital is absolutely homogeneous, and tends to receive an equal rate of interest which is daily determined by the total balance of the supply and demand of loanable money in prior to lending. An ideal of capital as being automatically and homogeneously self-augmenting money is represented by this form of capital. Actually this form of capital serves as a measure for the activities of other capitals with various rates of profit being compared with the rate of interest.

Inequality of the rate of value-increase among merchants' capitals is overcome, but merely externally, in the form of interest-bearing capital. The fundamental limitation of merchants' capital which is the absence of an internal basis for valorisation however, remains unsolved, and is shown rather more extremely in the form of interest-bearing capital. In these forms, capital cannot assure its motion of self-proliferation on an increasing scale, and cannot be fully established. At the same time the values of commodities in circulation are so far utilised and compared only externally, and are not regulated or unified internally in the motion of capital.

The form of industrial capital $M - C\left\{ Pm/L \cdots P \cdots C' - M' \right\}$ appears as a type of capital which overcomes such limitations by establishing the inner ground of valorisation. In this form capital produces commodities to sell dearer than the commodities purchased for their production. Surplus-value as profit is obtained here in the motion of capital containing the process of production ($P$) as well as the process of circulation. In order to perform the process of production thoroughly by means of commodities capital must find both various means of production ($Pm$) and labour-power ($L$) as commodities in the sphere of circulation.

Raw materials and instruments of labour, which comprise the means of production, could already generally be found together with the means of consumption in a commodity form in precapitalist markets, as a part of commoditisation of labour products. In contrast, labour-power, which is not a product of labour but a subjective human ability to work, is not obtainable so broadly in a commodity economy in general. In various precapitalist social formations, workers could not dispose of their own labour-power as an individual right, and they were closely tied to the land as the main precondition of labour activities within a variety of communal and authoritarian power structures. Therefore, for the transformation of money into industrial capital, a special historical condition of workers lives must be formed, and the workers must be turned into the *free worker* in the double sense as Marx defines it; 'This worker must be free in the double sense that as a free individual he can dispose of his labour-power as his own commodity, and that, on the other hand, he has no other commodity for sale, i.e. he is rid of them, he is free of all the objects needed for the realization [*Verwirklichung*] of his labour-power.' (I, pp. 272–3). Such a condition of workers 'has no basis in natural history, nor does it have a social basis common to all periods of human history. It is clearly the result of a past historical development, the product of many economic revolutions, of the extinction of a whole series of older formations of social production' (I, p. 273). Especially 'the expropriation of the agricultural producer, of the peasant, from the soil' (I, p. 876) in a process of transition from feudalism to capitalism was decisive for the birth of 'free' wage-workers, as Marx describes it later in *Capital* in Part VIII, 'So-Called Primitive Accumulation'.

Capital can thus be developed into industrial capital only in the sphere of circulation which contains the commodity form of labour-power. Since this 'precondition comprises a world history', industrial capital, unlike other forms of circulation we have seen beginning from commodities, 'announces from the outset a new epoch in the process of social production' (I, p. 274). Industrial capital appears not merely in a limited historical epoch in the world history, but also in the limited sphere(s) of commodity circulation with such a social precondition. It cannot emerge universally in the whole world of commodities, though its scope of activity widens as capitalism develops.

In a sphere of commodity circulation with certain preconditions for industrial capital, the values of commodities are internally measured and adjusted through the social process of production organised by capital. Value relations in such a sphere of circulation also serve as the standard for fluctuation of prices in the whole world of commodities. Apparently, how industrial capital internally increases its value, and regulates values of commodities through the process of production, can no longer be studied in a theory of the forms of circulation. The content of the capitalist process of production must further be analysed. But let us briefly review the problems left by Marx at this point before coming onto the theory of the capitalist process of production.

**Another Transformation Problem**

Although there have been many debates and studies on the 'transformation problem' from values into prices of production in the third volume of *Capital*, the problem in Marx's theoretical treatment of the transformation of money into capital has not yet attracted much attention among Western theorists. The exceptional to this was where Marx defined the value of labour-power, as we shall see later. Among Japanese Marxians, especially in the Uno School, however, the problem has been discussed no less seriously than the so-called 'transformation problem'. It may be called 'another transformation problem'. Though the problem here may seem remote and independent from the problem in the third volume of *Capital*, its solution can serve as a necessary precondition for a proper treatment of the other problem.

In the theory of the transformation of money into capital, Marx defines $M - C - M'$ as 'the general formula for capital' and refers to merchants' capital and interest-bearing capital as a kind of capital. However, in discussing 'contradictions in the general formula,' he emphasises the theoretical impossibility for capital to acquire surplus-value, properly understood, in the sphere of circulation. It is because commodities are assumed to be bought and sold generally at their value as the embodied labour time on the basis of the preceding labour theory of value. As a result, capital cannot arise from circulation, whereas 'it is equally impossible for it to arise apart from circulation' (I, p. 268). The contradiction can be solved only when the money-owner can find within the sphere of circulation a special commodity to be used as a source of value and surplus-value, namely the commodity labour-power. In this theoretical sequence money can eventually be transformed into capital only as industrial capital carrying out the production process by using the commodity labour-power. Thus, according to Marx's treatment, while commodities and money can appear along with many precapitalist economic formations of society, 'it is otherwise with capital. The historical conditions of its existence are by no means given with the mere circulation of money and commodities.' (I, p. 274).

Capital is conceived here narrowly only as industrial capital. As historical fact it is obvious that capital already appears also in the forms of merchants' capital and money-lenders' capital in precapitalist commodity economies from very early periods, or widely in the world not being confined to the central capitalist countries. Certainly Marx knew that and noticed that 'historically speaking, capital invariably first confronts landed property in the form of money; in the form of monetary wealth, merchants' capital and usurers' capital'[15] (I, p. 247). Also within the historical development of capitalism, at its first stage of mercantilism, merchants' capital in the world trade played a decisive role as leading capital. As Marx says, 'world trade and the world market date from the sixteenth century, and from then on the modern history of capital starts to unfold' (I, p. 247). The mercantile system reflected the initial stage of such capitalist development.

If capital is conceived theoretically as being feasible only on the social basis of the commodity labour-power, the concept of capital clearly can not include the forms of merchants' or money-lenders' capital. Then the theory of the transformation of money into capital cannot serve as a sufficient conceptual standard for understanding the structure of commodity economy in general, where certain forms of capital must usually arise along with the forms of commodity and money. The theory can neither properly imply or reflect the logic of the birth of capitalism in the world market accompanied by the mercantile system.

Taking these points into consideration Uno asserted that the theory of the transformation of money into capital had to refer to precapitalist merchants' and money-lenders' capital from the view of an economic theory to elucidate history.[16] In the theory of transformation of value into prices of production, Marx suggests, as very much emphasised by Engels and Hilferding, a historical-logical sequence following the development from a precapitalist simple commodity economy to a capitalist economy. In contrast Marx excludes a broad historical basis of abstraction from the theory of transformation of money into capital, by saying that 'we do not need to look back at the history of capital's origins in order to recognize that money is its first form of appearance. Every day the same story is played out before our eyes.' (I, p. 247). In my view Marx's treatments here must be contrary. The law of value is logically to be shown as the law of motion of a capitalist economy consistently, including both the process of production of surplus-value and its distribution through prices of production. A historical separation of the basis of abstraction between the theory of the law of value and that of prices of production can not solve the value controversy, but rather confuses its solution. Whereas, the theory of transformation of money into capital must define the historically specific social condition, i.e. the commodity-form of labour-power, for appearance of industrial capital, in contrast with historically older and broader existence of other forms of capital as well as the forms of commodity and money.

The theoretically wider concept of capital, including the forms of merchants' and interest-bearing capital, not merely enables us to see *both* the structural development of precapitalist commodity economy with its limitations, *and* the logic of the birth of capitalism with its necessary social preconditions. It also elucidates the nature of a capitalist economy in a triple sense. First, the anarchical, private moneymaking character of industrial capital originates from the form of merchants' capital as the general formula of capital, which arises externally outside of social communal reproduction. A capitalist economy, therefore, cannot basically be organised for the sake of co-operative harmonious economic order among human beings, along with their environmental relations with nature. Second, there remain the forms of merchants' and money-lenders' capital even after the establishment of industrial capital, especially between the capitalist centre and the periphery in the world market as well as within each capitalist country. Surplus-value or profit obtained in the capitalist centre actually contains not only surplus-value produced in its process of production, but also profit upon alienation from the trade with peripheral modes of production. Profit upon alienation obtained in world trade may well include the transfer of surplus-labour from the peripheral countries to the capitalist centre as suggested in the recent theory of unequal exchange,[17] though the point cannot be discussed any further here. Anyway, in spite of its expansion, capitalist production must remain in reality only a partial system of production in the world, because of its egoistic and money-grubbing nature. Third, the forms of distribution of surplus-value on the basis of capitalist production, such as profit and interest, are inherited from the forms of merchants' and money-lenders' capital, and are not unique to industrial capital. There are certain difficulties and unrealities in Marx's attempts in the third volume of *Capital* to show how these forms are *created* originally by the transformation of capitalistic surplus-value obtained in the process of production. A portion of the transformation problem from values into prices of production, with equalisation of profit rates, can thus be removed by renovating the theory of transformation of money into capital.

Uno's renovation in this regard, however, left us with a methodological problem in relation to his basic position of how to formulate the whole principles of political economy. In his methodological differentiation of three levels of economic research Uno maintains that 'the pure theory of capitalism must presuppose the abstract context of a purely capitalist society made up of the three major classes of capitalists, workers, and landowners'[18] on the basis of the historical tendency of British capitalism up to Marx's age. It seems inconsistent to refer to precapitalist merchants' and money-lenders' capital in his theory of the transformation of money into capital in so far as the theory should be a part of the basic principles or the pure theory of capitalism. In conjunction with the attempts to solve the inconsistency two major positions appeared among the followers of Uno.

One group of Uno theorists insist that the forms of merchants' and interest-bearing capital should be presented consistently upon the presupposition of a purely capitalist society without referring to a broader basis of abstraction or precapitalist history.[19] The practice of the form of merchants' capital, buying cheap and selling dear was theoretically impossible to exist so long as commodities were assumed to be traded at their embodied labour-value. It must be otherwise, when the theory of forms of circulation is purified without referring to the substance of value. The anarchical fluctuation of prices in a commodity circulation even within a presupposed purely capitalist society is then more easily observable, and it gives theoretical room for the form of capital to buy cheap in order to sell dear in the circulation. The opportunity may also be open for capitalists to purchase cheaper by accepting in quantity the burden and the subsequent risks of realisation from commodity owners.

In this context, however, the theory of the transformation of money into capital may not be very secure, or comprehensive in its implications. The attempt to utilise the fluctuation of prices in a market is speculative and may easily give a loss, not a gain. The transformation of money into capital remains so far a mere possibility, and cannot be a certainty. Besides, the speculative attempts to utilise the fluctuation of prices, as well as any possibility of purchasing cheaper by accepting the burden of realisation, is common to the practice of industrial capital or commercial capital in a capitalist society, and cannot present a different source of valorisation for the forms of capital appearing prior to or outside of capitalist production.

Therefore, another group of Uno theorists, to which I belong, wish to solve these difficulties by reformulating the methodological ground or the subject of the principles of political economy. Especially as for the purified theory of the forms of circulation, we need not confine our subject of study to the economic relations in a purely capitalist society. We can abstract the notion of the forms of commodity, money and capital by directly observing world capitalism from its most elementary form. The external character of the forms of circulation which originate inter-socially, outside of the social process of production, is then clearly implied in our basic principles of political economy. Unlike in the theory of pure capitalism, the notion of world money and the theory of transformation of money into merchants' capital between different spheres of commodity circulation is, as we have seen, easily conceivable in theory based directly upon world capitalism.[20] The form of merchants' capital which is defined in such a theory has a distinguishable source of valorisation outside of the capitalist process of production, and is thus also indicative of precapitalist merchants' origins and practice.

The theory of the transformation of money into capital in this regard reflects *as a result* the historical formation of capitalist production *from the view of expansion of the commodity economy*. Capitalist production is formed when an originally external commodity economy expands and invades the social process of production in the form of industrial capital. The theory explaining the development of the forms of value through which a commodity economy reaches capital however, should not be taken for a historical theory which depends on and fully reflects the essential logic of the birth of capitalist production. In particular, the formation of a class of free workers in the double sense, which was the indispensable precondition for capitalist production, could not be ensured merely by peaceful expansion of commodity economy. It was carried through heavily assisted by violence as the 'midwife' (I, p. 916) of a new social formation in the process of expropriating the small farmers and peasants. Such an internal social change, the so-called 'primitive accumulation', cannot be treated in the theory of the transformation of money into capital, even though the theory can contain more historical implications than those considered in *Capital*.

Practically, the immanent logic in the forms of commodity economy systematically unfolds from the elementary commodity form up to the forms of merchants' and interest-bearing capital as the development of the forms of value, but it cannot provide the commodity labour-power as an inevitable result of the preceding notions. From the limitations of the forms of merchants' and interest-bearing capital, we have seen that the form of industrial capital together with the commodity labour-power is theoretically *required* to appear as a more developed capital. The request is made possible only when certain historical social conditions are prepared behind the sphere of circulation, which provide a supply of the commodity labour-power. A systematic guarantee of finding such a specific social situation is given, in my view, not by the preceding theory of the forms of commodity economy, but by the initial setting of the subject of study in the basic principles of a capitalist economy.

Thus Marx's distinction of the *separate* historical characters between capital *and* the forms of commodity and money, must be valid if it is applied to the difference *between* capitalist social production under the form of industrial capital *and* the forms of commodity economy in general, including the forms of merchants' and interest-bearing capital. The historically special character of capitalist production is, however, not merely distinguished from the forms of commodity economy in general, but also dependent on them. Especially the anarchical autonomy of capitalist production in relation to other modes of production in the world market is derived from the fact that the capitalist mode of production, unlike any other, has converted the originally inter-social commodity economic order into its internal forms of organisation, as we discussed in Section 4.1 of this chapter. Then our theoretical system of analysing the internal law of motion of capitalist production, after studying the forms of commodity circulation in the world market, simultaneously elucidates a methodological secret of the self-reliant motion of the capitalist mode of production. So far as the labour products of other peripheral modes of production are obtained in the commodity-form in exchange for its own commodity products in the world market, the motion of capitalist production is not at all disturbed qualitatively but simply quantitatively amplified. *From the view of the internal logic of the motion of capitalist production*, a portion of capital and labour which is necessary to produce exports can be regarded as the portion which is necessary directly to produce commodities actually obtained in exchange as imports.[21]

Therefore the basic theory of capitalism can abstract a purely and completely capitalist society in the process of the analyses of the internal law of motion of capitalist productioi, on the basis of the forms of commodity economy. By formulating the theory of the forms of commodity circulation on the broad basis of world capitalism the basic principles of political economy can systematically assure that they contain the methodological ground for abstracting a purely capitalist society in the theory of capitalist process of production. We need not narrow our subject of study to a purely capitalist society prior to the theory of the forms of circulation as in Uno's *Principles*. Thus, the logic and the historical implications of the theory of the transformation of money into capital would become systematically richer and easier to see by improving the theory of both Marx and Uno at this point.

# 5 Capitalist Production and the Law of Value

## 5.1 LABOUR AS THE UNIVERSAL ECONOMIC CONDITION FOR SOCIETIES

### The Labour Process

It is always impressive to read how sharply Marx distinguishes three different historical characters, as presented in the forms of a commodity economy, the labour process and the capitalist economy, in just a small number of pages of chs. 6 and 7 of the first volume of *Capital*. In ch. 6 Marx has defined free workers in the double sense as an essential precondition for capitalist production in his theory of the transformation of money into capital. In ch. 7, after that definition however, he does not immediately analyse the capitalist process of production. In the first section of ch. 7, Marx investigates the labour process as the universal condition common to all forms of society. This is noteworthy, since the substantial content of capitalist production is designed to be studied from this ch. 7. The distinction between the labour process in general and the capitalist process of production is unique to Marxian economics, and important for Marxian socialism as well as for the economic theory.

In my view this distinction is coupled with the recognition of the difference in the historical character of commodity economy in general and that of capitalist economy. From a standpoint that the forms of a commodity economy *totally* subsume the labour process *only* in a capitalist society, the labour process must naturally be observed as a common universal condition for societies, being separated from the commodity economic order. Contrastingly, in the classical school, which believed the capitalist commodity economy to be a natural order of liberty, labour was regarded as 'the original purchase-money,'[1] and was not theoretically separated from the commodity economic order. Therefore, Marx's theory of the labour process is just as important as his theory of the forms of value as a means theoretically to overcome the naturalism in the classical and the neo-classical school, and to clarify the historical specificity of capitalism.

How can we derive the notion of the labour process as a common condition for all the forms of society from the historically specific capitalist cconomy which we are observing? Marx stresses here the aspect of the production of use-values by capitalism. 'What the capitalist sets the worker to produce is a particular use-value, a specific article. The fact that the production of use-values, or goods, is carried on under the control of a capitalist and on his behalf does not alter the general character of that production. We shall therefore, in the first place, have to consider the labour process independently of any specific social formation.' (I, p. 284).

This corresponds to the definition of use-values Marx gives in his initial analysis of the two factors of the commodity – that use-values 'constitute the material content of wealth, whatever its social form may be' (I, p. 126). Also in the subsequent analysis of the dual character of labour embodied in commodities, Marx stated: 'Labour as the creator of use-values, as useful labour, is a condition of human existence which is independent of all forms of society; it is an eternal natural necessity which mediates the metabolism between man and nature, and human life itself.' (I, p. 133).

These analyses seem clear and sound. As Marx says, labour as the creator of use-values must obviously be an universal condition for all human societies. A problem remains here, however, as we shall see later, if the other aspect of labour as abstract labour is to be excluded from such an universal condition. Let us presently follow Marx's notion of the labour process. Marx inquires as to what is characteristic to human labour as a process of metabolism with nature.

> Labour is, first of all, a process between man and nature, a process by which man, through his own actions, mediates, regulates and controls the metabolism between himself and nature. He confronts the materials of nature as a force of nature. He sets in motion the natural forces which belongs to his own body, his arms, legs, head and hands, in order to appropriate the materials of nature in a form adapted to his own needs. Through this movement he acts upon external nature and changes it, and in this way he simultaneously changes his own nature. (I, p. 283).

Marx then deliberately leaves out of consideration the 'first instinctive forms of labour which remain on the animal level'. There must have been an immense interval of time for human beings to pass through such instinctive forms of labour, by changing their own nature through labour. How should we define labour in an exclusively characteristic form different from the instinctive animal level?

> A spider conducts operations which resemble those of the weaver, and a bee would put many a human architect to shame by the construction of its honeycomb cells. But what distinguishes the worst architect from the best of beees is that the architect builds the cell in his mind before he constructs it in wax. At the end of every labour process, a result emerges which had already been conceived by the worker at the beginning, hence already existed ideally. Man not only effects a change of form in the materials of nature; he also realizes his own purpose in those materials. And this is a purpose he is conscious of, it determines the mode of his activity with the rigidity of a law, and he must subordinate his will to it. (I, p. 284).

We saw in Chapter 3, Section 3.1, of this volume that Marx's reversal of the Hegelian idealistic dialectic into a materialist dialectic was performed, not through merely metaphysical thinking or general reflection on natural sciences, but by way of overcoming Feuerbach's abstract humanistic materialism on the basis of critical studies of classical political economy. We see clearly here, at the base of Marx's economic theory, not a mechanical physical sort of materialism but historical materialism, in a sense a thrilling synthesis of humanistic idealism and critical materialism. For Marx, labour is not merely a materialistic process of metabolism between man and nature. In its human form, labour is also characterised by the role of the human idea and the conscious will to realise it. Both head and hands as the developed natural forces in human beings are mobilised in the labour process, and thus form a most basic ground for the historical development of human societeies through changes in the labour process.

As H. Braverman correctly pointed out, the power of conceptual thought which characterises human labour is also closely connected with the linguistic ability to use symbols and speech.[2] The various useful forms of labour as purposive human action have clearly been extended to various fields, and transmitted to other groups or succeeding generations by the spoken or written expression of conceptual thought. The wide range of useful forms of human work is thus related to the human power of conceptual thought.

Conception of work and its actual execution, however, are not always wholly unified in each individual. In Braverman's words: 'The unity of conception and execution may be dissolved. The conception must still precede and govern execution, but the idea as conceived by *one* may be executed by *another*. The driving force of labour remains human consciousness, but the unity between the two may be broken in the individual and reasserted in the group, the workshop, the community, the society as a whole.'[3] This possibility of dissolving the unity of conception and execution is important, for it may serve also as the basis for the separation of the ruling class and the direct workers in class societies. It must be noted that such a *possibility*, and a *possible* ground for class relations, do arise in the human power of conceptual thought itself. In class societies the role and the function of designing and ordering the conception or the idea for execution by labour are concentrated in the position of the ruling class with their monopolistic possession of the means of production. But the conception for the work, which may be broken down into pieces of individual work, is conveyed to each worker and must be internalised as his own purpose by means of his own power of conceptual thought. The human subjective ability has thus ironically been utilised as a hidden unconscious basis for keeping the masses in a subordinate position in various forms of class societies.[4] It must be a fundamental task for Marxism to reunify the conception and execution of labour for the associated individuals in classless societies.

From the view of the labour process, the distinction between human labour as purposeful subjective activity in work and the condition of labour is essential. The condition of labour is further divided into the object of labour and the instrument of labour. The object of labour which 'has been filtered through previous labour' is called 'raw material' as distinguished from natural resources. (I, p. 284). The instruments of labour, such as tools, machines, equipments, etc., which 'the worker interposes between himself and the object of his labour', are 'characteristic of the specificially human labour process', and 'supply a standard of the degree of development which human labour has attained'.[5] (I, pp. 285–6).

In the eyes of the master of the labour of others, especially in a capitalist market economy, the distinction between labour and the conditions of labour must appear unimportant. Labour, the objects and the instruments of labour are all regarded as 'factors of production' which are necessary to produce goods. In a capitalist economy in particular, they are considered just as alternative cost factors, to be selected in a market for a more effective or cheaper production of commodities. Such a point of view is linked with naturalism which sees the market economy as an eternal natural social order, and it governs ideologically not only the bourgeois ruling class, but also the common sense of the masses, as well as neo-classical economics.

The notion of the labour process offers a basic critique of such a narrow bourgeois point of view. A broader view of historical humanistic materialism serves as 'a guiding thread' for the notion of the labour process beyond the limitation of the bourgeois ideological framework. At the same time the theoretical recognition of the different historical characters of the commodity economy, capitalist production and the labour process, as we have seen, presents a scientific basis for historical materialism. The starting-point for the labour theory of value must be founded upon the notion of the labour process in this context. The concept of labour is, however, not yet fully unfolded theoretically as the basis of the value theory (or of social science in general) so far as it has been confined to the aspect of useful labour producing use-values.

**Abstract Labour**

Marx was the first to point out and examine the dual character of labour; i.e. the concrete useful character and the abstract human character of labour. However, in the theoretical system of *Capital* where the substance of value is presented from the very beginning in the initial analysis of two factors of the commodity, the dual character of labour tends to be observed as being embodied in commodities and is strictly correlated to value and use-value of commodities. As a result, Marx does not refer to abstract labour or the dual character of labour in analysing the labour process. He comes back to the aspect of abstract labour only when he proceeds to the theory of the valorisation process of capital in the separate second section of ch. 7 of the first volume of *Capital*.

There remains here an important problem-whether the abstract character of labour exists exclusively within commodity-value relations or is common to all societies as an aspect of human activity in its metabolic interaction with nature. The problem is fundamental to the theoretical basis of the labour theory of value and Marxian socialism. In my opinion Marx's notion of the labour process is still incomplete, and too narrow in this regard as an analysis of the universal conditions of societies based on labour. It may also be inconsistent with his observations in other places.

There has been, however, a group of Marxian value theorists who believe that the commensurability of various products, as the result of abstract labour exists only as the consequence of commodity-value relations. For instance, I. I. Rubin states that 'social or socially-equalized labour in the specific form which it has in the commodity economy can be called *abstract labour*',[6] while he distinguishes three types of equal labour, i.e. physiologically equal labour, socially equal labour and abstract labour. In recent debates a similar position, that abstract labour cannot exist apart from commodity exchange or money-relations has been presented by a series of theorists called 'the Rubin School'.[7] As an interpretation, this position can find some support in *Capital*.[8] Marx's treatment of the dual character of labour embodied in commodities and his distinction between the labour process and the valorisation process may also seem consistent with this position.

Indeed, there are some reasons which tend to complicate the conception of abstract labour. First, as a theory to clarify history, Marx's value theory defines the substance of value as crystals of abstract labour always through and behind the forms of value, as we have seen. Especially in so far as the dual concept of labour is presented in combination with use-value and value of commodities from the beginning, the Rubin type of interpretation of abstract labour may easily arise. Second, as a fact in the history of economic thought, equality in human labour beyond its useful concrete forms could not be considered until a thorough commodity economy began to develop with capitalism. The fact was suggested by Marx in his dialogue with Aristotle, along with the fact that the concept of human equality became a fixed popular opinion for the first time in a modern society. Actually the modern popular view of human equality since the Enlightenment coincided with the rise of the capitalist commodity economy. Third, not only such a tendency in ideology but also the fact 'that in our capitalist society a given portion of labour is supplied alternately in the form of tailoring and in the form of weaving, in accordance with changes in the direction of the demand for labour' (I, p. 134) under the established industrial capitalism, seems evidence of the abstract character of labour as arising from the development of a commodity economic order.

Thus, it must be true that the recognition of abstract labour was made possible by the development of the modern capitalist commodity economy. However, once obtained the recognition can possibly be applicable to other social formations. For instance, in the section on the fetishism of the commodity in the first chapter of *Capital*, Marx mentions Robinson Crusoe's life, medieval European feudal society, the patriarchal peasant family and an association of free men as illustrations where the amount of labour measured by time is allotted to various concrete useful forms. When Marx states that the relations between Robinson and his labour products 'contain all the essential determinants of value' (I, p. 170) he clearly sees abstract labour embodied in Robinson's products. Marx's usage of the value concept here, however, is incorrect and confusing, for there cannot be any commodity value in Robinson's economic life without commodity exchanges. To be more exact, we should say that the essential determinants of the economic norms concerning the allocation of labour time in Robinson's life, as well as in non-capitalist forms of societies, would form the substance of value once placed within the commodity economic order. Marx's incorrect usage of the value concept here may come from a residue of the classical labour theory of value which does not grasp the forms of value and tends to concentrate merely on the quantity of labour values. If we distinguish the forms and the substance of value, and purify the forms of value, then we can more exactly treat general economic norms, including the dual character of labour common to all the forms of societies, separately from the value concept. Anyway, Marx's analysis in the section on the fetishism of commodity, despite his confusing usage of the value concept, convinces us well of the existence of the general norms or rules of economic life common to all societies, including the necessity of allocating abstract human labour to various useful concrete forms.

Whereas concrete useful labour is qualitatively different in each form, producing different use-values, and it therefore seems impossible to aggregate or compare such labour simply by time, labour must also be treated as an homogeneous expenditure of human ability to work, as abstract labour and measured by time even outside of the commodity economic order. Marx also stated in the *Grundrisse* the law of economy of labour time as follows:

> On the basis of communal production, the determination of time remains, of course, essential. . . . Economy of time, to this all economy ultimately reduces itself. Society likewise has to distribute its time in a purposeful way, in order to achieve a production adequate to its overall needs; just as the individual has to distribute his time correctly in order to achieve knowledge in proper

> proportions or in order to satisfy the various demands on his activity. Thus, economy of time, along with the planned distribution of labour time among the various branches of production, remains the first economic law on the basis of communal production.[9]

It is thus obvious that Marx recognised the comparable measurability of labour in social formations outside of a commodity economy. If we insist on the concept of the dual, and no more, characters of labour, then both the concrete useful and its abstract human character must be found as the basis of general economic norms or rules common to all the forms of society.[10] In precapitalist societies the general norms of economic life determining the distribution of abstract labour time to various necessary useful forms, are generally more or less unconsciously performed by traditional communal customs linked with religious and political orders. But in an ideal socialist economy, the general norms or rules dealing with labour in its dual character must be consciously realised as communal social planning. Although the forms of commodity and money actually still remain in the existing 'socialist' societies, such a communal planning of labour allocation in an ideal socialist economy, as Marx describes in the quotation above or in an example of 'an association of free men' in the section of the fetishism in *Capital*, is fully conceivable as a goal to be reached through socialist revolution and the subsequent construction of an associational economic order. In so far as the functions of prices, together with a capitalist economic order, must be decreased and then *finally* abandoned in the process of constructing socialist associational societies, the role of labour time as a basic measure for qualitatively different use-values of social products would become indispensable, as Marx suggested.

Even Rubin notices that production and distribution of products in a socialist society needs evaluation by means of equalised labour time. He believes, however, that the equalisation of labour in a socialist economy is quite different from that in a commodity economy. Whereas evaluations of things and labour are separable and submissive to social policy in a socialist society, 'the equalization of various forms of labour is carried out only in the form and through the equalization of things' in the form of value on the market in a commodity economy.[11] This is why Rubin distinguishes the concept of socially equalised labour from that of abstract labour. For him the difference in the evaluation of labour time in different societies is quite important.

Apparently there is a danger for Marxian value theory in Rubin's argument. If the amount of abstract labour is not independent of the form of value or prices in the market, the quantities of labour can not be an objective social basis for the determination of prices, but must rather become a sort of dependent variable of prices. The labour theory of value as a theory of prices is thus very much weakened. When the objectivity of the quantities of labour necessary to produce goods is discounted or disregarded, then the conceptual basis for socialism may also be clouded. Though there must certainly be an elasticity in the changes in distribution of labour-products and services, according to the social policies of a socialist economy, the amount of labour embodied in each product must still be measured or conceived as being measurable, as objectively determined on the basis of technical conditions of production. Otherwise, the low evaluation of labour in certain industries, say in agriculture, may easily and arbitrarily endanger a sound reproduction and growth of those industries, bringing about unfair and unequal distribution of social wealth. A worst thing is that a critical theoretical standard which is needed to evaluate and revise any such distortion in the socialist process of economic construction is lost or made ambiguous by disregarding the objective determinableness of labour time on the basis of the conditions of production. Conversely, once the basic equality in labour time is neglected in the conception of a socialist economy, by allowing policies to evaluate the labour time of various works more or less arbitrarily, Marxian value theory must then also negate the objective determinableness of labour time outside of the value form or prices as in Rubin's argument.

Against such arguments how can we be sure of basic equality in labour time expended in different useful forms, as an aspect of general economic norms themselves independent of the different forms of society? The problem relates to the twin issues, first of how conceptually to reduce concrete useful labour to abstract human labour, and second how to reduce skilled or complex labour to simple labour. Since the second issue must be solved on the basis of the first, let us presently concentrate on the first. As we have seen in the analysis of the labour process, our ability to perform a wide range of useful work is based upon the common human power of conceptual thought. Even the simplest sort of work on a modern belt-conveyor system is made up of different physical actions performed according to a conscious purpose and will. Though the range of mobilisation of the human ability to work may be narrowly limited in most workers' tasks in a modern factory system, the contents of work cannot simply be a mere mechanical action, but must be an expenditure of human ability, in head and hands, to work in a series of different useful forms. The potential human ability to do various works is actually also shown when a worker is shifted to another position in a factory or to another field of industry. In this regard, concrete useful labour in a social division of work has in common the character of the expenditure of human basic ability to do any useful works. Labour time in different useful forms is equally commensurable as the expenditure of this human ability. Apart from such a fundamental view in the definition of abstract labour time, the evaluation of qualitatively different useful forms of labour could not have a homogeneous measure, which is objectively independent *both* from prices in the market *and* from more or less arbitrary political decisions in a conceivable planned economy or conventional managerial estimations within each capitalist firm.

In order to avoid possible confusions, three more points had better be mentioned here in advance. First, the problem is still in a sense at the halfway stage at least until we treat the skilled-labour problem (in the first section of next chapter). For the labour time of different useful products may not be simply homogeneous, if different degrees of complexity or skilfulness are assigned to them. It remains therefore to clarify how we may reduce skilled labour to simple labour. Second, in dealing with the problem of how to divide the labour time embodied in jointly produced goods, Rubin's type of theory may have certain relevancy, though in a particularly limited context and scope, as we shall see later (in Chapter 6, Section 6.2). Third, both political decisions in a planned economy, and the motion of prices reflecting demand and supply in a market may well affect the changes in technical conditions of production, and thus may indirectly affect the quantities of labour time embodied in each product. However, technical conditions of production linked with fixed capital are not so easily altered in a short run, and the directions and pace of changes are also relatively independent of market conditions or policies.

Once representative technical conditions of production, with simple labour and a single product assumed for the moment, the quantities of labour time necessary to produce each product are determinable as follows.

In Marx's numerical example in the section of the valorisation process, 10 lb. of cotton containing 20 hours of dead labour is converted into 10 lb. of yarn by 6 hours of a spinner's current or living labour. A quarter of a spindle, which represents the necessary used up portion of the instruments of labour in 6 hours of spinning, contains 4 hours of dead labour. In total, 30 hours of abstract labour is embodied in 10 lb. of yarn. Presupposing the labour theory of value from the beginning of *Capital* Marx simply assumes here that 20 hours and 4 hours of labour respectively, lie behind the 10 shillings worth of cotton weighing 10 lb., and 2 shillings depreciated value representing a quarter of the spindle. It may seem an endless and theoretically difficult task to try to decompose and then aggregate the quantities of labour time embodied in the means of production, say coal and iron, necessary to produce the raw material and instruments of labour, cotton and spindle in this case, by going back further and further into the past production processes. However we can solve the problem and determine the quantities of labour embodied in each product on the basis of the currently existing system of interrelated conditions of production.[12]

Let us assume, as a simple example, that cotton is produced by means of iron and coal, and that iron and coal are produced again by using iron and coal. The current representative technical conditions of production for each unit of products are exemplified in the following input–output relations.

$$\left.\begin{array}{l} \frac{1}{4}\text{ kg of coal} + \frac{1}{6}\text{ kg of iron} + \frac{1}{3}\text{ hour of labour} \rightarrow 1\text{ kg of coal} \\ \frac{1}{2}\text{ kg of coal} + \frac{1}{3}\text{ kg of iron} + \frac{1}{3}\text{ hour of labour} \rightarrow 1\text{ kg of iron} \\ \frac{3}{4}\text{ kg of coal} + \frac{1}{2}\text{ kg of iron} + 1\text{ hour of labour} \rightarrow 1\text{ lb. of cotton} \end{array}\right\} \quad (5.1)$$

By designating the quantities of labour time embodied in each unit of coal, iron and cotton $t_1$, $t_2$, $t_3$ hours, we can obtain following three simultaneous equations from the technical system in (5.1).

$$\left.\begin{array}{ll} \frac{1}{4}t_1 + \frac{1}{6}t_2 + \frac{1}{3} = t_1 & (1) \\ \frac{1}{2}t_1 + \frac{1}{3}t_2 + \frac{1}{3} = t_2 & (2) \\ \frac{3}{4}t_1 + \frac{1}{2}t_2 + 1 = t_3 & (3) \end{array}\right\} \quad (5.2)$$

Solution of these equations determines first $t_1 = \frac{2}{3}$, $t_2 = 1$ from (1) and (2), and then $t_3 = 2$. If a spindle is produced by 7 hours of current labour using 9 kg of coal and 3 kg of iron on the same technical basis, then 16 hours of labour in total is embodied in a spindle. We can conceive of these technical relations of production as an example behind Marx's assumption that 20 hours and 4 hours of labour are embodied in 10 lb. of cotton and a quarter of spindle. What assures aggregation of these amounts of past labour with 6 hours of living labour to make 30 hours embodied in 10 lb. of yarn is the concrete useful character of labour able properly to perform each process of production.

Let us generalise from this example, determination of the necessary labour time to produce various products on the basis of technical conditions of production. Assume that $n$ kinds of products are being produced respectively in $n$ sectors of production or industries in a society. In order to produce a unit of $i$th product, $a_{ij}$ units of $j$th product and $l_i$ hours of living labour are technically necessary. Let the total of past and living labour embodied in a unit of $i$th product be $t_i$ hours. Then, we have,

$$\sum_{j=i}^{n} a_{ij}t_j + l_i = t_i \ (a_{ij} \geqslant 0, \ l_i > 0, \ i = 1, 2, \ldots n) \qquad (5.3)$$

We see $n$ simultaneous linear equations in (5.3), where $n$ unknowns $t_i$ are determinable on the basis of technical conditions, as dependent variables of $a_{ij}$ and $l_i$.[13]

Thus the quantities of abstract labour embodied in a unit of each product are determined within the social relations of the technical conditions of production in a society based upon division of labour. The social relations of productive technologies as a whole also determine to certain degree, the objective basis for distributing past and living abstract labour into various useful concrete forms in a social division of labour. In the example of technical relations in (5.1) for instance, we can define the minimum quantitative relations of a self-reproducing system (maintaining the production of a unit of cotton as *a net product*) as follows:

$$\left.\begin{array}{l} \frac{9}{20}\text{ kg of coal} + \frac{3}{10}\text{ kg of iron} + \frac{3}{5}\text{ hour of labour} \rightarrow \frac{9}{5}\text{ kg of coal} \\ \frac{3}{5}\text{ kg of coal} + \frac{2}{5}\text{ kg of iron} + \frac{2}{5}\text{ hour of labour} \rightarrow \frac{6}{5}\text{ kg of iron} \\ \frac{3}{4}\text{ kg of coal} + \frac{1}{2}\text{ kg of iron} + 1\text{ hour of labour} \rightarrow 1\text{ lb. of cotton.} \end{array}\right\}$$

$$\begin{array}{l} (\frac{9}{5}\text{ kg of coal} + \frac{6}{5}\text{ kg of iron}) + 2\text{ hours of labour} \rightarrow \\ (\frac{9}{5}\text{ kg of coal} + \frac{6}{5}\text{ kg of iron}) + 1\text{ lb. of cotton.} \end{array} \qquad (5.4)$$

This is a case which Sraffa called a 'sub-system'.[14] This is an alternative way of showing how the abstract labour-time embodied in 1 lb. of cotton (2 hours in this example) is technically determinable. At the same time we see that the balance of the distribution of living and dead labour between different correlated industries as in the example above, must be based on objective technological conditions. However, the objective technological conditions of production cannot fully determine the socially necessary production of final products. If cotton is one of the final products, the technical conditions illustrated above cannot determine how much cotton must be produced in a year. As Marx mentions, 'the social need . . . here appears decisive for the quota of total social labour time that falls to the share of the various particular spheres of production' (III, p. 774). The system of social needs is determined and altered by complex factor in the process of the historical development of human cultural and social life, which is ultimately, though not very directly, regulated by the technical conditions available for the production of various useful goods.

In observing the basic conditions of the metabolism between human beings and nature as general economic norms in the analysis of the labour-and-production process, we must surely recognise that the system of technical conditions of production, as well as the system of social needs, are historically variable. These changes have been made possible by the human ability to produce surplus products over and above the necessary means of consumption for direct workers. An important aspect of the historical characteristics of societies can be seen in the way that changes in the conditions of production and social needs are controlled in each society, corresponding to the social relations which cope with surplus products. However, once the system of the technical conditions of production and the social needs to be satisfied by them are given within certain historical and social relations, then it must be clear that an essential element of general economic norms is the necessity of distributing dead and living abstract labour-time to various useful concrete forms, so as to enable the reproduction of socially necessary use-values, on the basis of the quantities of labour-time necessary to produce them. This holds irrespective of whether such economic norms concerning abstract and concrete labour are carried out consciously in socialist planning, or unconsciously as in a capitalist commodity economy.

**Surplus-labour**

To be more precise, we must ask how the quantities of abstract labour subject to the general economic norms determine the mutual relations which transfer products between the processes of production or industries. Let us examine the prerequisite for maintaining the production processes of goods necessary to meet social needs, presuming a social division of labour with a given system of technical conditions of production. Clearly the quantity of the means of production and living labour which are necessary to produce the output of the industry must be made available again to the industry in order that it may maintain production. Reciprocation is, conceptually, not confined here to commodity exchanges in a market, but may take various forms such as customary mutual presents, or mutual delivery under conscious socialist planning. Anyway, first of all, each time a unit of a product is delivered from one industry to another for use as means of production or consumption, at least the portion of labour time which is transferred from the consumed means of production must be returned to the industry in the same form of necessary means of production. Second, the portion of living labour, which is embodied to a unit of a product in addition to dead labour from the means of production, must also be made available. This is done concretely by providing the necessary labour-power to perform that amount of living labour.

In order to secure the necessary quantity of labour-power for a certain labour process or industry, it is essential continuously to supply workers with means of subsistence necessary to maintain the reproduction of that quantity of labour-power.[15] The maintenance and reproduction of labour-power is carried out by consuming a certain quantity of means of subsistence. The necessary range and amount of means of subsistence for a worker, such as food, clothing, housing, fuel, household furniture and instruments, not only 'vary according to the climatic and other physical peculiarities of his country', but also depend 'to a great extent on the level of civilization attained by a country' as the results of history (I, p. 275). The technological conditions of production do not directly determine the range and the amount of necessary means of subsistence for workers, though the former may indirectly influence the latter. The total socially useful net product in a year, being obtained after deducting the consumed means of production from the yearly gross product, embodies the social aggregate living labour-time expended on material production in a year. The range and quantity of useful net products produced by a certain aggregate amount of living labour-time are determined by the system of technologies and increase with the progress of technologies.

If the total social net products are less than the total necessary subsistence of workers, a part of the means of production cannot be replenished, and the scale of social production must be reduced. If this occurs, the general conditions of social economic life cannot be maintained apart from very exceptional short periods, say in the years of the failure of crops, sharp economic crisis or major wars. Conversely there must generally be surplus-products embodying surplus-labour as a difference between the total social net products embodying yearly living labour and the necessary means of subsistence of workers. The portion of living labour which is embodied in the necessary means of subsistence of workers is defined as necessary labour-time. The basic human ability to work with a broad range of power of conception is a fundamental source for changes and progress in the productivity of labour. This enables surplus-labour to produce and increase surplus-products beyond those embodying necessary labour as a general social economic norm. Certainly there is not any mere technological rule determining the ratio between the surplus and the necessary portion of labour-time within the total expenditure of social yearly living labour in the general economic norms. However, the existence of the division of labour-time into necessary and surplus-labour must thus be recognised as an aspect of human economic life common to all the social formations. The labour-time of an individual worker in an average working day can also be theoretically divided into necessary and surplus-labour-time.

In the section on the labour process of *Capital* Marx could not refer to the existence of surplus-labour as a general condition of human economic life, for he concentrated on the aspect of concretely useful labour. He presents the concept of surplus-labour first in the theory of the valorisation of capital. However, he notes later that 'capital did not invent surplus labour', and continues to state: 'Wherever a part of society possesses the monopoly of the means of production, the worker, free or unfree, must add to the labour-time necessary for his own maintenance an extra quantity of labour-time in order to produce the means of subsistence for the owner of the means of production.' (I, p. 344). More generally the social function of surplus-labour is not confined to the production of wealth for the owners of the means of production in class societies, although the antagonistic relation between the necessary and the surplus-labour-time will disappear in a classless society. In Marx's words:

> Surplus labour in some form must always remain, as labour beyond the extent of given needs. It is just that in the capitalist, as in the slave system, etc., it has an antagonistic form and its obverse side is pure idleness on the part of one section of society. A certain quantum of surplus labour is required as insurance against accidents and for the progressive extention of the reproduction process in keeping pace with the development of needs and the progress of population, which is called accumulation from the viewpoint of the capitalist.[16](III, p. 958).

When the antagonistic form of surplus-labour in class societies is abolished then the features of the extension of the production process will also be greatly changed. Although it would remain a basic economic norm to carry out the human metabolism with nature 'with the least expenditure of energy', the human metabolism must be realisable in a rational manner, including the more harmonious relations with the rest of nature as man's essential environment, by 'bringing that metabolism under the collective control of the associated producers instead of being dominated by it as a blind power' (III, p. 959). The pace and the direction of the development of productive power in capitalist industries should not be taken as an absolute natural path of the extention of the production process. At the same time, in an associational socialist society, the possible increase of surplus-labour-time made possible by the increase of productivity may well be switched either to the increase of necessary labour-time as accords with the development of needs in human life, or to the reduction of the working day in order to extend free time or 'disposable time for all'.[17] The antithetical relation between the necessary and the surplus-labour-time in class societies will disappear.

Thus, from the long-range view of human history, it must be noted that there are varying aspects in dealing with the human metabolic relation to nature, based as it is on labour, in different social formations. There is no natural destiny or mechanical rule of determination as a general economic rule especially in regard to the direction and the contents of the development of productive power, or in the ratio between necessary and surplus-labour-time, as well as in the ratio between the labour-time in a working day and the disposable free-time. However, once the technical system of production, the length of working day, the number of yearly working days, and the average physical amounts of the necessary means of subsistence of a worker are given, each including the historical and social factors of their determination, then the quantities of the necessary and the surplus-labour-time, as well as their ratio, are determined.

Whatever the ratio between the necessary and surplus-labour-time may become, it is a universal condition of economic life common to all social formations that the workers repeatedly obtain their historically determined necessary means of subsistence together with the necessary labour-time embodied in them. As a whole, this condition is also expressed in the universal social necessity of maintaining the reproduction of labour power itself by consuming the necessary means of production which are produced by a portion of the expenditure of labour. Let us come back again to the initial problem of this subsection and examine the quantitative relations intrinsic to the reciprocally transferred labour-time between industries.

Let us presently assume a set of representative technological conditions of production with simple labour and a single product for all the industries. Then the quantity of labour-time embodied in each unit of production from both past and living labour is determined as we have seen. In so far as each industry must maintain at least the current production levels to satisfy the social need for its product, the means of production and the living labour which are necessary for its reproduction must be reobtainable in a system of socially divided labour. The portion of living labour is, however, recharged indirectly by securing for the workers in each industry the means of subsistence containing the necessary labour-time, which is less than the total living labour expended. Consequently the portion of living labour embodied as surplus-labour in its product need not be fully reobtained in the form of products from other labour processes. So long as the necessary labour time in the form of necessary means of subsistence is obtained and consumed by the workers, they are able to expend a larger amount of living labour in the labour process. This is quite different from the portion of past labour which is transferred from the means of production, as this portion must be recharged at least in the same amount in the form of products from other labour processes.

These conditions form an expanded part of the general economic norms and can be illustrated by extending the previous numerical example of spinning. Let us assume a working day of 12 hours composed on average of 6 hours of necessary labour and the same length of surplus-labour under the present social conditions of production. The spinner in the previous example converts 20 lb. of cotton containing 40 hours of past labour into 20 lb. of yarn, by consuming half of a spindle representing 8 hours of past labour, in his 12 hours of labour in a day. Consequently 20 lb. of yarn embodies 60 hours of labour in total, or 48 hours of past labour and 12 hours of living labour in the spinning process. When every 20 lb. of yarn with 60 hours of embodied labour is delivered to another labour process, say weaving, or for personal consumption, at least 48 hours of labour in the form of means of production, or 20 lb. of cotton and a half of a spindle, together with 6 hours of labour in the form of necessary means of subsistence must on average be reciprocally recharged into the spinning process, in order to maintain its reproduction. By consuming the necessary means of subsistence with 6 hours of necessary labour-time, the spinner can repeat 12 hours of labour a day, manufacturing 20 lb. of yarn. Therefore the minimum necessary condition for maintaining the spinning labour process is not an equal exchange of labour with other industries. Against 60 hours of labour in 20 lb. of yarn, 54 (48+6) hours not 60 hours of labour in the form of products from other industries must be reallocated to the spinning process (both for labour-power and constant capital) as a minimum requisite for its reproduction.[18]

In contrast there is no such general economic rule for the allocation of labour in regard to surplus-labour. The portion of 6 hours of surplus-labour embodied in 20 lb. of yarn need not be reobtained by the spinning industry in the form of other products, unlike other portions of labour-time. More generally, it does not impede the general rule of social reproduction to distribute surplus-labour-time disproportionately to the amount of surplus-labour-time embodied in each process of production, or to consume the results of surplus-labour-time separately from where it is embodied. In other words there *can* be inequality *between* the amount of labour-time delivered from each labour process in the form of its product *and* that received by it (directly or indirectly) from other processes in the form of means of production and means of consumption. The portion of surplus-labour thus gives an elasticity or freedom to the general economic norms of labour-allocation.

This fundamental freedom in dealing with surplus-labour and its products has formed, on the one hand, the basis for the ruling classes to appropriate them in the various forms of class societies. On the other hand, this elasticity also gave room for a commodity economy to invade precapitalist societies where the central relations of production were subject to authoritative or communal social order. Capitalism has organised its central relations of production entirely through the commodity economic order, on the basis of the commodity form of labour-power, and has formed a very special class society, where appropriation and distribution of surplus-labour are realised through commodity transactions. In this thoroughgoing commodity economic society the general economic norms in the labour-and-production process have to be maintained completely through commodity relations. Then, the quantitative relations of abstract labour in the general labour-and-production process must appear as the social substance of the value relations of commodities, and become the substantive basis of regulating the values of commodities with social necessity. At the same time the labour-and-production process appears as the valorisation process of capital.

## 5.2 THE LAW OF VALUE AND THE VALORISATION PROCESS

### The Labour Theory of Value for Commodity Products

The labour theory of value in Marxian economics, unlike in the classical school, can be grounded upon the distinction between the forms of value and the quantitative relations of labour-time as general economic regulators. It is obvious by now that the embodied labour-time in labour-products is not always dealt with through the existence of value-forms in the different social formations. However, when labour-products are repeatedly exchanged as commodities, the quantities of labour embodied in them must more or less regulate their prices, and become the substance behind the form of values. For too unfavourable price of a commodity in comparison with the necessary labour time to produce it must sooner or later include a reduction of supply, and thus result in the rise in price; and vice versa. So far the law value, or the regulation of commodity values on the basis of embodied labour-time, must be carried out even in a precapitalist commodity economy. Its working, however, cannot be smooth and certain as long as the central relations of production are subject to authoritative or communal regulations. It is impossible to prove the social necessity of the law of value in a precapitalist commodity economy. It is otherwise in a capitalist economy, where the quantitative relations of labour in the general labour-and-production process totally become the social substance of value relations. The working and the role of the law of value in a precapitalist commodity economy is to be understood and studied by taking the law of value shown for a capitalist economy as a theoretical frame of reference.[19]

There are three aspects to be clarified in the law of value: i.e. (i) determination of the substance of values as the crystals of abstract labour-time necessary to produce commodities; (ii) regulation of the ratios of exchange through the form of value, or of the standard prices, by the substance of value; (iii) adjustment of the allocation of labour in various useful forms or branches of production to meet social needs through value relations. Not to have separated and often to have mixed up these three aspects, has been a source of confusion in the studies and the controversies on the labour theory of value. In particular, problems in respect of the second aspect are usually taken for grounds to doubt the first. If we separate the second aspect, concerning the exchange ratios as expressed in standard prices, we can easily understand the first, more basic content of the law of value from the previous discussion.

Let us continue to assume that each sphere of production produces a single product by unskilled simple labour in a social set of technological conditions of production. Then, the quantity of abstract labour necessary to produce a unit of each kind of product is determinable from the physical data of production. Though it certainly includes the portion of past labour transferred from the means of production, the size of that portion is determined by the current conditions of production, and not by historical conditions. Therefore, the socially necessary labour-time signifies the amount of labour necessary to *reproduce* a unit of product rather than the amount of labour actually expended in the historical past. In a capitalist economy all the products are basically produced as commodities to be sold by capital. The crystals of abstract labour-time embodied in products never fail to form the common substance of values of commodities in capitalism. So far as the commodity products in a capitalist economy are concerned we are theoretically bound to find and determine the crystals of abstract labour, as the social substance of value, behind the forms of commodity values.

Unlike commodity products, human labour-power is not a labour-product, and therefore does not directly embody any labour-time. Therefore the commodity labour-power does not directly have the substance of value in it, although the sale and purchase of labour-power as a commodity is an indispensable prerequisite for capitalism as a social system of production of commodities by means of commodities. However, labour-power must be reproduced by consuming the necessary means of subsistence together with the necessary labour-time embodied in them. So far as capitalism as a social system must ensure reproduction of labour-power, it must treat the labour-time embodied in the necessary means of subsistence as the necessary time to reproduce the commodity labour-power, or the substance of value of that commodity.

The substance of value of capital which is invested in the means of production is merely transferred into the substance of value of commodity products as the portion of past (dead) labour. It is called 'constant capital (*c*)' because its magnitude is simply maintained in the process of transferring past labour from means of production. In contrast the substance of value which is invested in the commodity labour-power is called 'variable capital (*v*)' because it is not transferred but fundamentally reproduced and variably augmented in the process of commodity production. To be more exact, the substance of value of variable capital is lost to capital when it is given to workers in exchange for the use of labour-power. However, in the process of consuming the use-value of the commodity labour-power, capital can obtain the whole result of living labour, which not only reproduces the substance of variable capital (*v*) but also adds the substance of surplus-value (*s*) by surplus-labour. As a whole, workers sell their labour-power to capitalists in exchange for wages as the form of value of commodity labour-power (*L*), and buy back by wages a portion of their own products from capitalists. Symbolically we can illustrate these relations as follows:

*Figure* 5.1

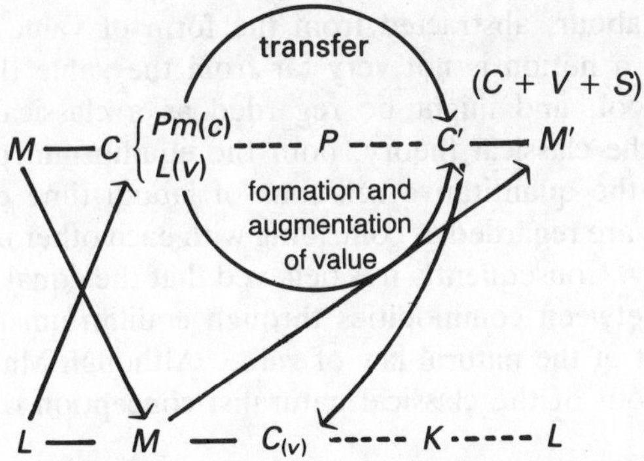

where $M$ designates money; $C$ commodities; $Pm$ means of production; $P$ process of production; $K$ consumption.

Let us suppose that 20 lb. of yarn in the previous example is now produced as a commodity product of capital. Then, 60 hours of abstract labour embodied in it in total becomes the substance of its value, while in 60 hours 48 hours is the transferred substance of constant capital, 6 hours being the reproduced value of variable capital, and another 6 hours forming the substance of surplus-value added. Or, 60 hours of the substance of 20 lb. of yarn = $(48c + 6v + 6s)$ in hours. More generally the substance of value of a unit of $i$th commodity ($a_i$, in hours) is composed of such three portions:

$$a_i = c_i + v_i + s_i \tag{1}$$

If all the problems in economics can be reduced only to the determination of prices in a market as the neo-classicist and the neo-Ricardians believe, the analyses of the labour substance of values may well be denounced as redundant at best. From a broader socio-historical view and of concern to Marxian economics, it is imperative to clarify the distinction and the relation between prices as the form of value and the crystals of abstract labour as the basic social substance of value. In this regard it depends on the scope of the tasks of economic theories whether the labour theory of value is to be judged redundant or not. The historically specific character of the capitalist economy is systematically elucidated in Marxian theory, by clarifying how the general economic rules common to different social formations, and operated through the forms of values in capitalist society, with its specific contradictions.

For such a theoretical theme, Marx's own notion of value, (as found at the very beginning of *Capital*) directly treated as the crystals of abstract labour, abstracted from the form of value, is not well suited. Such a notion is not very far from the value theory of the classical school, and might be regarded as a classical residue in *Capital*. In the classical theory, both the equilibrium prices in the market and the quantitative relations of labour-time embodied in commodities are regarded as coinciding with each other naturally and harmoniously. Consequently it is believed that the equal exchange of labor-time between commodities through equilibrium prices is the basic content of the natural law of value. Although Marx opened a critical way out of the classical naturalist conception of the law of value, by creating the theory of the forms of value, his qualitative distinction between the forms and the substance of value was not accompanied by a clear-cut quantitative critique of the classical notion of the basic content of the law of value. Just as in the classical school the equal exchange of labour-time embodied in commodities is also regarded as an essential content of the law of value in Marx. Consequently from a quantitative point of view standard prices as a form of value tend to be treated as a directly proportional and formal expression of the substance of value as embodied labour in commodities. Marx does not clarify in regard to the content of the law of value, a relatively autonomous aspect in the character of the forms of value which go to make up a market mechanism external to the substantial social relations of labour within the general economic norms.

Uno's purification of the theory of forms of value was an important theoretical step forward showing a relatively autonomous character of the value forms in clearer distinction from the social quantitative relations of labour-time. However, in his presentation of the labour theory of value in the theory of the capitalist process of value formation, he still follows Ricardo and Marx in showing the basic content of the law of value as the equal exchange of labour-time embodied in commodities through prices directly proportional to the labour-substance.

Generally speaking, there are four formally possible positions in which the law of value can be presented substantially as the equal exchange of labour-time between commodities in a capitalist economy, apart from the positions which show the law either as a mere theoretical hypothesis or as a precapitalist commodity economic order. Let us examine those four possible positions including Uno's, together with their problems. In a capitalist economy competition among capitals and workers usually tends to equalise the rate of surplus-value ($s_i' = \frac{s_i}{v_i}$) and the rate of profit ($p_i'$) across various industries. Workers would leave the industries where the working day is longer or wages are lower than in others, while they would rush into the industries with better working conditions, making them equalise through competition.

First, given thus an equal rate of surplus-rate, and if we can somehow disregard the competition among capitals which would equalise the rate of profit, we may be able to maintain a position seeing the law of value as the equal exchange of labour-time. A likely reason for this position would be that the competition among capitals need not yet be taken into consideration in the theory of capitalist process of production of surplus-value as a whole. When prices are assumed in this position to be directly proportional to the embodied labour-time in commodity products, then the rate of profit must be supposed to be unequal, reflecting the difference in the composition of capital ($\frac{c_i}{v_i}$) between industries with heterogeneous technological bases. (Marx calls this ratio ($\frac{c_i}{v_i}$), or 'the value-composition of capital, in so far as it is determined by its technical composition and mirrors the changes in the latter, the organic composition of capital', (I, p. 762). This concept applies to the whole economy as well as to the individual industries, and is often expressed simply as the composition of capital.) For the sake of simplicity let us assume that the period of turnover of capital is a year in all the industries, and also that there is no fixed capital lasting longer than a year. Then the rate of profit for *i*th industry under the assumed conditions of prices would be:

$$p_i' = \frac{s_i}{c_i + v_i} = \frac{s_i'}{c_i / v_i + 1} \tag{5.2}$$

Thus the rate of profit of industries with higher composition of capital, or greater $c_i / v_i$, must be lower than the social average, and vice versa. Although the competition among capitals surely need not be investigated in detail in the sphere of analysis of capitalist process of production, the concept of the law of value regularly causing such differences in the rates of profit must be too divorced from the actual features of a capitalist economy to be real and appropriate.

Then, second, if constant capital does not exist, or $c_i = 0$, the rate of profit $p_i'$ must be identified with the rate of surplus-value $s_i'$, and equalised between industries by prices being directly proportional to the labour substance expended in commodities. This position is quite close to Ricardo's presentation of the labour theory of value in his *Principles* prior to his modification of it by considering the effect of fixed and durable capital, which is really identical with the effect of constant capital. As Marx criticises the reiterative decomposition of $c$ into $v+m$ in the past as a classical dogma of $v+m$, a capitalist economy with no constant capital is not merely inconceivable, but also misleading as to the working of the law of value.

Third, if the composition of capital $c_i / v_i$ is assumed to be equal across industries, the rate of profit must be equalised by prices being proportional to the labour-substance. This position would be more plausible than others, and might be utilised as an initial hypothetical explanation of the capitalist process of production based on the working of the law of value. In following this sequence the unrealistic hypothetical character of the assumption ought to be noted from the start, together with the possible range of alteration when the assumption is removed.

Fourth, if surplus value does not exist, or $s_i' = 0$, maintenance of at least the current size of production in each industry would be possible only with prices proportional to the quantity of abstract labour embodied in commodities. The equilibrium prices would necessarily be such prices giving zero rates of profit ($p_i' = 0$), otherwise the size of some industries with lower prices must be reduced, and subsequently raising prices by failing to satisfy the social demand for their products in a market. The feasibility of the labour theory of value asserting such equilibrium prices under this fourth assumption (as well as under the third in a more exact mathematical definition), is generally recognised even by non-Marxian economists like P. Samuelson and M. Morishima.[20] Uno's presentation of the labour theory of value in his *Principles* can be interpreted as a theory which also depends on this assumption, for he initially presents it using the notion of the process of value formation within the range of the necessary labour-time of wage-labourers, prior to the notion of the process of value augmentation on the basis of their surplus-labour.

Although this fourth case is in a sense suggestive of the relation between the general economic condition of reproduction and the working of the law of value, as we shall see a little later, it is again unrealistic, by itself and even seems trivial, since a capitalist economy without surplus-value or the augmentation of capital is generally inconceivable, but for short critical periods. Sharp economic crises causing losses of capital must periodically occur, as we shall see later in Chapter 9 of this volume, but they are also actually overcome in so far as capitalism continues to exist. Therefore, presentation of the law of value can never be complete for a capitalist economy in particular, if we do not treat it in relation to surplus-labour.

Since all four typical positions showing prices in direct proportion to the labour-substance of commodities are unsatisfactory in one way or the other, we have to challenge them by forming a somewhat new theory of prices which does not fully maintain the equal exchange of labour-time embodied in commodities as a substantial content of the law of value.[21] While discussing the function of money as the measure of value (in Chapter 4, Section 4.2), we saw that standard prices in a fluctuating market would appear as the form of value for competitively reproducible commodities. Such standard prices are not actually certain to be directly proportional to the labour-substance in commodities. However, if the price of the *i*th commodity is insufficient to replenish the portion of labour expended $(c_i + v_i)$ in the form of means of production and subsistence, so maintaining the production process within the parameters of a set of prices in a market, then the amount of production of the *i*th commodity has to be reduced, and consequently its price must rise relatively so as to enable its producer to regain at least $(c_i + v_i)$ through commodity transactions. Therefore, standard prices as the gravitational centre for fluctuating prices must systematically replenish at least the portion of labour-time $(c_i + v_i)$ embodied in a commodity through commodity exchanges. Though the substance of value $(c_i + v_i + s_i)$ of a commodity does not proportionally regulate the standard price or the form of value, its portion $(c_i + v_i)$ must thus work as a substantial core regulator of the standard price in the mutual relations of commodities, on the basis of given technological conditions and living standard of wage-workers.

In the view of a capitalist a standard price of a commodity must cover at least the cost price which is necessary to purchase the factors of production in average. The need to recover the cost price of a commodity (from the view of the labour theory of value) reflects the regulation of prices by the portion of labour substance $(c_i + v_i)$ embodied in a commodity. If we put in parentheses both the role of profit above cost price in a commodity price, and correspondingly the portion of surplus-labour $(s_i)$ embodied in the value substance of a commodity, the standard prices must enable the equal exchange of labour time crystallized in commodities. Here is a rational essence of the fourth position, given above, which conceives the content of the law of value as the equal exchange of labour by excluding the portion of surplus-labour. At the same time it becomes clear how far standard prices may differ from those assumed in the third position assuming the precondition of an equal composition of capital throughout industries. When the composition of capital or the period of turnover of capital is unequal between industries the standard prices would not be proportional to the labour-substance in the commodities. Their deviation from prices proportional to the labour substance must, however, be restricted within the range of the redistribution of surplus-labour across industries. In other words the regulation of prices by the substance of value embodied in commodities has an elasticity in the process of exchanging surplus-labour through the form of profit.

For instance, by assuming that two hours of the labour-substance of value is expressed equally in a price of a shilling for every commodity, Marx illustrates the process of value formation and augmentation as follows. When 10 lb. of yarn are spun by 6 hours of living labour, consuming 24 hours of past labour embodied in 10 lb. of cotton and a quarter of spindle, then 10 lb. yarn contains 30 hours of labour-substance in total and must be priced at 15 shillings. If the necessary means of subsistence for a worker per day contains 6 hours of labour, the substance of value of a day's labour-power is 6 hours of labour and is expressed in 3 shillings. A spinning capitalist pays 12 shillings for means of production (the cotton and the spindle) and 3 shillings for labour-power to produce 10 lb. of yarn of 15 shillings in a process of 6 hours of value formation. If such a process of value formation without surplus-labour prevails throughout industry, standard prices must necessarily be in direct proportion to the labour-substance in commodities in this way. Suppose that the price of means of production (the cotton and the spindle) with 24 hours of labour-substance becomes 13 shillings instead of 12 shillings while other conditions remain unchanged, then the spinning capitalist must reduce his production. Any gain in an industry would entail some losses and the reduction of production in other industries.

When the process of value formation is extended into the process of value augmentation, such strict proportionality will not hold. The spinning capitalist now produces 20 lb. of yarn by 12 hours of living labour a day, consuming 48 hours of past labour in 20 lb. of cotton and a half of a spindle. If two hours of labour-substance is proportionally expressed in a shilling as Marx continues to assume, then the capitalist sells 20 lb. of yarn containing 60 hours of labour at 30 shillings and obtains 3 shillings of surplus-value after deducing both 24 shillings for prices of means of production and 3 shillings for price of a day's labour-power as costs of production. However, such strict proportionality between the labour-substance of value and prices of commodities need not be maintained so far as surplus-value represents the portion of labour-time elastically disposable and freed from the minimal requisites of reproduction. For instance, the price of means of production (the cotton and the spindle) with 48 hours of labour-substance may now become 26 shillings instead of 24 shillings while other prices remain unchanged. The spinning capitalist can still get surplus-value, but 1 shilling (30–26–3 = 1) giving a rate of profit of 3.4 per cent (1/29), instead of 3 shillings of surplus value giving a rate of profit of 11.1 per cent. Alternatively, the price of 20 lb. of yarn with 60 hours of labour-substance may become, say 29 shillings, while the price of means of subsistence with 6 hours of labour-substance is 3 shillings and the price of means of production with 48 hours is 25 shillings. Then the spinning capitalist would obtain 1 shilling of surplus-value with a profit rate of 3.6 per cent (1⁄28). Whatever the relative relations of prices may be, the standard prices must be in a condition to replenish at least 54 hours of labour-substance in the form of means of production and of subsistence to the spinning process in exchange for 20 lb. of yarn with 60 hours of labour-substance. The exchange of labour-substance through the form of value may thus be unequal, but inequality must be limited within the range of the redistribution of surplus-labour across industries.

As we shall see in Chapter 7, capitalist competition determines the standard prices so as to equalise the rate of profit across industries in the form of prices of production. We must keep it in mind, while analysing the inner logic of capitalist production, that the regulation of standard prices by the labour-substance in commodities as an aspect of the law of value, allows room for the unequal exchange of labour in the range of surplus-labour. Thus standard prices, as the form of value, are generally regulated by the labour-substance of value, with such slack in the range of unequal exchange of surplus-labour for the commodity products. The anarchical fluctuations of prices around the standard prices are also possible, *usually* within the range of the redistribution of surplus-labour, as a more concrete form of the law of value.

**The Value of Labour-power**

The substance of value of commodity labour-power must be defined indirectly as the labour-substance embodied in the means of subsistence necessary to reproduce labour-power, since labour-power is not produced directly by labour in the labour process. The physical scope of the means of subsistence necessary in average to maintain and reproduce labour-power a day, together with technological conditions of production, determines the magnitude of the labour-substance of the commodity value of a day's labour-power, or the necessary labour-time in a working day. The scope of the necessary means of subsistence is relatively independent of the technological conditions of production, and includes historical and social elements. More concretely, the lifestyle of wage-workers which is historically and socially formed has to be considered.

For instance, 'the sum of means of subsistence necessary for the production of labour-power must include the means necessary for worker's replacement, i.e. his children, in order that this race of peculiar commodity-owners may perpetuate its presence on the market' (I, p. 275). The average number of children, the ordinary level and costs of education are among the factors to determine the necessary means of subsistence. In case the aged worker after retirement ordinarily lives either on his own previous earnings or as a dependent member in a family, his costs of living must also be counted into the necessary means of subsistence in average. If a part of educational costs or a part of the subsistence of an aged person is supported by a social fund outside of taxes on worker's earnings, the necessary means of subsistence or the substantial contents of the value of labour-power may so much be reduced. The number of wage-earners in a family also affects the value of labour-power. 'The value of labour-power was determined, not only by the labour-time necessary to maintain the individual adult worker, but also by that necessary to maintain his family. Machinery, by throwing every member of that family into the labour-market, spreads the value of the man's labour-power over his whole family. It thus depreciates it.' (I, p. 518). Mobilisation of married women into the labour-market is reinforced in the recent decade especially under the pressure of great depression, having a similar effect on the value of labour-power. Certainly the total value earned by two workers in a family may become greater than the former value earned only by the head of the family, but the substantial value per head must be reduced when two workers in a family become the usual lifestyle. The change would also entail alteration in the division between what is carried by domestic (shadow) work and what is purchased as commodities, expanding the capitalist market internally and weakening the function of family life.[22] In the process of capital accumulation the real wages would rise and decline according to the motion of the condition of labour-market as we shall see later (in Chapter 9), and gradually through such fluctuations standardise the ordinary material lifestyle of workers for a certain period in a society. The business cycles in the process of capital accumulation thus form a concrete mechanism through which the material contents of real wages are changed and standardised including the social and cultural elements.

Anyway, once the average necessary means of subsistence for a wage-worker each day is given as the standard contents of real wages for the time being, the labour-substance embodied in them is determinable on the basis of present technological conditions of production as we have seen (in Section 5.1 of this chapter). Since a day's labour-power must be maintained and reproduced by consuming the necessary means of subsistence, the labour-time embodied in these means of subsistence, say 6 hours, is theoretically regarded as the necessary labour-time for reproducing the commodity labour-power. There is thus a roundabout in the definition of the substance of value of the commodity labour-power, reflecting the special native of its reproduction. From the quantitative aspect, however, there must be an equal exchange of the labour-substance between the commodity labour-power and the necessary means of subsistence through their prices. Though it may seem tautological to conceive equal exchange of labour-time between these commodities, it contains social significance. Wage-workers as a class must obtain in exchange for their commodity labour-power a portion of their labour-time expended in the production process; this portion is the necessary labour-time, in the form of the means of subsistence, leaving the other portion of their labour-time as a source of surplus-value. Therefore, the notion of the labour-substance of the value of labour-power forms the theoretical foundation of analysis of the capitalist production of surplus-value. (Review Figure 5.1. once more.)

It is worth noting that the commodity labour-power is an unique simple commodity in a purely capitalist society. Unlike any other commodity produced by capital, its reproduction does not contain the crystallization of surplus-labour. Whereas the other commodity products are to be priced elastically not in direct proportion to the labour-substance of value within the range of the redistribution of surplus labour-time, there is no such elasticity in the case of the commodity labour-power. The ratio between the price-form of the value of labour-power and the labour-time necessary to reproduce it must basically be equal to the ratio of the standard price against the labour-substance of the necessary means of subsistence, so as to maintain a sort of equal exchange of labour-time. When the nominal prices of the means of subsistence are enhanced, say by a change in the relative value of the money commodity, then *ceteris paribus* the nominal price as the form of value of labour-power must also duly be proportionally increased as a basic principle. In this regard Marx is a little confused when he says, concerning an effect of the deviation of the prices of production from value-prices: 'The workers must work for a greater or lesser amount of time in order to buy back these commodities (to replace them) and must therefore perform more or less necessary labour than would be needed if the prices of production of their necessary means of subsistence did coincide with their values.' (III, p. 309; cf. also III, p. 261). So far as the theory of the transformation from values into prices of production refers to the logic of the redistribution of surplus-value among capitals, the theory must be independent from the more fundamental logic of the relation of production of surplus-value. If the prices of production of the means of subsistence were higher than their value-prices, i.e. prices conceivable as proportional to the labour-substance, then the nominal wage-rate must be sufficient to purchase the necessary means of subsistence at that price-level. The relative inelasticity of nominal wage-rates, as Keynesians emphasise so much, would hold well in the short run particularly in the stage of monopoly capitalism with established trade unions and the subsequent labour-management strategies of big firms, but would not hold as a basic universal principle for a capitalist commodity in the long run. At least it is quite difficult to find persuasive theoretical reasons to explain such an inelasticity of wage-rates. This is an interesting problem to be noted and investigated further.

As a basic theory of the process of capitalist production, wages as the form of value of labour-power are to be conceived at a level which enables the equal exchange of labour-substance with the necessary means of subsistence. The standard level of wages is determined by the factors as we have discussed, including the basic social relations of production between capitalists and labourers, and is not merely a result of fluctuations in the labour-market nor a transcendentally inelastic condition of a capitalist economy. The socially standard wages must theoretically be defined as the form of the substantial value of labour-power, or the price-form of value for the labour-time necessary to reproduce the commodity labour-power by consuming the necessary means of subsistence purchased in a market.[23]

'However, on the surface of bourgeois society the worker's wage appears as the price of labour, as a certain quantity of money that is paid for a certain quantity of labour' (I, p. 675). Marx attempts to show 'the transformation of the value of labour-power into wages' in this sense, and says that the ordinary expressions like 'value of labour' arise 'from the relations of production themselves' (I, p. 677).

Though he clarifies how these common-sense notions like the value of labour or wages conceal the real social substance of exploitation, he does not seem successful in presenting a logic for why these notions arise from the nature of the capitalist relations of production. In retrospect the notion of wages as remuneration for the whole work or labour performed was not really established from the transformation from the value of labour-power. Already in precapitalist societies, various artisans or craftsmen like gardeners or barbers having their own tools used to be paid remuneration for all their work in the form of wages. Therefore, the wage-form itself is part of the forms of a commodity economy in general, and is not specific to capitalism. Capitalism took over such a wage-form for the wage-workers in completely differing social conditions. Although the propertyless wage-workers, unlike the independent craftsmen, actually have to sell their commodity labour-power for the daily means of subsistence which embody just the necessary labour-time in a working day to sustain their labour-power, wages with the notion of 'the value of labour' is conceived as the full remuneration for the whole labouring day. As Marx sharply points out, the wage-form in this sense conceals the source of surplus-value on the surface of bourgeois society.

Such a notion of wages as a full payment for all the labouring activity of workers is reciprocally intensified by a corresponding notion that capital is a creative subject producing surplus-value through its innovative development. In such a notion of capital the methods of increasing efficiency in producing surplus-value, as we shall see in the next item, are taken for the source of surplus-value. The general custom of paying wages after the total labouring-time in a day, or a week, or a month, also intensifies the commonplace notion of wages as a full equivalent for the total labour expended. The custom of post-payment of wages is grounded also in more substantial reasons. Capitalists cannot obtain the use-value and the value of the commodity labour-power instantly by the contract to purchase it, since it does not contain the embodied labour-substance and its use-value is obtainable only by the actual expenditure of labour in the production process. The custom of post-payment of wages serves for capital to secure the subordination of workers in the production process despite its form as a free and equal exchange of a commodity between capitalists and workers.

As Marx notices there are two fundamental forms in wages, i.e. time-wages and piece-wages. Given a capitalistic tendency to treat workers in the mass at factories and offices, the form of time-wages would be more suitable for the central work-places in capitalism. It is therefore doubtful whether 'piece-wages is the form of wage most appropriate to the capitalist mode of production' (I, p. 698) as Marx says. The wage per hour, called the wage-rate, is determined by dividing the monetary value of a day's labour-power by the average hours in a working day, and serves as the basis for daily, weekly or monthly time-wages. Since the amount of wage-payment in these forms is calculated from the total labouring-time as well as the wage-rate, the notion that the wage is the full equivalent for all the labour expended would seem quite natural. The form of time-wages also tends to force workers to offer longer labour-time voluntarily in order to increase their total earnings, especially in the phases of depression with reduced wage-rates.

Piece-wages are paid for each piece worked, and the rate is based upon the time-wage-rate and the estimated average number of pieces hourly producible. This form of wage-payment seemingly resembles remuneration for the piece-work of artisans, and further clouds the actual social function of wages in capitalism. Under the form of piece-wages, workers are compelled to intensify their labour voluntarily to produce as many pieces as possible, and so to secure the necessary means of subsistence. The costs and trouble of supervising workers are thus clearly dispensed of. Therefore, workers out of the direct control of capitalists in small separated work-places (like taxi-drivers nowadays) generally tend to be paid more or less in the form of piece-wages.

Thus, in either form, the wage is not merely a monetary expression of the value of labour-power, it also hides the actual substance of value of labour-power as the necessary labour-time in a working day beneath the notion of the value of labour, and further induces longer and more intensified labour by harnessing workers' own subjective will.

**Production of Surplus-value**

So far as capital pays wages for the value of the commodity labour-power, it duly gets the command of its use-value as the actual expenditure of labour-power, and obtains the whole results of labouring activity according to the rules of a commodity economy. As a whole, labourers have to purchase back from capitalists the means of subsistence which they have produced in the necessary labour-time, by repeatedly handing over the money obtained as the value of labour-power. The expenditure of labour-power which is performed in the capitalist process of production in exchange for the value of labour-power is not confined to the labour-time necessary to reproduce the means of subsistence for workers. Surplus-labour time beyond the necessary labour-time and the resultant surplus-products are appropriated by capital, and forms the social substance of surplus-value. Such a social relation between the substance of value of the commodity labour-power and that of surplus-value is the most basic inner relation of production of capital.

The portion of capital value invested in the commodity labour-power as variable capital is, in substance recreated and further augmented by the expenditure of labour-power in the process of production. Contrastingly, the portion of capital invested in the means of production as constant capital does not vary its labour-substance, though its functions to facilitate the working of variable capital. Therefore, in direct relationship, surplus-value ($s$) in regard to the labour-substance is a result solely of the working of variable capital ($v$) *invested in labour-power*. In order to increase the production of surplus-value, capital needs first of all to enhance the rate of surplus-value $s/v$. This rate of surplus-value signifies the social relation of the division of the value-product ($v + s$), which workers create in the process of production, between the portion belonging to capitalists as surplus-value and the portion coming back to workers as the value of labour-power. It represents the rate of exploitation of workers under capitalism.

The production of surplus-value by capital is substantially based upon the relation between the necessary labour-time and the surplus-labour-time as expressed in the rate of surplus-value s/v. Thus, appropriation of surplus-labour-time by extending a working day beyond the labour-time necessary to reproduce labour-power is the absolute method of the production of surplus-value for capital.[24]

Since a major motive of capitalist production is acquisition of ever greater surplus-value, capital attempts to prolong the working day as far as possible. Simultaneously, intensification of labour is also pursued. As we have seen the law of value determines the labour-substance of the value of labour-power on the basis of social and technological conditions, but it cannot define how long and how intensively labour is to be performed a day in the process of the utilisation of the use-value of the commodity labour-power. From the point of view of workers, labour in a capitalist process of production is basically alienated labour for others, and therefore the prolongation and intensification of labour does not at all accord with their own interest. So as long as skilled workers who were not easily substitutable could determine the tempo of the process of production, capital was unable effectively to remove workers' resistance against the prolongation and intensification of labour. As Marx elucidates, 'after capital had taken centuries to extend the working day to its normal maximum limit, and then beyond this to the limit of the natural day of 12 hours, there followed, with the birth of large-scale industry in the last third of the eighteenth century, an avalanche of violent and unmeasured encroachments. Every boundary set by morality and nature, age and sex, day and night, was broken down.' (I, pp. 389–90). Against capitalists' resistance a normal working day had then to be legislated as a result of workers' struggle, combined with the actual social necessity to maintain and reproduce a healthy labouring population. With the limit of the working day given, both physically and socially, capital still strives to increase the production of surplus-value relatively by developing productivity as well as the intensity of labour.

The production of relative surplus-value is realised by reducing the portion of necessary labour-time within the given length of a working day. As we have seen the necessry labour-time in a working day is indirectly determined by the labour-time necessary to reproduce the average means of subsistence for a worker per day. The portion of surplus-labour-time can be increased relatively, if the necessry labour-time in a day is shortened by the reduction of the labour-time embodied in the means of subsistence. When the productivity of labour is increased in the industries directly producing the necessary means of subsistence or in those producing the means of production for them, the embodied labour-time in a given unit of the necessary means of subsistence is reduced. Therefore, the increase of productivity of labour generally enables the enhancement of the rate of surplus-value $s/v$ by reducing the substance of the value of labour-power without altering the real wage-rate (i.e. the physical quantity of means of subsistence obtainable by hourly wages), or even with some increase in real wage-rate as long as it is less than that of productivity.

Here is the social basis to explain why capitalism strives to develop the natural sciences and technologies, realising much faster increases in the productivity of labour than in any other previous society. In the recent past, especially in phases of prosperity where the position of workers was stronger, so called guidelines to define the upper limit of an increase of real wages in proportion to that of productivity was usually requested by business circles. The request represented capitalists' desire not to reduce the rate of surplus-value $s/v$ by wage increases. On the other hand, in the phase of depression, as we are witnessing, the gap between stagnant real-wages and the increase of productivity of labour through 'rationalisation' tends to be widened, enabling a powerful production of relative surplus-value.

As Marx pointed out, 'an increase in the productivity of labour in those branches of industry which supply neither the necessary means of subsistence nor the means by which they are produced (e.g. industries producing luxury goods or weapons as non-basic products in Sraffa's terminology[25] – M. I.) leaves the value of labour-power undisturbed' (I, p. 432), and therefore does not directly contribute to the social production of relative surplus-value. However, technological inventions in such branches of industry may well be applicable to others, and thus indirectly relate to the production of relative surplus-value.

A driving force for the social production of surplus-value is actually in individual capitalists attempt to improve their own methods of production in order to obtain extra surplus-value. A capitalist who has managed to introduce an exceptionally superior technological method of production in comparison with the dominant representative method in an industry reduces the labour-time as well as the costs necessary to produce a unit of product, while he can sell it with a social value estimated on the basis of the general conditions of production in the industry. The extra surplus-value which is obtained by such a capitalist must disappear with the gradual diffusion of his method of production over the industry, and the social value of the product is accordingly reduced down. Therefore, the acquisition of extra surplus-value presupposes more or less difficulty in instantly introducing new technological methods of production on the part of other capitalists, generally because of the costs of abandoning the existing equipments with their remaining values. The legal patent rights system further serves to secure extra surplus-value for the initiating capitalists. Increasing investment into research and development (R & D) by giant corporations in our age also largely relate to the possibilities of obtaining this sort of surplus-value.

Since even the capitalists in industries producing luxury goods or weapons can obtain extra surplus-value by innovating technologies, extra surplus-value is obtainable even without directly contributing to the social production of relative surplus-value. There is a problem of how to conceive of the substance of extra surplus-value. According to Marx, 'The exceptionally productive labour acts as intensified labor; it creates in equal period of time greater values than average social labour of the same kind.' (I, p. 435). This conception is dubious as to the source of extra surplus-value, because the workers with same intensity of labour cease to bring about extra surplus-value after the generalisation of new technology. In my opinion the source of extra surplus-value is in the redistribution of social surplus-labour-time through the price mechanism (as the form of value), so that either less surplus-labour-substance may be distributed to other capitalists with old methods of production, or it is increased socially, with the gradual reduction of the price of commodity products in the process of the generalisation of new method of production. So long as a portion of social surplus-labour must cover, in one way or another, the costs of improving methods of production according to the general economic norms common to all human societies, the portion of capitalistic surplus-labour redistributed in the form of extra surplus-value has such a social function by its very nature.[26] Nevertheless there cannot be any objective standard set by general economic norms as to how large a proportion of social surplus-labour is to be spent for such a function. And the quantity of surplus-labour obtained in the form of extra surplus-value by capitalists often well exceeds the quantity of labour which is rationally and actually necessary for improving methods of production. Hence, it serves as a strong incentive for technological innovations.

As Marx elucidates, the capitalistic development of productive power, driven by the incentive to acquire extra surplus-value and resulting in the social production of relative surplus-value, takes three elementary forms: i.e. co-operation, division of labour and mechanised factory system.

In contrast with peasant agriculture and independent handicrafts until the medieval age, a large number of workers working together in co-operation in work-places characterised capitalist production from the beginning, although the form of co-operation itself is not newly created by capitalism, as exemplified by the case of ancient monumental constructions. 'When the worker co-operates in a planned way with others, he strips off the fetters of his individuality, and develops the capabilities of his species.' (I, p. 447). Co-operation 'excites rivalry between individuals and raises their animal spirits', 'economizes the means of production by use in common', and thus increases the productive power of labour (ibid.). At the same time capitalists can treat workers' abilities as average labour-power regardless of their individual difference in the form of co-operation.

Capital further organises workers in the form of the division of labour, on the basis of co-operation. When workers are divided and attached to specialised partial operations, the dexterity of workers is easily increased, the labour-time necessary for the transition from one operation to another is economised, improvement of specialised tools is facilitated, and thus the productivity of labour can be much increased. The classical shape of the division of labour in the work-place is found in the capitalist handicraft factory system called 'manufacture'. 'As a characteristic form of the capitalist process of production it prevails throughout the manufacturing period properly so called, which extends, roughly speaking, from the middle of the sixteenth century to the last third of the eighteenth century.' (I, p. 455).

Manufacture put workers under the discipline and command of capital more fully than simple co-operation, including a hierarchical structure amongst the workers. While it enhanced the productive power of capital it suppresses 'a whole world of productive drives and inclinations' of workers, by converting them into 'a crippled monstrosity' of partial fixed skills (I, p. 481). Whereas capitalism develops the division of labour between industries in society in a non-authoritative and anarchical order, it contrastingly develops the detailed division of labour inside the workshop in an authoritative order (cf. I, p. 477). In so far as manufacture still depends on the dexterity and skill of workers for its productivity, capitalist production has to remain within certain limit in respect to its rapidity of expansion, its degree of development of productivity, and its domination of the pace and content of work. Thus it could not thoroughly drive out smaller handicrafts and domestic industries through price competition, and often depended upon their production of parts through subcontract. Thus, 'manufacture was unable either to seize upon the production of society to its full extent, or to revolutionize that production to its core. It towered up as an artificial economic construction, on the broad foundation of the town handicrafts and the domestic industries of the countryside.' (I, p. 490).

The mechanised factory system develops the productive power of capital beyond the limitations of manufacture. On the basis of co-operation and the division of labour, the factory system, with the working machines or automatic production facilities after the Industrial Revolution, decomposed skills and converted a major portion of factory workers into unskilled simple labourers. Capital was not enabled elastically to expand its production without being restricted by the number of existing skilled workers. Workers as simple labourers have to be more subordinate to capital, and more fully controllable for capitalist management. As a result, intensity of labour tends to be increased easily and repeatedly. Even with the same degree of intensity of labour, productivity can also easily be enhanced by introducing new machines or facilities. Production of relative surplus-value on a social scale, driven by the possibility of individual acquisition of extra surplus-value, is thus much facilitated and promoted by the mechanised factory system. Depreciation of the substance of value of labour-power along with increase in productivity is often amplified by the effect of mobilising several workers from a family, as we have referred to.

The specific features of capitalist utilisation of machinery should not be taken for the generally inevitable features of utilising machinery in other types of societies. Capital uses machinery in order to reduce costs of production and increase individual and social surplus-value, as well as to facilitate the domination over workers by making them broadly convertible simple labourers. As Marx already points out, machinery 'is the most powerful weapon for suppressing strikes, those periodic revolts of the working class against the autocracy of capital' (I, p. 562). This weapon is effective not merely at the initial stage of introduction of automatic production system, but also repeatedly up until our own age along with introduction of newly 'rationalized' automation systems especially in the phase of depression. As such a weapon, machinery tends to be abused in capitalism, instead of being used to reduce the burden of labourers. On the other hand, the limit for capital to utilise machinery is narrowed from the view of costs. Capitalists do not directly attempt to lessen the labour-substance embodied in the product, but intend to reduce the costs of production. The limit for them to use a machine 'is therefore fixed by the difference between the value of the machine and the value of the labour-power (which is always less than the total labour-value created by the expenditure of the labour-power – M. I.) replaced by it' (I, p. 515). In this context the lower the value of the labour-power, or the lesser the necessary labour-time in a working day, the narrower the limit for capitalist utilisation of machinery. It might be a reason among others why it seems easier to introduce more expensive new machinery in advanced capitalist countries with higher real wages than in less advanced countries. On the other hand, large-scale machinery and facilities of production, once constructed, tend to restrict further innovation for a certain time period, as they need gradually to be depreciated through repeated turnover of capital before being scrapped. The dynamics of investment in machinery and facilities of production as fixed capital remains to be investigated more concretely in the theory of capital accumulation and business cycles which we shall discuss later in chapter 9.

Anyway, capital can treat a large central portion of labour-power as a simple convertible commodity, regardless of workers' individual difference or skill, and thereby elastically extend its production. The development of the method of production in pursuit of individual extra surplus-value and social relative surplus-value, thus clearly entails the social process of making the subordination of workers to capital more complete, strengthening the alienation of labour from its own products working as capital, and fostering the simplification of the commodity labour-power. Capital acquires here an objective technological basis by which to behave as an subjective agent of the production of surplus-value. At the same time the law of value can fully work socially including the aspect of adjustment of allocation of labour according to the anarchical fluctuations of demand, once labour-power is thus converted generally into a simple homogeneous commodity. As we shall discuss in the next chapter, our grounds for reducing skilled or complex work to simple labour in value theory are certainly related to, but not confined to, this capitalist social tendency to treat labour-power as a simple homogeneous commodity with the establishment of the mechanised factory system.

# 6 The Extension of the Theory of the Substance of Value

In treating the law of value and the capitalist production of surplus-value, we have assumed that each industry each produces a single product with simple labour. However, there have been fervent controversies over how to deal with skilled or complex labour, and with joint production, when defining the labour-substance of value. These problems have been focal issues in the debate on the feasibility of Marx's labour theory of value between neo-classists, neo-Ricardians and Marxians, in addition to the related issue of the transformation problem discussed in Chapter 7. In my view these problems still need clarification, especially from the point of view of our discussion of the distinction between and relation between the forms and the substance of value. Reconsideration of these problems from such an angle would strengthen our understanding of the law of value and the working of the capitalist economy, and thus would also serve to make sounder our frame of reference for a possible socialist economy.

A similar theoretical concern must be applied to the theory of the reproduction schemes. The theory of the reproduction schemes deals with how the general material conditions of reproduction are to be carried through in the process of the reproduction and circulation of the total social capital. So far as the law of value must maintain the general economic norms in the labour-and-production process through the value relations of commodities, its absolute social foundation in a capitalist economy is presented in the theory of the reproduction schemes. Therefore we have to confirm our understanding of the substantial content of the law of value, and examine whether the analysis of the reproduction scheme is compatible with possible disproportionalities between the price-form and the labour-substance of commodity products within the range allowed by the surplus-labour embodied in them.

## 6.1 SKILLED LABOUR IN THE VALUE THEORY

### The Origin of the Problem

Even though Marx uncovered the social substance of value relations in general in terms of simple average labour throughout *Capital*, he was aware that the effect of human labour was determined not merely by technology, but also by the different degrees of intensity and skill of the labour. For instance, just after defining values of commodities as crystallised human labour expended to produce them, Marx states that the quantity of the 'value-forming substance', the labour, must be of an average or a socially necessary labour-time, and he continues as follows: 'Socially necessary labour-time is the labour-time required to produce any use-value under the conditions of production normal for a given society and with the average degree of skill and intensity of labour prevalent in that society.' (I, p. 129). In the context where this is stated in the first section in the first chapter of *Capital*, Marx seems to consider the conditions of production and the character of labour mainly in relation to the same kind of labour producing the same sort of use-value. In the case of producing the same kind of use-value, it is not difficult to compare and measure the degree of skill and intensity of labour under the same conditions of production. We can easily assume that the labour-time of skilful workers is reduced to a certain amount of the socially necessary labour-time by comparing the resultant quantity of products. Moreover the mechanised factory system of capitalist production generally homogenises the efficiency of labour under the same conditions of production, making the instruments of labour the main determinants of productivity. The difference in the objective conditions of production, rather than in workers' ability, tend to be the decisive influence on productivity of the same sort of product. The determination of representative technical conditions of production for each kind of commodity can here be left to one side, and analysed separately in the theory of market value or market prices of production, as we shall discuss later in the second section of Chapter 7. Therefore let us presently assume representative conditions of production and average intensity and skill of each kind of labour producing the same sort of use-value.

However, the problem of the degree of skill and intensity of labour cannot conceptually be confined to the same kind of labour. Marx refers to complex labour in contrast with simple average labour, when he compares different kinds of useful labour. Complex labour can be regarded as expenditure of labour-power of skilled workers better trained or educated than the average unskilled or simple workers. It is certainly difficult, or rather impossible, physically to compare and measure the different degrees of skill and intensity of different kinds of useful labour, since the resultant different use-values are not directly commensurable. So long as Marx discusses the substance of value in a simple commodity exchange, the social mechanism by which capitalism treats the great majority of labour as interchangeable simple labour cannot yet be logically presented. A mere commodity-exchange relation, unlike a capitalist economy, cannot provide the *social* ground to make simple unskilled labour the common general substance of value-relations. Thus, Marx's explication of reducing complex into simple labour in the first chapter of *Capital* lacks an actual and unambiguous social basis and is really problematic:

> More complex labour counts only as intensified, or rather multiplied simple labour, so that a smaller quantity of complex labour is considered equal to a larger quantity of simple labour. Experience shows that this reduction is constantly being made. A commodity may be the outcome of the most complicated labour, but through its *value* it is posited as equal to the product of simple labour, hence it represents only a specific quantity of simple labour. The various proportions in which different kinds of labour are reduced to simple labour as their unit of measurement are established by a social process that goes on behind the backs of the producers; these proportions therefore appear to the producers to have been handed down by tradition. In the interests of simplification, we shall henceforth view every form of labour-power directly as simple labour-power; by this we shall simply be saving ourselves the troubles of making the reduction. (I, p. 135).

What does 'a social process that goes on behind the backs of the producers' mean? The process may well be interpreted in this context as the exchange relations in a market 'behind the backs of the producers'. At least Marx does not show how complex labour-time is socially measured as multiplied simple labour-time, apart from the reduction through commodity *value* which seems to imply that value in exchange here determines labour-values rather than the reverse. From the viewpoint of vulgar economics, which resolves all economic problems into the determination of prices within a market, this point naturally appears a great failure in Marx's labour theory of value. Böhm-Bawerk, the first major critic of Marx's value-theory, did not miss the point. Marx seems to define the measurement of labour-time here by the exchange-values given in the market, while he initially intended to explain the exchange-values from labour-time embodied in commodities. Does it not make a 'circular explanation'?[1]

Is there any other possible interpretation of Marx's treatment of complex skilled labour? Against Böhm's type of critique most Marxian value-theorists have attempted to show that complex labour can be reduced to multiplied simple labour by analysing the value of complex labour-power without referring to the role of market. They usually cite and rely on Marx's statement in the section of 'The Valorization Process' in chapter 7 of the first volume of *Capital* as follows:

> All labour of a higher, or more complicated, character than average labour is expenditure of labour-power of a more costly kind, labour-power whose production has cost more time and labour than unskilled or simple labour-power, and which therefore has a higher value. This power being of higher value, is expresses itself in labour of a higher sort, and therefore becomes objectified, during an equal amount of time, in proportionally higher values. Whatever difference in skill there may be between the labour of a spinner and that of a jeweller, the portion of his labour by which the jeweller merely replaces the value of his own labour-power does not in any way differ in quality from the additional portion by which he creates surplus-value. (I, p. 305).

There seems to be little difficulty in accepting Marx's definition of the value of complex labour-power. It is defined as the amount of labour-time which is necessary to produce this sort of labour-power, just like the value of simple labour-power. The real problem lies in the relation between the value of complex labour-power and the value created by the expenditure of this labour-power. The second sentence quoted above, which begins with the phrase 'This power being of higher value', can be interpreted variously.

(1) If the phrase means 'While this power is of higher value', but does not signify causality, the higher value objectified by the expenditure of this labour-power can still be interpreted as being determined by the exchange ratio in a market. Although the Rubin School's

tendency to accept this interpretation has been exceptional among Marxians, it may coincide with Marx's own suggestion in the preceding quotation from the second section of the first chapter of *Capital*. However, in opposition to Böhm's type of critique, most Marxians have interpreted the phrase differently, and maintained that the higher value of complex labour-power is causally related with the higher value created by that labour-power.

(2) As a formal interpretation of the sentences quoted above, a higher sort of skilled labour can be regarded as being able somehow to create higher values in proportion to its value. For example, E. Bernstein asserted such an interpretation.[2] This view apparently allows the theoretically convenient assumption that the rates of surplus-value ($s_i' = s_i/v_i$) are equal across different kinds of complex labour. However, this view contradicts Marx's basic theory, because Marx strongly demonstrated that the use-value of labour-power to be realised in the labour-time expended in a day, *and* the value-substance of labour-power as the necessary labour-time to reproduce labour-power for a day, are determined independently. In view of this basic position we cannot mechanically assume a direct proportionality between the values and the value products, or an equal rate of surplus-value, as between various kinds of complex and simple labour. Therefore, Hilferding opposed both Böhm's critique and Bernstein's formulation, and suggested a third interpretation as follows.

(3) According to Hilferding's interpretation[3], complex labour mobilises and transfers a series of simple labour which were necessary to produce skilled labour-power. Just as ten batteries combined can generate ten times the electric power of a single battery, a series or a combined set of necessary educational and training labour is potentially stored in the character of the skilled worker and is transferred to the commodity products through his labour. So long as educational or training labour in the past, constitutes part of the value of complex labour-power, it is transfered to the commodity product without varying its amount just like the value of constant capital. Then, for a capitalist who employs skilled workers, surplus-value is to be extracted only from labour newly expended by those workers. Therefore, even though skilled workers objectify greater quantities of labour in the commodity products during equal amounts of time, their rate of exploitation must be lower than in the case of simple labourers.

This third interpretation seems most consistent with the technological determination of values in terms of labour-time, and has been regarded as a classic solution of the skilled labour problem. However, it could not be a final solution. In recent value controversy the problem has continued to be discussed from various angles.

**The Recent Technological Analyses**

In Hilferding's solution the role of educational labour and that of the skilled worker's *own labour* were not very clearly distinguished. It was also ambiguous as to whether the skilled worker's own labour was to be regarded as simple common labour or not when it was separated from the educational labour stored in his ability. Further, it remained to be clarified how to decompose complex labour in the educational process into simple labour.

N. Okishio[4], and then B. Rowthorn[5] extended Hilferding's approach and gave it a more formal exposition. Let me abridge Rowthorn's exposition here, and begin with assuming $n$ different commodities labelled 1, 2, . . . , $n$, and $m+1$ different types of labour labelled 0, 1, 2, . . . , $m$. Suppose that to produce one unit of commodity $j$ requires $1_{rj}$ units of labour of each type of $r$, and $a_{ij}$ units of each commodity $i$. Then, if one unit of labour expended in an average lifetime of type $r$ is equivalent to $\phi_r$ units unskilled labour, the value of one unit of commodity $j$ is given by

$$\sigma_j = \sum_r \phi_r 1_{rj} + \sum_i \sigma_i a_{ij} \tag{6.1}$$

Since the terms $1_{rj}$ and $a_{ij}$ are technically determined, there are $n + m + 1$ unknowns ($\sigma_i$ and $\phi_r$) in $n$ equations. Let $\sigma^*_s$ be the amount of unskilled labour contained in one unit of skill of type $s$. It is in a sense assumed here, following Hilferding's point of view, that skill in the skilled-labour-power is producible by a certain amount of abstruct human labour, and thus accountable by units of unskilled labour. Then one unit of labour in an average lifetime of this type is equivalent to one unit of unskilled labour of the worker concerned *plus* $\sigma^*_s$ units of unskilled labour embodied in his skills. Then

$$\phi_s = 1 + \sigma^*_s \tag{6.2}$$

Suppose further that to produce one unit of skill of type $s$ requires $t^*_s$ units of unskilled labour by the person being trained, *plus* $1^*_{rs}$ units of labour of each type $r$, *plus* $a^*_{is}$ units of each commodity $i$. Since each unit of labour of type $r$ is equivalent to $\phi_r$ units of unskilled labour, and each unit of commodity $i$ contains $\sigma_i$ units of unskilled labour, $\sigma^*_s$ can be given by

$$\sigma^*_s = t^*_s + \sum_r \phi_r 1^*_{rs} + \sum_i \sigma_i a^*_{is} \tag{6.3}$$

From equations (6.2) and (6.3) we get

$$\phi_s = (1 + t^*_s) + \sum_r \phi_r 1^*_{rs} + \sum_i \sigma_i a^*_{is} \tag{6.4}$$

We can assume in this economy that labour of type 0 is simple unskilled labour, which means

$$\phi_0 = 1 \tag{6.5}$$

Taking (6.1), (6.4) and (6.5) together, we have now $n + m + 1$ equations, which under most conditions will be sufficient to determine both the values $\sigma_i$ and the reduction coefficient $\phi_r$.

Clearly this form of solution can define the substance of values independently from the wages and avoid the circular inconsistency. If we follow the same line of discussion we can suppose that workers of type $s$ perform $(1 + t^*_s)$ units of their own labour, as both employees and trainees, and receive a bundle of commodities $(b_{1s}, b_{2s}, \ldots, b_{ns})$ for each unit of labour through wages. Then, against their own total labour $(1 + t^*_s)$, their paid labour equals $(1 + t^*_s) \sum_i \sigma_i b_{is}$. The rate of surplus-labour, $e_s$, is calculated as follows:

$$e_s = \frac{(1 + t^*_s) - (1 + t^*_s)\, \Sigma\sigma_i b_{is}}{(1 + t^*_s)\, \Sigma\sigma_i b_{is}} = \frac{1 - \Sigma\sigma_i b_{is}}{\Sigma\sigma_i b_{is}} \tag{6.6}$$

Three points are noteworthy in this Okishio–Rowthorn type for formulation.

First, skilled workers' own labour is clearly separated from educational labour by others and is treated as unskilled simple labour. This point is not particularly emphasised nor theoretically grounded by Okishio–Rowthorn. However, it is not only a technically key point, but may also lead to an interesting insight as to the common character of human labour to which we shall soon come back.

Second, skill in workers' ability is treated just like an objective product of educational labour, and embodied labour in skill is regarded as being transferred to the products of skilled workers just as embodied labour in the means of production. This obscures, and may contradict, Marx's fundamental distinction between human labour-power and means of production in the valorisation process. In Marx the substance of the value of labour-power, which is obtained and consumed by workers in a bundle of commodities to sustain their lives, is not transferred to the value of commodity products, but always newly created and embodied in the products by newly expended labour-time together with surplus-value, whereas the value of means of production is transferred to the products (cf. I, pp. 316–17). This is basically why changes in wages or value of labour-power do not affect the amount of value-product or the substance of values of commodity products. In spite of their intention, Hilferdung, Okishio and Rowthorn have somewhat clouded over the basic position of the Marxian theory of value.

Third, in their treatment, the rate of surplus-value or that of exploitation must generally differ between simple and skilled workers, or among different kinds of complex workers.

According to M. Morishima, as a result of the introduction of heterogeneous labour this third point conflicts with Marx's law of the equalisation of the rate of exploitation and is not compatible with Marx's view of the polarisation of society into two classes. This anomaly is an important reason for Morishima to recommend 'a Marxian economics without the labour theory of value'.[6]

Opposing Morishima, S. Bowles and H. Gintis hold that the labour theory of value is perfectly compatible with the heterogeneity of labour. They also oppose the conventional Marxian way of reducing complex labour to simple labour, because they do not believe in the historical tendency of capitalism to homogenise all labour, and also because they want to have the conceptual tools of value theory to encompass the phenomenon of segmentation of workers. In their view, not simplification, but segmentation of workers has become increasingly important especially in the recent development of capitalist labour management. Therefore, Bowles and Gintis build an economic model containing heterogeneous labour, or various types of skilled or complex labour, the wage bundles of the various types of wage-labour, the matrix of input–output relationships among goods, and the matrix of direct labour inputs involved in their production. In this model they show that the structure of value-relations, including the vectors of rates of exploitation and the organic composition of capital, without being counted by units of simple labour, can determine the average rate of profit and the prices of production. It is also shown that there is normally a strictly inverse relationship between wages and the rate of profit.[7] The reduction of complex or skilled labour into simple labour is thus regarded as unnecessary.

These analyses are to be appreciated as a contribution to the feasibility of Marxian value-theory with heterogeneous labour. However, Bowles and Gintis's model and their formal technical exposition may possibly be utilised or extended in two opposite directions.

On the one hand, neo-Ricardians may easily utilise the model and the exposition in order to show the redundancy of the concept of abstract labour. Even though Bowles and Gintis maintain that they would not abandon the concept of abstract labour, their treatment of heterogeneous labour can directly be interpreted as a model which deals only with concrete labour without considering the abstract character of labour. In their basic theoretical model the role of the common abstract character of labour between different kinds of heterogeneous labour is not very clear, and may even seem dispensable. In fact, I. Steedman demonstrates a similar vector-value analysis of an economy with heterogeneous labour in his Sraffa-based critique of Marx, and clearly denies any need to reduce different kinds of concrete labour into abstract labour.[8] In the context of Steedman's critique of Marx, the technical possibility of determining the rate of profit and prices without reducing heterogeneous skilled labour to simple unskilled labour, is directly regarded as a logical basis for his criticism of the concept of abstract labour and the labour theory of value as being redundant.

On the other hand, Bowles and Gintis's model can also be interpreted in an opposite way as being compatible and in a sense mutually complementary with the more traditional treatment of complex labour. For one thing, the determination of the rate of profit and prices of production for an economy with heterogeneous labour in Bowles and Gintis's (*B–G*) model does hold even when the ratios of the reduction of heterogeneous to simple labour and the value of skilled labour-power are analysed by the Hilferding–Okishio–Rowthorn (*H–O–R*) theory. From the view of *H–O–R* theory, *B–G* model can be regarded as a useful complement precisely to determine the average rate of profit and prices in an economy with various rates of surplus-value for different kinds of labour. Conversely the *H–O–R* approach may be useful to clarify some ambiguous aspects of the *B–G* model. For instance, although *B–G* reject the technical determination of values of heterogeneous labour-power, in order to emphasise the role of other social and managerial factors of discrimination, it might still be useful to observe and consider the distinct technical factors such as educational costs in *H–O–R* even for a more accurate understanding of the effects of other factors of segmentation. Besides, *B–G*, unlike Steedman, maintain the theoretical need of the concept of abstract labour in order clearly to see the fundamental social relations. They add to their numerical example the rates of surplus-value in *common labour*, in terms of which the amount of labour-time is simply added together and compared without any weight or qualification across different kinds of labour.

As *B–G* point out in their reply to E. McKenna, their common labour is different from the simple labour in *H–O–R*, and is not reduced from complex labour with a technically determinant weight.[9] The economic and social meaning of this concept 'common labour' is, however, almost uninvestigated by *B–G*, so that it may even give an impression of being introduced for technical convenience. Let us recall here that *O–R* treated the skilled worker's own labour as simple labour, also without giving theoretical foundation. An interesting coincidence both in the direction of recognition and in the insufficiency of investigation, is thus found here concerning the simple or common character in skilled heterogeneous workers' own labour, in the apparently different models by *O–R* and *B–G*. Let us study this point anew from a wider view in a slightly roundabout way.

## The Historical and Universal Basis for a Solution

In retrospect, various difficulties in Marx's value-theory often originated from his reduction of values to crystals of labour based directly on the exchange relations of commodities in the first section of the first chapter of *Capital*. In spite of Marx's great discovery of the forms of value, the exchange-value as a form of value is abstracted from this section to reach the concept of values. As a result, so far as the definition of value in this first section is concerned, Marx's labour theory of value contains a lot of similarities with Ricardo's. Certainly, Marx's *Capital* as a whole presents us, unlike Ricardo's *Principles*, with a systematic articulation of the historically specific character of a capitalist economy. In such an articulation, Marx clarified *both* the trans-historical character of the labour process as the everlasting Nature-imposed condition of human existence common to all the social formations (I, p. 290) *and* the broad historical character of commodity exchange, money and certain species of capital which existed before and outside of the capitalist mode of production. Only when human labour-power is converted into a commodity on a social scale, can capitalism be established and completely embrace the social labour process within the value-forms of commodity economy. The labour theory of value, which unveils the social relations in labour-time hidden under value-forms, can be shown with a *social* necessity only by observing this specific economic system of capitalism, as we have discussed in the previous chapter.

In contrast, so far as the substance of value as embodied labour is abstracted and observed in a mere commodity-exchange relation, we can not define the social mode of production which has turned out the commodity observed. In a long precapitalist history, commodities are especially made by skilled artisans in towns and often exchanged with agricultural surplus-products extracted by landlords from various sorts of communal production. In such a precapitalist commodity economy, it must be impossible to find a social basis to recognise the homogeneous and common character of human labour as values. This is because social status or ranks, the division of labour and skilled works are traditionally related and fixed, and personal mobility across them is strictly forbidden. Thus, Marx was correct when he pointed out the historical limitation preventing Aristotle from recognising the equality of human labour in his analysis of exchange values (I, pp. 151–2).

In a capitalist society the majority of people have become *free* workers in the double sense (I, p. 272), and have to alter the concrete forms of labour, say from tailoring to weaving etc., 'in accordance with changes of the demand' (I, p. 134) for their labour-power as a commodity. The mobility of workers across various kinds of concrete labour is not only formally given in the commodity-form of labour-power, but it is also substantially grounded in deskilling of labour by capitalist utilisation of machinery. Marx's analysis of the production of relative surplus-value by means of machinery simultaneously clarifies how capitalism decomposes skills and simplifies labour in a miserable way. In view of such a development, Marx notes that 'we must not imagine that so-called "skilled-labour" forms a large part of the whole of the nation's labour. Laing estimates that in England (and Wales) the livelihood of 11 300 000 people [from about 18 000 000 total population – M. I.] depends on unskilled labour.' (I, p. 305.)

Marx could have treated simple labour as a dominant form of wage-labour on the ground that this was the actual development of capitalism. This was an important reason why Uno insisted on showing the labour theory of value in the context of the production process of capital, not in that of simple commodity exchanges.[10] In the Uno School the reduction of complex skilled labour into simple labour has been regarded as being guaranteed by the historical tendency of capitalism to generalise simple labour by means of the mechanised factory system. This view coincides with H. Braverman's position in *Labor and Monopoly Capital*. Braverman underlines that the strong tendency towards the degradation of labour by the increasing separation of the time-consuming process of design from the majority of worker's practice, continues to prevail in the history of US monopoly capitalism.[11] We may thus erase the problem of how to evaluate skilled labour in terms of simple labour, by abstracting the labour theory of value upon the basis of an historical tendency of capitalism in this direction.

However, the problem has not yet completely theoretically solved, in so far as it is simply dismissed from the basic theory contingent upon a factual tendency which was conspicuous particularly up to Marx's own age. Without giving a more substantial theoretical solution to the problem, we may not be able to offer a sound frame of reference for the analyses of actual segmentation of workers in recent capitalist societies. In fact, more recent studies of the segmentation of labour tend to oppose Braverman and emphasise actual trends to create anew and reproduce various discriminations between workers which are often regarded as relating to actual or possible differences in the degrees of skills or of complexity of labour. In my view, however, these actual trends of the segmentation of workers have become more and more dependent upon socially discriminatory factors such as racism, sexism and schooling, and have been utilised and fostered more or less artificially in order to facilitate a managerial 'bureaucratic' control of working people.[12] Therefore, the trends towards segmentation do not really relegate, but are rather coupled with, the degradation and the deskilling of labour for the majority of working people, especially for those engaging in the material reproduction process.

Thus, if we disregard the artificial managerial segmentation of workers as for wages, etc., capitalist production has powerfully dissolved any fixed traditional skills like in craftsmanship, simplifying labouring operations in most workplaces, especially in industries susceptible to mass production, and thus technologically facilitating interchangeability of workers across jobs and industries. However, what enables such mobility of labour-power is not merely the capitalistic achievement of deskilling by means of machinery and equipment. More fundamentally, it is grounded upon the wide range of applicability of human labour-power linked with the mental, such as the linguistic, ability which is specific to human beings in distinction to other animals. As we have seen, Marx's treatment of the labour process clearly implied his recognition of such human labouring ability. Extendible human labour-power, based upon a rich mental as well as physical ability, has enabled workers to perform surplus-labour beyond necessary labour-time, working for a purpose given by others in class societies, simultaneously offers a most basic ground for the actual mobile interchangeability of workers which is realised under capitalism.

Traditionally the twin problems of how to deal with concrete and abstract labour and how to reduce skilled to simple labour are regarded as theoretically distinct, and to be handled separately. However, the solution of these problems must now be linked, and mutually cross over to the basis of the basic human ability to work. In treating the skilled-labour problem it is generally assumed that skilled labour is more intensive labour creating more value than simple labour in the same labouring time. In view of the basic ability of human labour-power, we must now understand that even most de-skilled and monotonous work is the expenditure of the commonly extendible potential power of human beings. Indeed as Marx suggests, 'The less he is attracted by the nature of the work, and the way in which it has to be accomplished, and the less, therefore, he enjoys it as the free play of his own physical and mental powers, the closer his attention is forced to be' (I, p. 284), and the more tiring his work must be. In this regard simple unskilled labour is also expenditure of the complex human ability to work, using different combinations of the various aspects of human mental and physical abilities in accord with different forms of concretely useful work. This makes a comprehensive and comparative assessment or measurement of the intensity of labour even in the ordinary unskilled grade of work theoretically hard, or rather impossible. This serves also as a hidden basis enabling managerially convenient introduction of artificially fine gradings and segmentations into various works which can basically be performed interchangeably without difficulty. However, we should see that beyond managerial differentiations each sort of work is equally expenditure of a composite human labouring ability in a specific form, and that different concretely useful labour so qualified is reducible to abstract human labour, being comparable simply according to the physical hours of labour performed.

From this point of view, complex skilled labour must also be regarded as the expenditure of general human ability to labour in special forms. So far as skilled labour-power needs a certain education or training beforehand, simple labour-power cannot instantly be converted to some sort of skilled work, whereas skilled labour-power can be used in simple work. Hence, grading and categorisation of wages, etc., can easily be imposed on skilled workers. However, if we disregard this aspect of differentiation for the moment, a skilled worker's own labour is basically nothing but the expenditure of the composite human ability to labour just as in the case of simple labour. With this qualification, skilled labour is also reducible to abstract human labour, being commensurable with other types of work simply in terms of physical hours of labour, as a part of the total social human activity of maintaining material reproduction. In comparison with simple labour, which covers various forms of the expenditure of human abilities, skilled labour cannot be regarded as especially intensified labouring activity. Skilled work may often be even less intensive and less tiring, since skilled workers have been given special training or education for their jobs and tend to work under a relatively lesser pressure of competition.

Therefore there is a certain rationality and justification in the direction of the recognition by *O–R* and *B–G* that skilled workers' own labour can be treated as simple or common labour being measurable simply in terms of physical labour-time just as simple workers' labour. Since Marx tended to analyse the labour-substance of value too closely linked with the forms of value from the initial theory of commodities, he was inclined to assume that skilled workers could perform in some (a little mystically in my view) intensified manner, more labour than simple workers in the same labour-time, behind the relatively higher exchange values of skilled workers' products in the market, including higher wages for them. If we theoretically separate the forms and the substance of value as dimensionally different orders for a more proper, non-mystical understanding of their relations, we need not follow Marx's lead here and must conclude from our re-examination that skilled workers' own labour embodies the same amount of labour-substance of value as simple workers do in a unit of labour-time, independently of the relatively higher exchange values in the market given to skilled workers' labour-power and products.

Contrastingly the Rubin School believes that the commensuration of concrete useful labour to abstract labour is inseparable from the form of value or exchange value in the market. In this tradition, S. Himmelweit argues, on the assumption of an equal organic composition of capital and an equal rate of profit across industries, that 'workers who are paid less or more produce correspondingly less, or more, value. Or equivalently that the value of any labour-power is proportional to its value producing power.'[13] The quantities of abstract labour as the substance of value are qualitatively treated here as a completely subordinate shadow of the equilibrium prices determined in the market, and are not conceived as an objective entity being independent of market relations. The labour theory of value as a theory to determine prices and to examine their functions from behind the market relations, in terms of objective human labouring activity, must be very much weakened by this way of reasoning. As a result Himmelweit's inference seems to include a circular reasoning between the assumed equal organic composition of capital and the deduced determination of the value of skilled labour-power. The proportional evaluation of the values of products and of the labour-power of skilled workers in the market would not hold in a real capitalist economy with differing organic compositions of capital, and it therefore cannot be a solid solution for the skilled-labour problem.

In our view the values of skilled workers' labour-power must be discussed independently from the labour-substance of value of their products. At first sight there is not any problem in defining the value of skilled labour-power. According to Marx it is the amount of labour-time which is necessary to produce and maintain this sort of labour-power. It seems just like the definition of the value of ordinary simple labour-power, and has been basically followed by most Marxians, though *B–G* technically redefined it in the vector value. In Marx's words, 'The costs of education vary according to the degree of complexity of the labour-power required. These expenses (exceedingly small in the case of ordinary labour-power) form a part of the total value spent in producing it.' (I, p. 276).

However, as we have seen in the previous chapter, labour-power is a special commodity, and is reproduced not in a production process but in a consumption process. Further, since its owner is mortal, 'the labour-power withdrawn from the market by wear and tear, and by death, must be continuously replaced by, at the very least, an equal amount of fresh labour-power' (I, p. 275). The replacement of workers by their children with the common level of education and civilisation attained by a country must be accounted for in the value of labour-power, in the case of workers in general, or simple common workers. Should we then straightforwardly understand that the same is true for the replacement of complex skilled workers? If we should, (as suggested in the ordinary analyses of the problem even among Marxians), we must also understand that the reproduction of skilled workers through generations is to be done fixedly within the same grade of skilled workers' families. As a result the families of skilled workers may functionally become similar to those in a fixed privileged social status or caste in precapitalist societies. This seems to be an inevitable consequence of a type of understanding of the law of value in accord with the traditional technological approaches since Hilferding. This is so especially where the embodied labour-time in skill is regarded as being transferred to the commodity products just like the substance of value of constant capital on the one hand, and is regarded as the value substance to be paid to the sellers of skilled labour-power to secure its reproduction on the other. This logical consequence seems at least partly consonant with the social function of higher wages of complex skilled workers.

However, in case Marx's more basic view that the amount of labour-time necessary to reproduce the human ability to work is just consumed in the form of means of consumption and not transferred to the commodity products is true, it should consistently be applied to educational labour-time as well. In addition, if we see that the skilled workers' own labour does not contain any mysteriously intensified labour which creates more substance of value compared with common simple labour, then there is no counterpart in the embodied labour-time of skilled workers products to match against the higher value of skilled labour-power. Thus, the law of value does not assure any socially or technologically fixed proportional relation between the amount of labour-time necessary to develop the skill and that embodied in the products of skilled workers. Certainly it must be obvious that a social fund, a certain amount of labour-time, is always to be spared for educational materials and labour-power in order to reproduce socially necessary sorts of skilled labour-power. As skilled workers do not expend any specially intensified labour nor transfer any past labour consumed during their life and education, and also as the necessary labour-time to reproduce *common* labour-power apparently cannot bear such an educational or training fund for skilled labour-power, the fund must generally be regarded as a deduction from total social surplus-labour. The forms to deal with such a fund would vary according to the different social systems.

For instance, without a lifelong employment system, a private capitalist firm will not directly bear educational costs of skills, since educated skilled workers may 'escape' to other competitive firms in order to sell their labour-power dearer. In a competitive capitalist economy without a public sector, educational costs thus tend to be borne by families, and thus ironically reduce competitive mobility independent of families, each of which are connected with certain different grades of skilled labour. Wages or the form of value of skilled labour-power on this occasion function as a channel of distributing educational funds deducted from social surplus-labour to the families of skilled workers. If wages of a certain type of skilled workers are higher than the costs necessary both to maintain their families and to replace their ability through their children, then other children of the families which can afford such educational costs will come in sooner or later, and vice versa. This is exactly the case, in fact, consonant with the *H–O–R* model as we have seen. In such a case wages as the form of value of skilled labour-power are maintained in a market by the inconvertibility of such labour-power just at the level tendentially being equivalent to the educational costs plus the ordinary wages for simple labourers, and this enables skilled workers to obtain more substance of value than simple workers. The higher wage-costs of technologically necessary skilled workers force capitalist firms to set much higher prices of production for their products in a competitive market, so as to enable these firms to maintain reproduction through price-relations with an average rate of profit, as substantially shown by the *B–G* model. So long as the extra portion of the substance of value obtained by the skilled labourer as compared to the common simple labourer remains within the quantity of surplus-labour-time in his life, the skilled worker may be conceptually classified as being exploited, nevertheless he must have a more or less petit-bourgeois character as well. This is probably what is implied by the degree of 'the rate of exploitation in common labour' in the *B–G* model. It must be noted, however, that even when a skilled worker is not exploited and is rather exploiting in this context, he may indirectly add to total surplus-value by increasing the productivity of *other* workers in various cases.

In an opposite case where educational costs of skills are entirely borne by the state or the public entity from taxes on surplus-value, the substance of value acquired personally by skilled workers through the form of value of labour-power or wages need not contain any social funds from surplus-labour, and must theoretically be reduced to the same level as that of the common simple workers. We assume here no shortage of skilled workers, nor special managerial strategies for their segmentation. Our view is substantially the same, with a different interpretation of the case, as analysed in the supplementary part of Rowthorn's essay. A skilled worker in a capitalist sector is assumed there to receive value $V_p$, just the same as unskilled workers. In Rowthorn's example, even though educational labour ($V_G+U_G$) in the state sector is expended for the skilled worker and is transferred to the output of capitalist sector, the total cost in value terms to produce the skilled labour-power ($V_p+V_G+U_G$) is not totally given to the skilled worker through wages. In Rowthorn's treatment there seems to be a considerable gap between wages as a form of value and the substantial definition of the value of skilled labour-power. In my interpretation educational labour ($V_G+U_G$) is neither transferred to the output of skilled workers nor to be counted in the value of his labour-power in this case.

In an actual capitalist society these two opposite cases are more or less combined together. Financial institutions from which personal funds for educational costs can be borrowed may also affect the manner in which the reproduction of skilled labour-power is managed between generations.[14] Various types of segmentation of labour are usually linked with different educational costs, but within contemporary capitalist firms they are mostly more in accord with managerial convenience than with the social need to reproduce necessary sorts of skilled-labour-power. We can criticise more thoroughly the social function of segmented work in a capitalist economy, with its differentiation of wages and revenues, when we properly recognise the basic common character of skilled and unskilled labour as well as the various possible ways to secure the reproduction of necessary skilled workers.

Our alternative solution of the skilled-labour problem further relates to two more important issues: one concerns international trade and the other socialism.

Closely linked with his treatment of skilled labour as intensified labour, Marx has this to say concerning international trade: 'the law of value is . . . modified in its international application by the fact that, on the world market, national labour which is more productive also counts as more intensive, as long as the more productive nation is not compelled by competition to lower the selling price of its commodities to the level of their value' (I, p. 702). Certainly there may be international differences of labour productivity due to a different degree of intensification of ordinary workers' labour. However, actual intensification of labour would rather be strengthened in the less-advanced nations with weaker trade unions and stronger competition among workers, as capitalist production extends its domination over workers in such nations. So far as labour productivity in the advanced country is greater for the same industry than in the less-advanced country because of better objective conditions of production, such as machinery and equipment, more productive labour in the advanced country should not be regarded as actually more intensive simply for the reason of its productivity. Comparison of labour productivity itself must lose its essential meaning where products are not homogeneous. Actually, when the advanced and the less-advanced countries produce and trade different use-values, as is often the case in the international division of labour, comparison of labour productivity in physical terms cannot have a theoretical sense, because the results of labour in different use-values are not commensurable. Therefore, the commensurability of labour products is conventionally based upon the prices given in the international market. Comparison of labour 'productivity' then must depend heavily upon evaluation in the sphere of market or the fluctuating relations between demand and supply. Such treatment, especially when combined with the assumption of more intensive labour behind higher labour productivity, becomes too remote from the basic position of the labour theory of value, where the social relations in the expenditure of labour are theoretically defined independently of the market relations as a fundamental determinant of prices. Our discussion here cannot be a final solution, but is rather an examination of a starting-point for the issues of international value relations or the international unequal exchange. However, it must be clear by now that a position recognising more productive national labour directly as more intensive labour following the Rubin School among others, as well as Marx's own statement cited above, cannot be based on a proper and sound understanding of the skilled-labour problem.

In a socialist society, where a part of total social product necessary for the common satisfaction of needs has to be deducted before the product is divided among the individuals,[15] such as for schools, health services, together with the portions of product for the replacement of the means of production, for the expansion of production, for reserves or insurance funds, for the general costs of administration and for those unable to work. The educational funds for skilled or complex labour-power should also be theoretically dealt with in such a society on a social communal, and not on an individual basis. Then, a skilled worker should not get back from society – after the socially necessary deductions have been made – more than a common simple worker either for what he contributes to society in his own labour-time, or for the costs of maintaining the socially necessary sorts of skilled labour-power. The economic position of such a skilled worker would correspond to that of the skilled worker of a capitalist society in the second theoretical case examined above with an entirely state educational system.

In the *Critique of Gotha Programme*, however, Marx assumes workers' unequal right to products proportional to the labour they supply in a lower phase of communist society, as a 'bourgeois right' in principle since 'one man is superior to another physically or mentally and so supplies more labour in the same time, . . .'. In contrast 'in a higher phase of communist society, after the enslaving subordination of the individual to the division of labour, . . . after the productive forces have also increased with the all-round development of the individual, and all the springs of co-operative wealth flow more abundantly – only then can the narrow horizon of bourgeois right be crossed in its entirety and society inscribe on its banners: from each according to his ability, to each according to his need!'[16] So long as this 'bourgeois right' is based on the concept of skilled or complex labour-power as being able to supply more labour in the same time, we have a theoretical ground to oppose to it. It is related to Marx's ambiguous and problematic treatment of skilled labour, as we have discussed. In a Soviet type of society, this 'bourgeois right' in the lower phase of communist society as described in Marx's writing has undoubtedly been fully utilised in order to legitimate the hierarchical and stratified privileges of the state and party bureaucrats in regard to material goods and social services. It tends also to be perpetuated in so far as the higher phase of communist society is regarded as a goal too far a way actually to be achieved.

Thus in my opinion, the Marxian labour theory of value even on the skilled labour problem, if properly developed, must be able to offer a basis for the fundamentally egalitarian point of view of social relations, which should always be *a* crucial element of Marxism. From this point of view the social function and the historical meaning of artificially segmented work in modern capitalist labour management, as well as *a* justification for hierarchical social orders in 'real existing socialist' societies, must be given a deeper and more critical frame of reference for re-examination, as we have suggested.

## 6.2 THE JOINT PRODUCTION PROBLEM

### Steedman's Critique of Marx

How can we define the labour value of jointly produced commodities like beef and cowhide as the joint products of raising cows, when our previous assumption of single product for each process of production is removed? The way of determing the labour substance embodied in each kind of product by solving the simultaneous equations such as (5.3) in Section 5.1 of Chapter 5, does not suffice, because the number of unknowns to be determined (the labour-substance in each product) must become more than the number of equations given by the number of processes of production. The problem, along with the skilled labour problem, has become a focus of the value controversy between neo-Ricardians and Marxians as well as between Marxians.

A clue to the issue is found in P. Sraffa's *Production of Commodities by Means of Commodities*. Sraffa there took up the case of joint production, while formulating his theory of prices deduced from the physical data of real wages and the technical system of production as a prelude to a critique of marginalist economic theory. In the case of 'two of the commodities to be jointly produced by a single industry', he assumed 'a second, parallel process which will produce the two commodities by a different method and, as we shall suppose at first, in different proportions',[17] so as to equalise the number of equations to the number of unknowns (i.e. prices of all products except one to determine relative prices and the rate of profit). Though Sraffa did not refer to Marx's value theory at all, his analytical techniques were easily applicable to the determination of the labour substance in commodity products from the same physical data. Therefore the theoretically interesting question was asked as to how Sraffians would see the Marxian labour theory of value.

As a representative Sraffian, I. Steedman in *Marx after Sraffa* denounced Marx's labour theory of value in favour of Sraffa's theory of prices. It has renewed the value controversy from a new angle and has managed to perplex Marxians to some extent. As was often the case with previous controversies this recent issue is also a good opportunity to deepen our understanding of the Marxian value theory.

Steedman claims that Marx's value theory is redundant and inconsistent. In general it is claimed to be redundant. Steedman admits that 'the labour-time required (directly and indirectly) to produce any commodity – and thus the value of any commodity – is determined by the physical data relating to the methods of production'.[18] However, he asserts that 'the value magnitudes are, at best, redundant in the determination of the rate of profit (and prices of production)',[19] because the same physical data and the specification of real wages suffice to determine the same results.

In the case in which some production processes produce joint products, values, reckoned as the quantities of embodied labour-time, may be indeterminate. Even when values are determinate, they can be negative, and surplus-value can consequently be negative even when the rate of profit and prices are positive. Let us see Steedman's example.[20]

Suppose there are two different processes of production which produce commodities *A* and *B* jointly as follows:

I. 5 units of commodity *A* + 1 unit of labour →
6 units of commodity *A* + 1 unit of commodity *B*.
II. 10 units of commodity *B* + 1 unit of labour →
3 units of commodity *A* and 12 units of commodity *B*.

The real-wage bundle for a unit of labour is assumed to contain $\frac{1}{2}$ unit of commodity *A* and $\frac{5}{6}$ unit of commodity *B*. Let its price be 1, prices of commodities *A* and *B* be $p_1$ and $p_2$ respectively and the uniform profit rate be $r$. Following Sraffa, we assume that the profit rate marks up only the prices of means of production. Then we can formulate the following three simultaneous linear equations:

$$(1+r)\,5p_1 + 1 = 6p_1 + p_2 \tag{6.7}$$

$$(1+r)\,10p_2 + 1 = 3p_1 + 12p_2 \tag{6.8}$$

$$1 = \tfrac{1}{2}\,p_1 + \tfrac{5}{6}\,p_2 \tag{6.9}$$

The positive solutions to (6.7), (6.8), (6.9) are:

$$r = 20 \text{ per cent}, \; p_1 = \tfrac{1}{3}, \; p_2 = 1.$$

Let the quantities of labour embodied in a unit of the same commodities *A* and *B* be $\ell_1$ and $\ell_2$. They are determined by the following simultaneous equations:

$$5\ell_1 + 1 = 6\ell_1 + \ell_2 \tag{6.10}$$

$$10\ell_2 + 1 = 3\ell_1 + 12\ell_2 \tag{6.11}$$

The solutions to (6.10) and (6.11) are:

$$\ell_1 = -1, \quad \ell_2 = 2.$$

Thus the value of the first commodity, $A$, the labour embodied in it must be negative, whereas its price and the rate of profit are positive. If 6 units of labour are employed, 5 operating the first process and 1 operating the second, then the surplus product (5 units of commodity $A$ + 2 units of commodity $B$) remains after deducing the necessary wage bundle (3 units of commodity $A$ + 5 units of commodity $B$) from the net product (8 units of commodity $A$ + 7 units of commodity $B$). The value of labour power $V$, and the surplus-value $S$ can be calculated in this case as follows:

$$V = 3 \times (-1) + 5 \times 2 = 7$$
$$S = 5 \times (-1) + 2 \times 2 = -1$$
$$V + S = 6.$$

Thus, surplus-value appears negative, while the rate of profit is positive.

Steedman concludes from this analysis that Marx's labour theory of value is not merely redundant, but also inconsistent, and that it should be abandoned and replaced by the Sraffian theory of prices.

**Anti-Critiques**

Steedman's critique is clearly based on a narrow point of view. He takes the point of Marx's theory of value to be the *determination* of equilibrium prices just as in the case with the neo-classical or the Sraffian theories of prices. From such a standpoint, analysing the quantities of labour appears redundant, since the prices of production can be determined directly by the physical data on production techniques and the real wages. This sort of critique, however, does not correctly understand the essential subject of Marx's value theory.

For Marx, the theory of value is not at all a means by which merely to determine equilibrium prices. It is, above all, a theory designed to clarify the historical specificity of the capitalist economy. As we have seen, Marx discovered that the labour process is 'the everlasting Nature imposed condition of human existence' (I, p. 290), and analysed how this fundamental condition of human societies became the *social* substance of value-relations under capitalism. In particular, the capitalist social mechanism for obtaining surplus-labour, which is the substance of surplus-value, is central for such an analysis. It is thus essential for Marx's theory of value to elucidate capitalist social relations based on human labour, together with its specific forms and mechanisms. From this standpoint the observation of the quantities of labour as the substance of value and surplus-value cannot be dispensed with. It is not at all redundant, despite Steedman's critique. By assessing Marx's labour theory of value as generally redundant Steedman shows an inability or reluctance to understand the significance and the task of Marx's value theory as the foundation of historical and social sciences. His total neglect of Marx's theory of value-forms is closely related to this weakness.

Steedman's critique of the inconsistency of Marx's value theory is presented exactly by neglecting the theory of value-forms and by a one-sided technological understanding of the concept of value. The seeming anomalies, as in the case of negative value and negative surplus-value, spring from the Sraffian interpretation, which derives the quantities of embodied labour, or values, of joint products in a mechanical way from a number of parallel, different, production processes equal to the number of joint products. This interpretation does not care which of the existing techniques is the dominant condition of production meeting social demand. Besides it cannot define the values or the equilibrium prices in cases in which there is only a unique joint-production method or more methods than the number of products.

However, Marxian anti-critiques of Steedman's treatment of the joint-production problem have been diverse and not yet very satisfactory, though they have almost unanimously pointed out the significant task of Marx's value-theory to reveal the social substance of surplus-value in rejecting Steedman's claim that Marx's value-concept is redundant.

For instance, P. Sweezy has criticised Steedman and correctly pointed out that the key concept of the rate of surplus-value has to vanish from an analysis made in terms of prices.[21] But Sweezy left Steedman's points on the joint production problem untouched.

N. Okishio treats this problem assuming a single technique of production for jointly produced commodities, say *A* and *B*. Then the value of *A* can be between zero and the maximum given in the case where *B* is zero. So the total value of both *A* and *B* is determinate, but the value of *A* or *B* is not, since Okishio analyses values only in a purely technical fashion. As a result the values of surplus-products and of the wage-goods become indeterminate when some of them are jointly produced. At the same time Okishio's fundamental Marxian theorem, that the general rate of profit is positive only when the rate of surplus-value is positive, becomes untenable. Okishio revises it substantially and says: 'The existence of exploitation is determined by whether labourers are forced to produce the surplus products or not'; 'The necessary condition for the existence of profit is that labourers are exploited' in this sense.[22] Sad to say, the essence of Marx's value-theory, as an analysis of the capitalist exploitation of surplus-*labour* of wage-labourers, seems abandoned by Okishio in this context, for his revised fundamental Marxian theorem defines exploitation just in terms of physical quantities of surplus products, not referring to the quantities of labour-substance embodied in them, as even Steedman would consent.

Armstrong, Glyn and Harrison also agree that 'values cannot be attributed to individual commodities' in the case of joint products.[23] However, they attempt to define the value of labour-power as the total labour embodied in a group of production processes which are necessary to produce at least the wage bundle with the smallest possible extra joint products. The rate of exploitation is present in labour-value terms on the basis of this definition. As they admit, 'the method is not perfect'.[24] It tends systematically to underestimate the rate of exploitation, and cannot be very accurate. The more joint production is interlinked, the more their definition of the rate of exploitation will become meaningless.

Himmelweit and Mohun argue from a different angle from Rubinite view. According to them, as a Sraffian Steedman is not concerned with the social logic of commensuration of different sorts of useful concrete labour into abstract labour *through* the exchange of commodities. Consequently he cannot understand the logic of a second commensuration of labour-time in capitalism *through* the competitive equalisation of the rate of profit. The anomalies that cause negative surplus-value with a positive profit 'arise from the contradiction between the fundamental concept of socially necessary labour-time and the development of its full consequences in capitalist competition'.[25] Himmelweit and Mohun attempt to counter Steedman by emphasising the development of the value-concept in Marx from commodity values into prices of production. In their treatment, however, it is unclear why and how the anomalies concerning the joint-production problem arise from the contradiction in the development of the value-concept. The anomalies are not solved but rather recognised as a really existing contradiction in a capitalist commodity economy. Basically the first 'commensuration' in Himmelweit and Mohun entails, in my opinion, a misunderstanding: that abstract labour, unlike concrete labour, cannot exist without the exchange of commodities.[26] It is also basically dubious whether the logical development from values to prices of production in itself can establish the contradiction in a capitalist economy, in contrast with the logical analysis of crisis.

In sum, in so far as the anti-critiques maintain merely a technical approach regarding values as determinable only by physical data of production, they cannot satisfactorily overcome the difficulties with joint production emphasised by Steedman. Himmelweit and Mohun's attention to the role of market was not consistently theorised in combination with such an approach to solve the problem.

**An Alternative Solution**

In my view what is missing in this recent controversy is a correct understanding of Marx's concept of forms and substance of value. A fundamental defect of the classical school was that it did not analyse the development of the forms of values and concentrated on the quantitative analyses of values. The presentation of the joint-production problem by Steedman, a neo-Ricardian and the succeeding controversy have not been immune from this defect. As we have seen in the previous chapters, K. Uno has emphasised precisely the significance of Marx's theory of the forms of values and distilled it as a basic theory of circulation.[27] He has also clarified the labour process and the dual character of labour as the common economic *norm* or *rule* for any forms of society. Then he attempted to show the logical necessity of the *law* of value as the law of motion of the capitalist production where the common economic rule in the social labour process must be effected completely through value-forms. From such a point of view the commodity market composed of forms of values should not be neglected, but must be treated as an integral part of the working of the law of value. Extending such a view, we can offer an alternative solution to the joint-production problem, as follows:

Steedman deduced negative values and negative surplus-value from an assumption that there were as many different techniques of production as there were different joint products. This assumption was obviously arbitrary. Even when there actually are different techniques of production, one of them must be chosen as representative for the standard of social allocation of labour. Let us come back to Steedman's numerical example. If we calculate the net products of a unit of labour in the process I and II, we get (A 1, B 1) for I and (A 3, B 2) for II. As far as circumstances permit, the more effective process II must increasingly be selected as a common rule of economic life. However, if process II remains in only limited use for a time, while process I is an overwhelmingly dominant condition of production, then the process I must be regarded as the standard condition of production of A and B in the social allocation of labour. In a commodity economy, as long as the dominant condition of supply to meet the fluctuations of demand in the market is process I, the market values of the market prices of production of A and B must be regulated by this technical process according to the theory of market prices of production as I shall discuss later in section 7.2 of the next chapter more generally.[28]

Let us suppose then, that process I is the current representative condition of production. Since the net products (A 1, B 1) are obtained by a unit of labour in this process, the amounts of embodied labour in a unit of A and B together must clearly be $\ell_1 + \ell_2 = 1$. Each of $\ell_1$ and $\ell_2$ can be between zero and one within the constraint of this equation. There is no common technical rule in various social formations to determine the ratio $\ell_1 / \ell_2 = \alpha$. In other words, we can recognise a basic freedom or elasticity in the apportionment of labour-substance between the joint products, just like the elasticity in the disposal of social surplus-labour. For instance, in a communal planned economy without market prices, the ratio $\alpha = \ell_1 / \ell_2$ can be lowered when a consensus is made to foster the direct or indirect consumption of A in comparison with B, under a certain social ordering of needs in relation to given technical production processes. The ratio can be adjusted to an appropriate level, by observing the reactions in consumption and production caused by its alteration.

Generally speaking, so far as we can with actual appropriateness assume that a representative condition of production is determinable for the time being in each industry, and that the same product is not produced in different industries, the amount of labour-substance allotted to each unit of joint products can be determined on the basis of social physical conditions of production when the ratios of allotment, such as $\alpha$, are somehow decided. Moreover, we can use the ratios such as $\alpha$ theoretically to reduce a joint-production industry to separate single production industries with the same technical composition and with sizes differing according to those ratios. These ratios by which the labour-substance is allotted between or among jointly produced use-values are not determined merely by the physical system of production. Neither are they deduced from individual subjective utility functions. As a common economic rule they are determined in conjunction with both the technical system of production and the system of social needs, always more of less elastically or freely, including social and political decisions in the case of a socialist economy.

In the basic theory of a capitalist economy these ratios by which to allot labour-substance in joint products are determined anarchically through the form of the measure of commodity values, by means of a function of money. As we have discussed in Section 4.1 of Chapter 4 of this volume, the repetitive purchasing of commodities by means of money compels the owners of commodity products to revise their arbitrary prices and reveal the gravitational centre of prices as the form of commodity values. This function of money, to measure the form of commodity values, implies a market mechanism adjusting labour-allocation among industries to meet a social system of material needs. This simultaneously clarifies the dominant or representative technical condition of supply in each industry. Such a function of money, to measure values in a market, also serves as a mechanism to determine the ratios by which to allot labour-substance between or among the jointly produced commodities, according to the ratios of their equilibrium price-levels. In this very limited context we see certain relevancy of Rubin's type of value-theory which defines abstract labour always through the price-form of value, as we have suggested in Section 5.2 of Chapter 5.

Our position here does not at all mean that the substance of value in commodity products can be created or increased by their circulation or by degrees of demand. For instance, the substance of value of jointly produced commodities A and B in the above case must each be between zero and one, and their total must be one. These conditions substantially constrain the formation of their equilibrium prices in a market. These prices, and therefore their ratio as well, are certainly further conditioned by the prices of production of their substitutes, if available from different industries. While Steedman's numerical example above is simple, in a more general case the joint products A and B are interrelated with other industries in the process of reproduction. The total labour-substance of value ($\ell_1 + \ell_2$) in A and B may be somewhat altered depending on their ratio $\alpha$, in so far as α can affect the amounts of embodied labour of other products which are again utilised directly or indirectly for reproducing A and B. Suppose for instance that B is just consumed as a 'non-basic' product in Sraffa's terms, whereas A is used directly or indirectly in the reproduction process of the means of production for A and B. Then, a decline in α would more or less reduce the total labour-substance ($\ell_1 + \ell_2$). Therefore, strictly speaking, the ratios for allotting the labour-substance among joint products may affect the total amounts of embodied labour as a result of changes in the estimated amount of dead labour in the means of production. This effect should not be interpreted as a fundamental difficulty of the labour theory of value. In my view the effect implies that the social estimation of embodied labour-time being transferred from the means of production is to be altered according to a change in the social conditions of reproduction caused by an alteration of α, just as in the case where re-estimation of embodied past labour-time is required by the alteration of technical conditions of production.

In any case the amounts of embodied labour in the necessary means of subsistence for wage-labourers and in the social surplus products, and hence the rate of surplus-value, are thus always determinable positively even when some commodities are jointly produced. This holds so long as the ratios by which to allot labour quantities between or among joint products are determined through the function of money in measuring commodity values in a market. This solution of the joint-production problem concerning the rate of exploitation may be meaningless in an extreme case, where a society involves only one industry jointly producing, for instance, commodities A and B. Though the case is conceivable when we follow such a model as Ricardo's corn-rate theory of profit, it is too simplistic to be relevant to the determination of the value substance of joint products. If we exclude the case of fixed capital, in spite of Steedman's claim (since the residual fixed capital is not really jointly produced in the process of its utilisation, and so its value substance should be treated differently), then joint production occupies not all but a part of many industries, and is far from dominant in a society. Our solution of the values of joint products and the related rate of exploitation can thus be relevant on the basis of a more realistic social position of joint-production industries.

In sum, the joint-production problem presented by Steedman to show the anomalies of Marx's theory of value, reveals rather the narrow limitations of the neo-Ricardians' one-sidedly abstract, technological approach to the theory of value. In order to overcome such limitations, together with some of those confusions among Marxians caused by the problem, a correct understanding of Marx's unique theory of the forms and the substance of value is quite essential. From this view the joint-production problem must be solved by clarifying the historically specific forms and mechanisms of the capitalist economy (including the role of market), which fix the allocation of labour-substance among the joint products (even though this allocation is technically indeterminate). This must be done by considering what the problem means in relation to the trans-historical common social economic rule, as we have seen. In my opinion, this solution will not only clear up the issues of the joint-production problem, but can also positively show, in this special case, how capitalism treats social labour anarchically and unconsciously in a historically specific manner.

## 6.3 THE REPRODUCTION SCHEMES AND THE LAW OF VALUE

### Marx's Reproduction Schemes

Marx's reproduction schemes represent the basic material conditions for the reproduction-process of a capitalist economy. The schemes are constructed in equilibrium conditions in value terms. The conditions shown in the schemes cannot be statically maintained. However, so far as capitalism does exist as a social formation it must satisfy the conditions more or less through anarchical fluctuations and disturbances. Actually, capital can produce in principle all the socially necessary products to maintain a complete social reproduction, on condition that the commodity labour-power is sufficiently obtainable in the market. The anarchical fluctuation of prices in the market does not necessarily bring about one-sidedly destructive effects upon capitalist reproduction. Usually it rather serves as a signal for capital to readjust its social content of production, redirecting labour-power and the means of production (living and dead labour) to various branches of production, so as to meet the social demand for the products.

The social demand itself is fundamentally formed in the reproduction-process of the value-relations of capital on the basis of embodied labour-time in the commodity products. The working of the law of value depends upon the feasibility of the readjustment of the social relation between supply and demand for the products in the reproduction-process of capital. In particular the means of production and the means of consumption which are basically necessary to maintain the social metabolism must be reproduced in the two major departments of production, mutually supplying what the other demands. The economic norm common to all societies requires the maintenance of the reproduction of the means of production and the means of consumption in accord with the labour-time technically necessary for their reproduction. A capitalist commodity-economy must satisfy this norm, through the price-form, as the substantial content of the law of value. The absolute foundation of the law of value thus rests upon the social necessity of maintaining reproduction of the means of production and those of consumption according to the necessary labour-time under the price-form.

Marx elucidated these social relations of capitalist reproduction of commodity products in his reproduction schemes with simple numerical examples. The schemes were formulated by developing F. Quesnay's *Tableau Économique*,[29] and theoretically anticipated later input–output analyses of W. Leontief's type. Unlike Quesnay and Leontief however, Marx sees in the schemes not merely the material conditions of reproduction, but also the necessary social relations of labour-time embodied in the products under price-form as the social content of the law of value in a capitalist economy. The schemes show how the material conditions necessary to maintain the reproduction of the means of production and consumption are to be prepared in the aggregate annual commodity product of capital, and how this mass of products are to be exchanged through value-relations so as to enable the production process of capital in the following year. The basic point of view of the schemes is thus in the circuit of commodity capital, $C' - M - C \ldots P \ldots C'$.

The total social production process is divided into two great departments: Department I produces means of production, and department II produces means of consumption. Marx first assumes simple reproduction, where surplus-value ($s$) is all consumed by capitalists, and as a resultant reproduction simply of the same scale is repeated. The social relations which are exhibited in simple reproduction serve as the basis of further analyses of expanded reproduction. In Marx's numerical examples of simple reproduction in ch. 20 of the second volume of *Capital*, 'the figures may be in millions of marks, francs or pounds sterling' (II, p. 473), so let them be in millions of pounds here.

For instance, the social total annual commodity products are 9000, of which 6000 are the means of production produced in the department I and 3000 are the means of consumption produced in department II. The composition of capital between constant capital ($c$) and variable capital ($v$) is assumed to be 4:1 in both departments, and the rate of surplus-value ($s' = s/v$) is assumed equally 100 per cent. It is also assumed that the turnover of capital is once a year, and the particular turnover of fixed capital over years is abstracted for the moment. Then, the value-relations of commodity products from both departments for the process of simple reproduction must be such as follows:

$$\text{I} \quad 6000 = 4000c + 1000v + 1000s$$
$$\text{II} \quad 3000 = 2000c + 500v + 500s$$

In 6000 commodity products of the department I, 4000$c$ are to be used within the same department in order to replenish the means of production consumed, through transactions among capitalists in the department. Of the 3000 commodity products of the department II, 500$v$ are to be consumed by workers, and 500$s$ are by capitalists in the same department. The remaining 2000 (1000$v$ + 1000$s$) in I are to be consumed by workers and capitalists in I as the value composition, but are produced in the form of means of production. Whereas, 2000$c$ in II are to be used to replenish the means of production as the value composition, but are produced in the form of means of consumption. Therefore, these portions, (1000$v$ + 1000$s$) and 2000$c$, must be exchanged between the departments through transactions among capitalists and workers. Generally the basic condition of simple reproduction is condensed to I $(v + s)$ = II$c$ as Marx summarizes (II, p. 478), since the products of I in the form of means of production must be just equal to the means of production consumed in both departments, i.e. I $(c + v + s)$ = I$c$ + II$c$, or alternatively since the products of II in the form of means of consumption must be just equal to $v + s$ in both departments, i.e. II $(c + v + s)$ = I $(v + s)$ + II $(v + s)$. All the transactions within and between both departments are performed through expenditure of money posessed by capitalists in order to buy labour-power or means of production and consumption. Money functions here as the means of circulation, and goes back to capitalists, the points of departure, partly via expenditure of wages by workers, so as to be used similarly in the next year.[30] It is obvious that capital in both departments with replenished material compositions, I (4000$v$ + 1000$v$) and II (2000$c$ + 500$v$) in the above example, can reproduce the same amount of total commodity products with the value of 9000 again at the end of the next year.

Usually capitalists do not consume all the surplus-value. As the personification of self-expanding capital, they have to attempt to accumulate a portion of surplus-value to extend reproduction as much as possible. An additional mass of labour-power necessary for capital to expand reproduction is assumed here to be obtainable. The value relations in commodity products of both departments I and II can be illustrated as follows, according to Marx's example in ch. 21 of the second volume of *Capital*, to suit reproduction on expanded scale.

$$\left.\begin{array}{ll} \text{I} & 6000 = 4000c + 1000v + 1000s \\ \text{II} & 2250 = 1500c + 375v + 375s \end{array}\right\} \text{Total} = 8250$$

Suppose that half of the surplus-value of I is accumulated, and in the same composition, added to the original capital to expand the scale of production in the next year. In accord with such accumulation (or addition of $400c + 100v$) in I, there must be accumulation also in II. The total amount of consumption in I for the next year will not be $2000 = 1000v + 1000s$, but $1600 = 1000v + 100s(v) + 500s(k)$, where $s(v)$ and $s(k)$ are respectively the portions of surplus-value to be used as additional variable capital and the consumption of capitalists. So as to balance with this amount 1600 of demand for the means of consumption from I, constant capital of II must be increased to 1600 from $1500c$, by adding $100s(c)$ from surplus-value. Corresponding to this increment of II$c$, $25s(v)$ must be added to II$v$ from II$s$. Then, the values of commodity products of both departments are now redivided as follows, preparing for expanded reproduction in the next year.

$$\begin{array}{ll} \text{I} & 6000 = 4000c + 400s(c) + 1000v + 100s(v) + 500s(k) \\ \text{II} & 2250 = 1500c + 100s(c) + 375v \ + 25s(v) \ \ + 250s(k) \end{array}$$

In this scheme $4000c + 400s(c)$ are used within I to replenish and expand its own constant capital through transactions among capitalists, and $375v + 25s(v) + 250s(k)$ are consumed within II through transactions among capitalists and workers in it. The remaining portions, I $1000v + 100s(v) + 500s(k) = 1600$ and II $1500c + 100s(c) = 1600$, are exchanged between the departments, just like I $(v + s) =$ II$c$ in the case of simple reproduction. As a result, production capital for the second year will become I $4400c + 1100v$, and II $1600c + 400v$.

They will bring about at the end of the second year the commodity products of I 6600 and II 2400, or 9000 in total, which are beyond 8250, the value of commodity products of the first year, by realising reproduction on expanded scale.

Expanded reproduction in any form of society must necessarily be performed through expansion of the production of means of production. This general norm of economy appears in the value-relations of capital, as a condition I $(v + s) > \text{II}c$, instead of the condition I $(v + s) = \text{II}c$ for simple reproduction. The basic condition for expanded reproduction is thus I $(v + s) > \text{II}c$ (II, p. 590). It is because the products of I in the form of means of production must be greater than the means of production consumed in both departments, i.e. I $(c + v + s) > \text{I}c + \text{II}c$, or alternatively the products in II in the form of consumption goods must be smaller than the social total of variable capital and surplus-value, i.e. II $(c + v + s) <$ I $(v + s) +$ II $(v + s)$. More precisely the basic condition for a balanced expanded reproduction can be summarised into an equation $\text{I}v + s(v) + s(k) = \text{II}c + s(c)$, as shown in the numerical example above.

**The Form and Substance of Value in the Reproduction Schemes**

Marx's reproduction schemes with the further detailed examination of the circulation of money, or the social relation of depreciation and replacement of fixed capital, etc., have often been utilised as a theoretical basis of Marxian crisis theories. However, the specific character of the reproduction-process of the capitalist mode of production is not wholly presented in the reproduction schemes. Especially the capitalist mechanism of reproducing the commodity labour-power is not directly included in the schemes. It is assumed there that the necessary number of workers are obtainable by capital in the market in exchange for the necessary means of livelihood. If we compare the theory of capital accumulation in the first volume of *Capital* and the theory of reproduction in the second, it is clearly the former which deals with the specific character of the capitalist process of reproduction with its inner difficulty of securing the necessary supply of the commodity labour-power. The equilibrium conditions in the reproduction schemes may be incessantly broken as a result of the anarchical motion of capitals, but the disequilibria may also be constantly readjusted through the working of the law of value in the process of reproduction and the accumulation of capital, in so far as the commodity labour-power is assumed to be obtainable in exchange for the necessary means of consumption. Therefore the reproduction schemes can only show that economic crisis is *possible* for a capitalist society.

The function of the reproduction schemes is to show that capitalist production can continuously exist, by satisfying the basic material conditions of reproduction common to all societies, rather than revealling the inner contradictions of capitalism.[31] The schemes show in particular that labour-time, which serves as the standard for the distribution of yearly products and labour-power consciously under socialism, appears as the substance of value of commodities in capitalism with its social necessity of material reproduction. The law of value is founded in this regard on the general economic norms of material reproduction which are to be maintained by social disposition of past and current labour-time. Prices as the form of value must actually carry through this social foundation of the law of value in a capitalist market.

By following Marx's definition of the value-concept at the beginning of *Capital*. Prices in the reproduction schemes are generally assumed to be directly proportional to the quantities of labour-time embodied in commodity products. As a result, the equilibrium conditions in the schemes are theoretically understood to signify the equal exchange of labour-time. The general economic norms, which must be realised consciously in socialism instead of through the anarchical market mechanisms in capitalism, might be understood to entail the social necessity of the equal exchange of labour-time. This would be a source of theoretical confusion in perceiving both the social contents of the necessity of the law of value and the way of applying Marxian value-theory to the process of socialist economic construction. The confusion is anyway related to the neglect of the room for elasticity in the social relations of the exchange of labour-time embodied in products. Let us investigate, therefore, whether and how far the economic conditions summarised in the reproduction schemes may entail the unequal exchange of labour-time.

When simple reproduction is assumed, all the surplus products are to be consumed, and exactly the same scale of reproduction of both departments I and II must be maintained yearly with the same technical composition. It is obvious that under such conditions the total means of production yearly consumed in both departments must be replenished by the same quantities of yearly products of the department I, the same in terms of labour-time embodied as well as physical quantities. This must be true, whether or not the economy is under a commodity order or not. Therefore, if we designate the quantities of labour-time in yearly consumed means of production as $c_i$, labour-time in the necessary means of consumption or the necessary labour-time as $v_i$, and surplus labour-time as $s_i$, and their total as $a_i$ (a unit may be, say, a billion hours. $i$=1, 2), the social conditions must be as follows:

$$a_1 = c_1 + v_1 + s_1 = c_1 + c_2 \tag{6.12}$$

$$v_1 + s_1 = c_2 \tag{6.13}$$

In spite of conventional perceptions, the relation expressed in equation (6.13) does not socially require an equal exchange of labour-time in the form of means of production and that of consumption between the two major departments. As we have seen in Chapter 5, there must be fundamental elasticity or freedom as to the disposal of surplus-labour in general economic norms. In this regard the basic conditions for simple reproduction are not destroyed by the unequal exchange of labour-time within certain limits. While the means of production embodying $v_1 + s_1 = c_2$ billion labour hours necessary to maintain the reproduction of department II are transferred from department I to II, the means of consumption more than the quantity embodying $c_2 = v_1 + s_1$ may be transferred interchangeably from the deparment II to I without reducing the scale of reproduction in department II, only by increasing consumption of surplus-products in the department I, so far as the amount transferred from department II remains within the upper limit of $c_2 + s_2$ billion hours. Conversely, the quantity of the means of consumption transferred from department II, in exchange for the means of production with $c_2 = v_1 + s_1$ billion hours of labour, can be less than the quantity embodying $c_2$ million hours of labour, so much increasing the consumption of surplus products in department II and decreasing it in department I. This transaction would not damage the material conditions of simple reproduction, in so far as the transfer from the department II is above the minimum quantity required to replenish the necessary means of consumption embodying $v_1$ billion hours of labour-time. Within these limits in either direction consumer goods to the value $s_1 + s_2$ may be distributed variously without threatening the basic conditions for simple reproduction.

Let us now suppose that social reproduction is embraced totally by capital, and therefore that the allocation of labour necessary to maintain reproduction must be carried out through the form of value or the price-form. The products of department I are further assumed to be priced in pounds sterling, nominally $x$ times the labour-substance (in billions of hours) embodied, whereas the products of the department II are also priced in pounds at $y$ times the labour-substance. Accordingly capitalists in department I as a whole acquire $a_1x$ billion pounds as the form of value of their yearly products, and capitalists in department II acquire $a_2y$ billion pounds from their yearly products. From these amounts of total sales $c_1x$ billion pounds must be expended in order to replenish the means of production used up, and $v_1y$ pounds must be expended as the price of labour-power. Therefore the amount of surplus-value obtained by capitalists of department I in the money-form must be $a_1x - (c_1x + v_1y)$ billion pounds. The total of this amount plus $v_1y$ billion pounds received by workers in department I is assigned to purchase the means of consumption produced in department II in a model of simple reproduction. The total amount must then be as follows:

$$a_1x - (c_1x + v_1y) + v_1y = (a_1 - c_1)x = (v_1 + s_1)x \qquad (6.14)$$

On the other hand, department II must spend $c_2x$ billion pounds for the purchase of the products of department I, in order to replenish the means of production used up. Therefore, purchase and sale mutually performed between the departments can be balanced when the following equation holds:

$$(v_1 + s_1)x = c_2x \qquad (6.15)$$

This equation holds, being indifferent to the magnitude of $x$ or $y$, in so far as the previous equation, (6.13), is effectual. Department II can replenish the consumed means of production of $c_2$ billion hours by the same quantities of newly produced means of production with $(v_1 + s_1)$ billion hours, through the transaction in price terms expressed in (6.15). Thus, equation (6.13) or $v_1 + s_1 = c_2$ must hold as the essential condition for the balance between social demand and supply of the products in the case of simple reproduction, even when the prices of the products of the both departments are not proportional to their labour-substance, and resultantly $x/y = k$ is not 1.

The key relation expressed in equation (6.13) $v_1 + s_1 = c_2$, however, does not necessitate the equal exchange of labour through prices between the departments. Department II must always purchase the means of production which embodies $(c_2 = v_1 + s_1)$ billion hours of labour-substance from the department I, by expending $c_2x$ billion pounds. Then, department I throws back the same amount of money $(v_1 + s_1)x$ billion pounds to department II in order to purchase the means of consumption for the price of labour-power and for capitalists' expenditure of surplus-value. Since the labour-substance contained in the products of department II is $1/y$ of their prices, the labour-substance obtained by department I through these transactions must be $(v_1 + s_1)x/y$ billion hours. This does not generally coincide with $(c_2 = v_1 + s_1)$ billion hours, except in the case of $x/y = 1$. The difference is to be written as follows:

$$(v_1 + s_1)x/y - (v_1 + s_1) = (v_1 + s_1)(k - 1) \tag{6.16}$$

As the workers in department I must theoretically get the necessary labour-time, $v_1$ billion hours in the form of the means of livelihood, through $v_1y$ billion pounds of wages regardless of the magnitude of $k$, formula (6.16) exhibits the amount of surplus-labour-time which capitalists in department I additionally obtains (in the case where $k > 1$), or conversely transfer to department II (in the case where $k < 1$), through price-relations. The upper limit in the former case is given by $s_2$, and that in the latter case is given by $s_1$. Accordingly the magnitude of $k$ must be within the following range, in so far as the social condition of simple reproduction is to be maintained:

$$-s_1 < (v_1 + s_1)(k - 1) < s_2$$

$$\therefore v_1/(v_1 + s_1) < k < 1 + s_2/(v_1 + s_1) \tag{6.17}$$

Needless to say, in a special case where $k = 1$ within this range, the corresponding relation of labour quantities expressed in the formula (6.13) $v_1 + s_1 = c_2$ must simultaneously entail the equal *exchange* of labour through prices between the departments without causing any additional transfer of surplus-labour across the departments. (The following paragraphs until the inequality (6.22) can be skipped by general readers.)

When expanded reproduction is to take place, surplus-labour-time embodied in the products of each department $s_i$ must be divided into $s_{i(c)} + s_{i(v)} + s_{i(k)}$. The first two items $s_{i(c)} + s_{i(v)}$ are for the additional means of production and necessary means of livelihood to be secured for the expanded scale of reproduction. The products of department I in this case must both replenish the consumed means of production and provide the additional means of production for both departments. Therefore, the following relation must exist in terms of labour-time:

$$a_1 = c_1 + v_1 + s_{1(c)} + s_{1(v)} + s_{1(k)}$$

$$a_1 = c_1 + s_{1(c)} + c_2 + s_{2(c)}$$

$$v_1 + s_{1(v)} + s_{1(k)} = c_2 + s_{2(c)} \qquad (6.18)$$

It is obvious that the relation $v_1 + s_1 > c_2$ must exist here as a basic condition for expanded reproduction. Let us suppose here, as in the previous case of simple reproduction, that the products of departments I and II are given prices in pounds respectively $x$ times and $y$ times labour substance. The amount of money to be expended by department I for the purchase of commodities from department II is composed of both wages to be paid in the expanded reproduction, i.e. $v_1y + s_{1(v)}y$, and the portion for capitalist consumption as a residue of the total price of the products after deducing the expenditures necessary for expanded reproduction, i.e. $a_1x - (c_1x + v_1y + s_{1(c)}x + s_{1(v)}y)$. The amount must thus be as follows:

$$a_1x - (c_1x + v_1y + s_{1(c)}x + s_{1(v)}y) + v_1y + s_{1(v)}y = (a_1 - c_1 - s_{1(c)})x = (v_1 + s_{1(v)} + s_{1(k)})x \qquad (6.19)$$

Whereas department II has to purchase $(c_2 + s_{2(c)})x$ billion pounds of means of production in order replenish and expand them. Accordingly the following equation must hold, so that sales and purchases of both departments mutually balance:

$$(v_1 + s_{1(v)} + s_{1(k)})x = (c_2 + s_{2(c)})x \qquad (6.20)$$

This equation (6.20) holds regardless of $x$, $y$ or $k = x/y$, so far as equation (6.18) above is effective. Therefore, the existence of such interdepartmental relations of labour-substance embodied in the products is the essential condition for the expanded process of production even when the price-form is not directly proportional to the labour-substance. The labour-substance as exhibited in equation (6.18) must be transferred from department I to II, in the form of means of production through their price in pounds being $x$ times their labour-substance. When the same amount of money is expended by the capitalists and workers in department I for the purchase of their means of consumption from department II, the labour-substance must be obtained by $1/y$ of their price. The difference between what is transferred from department I to II and what is conversely transferred from II to I must be as follows:

$$(v_1+s_{1(v)}+s_{1(k)})x/y-(v_1+s_{1(v)}+s_{1(k)})=(v_1+s_{1(v)}+s_{1(k)})(k-1) \quad (6.21)$$

Apparently the quantity of surplus-labour defined in (6.21) is transferred from department II to I when $k$ is greater than 1, whereas equal exchange of labour is effected when $k$ is 1, and the quantity of surplus-labour in (6.21) is transferred conversely from I to II when $k$ is smaller than 1. Therefore the maximum possible range of $k$ must be within in an inequality as follows:

$$1-s_1/(v_1+s_{1(v)}+s_{1(k)})<k<1+s_2/(v_1+s_{1(v)}+s_{1(k)}) \quad (6.22)$$

Simple numerical examples will clarify our investigations above. Since Marx assumed labour-substance in direct proportion to prices in the reproduction schemes, let us redefine Marx's numerical example for simple reproduction as follows are in terms of billions of labour-time, not directly in pounds:

$$\begin{array}{ll} \text{I} & 6000 = 4000c_1 + \underline{1000v_1 + 1000s_1} \\ \text{II} & 3000 = \underline{2000c_2} + 500v_2 + 500s_2 \end{array}$$

It is clear that the quantitative relation formulated in (6.13) above holds here between the underlined numbers in both departments. If the inequality (6.17) is applied here, the possible range of $k$ is defined as $0.5 < k < 1.25$. Suppose that $k = 1.1$, $x = 0.11$ and $y = 0.1$, then the prices of the total products, their costs and profits ($p_i$) must be as follows in billion pounds:

$$\begin{array}{ll} \text{I} & 660 = 440c_1x + 100v_1y + 120p_1 \\ \text{II} & 300 = 220c_1x + 50v_2y + 30p_2 \end{array}$$

From 300 billion pounds obtained by capitalists in department II, 220 billion pounds is to be expended in order to purchase the means of production embodying 2000 billion hours of labour in department I, and 50 billion pounds must be paid to the workers in the same department II so as to enable them to purchase the necessary means of livelihood with 500 billion hours of labour-substance. By these transactions, capitalists in the department II are able to repeat exactly the same scale of production as in the previous year. Similarly capitalists in the department I can maintain the same scale of production as in the previous year, by mutually purchasing the means of production with 4000 billion hours of labour-substance by 440 billion pounds, and also by paying 100 billion pounds to workers for them to reobtain the necessary means of livelihood with 1000 billion hours of labour-time. After deducing these items of costs necessary to maintain reproduction, capitalists in department I get 120 billion pounds, and those in department II 30 billion pounds of profit as the money-form of surplus-value from what they obtain as the total price of their products. As a result capitalists in I get surplus-products to consume with 1200 billion hours of labour-time, or 200 billion hours more than the surplus labour-time embodied in their commodity products, and capitalists in II conversely get 200 billion hours less than the surplus-labour-time embodied in their commodity products. Such redistribution of surplus-labour-time between the departments through the price-form does not hamper the maintenance of social reproduction, since the surplus-products in this case totally drop out of reproduction simply to be consumed by capitalists.

However, if the turnover of capital is assumed to be equally once a year, being abstracted also from the special turnover of fixed capital, then the rate of profit $p_i' = p_i/(c_i x + v_i y)$ must become uneven in the numerical example above; i.e. 22.2 per cent in the department I, and 11.1 per cent in II. Under a socialist planned economy, the room for coping with the result of surplus-labour would be much more flexible and free. But in a capitalist economy, distribution of surplus-products must accord with the tendential motion of capitals to equalise the rate of profit across departments and industries through their competition. In the case above, capital tends to move from department II to I to acquire higher rate of profit, causing changes in prices in the market, and tending to equalise the rate of profit around the gravitational centre of 20 per cent, making the rate of comparative prices of the products of both departments $k = x/y$ fluctuate tendentially around 1. The reason why the standard prices equalising the rate of profit become such as to realise the equal exchange of labour in their substance is in this case clearly due to the assumption of equal organic compositions of capital $(v_i/c_i)$, in concrete terms equally $\frac{1}{4}$, across the departments. As we have discussed, we have to assume either that there is no surplus-labour, or that the compositions and the turnover periods of capitals are identical as in this case, in order to prove the social necessity of equal exchange of labour as the substantial content of the law of value on the basis of the logic in the process of capitalist production.

Needless to say, the compositions of capital (and the turnover periods of capital, having similar effects on the efficiency of production of surplus-value by capital as the compositions of capital) can not actually be identical across the departments. Marx also presents numerical examples of reproduction schemes with uneven compositions of capital. For instance, his 'initial schema for reproduction on expanded scale' is shown in the following figures:

$$\begin{aligned} &\text{I} \quad 4000c + 1000v + 1000s = 5000 \\ &\text{II} \quad 1500c + 750v + 750s = 3000 \end{aligned}$$

In this example, where the composition of capital in II ($v_2/c_2 = \frac{1}{2}$) is twice of that in I ($v_1/c_1 = \frac{1}{4}$), the rates of profit would be $p_i' = 20$ per cent, $p_2' = 33.3$ per cent, and clearly different under the prices directly proportional to the labour-substance, or the prices which cause an equal exchange of labour. Let us suppose that the numbers in this scheme are in terms of billions of labour-time, and also that the commodity products of departments I and II are respectively given prices in pounds nominally $x$ times and $y$ times of the labour-substance embodied under an equalised rate of profit. Then there must simultaneously be the following equations;

$$\begin{aligned} (4000x + 1000y)\,(1 + p') &= 6000x \\ (1500x + 750y)\,(1 + p') &= 3000y \end{aligned}$$

By solving these simultaneous equations only for a positive range of answers, we get $p' = 22.8$ per cent, and $k = x/y = 1.1287$. Thus, if $y = 0.1$, $x$ must be 0.11287. Unequal exchange of labour transferring some portion of surplus-labour from department II to I must take place. According to Marx's assumption that a half of $s_1$ in department I is accumulated and added to initial capital in the same composition of capital, the surplus-value of each department must be divided as follows to make possible the balanced reproduction on an expanded scale in the next year:

$$\begin{aligned} &\text{I} \quad 6000a_1 = 4000c_1 + 1000v_1 + 400s_{1(c)} + 100s_{1(v)} + 500s_{1(k)} \\ &\text{II} \quad 3000a_2 = 1500c_2 + 750v_2 + 100s_{2(c)} + 50s_{2(v)} + 600s_{2(k)} \end{aligned}$$

These items of labour-substance would be capitalistically transacted through such prices as follows to suit out calculations above:

$$\text{I}\quad 677.22a_1x = 451.48c_1x + 100v_1y + 45.15s_{1(c)}x + 10s_{1(v)}y + 70.59p_{1(k)}$$
$$\text{II}\quad 300a_2y = 169.3c_2x + 75v_2y + 11.29s_{2(c)}x + 5s_{2(v)}y + 39.41p_{2(k)}$$

In this case the price relations entail an unequal exchange of labour transferring 205.9 billion hours of surplus-labour from department II to I. But under these prices actual demand and supply in both departments are balanced, the means of production and consumption necessary for the expanded reproduction of both departments are mutually secured and the rates of profit are equalised.

### The Social Foundation of the Law of Value

Let us briefly summarise what we have found in our analyses of the reproduction schemes from the view of the law of value. The reproduction schemes clarify basic social norms of labour-allocation maintaining social material reproduction. In particular there must be such social relations in labour-time embodied in the products of department I and II as capitalistically expressed in $v_1 + s_1 = c_2$ for simple reproduction, and $v_1 + s_1 > c_2$, or $v_i + s_{1(v)} + s_{1(k)} = c_2 + s_{2(c)}$ for expanded reproduction, so long as technical conditions are not altered. These relations, in the quantities of labour embodied in the social annual products, must hold in their nature as an aspect of the general economic norms common to all societies, and are basically independent of value-relations in a commodity economy. The absolute basis of the law of value in a capitalist economy is shown in the social necessity of achieving such general economic norms of labour-allocation entirely through the value-relations of commodities. Generally speaking, the law of value is conceivable from three aspects, as we have suggested in the previous Chapter 5, Section 5.2. The basic foundation of the law is the determination of the substance of values by the labour-time necessary to produce commodities. The regulation of the exchange of commodities by values, together with the adjustment of the labour-allocation, are to be regarded as effects of the working of the law. These three aspects, namely the determination of values by labour, regulation of exchange, and adjustment of labour-allocation are simply transparent in models either excluding surplus-labour or with an equal composition of capital and turnover period across industries. In such models standard prices regulating commodity exchanges in a capitalist economy become directly proportional to the labour-substance of commodity products, and the labour-allocation necessary to satisfy social needs, given existing technological conditions of production, is achieved tendentially around such standard prices so realising equal exchanges of labour. However, the capitalist process of production cannot but entail the exploitation of surplus-labour in the valorisation process, and the composition as well as turnover periods of capital cannot be guaranteed to be equalised. Thus, one aspect of the law of value which regulates commodity exchanges, must not be identified as the social necessity of realising an equal exchange of labour-substance in commodity products. The socially necessary balance of labour-time in the commodity products of both departments, expressed as $v_1 + s_1 = c_2$ for simple reproduction, and $v_1 + s_{1(v)} + s_{1(k)} = c_2 + s_{2(c)}$ for expanded production, would not necessitate prices being directly proportional to labour-substance, but can be coped with through prices which bring about unequal exchange of labour in the range permitted by the transfer of a portion of surplus-labour from one department to the other, *as we have seen*.

Nevertheless, determination of the substance of values by the labour-time necessary to reproduce commodity products cannot be negated by such a recognition of the unequal exchange of labour within the range of surplus-labour through prices, any more than by the theoretical issues of skilled labour and joint production. The regulation of exchanges of commodities by values is not actually performed by prices directly proportional to their labour-substance, but by prices having a certain relation with the labour-substance. The working of the law of value in regulating the exchange of commodities is still logically discernible in that the maximum range of unequal exchange of labour through standard prices must lie within the transfer of surplus-labour across departments or industries. In other words, standard prices as the form of value must be determined in mutual relation to enable each department or industry to replenish at least the portion of the labour-substance $c_i$ and $v_i$ embodied in the commodity products.

It is particularly noteworthy that wages as the form of value of the commodity labour-power must theoretically be at a level which lets workers purchase back the necessary means of consumption containing necessary labour-time, regardless of the possible deviation of prices of commodity products from a direct proportionality with their labour-substance. As a special 'simple' commodity not produced by capital, labour-power has a basic key position for the law of value. There must be a social necessity for the equal exchange of labour, particularly between the commodity labour-power and its equivalent necessary means of consumption, through the social process of consumption and production under capitalism. This social relation of the equal exchange of labour concerning the value of labour-power (factually having been recognised since the classical school), is an essential basis for the labour theory of value, as well as for the theory of the capitalist process of the production of surplus-value. If we shift our position to a neo-Ricardian type of theory and determine prices simply by the physical data of production, because of the possible deviation of prices of commodity products, we naturally have to lose sight of the secret of the central class relation under capitalism, the process of exploiting the surplus-labour of wage-workers.

From the view of the adjustment of labour-allocation the flexible range of unequal exchange across industries or departments is essential for the law of value to operate as a principle by which material reproduction is organised through the anarchical capitalistic market mechanism. Without such flexibility in the social relations of labour expended, the capitalistic way of distributing surplus-products and surplus-labour through the equalisation of the rate of profit across industries, with various compositions and turnover periods of capital, must turn out to be incompatible with the law of value. Competition among capitals which forms prices of production with an equal rate of profit across industries is not a deviation as it is often conceived in the conventional labour theory of value. Rather it is the concrete mechanism of the law of value to adjust the labour-allocation to suit a social system of need through the anarchical market in capitalism. Incessant misallocation of both past and present labour in anarchical capitalist production is also incessantly readjusted through competition among capitals guided by fluctuating rates of profit gravitating around the general average rate. The rationality and efficiency of capitalism in this regard is not in its ability to achieve an ideal labour-allocation statically and without failure, but in its function of incessant readjustment. The substantial content of the law of value must be compatible with such incessant fluctuations in prices and profit rates in a market, in so far as it generally contains room for the unequal exchange of labour within the range of surplus-labour.

These aspects of the law of value must be carefully taken into account in the socialist process of economic construction as we shall discuss in Chapter 10. Marx's reproduction schemes have often been used as a frame of reference for socialist planning. Since the schemes include insight into the general economic norms of human societies, they can indeed be useful for a socialist economy as well, to certain degree. For instance, the basic conditions of material reproduction, such as $v_1 + s_1 = c_2$ for simple reproduction and $v_1 + s_{1(v)} + s_{1(k)} = c_2$ $s_{2(c)}$ for expanded reproduction, must exist in terms of embodied labour in the products of departments I and II even under socialism. However, the balanced relations of the labour contents of products of both the departments under socialism does not require an equal exchange of labour, as we have seen for a capitalist economy. The mutual transfer of products across industries must realise the replenishment of the means of production and consumption for simple reproduction, as well as an additional supply of goods necessary in the case of expanded reproduction, but a society in any form need not distribute the materialised surplus-labour so as to realise an equal exchange of labour. Flexibility or the freedom of coping with surplus-labour should certainly not be abused to distort the socialist principle of equal distribution of income, or the rationally balanced growth of various industries, but must surely give a basic elasticity in many ways to the process of socialist construction. Ridding itself of the capitalistic principle of distributing surplus-labour through the competition of capitals to equalise the rate of profit, a socialist economy would basically have wider freedom to dispose of social surplus-labour. Before considering further the possible implications for socialism of the basic theory of capitalism discussed in the final part, Part IV, we have further to examine, in the following part, Part III, the full motion of capitals as a concrete mechanism distributing surplus-value among themselves, carring out the working of the law of value in their actual forms.

# Part III
# The Motion of Capitals as a Concrete Mechanism

Capitalism is established when the forms of a commodity economy comprise a social process of production. The quantitative commensurability of the forms of value in a commodity economy, which is expressed in prices, should not be identified with the more substantial commensurability of labour-time embodied in social products. Once the basic structure of a capitalist commodity economy is clarified in the light of the forms and the substance of value, then the social relation of labour-time and its adjustment in accord with social needs are clearly separable from and conceivable without the forms of values in the central areas of precapitalist social formations as well as of socialist societies. The forms of value which are specific to commodity economy originated from inter-social economic relations external to the central labour-and-production process of those societies. Capitalism is a historically unique social formation where such originally external inter-social forms of a commodity economy have been turned into the internal economic order. By comprising a social process of labour and production, the forms of value in capitalism must be related with social necessity to the social relations of dead and living labour, and must be regulated by them. Thus, the quantities of labour-time necessary to reproduce commodities are proved to be the substance of value, which regulate from behind the forms of value. At the same time the socially necessary labour-time to reproduce the necessary means of consumption of wage-workers, which is determinable by the physical data of the contents of real-wages and the technological conditions of production, defines the substance of value of the commodity labour-power. The social surplus-labour beyond it must correspondingly be turned into the social source of surplus-value for a capitalist process of production. The analysis of the social mechanism for capital to extract surplus-labour does not merely elucidate the material basis of the class-relations in capitalism, but also serves as a theoretical frame of reference for studies of all the class societies in human history, and hence serves as a theoretical foundation for socialist argument to move beyond the history of class societies.

Extraction of surplus-labour by capital is by no means a clear social relation. The forms of value, which seem to treat individuals equally as owners of commodities to be exchanged more or less according to proper values, disguise the substantial social process of the exploitation of surplus-labour under the surface of commodity circulation. Wages tend to be regarded as proper reward, full payment for labour performed by workers. Correspondingly, profit, ground-rent and interest are conceived as fair sums or prices which are determined and offered in a market for the services or the contributions of capital, land and loan capital to economic activities. This way of viewing the main categories of income prevails in daily 'common sense' as well as in conventional neo-classical economics. Such a view is not a mere deceptive ideology without any actual reality or rational function. On the contrary, the daily economic life of capitalism is founded upon such a view, with no insight into the social relations of labour-quantities. We have to recognise further that the forms of revenue from capital and land have a certain rational function in organising and maintaining the economic process of reproduction under capitalism. Of course, there are weaknesses or absences in such a conventional view. Among others, it cannot provide a consistent theory to define commensurable values for heterogeneous economic subjects such as labour, capital, land and loanable capital, beyond evaluation in a market; containing a theoretically circular definition in one way or the other. Hence it cannot explain the commensurable common source of surplus-values and incomes. A socio-historical analysis of the capitalist economy, viewing the long historical development of human societies organising the common labour-and-production process in different ways, must also be theoretically impossible from such a conventional standpoint.

Hence, the importance for political economy, as a socio-historical science, to explore the substantial social relations of the quantities of labour behind the forms of value, along with the social mechanisms of production of surplus-value, is clear. However, our studies into the basic law of motion of a capitalist economy are so far still at the half-way stage. Upon clarification of the social substance of values and surplus-value, we have further to investigate the more concrete forms and mechanisms of a capitalist economy. There are four interrelated aspects to be investigated. First, the main categories of incomes for capitalists and landowners, like profit, ground-rent, commercial profit, interest, dividends as they appear in the everyday consciousness of a capitalist economy, must be examined for their rationale in relation to the social surplus-labour, or as the concrete forms of the distribution of surplus-value. Second, corresponding to these concrete forms of distributing surplus-value, concrete forms of capitals, such as industrial capital, commercial capital, loanable capital, bank capital, joint-stock capital, as well as the social position of landowners in capitalism are to be clarified in their mutual relations. Third, the actual working of the law of value in regulating the motion of forms of value and adjusting the labour-allocation must also be examined through these concrete forms of surplus-value and capital. Fourth, although the concrete forms of surplus-value and capitals generally have a rationale in functioning positively to promote capitalist economic efficiency (as neo-classicists would tend to one-sidedly emphasise), these forms also serve as concrete mechanisms through which the actual process of accumulation of capital in the form of business cycles and periodical crises, proceed inevitably leading to the contradictory self-destruction of capital value. We must examine the basic logic of such an actual process of accumulation of capital and its theoretical implication for the working of the law of value.

Marx explored these four aspects more or less in the third volume of *Capital*. The basic theories of competition among capitals, which were put outside of the framework of 'capital in general' in the *Grundrisse*, as well as the basic theory of the economic position of landownership in a capitalist society, which was further outside of the framework of 'capital; capital in general, competition, credit, and joint-stock capital', became necessarily included in the theoretical system. However, the third volume was the most unfinished of the three volumes in *Capital*, mostly based upon Marx's manuscript written in 1863–5, earlier than his writing the first volume for publication. Much of the controversial character of that volume at least partly originates from this fact. It must spring also from the theoretical difficulties to be pursued here, in addition to some basic theoretical problems which are already raised in the previous volumes, especially as to the logical contents of the working of the law of value. On the basis of our investigations in the previous parts especially focusing upon the distinction between the forms and the substance of value, we may now be qualified to discuss more properly the forms and functions of competition among capitals, through the so-called 'transformation problem', the theory of market value or market prices of production, and theory of ground-rent in Chapter 7. Then, in Chapter 8, the forms and the role of commercial capital, the credit system and joint-stock capital will be examined as higher capitalistic organisations for the motion of capital. One central issue for the basic theory of a capitalist economy is surely the theory of capital accumulation, business cycles and crises, which will be consciously withheld until Chapter 9 below so as to be concentrated there. The chapter must treat the most concrete dynamic mechanisms of a capitalist economy in a basic theory.

# 7 Competition among Capitals

## 7.1 THE LAW OF VALUE AND PRICES OF PRODUCTION

### Marx's Theory of Prices of Production

Upon the theories of the processes of production, circulation and reproduction of capital in the first and the second volumes of *Capital*, the third volume 'The Process of Capitalist Production as a Whole' is designed 'to discover and present the concrete forms which grow out of the *process of capital's movement considered as a whole*', examining step by step the forms 'in the action of different capitals on one another, i.e. in competition' (III, p. 117). Its first two parts investigate 'the law that govern the general rate of profit and the so-called prices of production determined by it', as 'the basic law of capitalist competition' (III, pp. 127–8). The forms of distribution of surplus-value, such as commercial profit, interest and ground-rent, which are presented in the following parts, elucidate the concrete mechanisms by which the law of capitalist competition is carried out basically gravitating around the prices of production. A controversial problem is the logical consistency between the law of value and the law that governs the prices of production. Marx clearly intended to show that the forms and the mechanisms of capitalist competition are not merely consistent with, but also essential for, the social working of the law of value. For instance, reviewing his whole analyses in the very last part of *Capital*, Marx has this to say;

> '. . . the two . . . characters of product as commodity and the commodity as capitalistically produced commodity give rise to the entire determination of value and the regulation of the total production by value. In this quite specific form of value, labour is valid only as social labour; on the other hand the division of this social labour and the reciprocal complementarity or metabolism of its products, subjugation to and insertion into the social mechanism, is left to the accidental and reciprocally countervailing motives of the individual capitalist producers. Since these confront one another only as commodity owners, each trying to sell his commodity as dear as

possible (and seeming to be governed only by caprice even in the regulation of production), the inner law operates only by way of their competition, their reciprocal pressure on one another, which is how divergences are mutually counterbalanced. It is only as an inner law, a blind natural force *vis-à-vis* the individual agents, that the law of value operates here and that the social balance of production is asserted in the midst of accidental fluctuations.' (III, p. 1020).

Since the classical school regarded the capitalistic commodity economy as a natural harmonious order of things, its labour theory of value could not pay theoretical attention to the historically specific forms of value through which social labour is treated. Hence, it failed to formulate the theory of prices of production consistently on the basis of the labour theory of value. Marx overcame this failure by showing the prices of production as a basic form of competition among capitals, through which the law of value actually operates. The distinction between the forms and the substance of value is essential here, in order to see the logical consistency between the labour theory of value and the law of the equalisation of the profit rate in the form of prices of production. As we have seen, there is a technically indeterminate elasticity or freedom as to how to cope with the portion of surplus-labour embodied in products consistent with the general economic norms in societies. Through the theory of prices of production, in which a basic capitalist principle of distributing surplus-labour is presented, the whole regulation of standard prices as the form of value by the labour-substance is clarified. The actual working of the law of value is shown in the process of competition among capitals where fluctuating market prices are repeatedly guided and regulated from behind by the substance of value, being determined on the basis of the technical conditions of production and the real wages. Seemingly accidental fluctuations in prices in a market are not an external distortion for the law of value, but an indispensable mechanism to adjust the allocation of labour to meet the social system of needs for various use-values in an anarchical commodity economy. The regulation of prices from behind by the labour-substance of value cannot really be effective without having a process of labour-allocation readjustment in the anarchical market economy, where the discrepancy between demand and supply must incessantly occur.

So far as the prices of production serve as a basic form of capitalist competition in such a fluctuating market, they must appear qualitatively of the same dimension as market prices, measured in quantities of money. Corresponding to the theory of forms of value in the first two parts of the first volume of *Capital*, where the logical formation of the price-form and the formula of capital obtaining surplus-value in money terms was presented, the prices of production with their categorical elements such as cost-price and profit, can be conceived as a concrete developed form of value on the basis of capitalist production.

Marx actually begins his theory of prices of production by examining 'cost-price and profit'. He defines the cost-price as follows: the 'part of the value of the commodity, which replaces the price of the means of production consumed and the labour-power employed, simply replaces what the commodity cost the capitalist himself and is therefore the cost price of the commodity, as far as he is concerned' (III, p. 118); or, 'the cost price of the commodity is by no means simply a category that exists only in capitalist book-keeping. The independence that this portion of value acquires makes itself constantly felt in practice in the actual production of the commodity, as it must be constantly transformed back again into the form of productive capital by way of the circulation process, i.e. the cost-price of commodity must continuously buy back the elements of production consumed in its production.' (III, pp. 118–19).

It is noticeable that Marx defines here the cost-price as the part of commodity value which is necessary to replace the *price* of the means of production consumed and the labour-power employed. He clearly examines the elementary concept for the basic law of capitalist competition in the price-form of commodity value. At the same time the cost-price in the form of value is conceived as the necessary portion to buy back, through the circulation process, the elements of production consumed in the production of a commodity. In this regard the cost-price surely presents an elementary form of capitalist pricing which is subject to the regulation by the quantity of the labour-substance necessary to reproduce each commodity. This is because the cost-price must be determined in accord with its function of enabling capitalists in each industry with given representative conditions of production to replenish the means of production and labour-power as well as their substance of values ($c_i + v_i$). Through this function the cost-price also enable capitalists to reobtain continuously the whole substance of value of their commodity products ($c_i + v_i + s_i$) through the successive process of production.

It must further be noted that the relevancy of the definition of cost-price above is not confined to the case where the prices of commodities are assumed to be directly proportional to the amounts of labour-time embodied in them. In other words, the definition of the cost-price above is separable from the conventional understanding of the content of the law of value as the equal exchange of labour embodied in commodities. We might extend this line of argument to construct the theory of prices of production, not depending on the concept of the law of value as the equal exchange of labour, but by examining the concrete forms of value in the sphere of capitalist competition which reflect the regulative social relations of the labour-substance of value from behind. Corresponding to his treatment of the cost-price as a concrete form of value, Marx presents profit also as a form of value appearing in the process of circulation in terms of price. He begins the second chapter 'The Profit Rate' in the third volume of *Capital* by returning to the general formula for capital, $M - C - M'$. He says for instance; 'surplus-value itself does not appear as having been produced by the appropriation of labour-time, but as the excess of the sale price of commodities over their cost price' (III, p. 135). The theory of prices of production beginning from the concept of the cost-price and profit could be formulated in this line of discussion as a concretisation or development of the forms of value in relation to the social regulation of the substance of value in the sphere of capitalist competition, and not as the theory of a transformation from the labour-substance of values, or a set of prices directly proportional to those (i.e. value-prices) into another set of prices.

However, Marx did not thoroughly follow up and finish this line of argument. It is because he defined value one-sidedly as crystals of human labour by abstracting from the forms of value at the initial section of *Capital*, and assumed equal exchange of labour as the content of the law of value throughout in his examination of the inner structure of a capitalist economy. Accordingly Marx defines the cost-price also as 'replacement value' ($c_i + v_i$) within the value of a commodity ( $a_i = c_i + v_i + s_i$), presupposing value-prices directly proportional to labour-substance embodied in commodities. In line with this the portion of surplus-value ($s_i$) in the vlue of a commodity is directly defined as profit when it is supposed to be derivative of the total capital advanced. Hence, commodity value = cost-price + profit (III, p. 127), or 'the surplus-value or profit consists precisely in the excess of commodity value over its cost price, i.e. in the excess of the total sum of labour contained in the commodity over the sum of labour that is actually paid for' (III, p. 133).

In so far as cost-price and profit are thus treated as the internal divisions within the substance of commodity value directly measurable in terms of labour-time, capitals would acquire surplus-value as profit just as much as surplus-labour expended in each of their own process of production. As a result, the yearly rate of profit against the total advanced capital, which is hereafter simply called 'the rate of profit' in accord with usual terminology must necessarily vary across different branches of industry with a different number of workers employed against the total advanced capital, due to different organic composition and/or different turnover period of capital. We can reasonably assume here that the length of the working day as well as the real wages, and therefore the rate of surplus-value ($s_i = s_i/v_i$) tend to be equalised across industries through competition among capitals and workers. There cannot be any theoretical reason, however, to expect the equalisation of the organic composition of capital ($v_i/c_i$) or of the turnover period of capital across industries having different technical bases. The industries with lower compositions of capital, employing more labourers with a given amount of capital, or those with faster turnover, must obtain a higher rate of profit than otherwise, so long as the law of value is identified here with the equal exchange of labour embodied in commodities.

Marx examines these points in chapter 8, 'Different Compositions of Capital in Different Branches of Production, and the Resulting Variation in Rates of Profit', in the third volume of *Capital*, and summarises the problem further to be clarified as follows:

> We have shown, therefore, that in different branches of industry unequal profit rates prevail, corresponding to the different organic composition of capitals, and, within the indicated limits, corresponding also to their different turnover times; so that at a given rate of surplus-value it is only for capitals of the same organic composition – assuming equal turnover times – that the law holds good, as a general tendency, that profits stand in direct proportion to the amount of capital, and that capitals of equal size yield equal profit in the same period of time. The above argument is true on the same basis as our whole investigation so far: that commodities are sold at their values. There is no doubt, however, that in actual fact, ignoring inessential, accidental circumstances that cancel each other out, no such variation in the average rate of profit exists

between different branches of industry, and it could not exist without abolishing the entire system of capitalist production. The theory of value thus appears incompatible with the actual phenomena of production, and it might seem that we must abandon all hope of understanding these phenomena.' (III, p. 252).

The incompatibility pointed out here between the law of value, as the equal exchange of labour, and the law of the equalisation of the rate of profit across industries with different organic compositions or turnover times of capital was a crucial problem for the labour theory of value since the classical school. Marx's solution is presented in the following chapter 9, 'Formation of a General Rate of Profit (Average Rate of Profit), and Transformation of Commodity Values into Prices of Production', starting from Table 7.1, where turnover of capitals is assumed equally once a year.

*Table* 7.1

| | *Capitals* | *Rate of surplus-value* % | *Surplus-value* | *Value of product* | *Rate of profit* % |
|---|---|---|---|---|---|
| I | $80c + 20v$ | 100 | 20 | 120 | 20 |
| II | $70c + 30v$ | 100 | 30 | 130 | 30 |
| III | $60c + 40v$ | 100 | 40 | 140 | 40 |
| IV | $85c + 15v$ | 100 | 15 | 115 | 15 |
| V | $95c + 5v$ | 100 | 5 | 105 | 5 |

Upon this numerical example Marx proceeds to define the average rate of profit and then the price of production as follows:

If we treat the 500 as one single capital, with I–V simply forming different portions of it, – then the average composition of the capital of 500 would be $500 = 390c + 110v$, or in percentages $78c + 22v$. Treating the capitals of 100 as each simply a fifth of the total capital, its composition would be this average one of $78c + 22v$: in the same way the average surplus-value of 22 would accrue to each of these capitals of 100, the average rate of profit would thus be 22 per cent, and the price of each fifth of the total product produced by this capital of 500 would be 122. (III, p. 255). Taken together, commodities are sold at $2 + 7 + 17 = 26$ above their value, and $8 + 18 = 26$ below their value, so that the divergences of price from value indicated above cancel each other out when surplus-value is distributed evenly, i.e. through adding the average profit of 22 on the capital advance of 100 to the respective cost prices of commodities I–V. – The prices that arise when the average of different rates of profit is drawn from the different spheres of production, and this average is added to the cost prices of these different spheres of production, are the *prices of production*. (III, p. 257).

To express Marx's definition here in general terms, the value of yearly commodity product of *i*th industry $a_i = c_i + v_i + s_i$ is transformed into the price of production $P_i = (c_i + v_i) + r\,(c_i + v_i)$, or cost-price-plus average profit, where the average rate of profit is defined as $r = \Sigma s_i / \Sigma(c_i + v_i)$. According to this procedure Marx's two propositions on the aggregates duly hold, i.e. 'The sum of the profits for all the different spheres of production must be equal to the sum of surplus-values, and the sum of prices of production for the total social product must be equal to the sum of its values' (III, p. 273), or $\Sigma p_i = \Sigma s_i$ and $\Sigma P_i = \Sigma a_i$, where $p_i$ designates yearly average profit for *i*th industry.

Thus, there were two lines of discussion in Marx's theory of prices of production. In the first line the cost-price and profit are shown as developed forms of value measured from the beginning in terms of certain quantities of money. If we follow and extend this line we may be able to treat the prices of production as the transformation of value-forms from those in the simple and general commodity circulation into the concrete forms belonging to the sphere of capitalist competition, and not as transformations from the labour-substance of values. In the second line the cost-price and profit are defined as an internal redivision within the labour-substance of values, and the prices of production are shown as a transformation of the labour-substance of values, or a set of prices directly proportional to that substance into another set of prices to equalise the rate of profit. Along this second line the dimension or the unit of cost-price, profit and prices of production is ambiguous. The prices of production, e.g. 122 in the numerical example deduced from Table 7.1 above, as well as the cost-price and profit, seem directly deducible from and comparable with the labour-substance at the same dimension, although they are sometimes designated also in terms of pounds sterling deduced from value-prices.

As the second line dominates, the first line was not fully extended nor utilised, leaving us some controversial problems. For instance, in the process of deducing the prices of production starting from the numerical example above, the general rate of profit and average profit are defined as average distribution of surplus-value to capitals in different spheres of production by regarding those capitals as 'a single total capitals' (III, p. 256), or 'shareholders in a joint-stock company' (III, p. 258). So far the cost-prices and the sale prices as the forms of individual capitalist competition are somewhat neglected, and treated as if they were measurable directly in terms of labour-substance. However, without referring to the forms of value, the concept of profit and that of the average rate of profit themselves would not properly be deduced from the basic value theory. Marx titles part I of the third volume of *Capital*, 'The Transformation of Surplus-Value into Profit, and of the Rate of Surplus-Value into the Rate of Profit', and seems to attempt to deduce the concept of profit itself from the function of capital to produce surplus-value in the process of production. He asks himself in this context why surplus-value is supposed to be a derivative not merely of the variable capital, but of the total capital advanced, in being transformed into profit, and then explains the reason as follows: 'The entire capital is materially involved in the labour process, even if only a part of it is involved in the process of valorization. This is perhaps the very reason why it contributes only in part towards the formation of cost price, but in full toward the formation of surplus-value.' (III, p. 126). The reason presented here is not persuasive. From the view of the function of capital in the process of labour and valorisation, the distinction between variable and constant capital as well as that between fixed and circulating capital might not be disregarded theoretically. Therefore, Marx offers another explanation in saying: 'Because the price of labour-power appears at one pole in the transformed form of wages, surplus-value appears at the other pole in the transformed form of profit.' (III p. 127). But the concept of wages as full remuneration for the whole labour was itself difficult to deduce 'from the relation of production', and had better regarded as originating in the forms of commodity economy in general, wider and older than capitalist production, as we have argued in Chapter 5, Section 5.2. Similarly, profit is also quite conceivable in the forms of commodity economy in general, as we have discussed in the theory of transformation of money into capital in Chapter 4, Section 4.3.

Capitalist production did not *create* the form of profit or capitalist competition equalising the rate of profit, though they seem specific to the transformed form of capitalistic surplus-value in the theoretical system of *Capital*. The task of the theory of prices of production must, therefore, be reconsidered. It must not be in deducing the forms of profit and average profit from the labour-substance of surplus-value, but in analysing the social regulation, on the basis of substantial relations of labour quantities, of these forms which capitalism takes over from the commodity economy in general. Along with this problem, Marx solidly presupposed the content of the law of value as the equal exchange of labour embodied in commodities. As a result he must introduce the law of the equalisation of the rate of profit across industries from 'the actual phenomena of production', externally to the value theory and the working of the law of value at the end of chapter 8 of the third volume of *Capital*, as we have seen. There is clearly a theoretical restriction in Marx resulting from a residue of Ricardo's value theory. Consequently Marx's presentation of the prices of production, which doubtlessly surpassed a basic weak point of Ricardo's theory, had to leave us further problems to be cleared up in relation to the content of the law of value. Two problems especially were crucial, and Marx was already aware of both of them.

First, if the standard prices of commodity products of capitals turn out to be prices of production, then equal exchange of labour among commodity products from various spheres of production with different composition of capital and different turnover periods cannot hold, in particular as for the portion of embodied surplus-labour. So far as transactions of commodities at their values are supposed to be substantially identical with an equal exchange of labour, then 'it is, *prima facie*, a very different matter whether commodities are sold at their values (i.e whether they are exchanged one another in proportion to the value contained in them, at their value-prices) or whether they are sold at prices which make their sale yield equal profits on equal amounts of the capitals advanced for their respective production' (III, p. 275). In retrospect, Marx further asks himself: 'How therefore is this exchange of commodities at their actual values supposed to have come about?' (ibid.). This is essentially the point which has been repeatedly criticised since Böhm-Bawerk as the contradiction between the first and the third volume of *Capital*. Marx suggests here, as 'the salient point', exchanges of commodities among simple producers who possess their respective means of production. This position of showing the actuality of transactions of commodities at their values by relations among simple producers, historically prior to capitalist prices of production, is extended by Engels in his

'Supplement to Volume 3 of *Capital*', and emphasised also by Hilferding in his anti-criticism of Böhm-Bawerk. Although the position has been regarded as an orthodox Marxian view since then, it cannot be very persuasive. For one thing, simple commodity producers could not constitute a full social formation except in an assumed imaginary classless society; whereas the substance of value as well as the working of the law of value must be shown with the necessity of the allocation of labour on a social scale through commodity exchanges, as discussed in Chapter 4, Section 4.1. The position in question cannot be held strongly even as an interpretation of the theoretical system of *Capital*, because the whole investigation into the processes of production and circulation of capital in the first and the second volume of *Capital*, prior to the theory of prices of production, is firmly based upon the law of value. The law of value must, above all, be understood as the inner law of motion of a capitalist economy, the only state in which a commodity economy is turned into a fully socio-economic order. Therefore, in recent studies and controversies on the value theory, an increasing number of Marxians tend to avoid the position of explaining the relation of values and prices of production in a conventional historical-logical theory of transformation.

The law of value must then be shown as an actually relevant law of commodity exchanges in a capitalist economy. For convenience's sake in an introductory explanation, we might well assume equal composition and turnover periods of capital across industries, to show the law of value as the equal exchange of labour among commodity products. However, this explanation, as well as three other plausible sorts of explanation showing the law of value as an equal exchange of labour, depends upon a clearly unrealistic hypothesis, and is not yet satisfactory in showing the actual relevancy of the law of value, as we have examined in Chapter 5, Section 5.2. In this regard the problem which Marx himself noticed here concerning the actual relevancy of commodity exchanges at their values still remains to be solved in the basic theory of capitalism. My own attempt more clearly to distinguish the forms and the substance of value and clarify their relations more consistently by admitting the fundamental elasticity or freedom in the part of surplus-labour embodied in commodity products, as presented in the preceding chapters, certainly aims at overcoming this problem among others. Though it surely requires restructuring the basic theory, I trust the readers' judgement as to whether the essential points in Marx's value theory are lost or strengthened by it.

Second, Marx's theory of transforming values into prices of production is incomplete and seems at the half-way stage, so far as it defines cost-price as an internal portion $(v_i + s_i)$ within labour value $(c_i + v_i + s_i)$ embodied in commodities. It appears inconsistent to conceive that all capitalists sell their commodity products at the prices of production and buy the elements of production at values or value-prices. There remains a problem in Marx's theory as how to consistently transform cost-prices into prices of production. The problem may threaten Marx's two propositions on the equality of aggregates between profit and surplus-value, and that between prices of production and values. Marx was aware of this problem when he has this to say, after stating that the sum of prices of production is equal to the sum of their values: 'This seems contradicted by the fact that the elements of productive capital are generally bought on the market in capitalist production, so that their prices include an already realised profit and accordingly include the price of production of one branch of industry together with the profit contained in it, so that the profit in one branch of industry goes into the cost price of another.' (III, pp. 259–60). In another place he points to the same problem more decisively, saying: 'It is necessary to bear in mind this modified significance of the cost-price, and therefore to bear in mind too that if the cost-price of a commodity is equated with the value of the means of production used up in producing it, it is always possible to go wrong.' (III, p. 265). Modification of the cost-price is surely not limited to the means of production or the portion of the constant capital. 'As for the variable capital, the average daily wages is certainly always equal to the value product of the number of hours that the worker must work in order to produce his means of subsistence; but this number of hours is itself distorted by the fact that the prices of production of the necessary means of subsistence diverge from their values.' (III, p. 261). In case where the prices of production diverge from values of the necessary means of subsistence 'the workers must work for a greater or lesser amount of time in order to buy back these commodities (to replace them) and must therefore perform more or less necessary labour than would be needed if the prices of production of their necessary means of subsistence did coincide with their values.' (III, p. 309).

As we have already mentioned in Chapter 5, Section 5.2, Marx's statement here that the length of necessary labour would be altered in accord with transformation of values into prices of production sounds peculiar, since his theory of prices of production is basically designed to show the forms of distribution of surplus-value among capitalists through competition, based upon the relation of production between total capitalists and wage-labourers. It is confusing to conceive that the competition among capitalists to equalise the rate of profit as a form of redistributing surplus-value simultaneously affects the more fundamental relation of production of surplus-value itself. In the actual capitalist economy the workers may have to work for a greater or lesser amount of time when nominal wages lag behind the changes in a system of prices of commodity products. But such a lag and its adjustment process must be outside of the task of the theory of prices of production. The analyses of the substantial content of the capitalist process of production in the first and the second volumes of *Capital* are dimensionally separable from the theory of distribution of surplus-value in the third volume, and can well be supposed valid during the analyses in the third volume. We should then conceive here that workers must obtain wages at the prices of production of the necessary means of subsistence containing necessary labour-time, in accord with concretisation of the standard prices of commodity products. Marx's peculiar confusion on this point originates partly from the first problem discussed above, but also for sure from his incomplete analysis of the exact procedure and the result of defining cost-prices in terms of prices of production.

## The Transformation Controversy

A controversy has continued on and off since the end of the nineteenth century concerning the two problems discussed above. In the period after the Second World War particularly until the 1950s, the focus of discussion among some Western scholars was on the second problem of how to transform values into prices of production consistently, including the elements of cost-prices. In this first phase of the Western controversy on the transformation problem, the first problem was untouched, and all the participants, Marxians and non-Marxians alike, assumed the labour theory of value or value prices as a given precondition for the debates. However, in the second phase of the controversy since 1970s, the scope of the debate has no longer been confined to the second problem, as the number of participants and the contents of controversy have largely extended. The growth of a neo-Ricardian School after the publication of Sraffa's *Production of Commodities by Means of Commodities* in 1960, and the following revival of the Western Marxian School, caused a rekindling of the controversy on Marx's value theory across the two problems, forming a common triangular battlefield between Marxians, neo-Ricardians and neo-classicists in a broad sense. Following the first phase of the controversy on the transformation of cost-prices into prices of production, the controversy in the recent second phase has tended to inquire more and more basically into the soundness, consistency and relevancy of Marx's labour theory of value itself. The debates on the joint-production problem and the skilled-labour problem, which have derived from the transformation controversy, have thus become focal points and crucial for the basic stand of Marxian political economy in this context. Since we have already treated these aspects of the debates concerning the first problem in the previous Chapters, let us concentrate here on the second problem.

Just as Böhm-Bawerk is to be referred to as a conspicuous initiator of the controversy on the first problem, it is L. von Bortkiewicz (1868–1931) who initiated the controversy on the second problem.[1] Although Bortkiewicz's treatment of the problem did not gather much attention for more than three decades, it was endorsed as an essential contribution to the problem by P. Sweezy in chapter 7 of *The Theory of Capitalist Development* in 1942, and became generally known as a starting-point of the debate since then. Let us therefore briefly review first the Bortkiewicz–Sweezy (*B–S*) solution.

Suppose there are three main departments of production. The department I produces means of production, II produces means of subsistence for workers and III produces consumption goods for capitalists or luxury goods. Using the same notation as in the previous item of this chapter, the relation of simple reproduction in terms of value is then described as follows:

$$\begin{array}{ll} \text{I} & c_1 + v_1 + s_1 = c_1 + c_2 + c_3 \\ \text{II} & c_2 + v_2 + s_2 = v_1 + v_2 + v_3 \\ \text{III} & c_3 + v_3 + s_3 = s_1 + s_2 + s_3 \end{array} \tag{7.1}$$

Marx's definition of prices of production was $P_i = (c_i + v_i) + r(c_i + v_i)$, where the average rate of profit was defined as $r = \Sigma s_i / \Sigma(c_i + v_i)$. The cost-price $(c_i + v_i)$ was in terms of value, and not yet transformed into prices of production. So as to clear up this residual incompleteness, *B–S* introduce three unknowns, $x$, $y$, $z$, which designate the ratios of the price of production to the value of the commodity products of departments I, II, III. For example, the price of production of the means of production is assumed to be $x$ times of its value when complete transformation including the elements of cost-prices is performed. The equations in terms of the prices of production must then be as follows:

$$\begin{array}{ll} \text{I} & c_1x + v_1y + r(c_1x + v_1y) = (c_1 + c_2 + c_3)x \\ \text{II} & c_2x + v_2y + r(c_2x + v_2y) = (v_1 + v_2 + v_3)y \\ \text{III} & c_3x + v_3y + r(c_3x + v_3y) = (s_1 + s_2 + s_3)z \end{array} \qquad (7.2)$$

There are four unknowns ($x, y, z, r$) in three equations. Either one more equation or one less unknown is necessary to get a unique solution. *B–S* recommend reducing the unknowns by making $z = 1$, assuming that 'the number of units of labour necessary to produce one unit of the money commodity (which is classified as a luxury good – *M.I.*) would provide a direct link between the two systems of accounting.'[2]

For the sake of simplicity, notations as follows are added; $1 + r = \sigma$, $v_i/c_i = f_i$, $(c_i + v_i + s_i)/c_i = g_i$. Then, from equations (7.1) and (7.2), we get:

$$\begin{array}{ll} \text{I} & \sigma(x + f_1y) = g_1x \\ \text{II} & \sigma(x + f_2y) = g_2y \\ \text{III} & \sigma(x + f_3y) = g_3 \end{array} \qquad (7.3)$$

From the first two equations in (7.3) we can deduce a solution which is non-negative and consistent with the equations, as follows:

$$\sigma = \frac{-(f_2g_1 + g_2) + \sqrt{(f_2g_1 + g_2)^2 + 4(f_1 - f_2)g_1g_2}}{2(f_1 - f_2)}$$

Once $\sigma$ is determined, then $x$ and $y$ can be deduced easily from the equations in (7.3). *B–S* set up a numerical example as follows to show the result of the solution:

*Table* 7.2 Value calculation

| *Dept of production* | *Constant capital* $c_i$ | *Variable capital* $v_i$ | *Surplus-value* $s_i$ | *Value of Products* $a_i$ |
|---|---|---|---|---|
| I | 225 | 90 | 60 | 375 |
| II | 100 | 120 | 80 | 300 |
| III | 50 | 90 | 60 | 200 |
| Total | 375 | 300 | 200 | 875 |

Given these numbers with $z = 1$, deduced are $\sigma = 5/4$, $r = 25$ per cent, $x = 32/25$, $y = 16/15$, and therefore:

*Table* 7.3 Price calculation

| *Dept of production* | *Constant capital* $c_i x$ | *Variable capital* $v_i y$ | *Profit* $p_i$ | *Price of product* $P_i$ |
|---|---|---|---|---|
| I | 288 | 96 | 96 | 480 |
| II | 128 | 128 | 64 | 320 |
| III | 64 | 96 | 40 | 200 |
| Total | 480 | 320 | 200 | 1000 |

Bortkiewicz, as a modern Ricardian, was rather critical of Marx's theory of prices of production as a result of these analyses. For one thing, determination of the general rate of profit $r$, or $\sigma$ above, is indifferent to the conditions of production in the department of luxury goods production, expressed in $f_3$ and $g_3$, whereas in Marx's formulation the general rate of profit depends on the conditions of production of the total social capital including department III. It is surprising to recall, as Bortkiewicz indicates, that Ricardo was already aware of the point. Ricardo stated that a change in the conditions of production of such goods as do not enter into the consumption of workers do not affect the height of the rate of profit. More recently Sraffa formulated the same point in his conception of non-basic commodities. Bortkiewicz also criticises Marx's proposition that total value equals total price. In Table 7.3, for example, the total price 1000 exceeds the total value 875, because production of the money commodity in department III is performed with lower organic composition of capital than social average. Assuming $z = 1$ with a lower composition of capital in department III, the purchasing power of the money commodity in the price scheme with an equalised rate of profit must be lowered than in the value scheme by elevating the prices of other commodities as a whole.

In contrast, Sweezy believed that Bortkiewicz's treatment of the problem was not substantially contrary to Marx's theory, but an important contribution making more consistent the logic of transforming the labour-values into the prices of production. Basically Sweezy's view is fair and positively sound. We should admit with Sweezy that Bortkiewicz's criticism of Marx concerning the role of the composition of capital in department III (luxury goods) in determining the general rate of profit is logically correct. 'Marx's criticism of Ricardo on this score was unjustified.'[3] However, this point is far from being fatal to Marx' theoretical system of value, exploitation and capitalist development as a whole. Practically such industries as cater only to capitalists' consumption would be relatively few and unimportant, excepting military industry. Besides, technical changes in such industries cannot be isolated, and would be applied to other industries in one way or the other, and vice versa. As for Bortkiewicz's critique of Marx's proposition on the equality between total value and total price, Sweezy has this to say in defence of Marx:

> It is important to realize that no significant theoretical issues are involved in this divergence of total value from total price. It is simply a question of the unit of account. If we had used the unit of labour time as the unit of account in both the value and the price schemes, the totals would have been the same. Since we elected to use the unit of gold (money) as the unit of account, the totals diverge. But in either case the proportions of the price scheme . . . will come out the same, and it is the relations existing among the various elements of the system rather than the absolute figures in which they are expressed which are important.[4]

There remained, however, a problem which was a source of later controversy. It is by no means an insignificant conventional matter how to conceive the unit of account of the value and the price-schemes. When *B–S* assumed $z = 1$, one unit of gold (say one-thirty-fifth of an ounce called a dollar) is conceived as the unit of value as well as of price. What does it mean to measure value by units of gold or in terms of dollars? There can be two possible interpretations: (i) One unit of gold is assumed to be produced by one hour of labour-time, since values must substantially be measured by units of labour-time. Or (ii) Some amount of labour-time embodied in one unit of gold is supposed to be a unit of value. But neither of these two are satisfactory. There is no theoretical or technical reason to guarantee the assumption (i). Units of measure of the substance of value in (ii) would be unstable, being subject to changes in the conditions of production. Besides, it is not clear in its meaning and theoretically improper to use a unit of labour-time as the unit of account in the price-scheme, though Sweezy recommended it as a device to restore the equality in the totals of values and prices.

In our understanding of the distinction between the forms and the substance of value, the prices as a form of value must be expressed and measured by physical quantities of the money commodity, gold, whereas the substance of value behind them must be measured by unit of labour-time. There is a confusion across these different dimensions in the *B–S* solution. The divergence between the total value and the total prices is further to be considered. Moreover, the equality between total surplus-value and total profit cannot be guaranteed, if the composition of capital in the production of the money commodity, gold, is separated from that in the production of other surplus products. Thus a focus in the first round of the Western transformation controversy until the 1950s, was how to match the *B–S* type of solution with Marx's propositions on the equality in the two sets of totals.

For instance, J. Winternitz asserted that a fourth equation $\Sigma c_i + v_1 + s_i) = \Sigma(c_i x + v_i y + s_i z)$ representing the equality between total value and total prices of production should be added, instead of $z = 1$, to get a proper solution in accord with the spirit of Marx's system.[5] K. May supported this, and further showed that the *B–S* type of solution really did not depend on the assumption of simple reproduction or of a three-department model, but could be generalised into an n sectors model of extended reproduction.[6] Although this generalisation is surely a contribution, the solution by Winternitz and May cannot normally satisfy the other required equality between total surplus-value and total profit. In order to satisfy this condition, R. Meek substituted $\Sigma s_i = \Sigma s_i z$ as a fourth equation.[7] Then, the equality between total value and total prices of production would not generally be guaranteed. F. Seton summed up the debate and pointed out that all the conditions proposed, including (i) $z = 1$, (ii) $\Sigma(c_i + v_i + s_i) = \Sigma(c_i x + v_i y + s_i z)$, and (iii) $\Sigma s_i = \Sigma s_i z$, can be simultaneously satisfied if the organic composition of capital in department III is equal to the social average.[8] This supposition, however, clearly lacks generality, as Seton himself recognises. The general appropriateness of Marx's theory of value and prices of production was still at stake.

H. D. Dickinson cut in to say that the fourth condition is unnecessary for determining a general rate of profit and relative prices (two ratios $x{:}y{:}z$ in *B–S* equations).[9] According to Dickinson, the size of the numéraire required to get actual prices from relative prices is not important, and it does not make sense to try to equalise total prices and total values because they are quantities in different dimensions and to be measured by different units. This was a sharp comment.

The dimensional difference, however, must not be a simple separation, but should be grounded in Marx's theory of the forms and the substance of value in solving the transformation problem. The money commodity, gold, cannot be regarded as a formal numéraire, something referred to for the sake of convenience for accounting. Its role and position between the substance of values and the form of values as prices must theoretically be clarified. It also remained as a problem to be further examined what Marx intended to express in his propositions on the equality in the two sets of totals, or if it really made sense. The transformation controversy in its first round did not thus reach a very satisfactory conclusion, leaving room for doubt as to the general appropriateness of Marx's theory of value and prices of production, especially in their actual link, though the controversy contained interesting contributions to our understanding of the depth and the technical aspects of the problem.

Actually, in the second round of the controversy since the 1970s, the extent of the analysis has been substantially extended. The relevancy of the labour theory of value itself has has been seriously reconsidered, and doubt thrown on it by various non-Marxian economists including neo-classicists and neo-Ricardians. P. Sammuelson represents a typical example of a recent neo-classicist critique of Marx's theory of value and prices of production. According to him, Marx's labour theory of value as a theory of relative prices of commodity products holds only on condition that either the means of production or surplus-value do not exist, or that the organic composition of capital in all industries is equal.[10] Further, Marx's theory of prices of production, defining the elements of cost-prices in terms of value, holds only in so far as 'the equal internal composition of capital' exists, maintaining exactly the same proportion of various inputs of products to every industry as the proportion of these products in the social output as a whole, and also the same proportion of goods in the content of the means of subsistence for the workers. This case surely lacks generality. Furthermore, the transformation procedure which alters all the elements of cost-prices into prices of production in a *B–S* type argument does not make much sense in Samuelson's view. We can certainly deduce the prices of production by determining the rates of transformation from the labour values embodied in each commodity on the basis of the given technological system as the quantitative physical relations of inputs and outputs. However, the result is just the same as the solution of the price equations directly based upon a physical system of the relations between inputs and outputs *determined technologically*. Therefore, the value analysis in the first volume of *Capital* is nothing but an unnecessary detour. M. Morishima followed up this discussion, partly resisting Samuelson's criticism of Marx. Morishima is more favourable to Marx's intention than Samuelson in his formulation of the relation between the rate of surplus-value and the general rate of profit, depending on N. Okishio's works. However, he underlines the point that Marx's concept of prices of production, defining cost-prices in terms of value, must be subject to a very restricted condition for industries to be 'linear dependent', though mathematically it is somewhat a broader condition than Samuelson's 'equal internal composition of capital'.[11] Moreover, he finally recommends the abandonment of Marx's labour theory of value and the adoption instead of a von Neumann type of theoretical model, on the grounds of the theoretical difficulty of treating heterogeneous labour, joint products or fixed capital.[12] I. Steedman echoed these critiques in favour of Sraffa's price theory. Besides his critiques of the problems concerning heterogeneous labour and joint products that we have seen, Steedman also asserts the redundancy of the labour theory of value on the grounds that the prices of production as equilibrium prices can be fully deduced from the physical data of the production processes.[13]

It is apparent in these criticisms that the transformation problem in the narrow sense since Bortkiewicz has been combined or fused with the more fundamental value controversy since Böhm-Bawerk. However, unlike Böhm-Bawerk, who totally rejected the possibility of theoretically recognising the labour values embodied in commodity products in favour of the marginal utility theory of value, these recent critics all accept such a possibility excepting special problems such as those of heterogeneous labour or joint production. Nor is the *B–S* type of procedure deducing prices of production from labour values denounced as logically wrong. Therefore, so long as we are convinced both that the task of economic theory (in the tradition of the classical and the Marxian schools) is to reveal the social relations based upon human labour behind prices, and the logical feasibility of determining prices of production including cost prices upon the basis of labour values in the *B–S* type of procedure, critical examinations by Samuelson and Morishima to show the narrow limits of the conditions under which Marx's concept of prices of production, with cost-prices in terms of value can hold, do not seem of much sense or point. What is required of the Marxian school is thus to clarify the theoretical relevance and meaning of the labour theory of value and the procedure by which prices of production can be consistently defined by labour values, besides solving the special problems on heterogeneous labour and joint production. Marxian theorists like A. Medio, D. Laibman, M. Desai, D. Yaffe and A. Shaikh among others have attempted to respond to such requests by emphasising the following points.

First, in contrast with the neo-classicals or neo-Ricardians, the Marxian theory of value is not merely a theory of the relative prices of commodity products. It is above all a theory of the production process of surplus-value, which is the economic basis of the relationship between capitalists and labourers. Moreover, especially in order to clarify the historically specific character of capitalist production, theoretical concern about the labour process, as a general economic norm common to all societies, is indispensable. In view of these points, the labour theory of value is far from being redundant, but rather a very relevant basis for social and historical economic theory, although its content need not be understood as the exactly equal exchange of labour embodied in commodity products in the light of our preceding analyses.

Second, on the common basis of recognising the relevancy of the labour theory of value as the theory of capitalist production of surplus-value, the distinction of dimensions and tasks between the theory of value and the theory of prices of production is newly stressed by some Marxians. For example, Desai emphasised the dimensional difference between the visible price domain and the invisible labour-value domain, and therefore the incomensurability of value and price.[14] His position would become almost identical with that of some Japanese followers of Uno, if he located the prices of production in the context of the development of the forms of value. The problem of how to consolidate the *B–S* type of transformation procedure, with Marx's propositions on two sets of totals, could be avoided in this position just as in Dickinson's treatment, though it did not seem to me substantially and positively solved.

Third, the notion of value has been reconsidered so as to include not merely labour value embodied in commodities, but also exchange value or form of value. However, it would be misleading and in correct if exchange value or the form of value is conceived directly in terms of labour-time, in the same dimension as the substance of value. For instance, from the view of the Rubin School, some Marxians tend to argue that exchange value is a specific way of measuring labour-time in a commodity economy. Then, prices of production as a developed form of exchange value would signify the equal exchange of labour-time measured in a capitalistic market.[15] Such a position, is a serious distortion of the labour theory of value, since it sees labour substance upside-down as being determined by market pricing, and does not clarify the internal structure of that process which determines the rate of profit and prices of production on the basis (independently of the market) of objectively determinable labour-time embodied in commodities.

Exchange value or form of value can be also conceived directly in terms of labour-time when it is counted by labour-time embodied in money. Yaffe presented this line of argument, and believes that prices of production as a transfigured form of value should have the same dimension as the value system. He further stressed that total prices must be equal to total values in a *B–S* type of transformation procedure, on the grounds that new value can not created in the process of circulation.[16] This reasoning is weak and insufficient to support the conclusion, without referring to a necessary special precondition for the composition of capital in the production process of the money commodity, gold, to be the social average. Furthermore, total profit must become different from total surplus-value in spite of their dimensional commensurability in Yaffe's treatment. Laibman maintains that the rate of exploitation should be constant between the system of value and price, and does not mind giving up both propositions on the equality of the two sets of totals.[17]

Another possible theoretical way forward would be to distinguish dimensionally the form and the substance of value, and locate the prices of production as a developed value-form measured by physical quantities of money. Shaikh attempts to pursue this line, and recognises that the transformation problem does not really concern the transformation from values to prices, but does require the transformation from direct prices as a form of value to prices of production as another form. The transformation in the form of value in circulation can not entail any substantial changes in total value and total surplus-value, except a change in distribution of surplus-value among capitals. A *B–S* type of transformation procedure is applicable in transforming direct prices to prices of production. Equality in two sets of total prices (or alternatively equality between total surplus-value and total profit in these sets of prices) is presupposed by Shaikh in solving the equations. He also shows that Marx's own transformation procedure was completely correct as a primary step forward to a correct prices of production in the following sense.[18] If we feedback the prices of production obtained by Marx's procedure into the elements in the cost-prices to get the secondary step of more correct prices of production, and continue such reiteration of correction of both cost-prices and prices of production, then we never fail to reach the same result as the solution of *B–S* type of procedure. Shaikh's demonstration in this regard is substantially identical with Okishio's preceding treatment of the same point,[19] though their works were done independently. The dimensional distinction between the forms and substance of value is quite close to our own view throughout this volume. What remains to be considered for him is, in my view, two questions. First, it remains as a problem how to prove the actual relevance of direct prices or prices directly proportional to embodied labour in commodities, as we have argued, concerning the substantial content of the law of value. Second, so far as the equality between direct prices and prices of production is assumed, Shaikh in fact also presupposes a special case of the social average composition of capital for the production process of the money commodity, gold. The case cannot be generalised. Further, it is unclear what the divergence between the total surplus-value in direct prices and the total profit in prices of production (or alternatively between the total prices in one set and that in another when the total surplus-value and the total profit are assumed to be equal), generally entailed in Shaikh's procedure, means.

Thus, in view of the current progress and the remaining limitations on the transformation issue, it must be further clarified as to how we should understand the structural relation between the substance of value and the prices of production, particularly in the context of what Marx intended to express in his propositions on the equality in the two sets of totals.

## The Theory of Prices of Production Reconsidered

Let us try to make clear the structural logical relation in the dimensionally distinct concepts of value so as to construct a more satisfactory theory of prices of production. In my view we must investigate the three aspects of value in their relation in order to solve the confusing transformation problem. It is not sufficient to see how (i) the substance of values, or the amounts of labour embodied in commodity products on the basis of given social and technical conditions of production determine (ii) the prices of production as a form of value. We have to analyse also (iii) what quantity of labour is obtainable as the acquired substance of value through the prices of production for each class and industrial branch. The prices of production as a form of value are not only determined by the substance of value upon the basis of the physical conditions of production, but also serves as the intermediary for the allocation of the labour-substance of values. Therefore, the conventional analyses of the relation between values and prices of production in two tables which have been used in one way or the other since Bortkiewicz no longer suffice. Three tables are definitely necessary. Let me reformulate the tables presented by *B–S* (Tables 7.4, 7.5, 7.6), to show my own solution of the problem in simplest expression.[20]

Table 7.4 designates the labour-substance produced and incorporated in commodity products of each department of production. The same numerical example in 'Value Calculation' of *B–S* is used, by adding a dimensional unit, millions of hours, to suit its content as the substance of value. The labour quantities in this table are given by the physical data both of the technological conditions of production and of the necessary means of consumption of employed workers which include social and cultural elements. It is noteworthy that the general rate of profit, $r$, is determined independently of the absolute level of $x$, $y$, $z$.

Table 7.5 shows a set of prices of production which are formed on the basis of the substance of value embodied in commodity products as listed in Table 7.4. This table corresponds to the 'Price Calculation' in *B–S*, although its dimensional unit should also here be added. Let us assume that one-thirty-fifth of an ounce of money commodity gold is socially called a dollar, and that the unit of prices in Table 7.5 is millions of dollars. If we assume further that two hours of (dead and living) labour is necessary to produce one-thirty-fifth of an ounce of gold, then $z$ must be ½ (dollars/hours) instead of 1 in *B–S*. The size of numbers in Table 7.5 must then be reduced to one-half of that in 'Price Calculation' table by *B–S*. The numbers $x$, $y$, $z$ are to be called the price–labour coefficient.

Table 7.6 designates the substance of value acquired through the prices of production in Table 7.5. The dimensional unit here must again be millions of hours, as in Table 7.4.

There is no equality as a rule between total value $\Sigma a_i$ and total price $\Sigma P_i$, or total surplus-value $\Sigma s_i$ and total profit $\Sigma p_i$, in Tables 7.4 and 7.5. Further, the rate of surplus-value $\Sigma p_i/\Sigma v_i$ and the ratio of

*Table* 7.4 The substance of value produced ($a_i$)
(millions of hours)

| *Department of production* | *Constant capital* $c_i$ | *Variable capital* $v_i$ | *Surplus-value* $s_i$ | *Values of products* $a_i$ |
|---|---|---|---|---|
| I | 225 | 90 | 60 | 375 |
| II | 100 | 120 | 80 | 300 |
| III | 50 | 90 | 60 | 200 |
| Totals | 375 | 300 | 200 | 875 |

$s_i/v_i = \frac{2}{3}$, $a_i = c_i + v_i + s_i$. From the numbers in this table the general rate of profit $r$ is determined to be 25 per cent. Assume $z = \frac{1}{2}$, then $x = \frac{16}{25}$, $y = \frac{8}{15}$.

*Table* 7.5 The prices of production ($P_i$)
(millions of dollars)

| *Department of production* | $c_ix$ | $v_iy$ | $p_i$ | $P_i$ |
|---|---|---|---|---|
| I | 144 | 48 | 48 | 240 |
| II | 64 | 64 | 32 | 160 |
| III | 32 | 48 | 20 | 100 |
| Totals | 240 | 160 | 100 | 500 |

$p_i = r(c_ix + v_iy)$, represents the average profits.
$P_i = (c_ix + v_iy) + p_i$, the prices of production.
$c_ix$ and $v_iy$ represent constant and variable capital of each department in terms of prices of production. The sum of them $(c_ix + v_iy)$ is, therefore, cost-prices.

*Table* 7.6 The substance of value acquired ($a_i'$)
(millions of hours)

| *Department of production* | $c_i$ | $v_i$ | $s_i'$ | $a_i'$ |
|---|---|---|---|---|
| I | 225 | 90 | 96 | 411 |
| II | 100 | 120 | 64 | 284 |
| III | 50 | 90 | 40 | 180 |
| Totals | 375 | 300 | 200 | 875 |

$s_i' = p_i \div 1/z = \Sigma s_i \times p_i/\Sigma p_i$, $a_i' = c_i + v_i + s_i'$

total profit against total wages $\Sigma p_i/\Sigma v_i y$, or the ratio of total surplus value against total capital $\Sigma s_i/\Sigma(c_i + v_i)$ in terms of labour-substance and the rate of profit in terms of prices $\Sigma p_i/\Sigma(c_i x + v_i y)$ do not generally coincide in these tables. It is no longer any wonder, in spite of all the criticisms against Marxian value theory on this point, causing continuous perplexity among serious Marxians, since the total quantities and ratios compared belong to different dimensional orders and are counted by different units. It must be noted that the labour-substance of value acquired through prices of production are not directly proportional to prices (and their components) in Table 7.5. So long as capitalists in each department continue their production they have to reinvest the money obtained by selling their commodity products at the prices of production, and must repurchase the factors of production consumed. The money representing the portion of prices of constant capital $c_i x$ within the cost-prices must be expended in order to repurchase the means of production which contain $1/x$ of prices in labour-hours, or $c_i$ hours of value-substance. The money obtained as the portion of the price of variable capital $v_i y$ in the cost-prices must also be expended to repurchase labour-power of workers, enabling them to get $1/y$ of wages in labour-hours as the substance of value of their necessary means of consumption. The same number of workers can thus be employed by each department of production, and they will replenish the labour-substance of variable capital $v_i$ as well as that of surplus-value $s_i$ through their living labour again in the next year. Therefore, $c_i$ and $v_i$ together with their totals in Table 7.4 reappear in each corresponding items of the same quantities in Table 7.6, representing the substance of value acquired through transactions performed this year at prices of production.

Correspondingly, the surplus-labour embodied in the social surplus products appears as the only portion of the substance of value that are to be treated socially through the form of profit. Unlike $c_i$ and $v_i$, this portion of the value substance $s_i$ need not be reobtained by each department in the same amount as is produced in that department. Competition among capitals determines the distribution of the substance of surplus-value, by equalising the rate of profit across industries in the form of prices of production. So far as simple reproduction and equal composition of capital (or a single product) in department III are assumed here, the quantity of the substance of value of the surplus product obtained by the average profit $p_i$ resultingly coincides with the social distribution of the total substance of surplus-value in direct proportion with $p_i$, as shown in Table 7.6. By adding the resultant distribution of surplus-value $s_i'$ *to* $c_i$ and $v_i$, we get the substance of value acquired by each department of production $a_i'$ in Table 7.6.

Comparing the resultant Table 7.6 with Table 7.4 we see that departments I, II, III each interchange 375, 300 and 200 million hours of labour embodied in their products into 411, 284 and 180 million hours of labour. As a result the equalities between $a_1'$ and $\Sigma c_i$, $a_2'$ and $\Sigma v_i$, $a_3'$ and $\Sigma s_i'$ in Table 7.6 do not hold, whereas similar equalities between the corresponding items do hold in Table 7.4. This is no anomaly, as Table 7.6 represents the result, not the starting condition of the social exchanges. Its $s_i'$ is merely consumed and $c_i$ and $v_i$ are replenished without loss and used to reproduce the same subtance of values as in Table 7.4 in the following period.

The prices of production as the form of value in Table 7.5 are regulated fundamentally by the substance of values in Table 7.4 based upon the objective conditions of production. Even though prices of production and the substance of values belong to different orders and cannot nominally be equal, it is clear by now that total prices and total profit are nothing but the representation of the substance of total value or of surplus-value in the concrete form of value. The intermediary form of value, as prices of production, cannot alter the total substance of value and surplus-value which is produced and exchanged as shown in Tables 7.4 and 7.6. Thus, by comparing Tables 7.4 and 7.6, we recognise that Marx's intention, in his proposition concerning the equality of total value and total prices and between total surplus-value and total profit, was not so irrational or inconsistent. The essential content of what Marx intended to say in the proposition are, in my view, not at all undercut, but rather consistently proved by distinguishing the different dimensions between the substance and the forms of value.

The basic logical structure of Tables 7.4, 7.5 and 7.6 would remain unchanged even when the model is extended to *n* sectors. It has already been shown that a B–S type of solution presented in three-sectors model can be applied to the extended *n* sectors model by Seton and Medio among others.[21] Though a numéraire is assumed either arbitrarily or as an ideal composite by Seton or Medio, given the gold-standard system, numerical linkage between the substance of values and prices of production is in principle more objectively determinable by both the physical unit of the money commodity gold as the standard of prices, and the quantity of socially necessary labour to produce it. Through such a linkage as $z = \frac{1}{2}$ in our example above, the absolute level of the prices of production in correspondence with the substance of values of commodity products is systematically determined. This price-level must also guarantee the general rate of profit to capital producing gold in department III.[22] The social function in particular of replenishing the substance of value of constant capital and variable capital consumed in each department through the transactions of each commodity product at such prices of production, would surely be unchanged and remain relevant in the extended *n* sector model as well.

If capitalists in all sectors are assumed to consume the same composition of commodities in an *n* sector model (still keeping to simple reproduction), all the relations between the substance of value produced and acquired through the prices of production must be of the same character as in Tables 7.4–7.6. When the composition of commodities consumed by capitalists differ, then the substance of surplus-value obtained $s_i'$ cannot be proportional to profit of each sector $p_i$. This would cause a change also in $a_i'$, or the substance of values obtainable for each sector. But all the other items will remain unchanged, including $\Sigma s_i'$ and $\Sigma a_i'$. The same will be true when some portion of surplus-value disposed of through $p_i$ is used to expand the scale of reproduction.

We have to admit that our analyses of prices of production have assumed stable technical conditions of production determining objectively the social relations of the substance of values lying behind prices for a period, even if it does not last long. However, Marxian value theory cannot be a merely static theory. Dynamic motion in the market, including various disequilibrium and the destruction of values, must be further investigated beyond the theory of prices of production.

Even given stable technical conditions of production the anarchical competition among capitals causes an incessant imbalance between the demand and supply of commodities and resultant fluctuations in market prices. From the point of view of the substance of value, such deviations of market prices from prices of production usually cause changes only in $s_i'$, and correspondingly in $a_i'$, though they may be more destructive from time to time especially in the process of business cycles and crises. The deviation of market prices from the prices of production does not signify by itself a negation either of the law of value or the regulation of prices by the labour-substance of values. Rather it forms a necessary part of the concrete mechanism which carries through the law of value. By its nature the regulation of prices of production presupposes a social process of adjusting the anarchical misallocation of dead and living labour to the various branches of production in accordance with a similarly anarchic fluctuation in demand. The incessant motion of the market prices of commodity products, representing the anarchical disturbance of the allocation of labour, simultaneously guides capitals so as to correct the disturbance. Prices of production actually appear only as the gravitational centre of these fluctuations in market prices.[23]

The price-form of value thus divides itself concretely into fluctuating market prices and central prices of production. Both of them in a set constitute, as the concrete form of value, the necessary mechanism for the regulation of the substance of value. The elasticity within the range of $s_t$ in the social substance of value, as we have seen, both allows and necessitates the anarchical disturbance and readjustment of the labour-allocation through these concrete forms of value.

## 7.2 THE MARKET PRICES OF PRODUCTION

Competition among capitals, which concretely expresses itself in fluctuating market prices, tends to equalise the rate of profit across industrial branches by forming prices of production as the gravitational centre of market prices. However, the same competition cannot equalise the rate of profit among individual capitals within each branch of production according to their different conditions of production and circulation. Since capitals in a certain branch of production tend to sell their commodity product at a same price in a market, the difference in their conditions of production and circulation, or the resultant difference in their costs must naturally create differences in their rate of profit. Although we have hitherto abstracted from such differences, we have to reconsider how to define the representative condition of production and circulation in each branch as a theoretical basis to see how capitalist competition equalises the rate of profit.

This problem, particularly in its aspect of the different conditions of production, is directly related with Marx's theory of market value or market prices of production, which is presented in chapter 10 of the third volume of *Capital*. Let us consider the problem first from the aspect of possible differences in conditions of circulation.[24]

Generally speaking there must always be some shorter or longer period of circulation besides the period of production in the turnover of capital in an anarchical and fluctuating market. As Marx analyses in the parts I and II of the second volume of *Capital*, the whole turnover period of capital includes circulation time as well as production time. Each industrial capital must divide itself into production capital and circulation capital in its circuit. Along with the function or existence of circulation capital acting as commodity and money in circulation, the costs of circulation are more or less necessary. Since the process of selling takes more time and costs than that of buying due to the different position of commodities and money, circulation capital in the form of a commodity to be sold $C' - M'$ usually needs more circulation costs. Marx classifies the costs of circulation into three categories, i.e. pure circulation costs, costs of storage and transport costs. Unlike pure circulation costs such as book-keeping and advertising costs which are *faux frais* specific only to a commodity economy, some portions of the costs of storage and transport belong substantially to production processes that are continued in the circulation sphere, and therefore add to the substance of value and surplus-value just as production costs. The rest of the costs of storage and transport, together with pure circulation costs, proceed from the mere change in the form of value, and cannot enter into the substance of value of commodities. Such circulation costs are *faux frais* which must be maintained by a part of surplus-value.

Therefore, the social surplus-value to be distributed among capitals in the form of profit is actually so much deduced. Let the circulation costs as *faux frais* ($D$) represent the whole circulation costs, for the rest of the costs function just like production costs from the view of substantial valorisation. Then the substance of surplus-value to be distributed through profit would be $(s - D)$. Moreover, capitals in the concrete process of competition must count circulation costs as well as production costs as part of the capital invested. The portion of circulation capital ($B$), which is handled by adding the circulation costs, does not create any surplus-value, unlike production capital ($A$). The substance of value of circulation capital is repeteadly supplied by the transformation of value functioning as production capital, which is replenished through the transformation of value in circulation back into the elements of production. Therefore, it need not be subtracted from surplus-value unlike the circulation costs, but would reduce the rate of profit if it increases relatively due to stagnation in the process of circulation. The social relation of the substance of values defining the rate of profit can not simply be $r = s/A = s/(C + V)$, but must be $r = (s - D)/(A + B + D)$, though the price – labour coefficients such as $x$, $y$, $z$ in the previous section must actually be multiplied into the composite elements of items $s$, $A$,$B$, $D$, precisely to reach the rate of profit in price terms.

When relative quantities of circulation capital and circulation costs in a certain industrial branch ($B_i$, $D_i$) fluctuate, the rate of profit of the industry ($r_i$) has accordingly also to vary even with a fixed commodity product price on the basis of stable conditions of production. How can we conceive of the basis of the equalisation of the rate of profit, including such possible fluctuations of capital and costs in circulation? There are three factors to be considered in this regard. First, there must, at least to some degree be some technologically determining condition even in the process of circulation. About one-half of the cotton cropped once a year must be stored, usually in the form of commodity capital in circulation in the middle of a year between the crops, so long as the spinning industry productively consumes cotton more or less evenly in every month. This is an example of how technologically determined conditions of production among industries can be a basis of ruling the relative size of circulation capital. In addition to such conditions of production, there must be certain stratified structures of wholesalers and retailers, which are more or less stable in a given period of time, partly upon the degree of technological development of communication and transport systems besides commercial customs. Second, so far as the period of circulation or the relative size of circulation capital is more than technologically necessary, its fluctuation seemingly depends on an anarchical market, lacking any objective standard. However, since the period of circulation and the size of circulation capital can be reduced by sales at discounted prices, they are not independent from the motion of market prices. Reducing selling prices so as to shorten the extended period of stagnant circulation might well reduce the rate of profit for the industries concerned. Then, however, the reduction of (the growth rate of) production in accord with the motion of the profit rate would eventually improve the market for the industries to enable them to sell their commodities faster at better prices. As the market prices have their gravitational centre of fluctuation in the prices of production, the period of circulation and the relative size of circulation capital must thus also be indirectly regulated on the basis of the law of value. Third commercial capital tends to increase purchase of the commodities which become easily and rapidly saleable, reflecting the relative shortage of supply, and thus helps to speed up the expansion of production of such commodities. This consequently facilitates the readjustment of the imbalance in demand and supply, and thus helps to normalise the period of circulation, although it seems directly to increase the imbalance by shortening the period of circulation mostly for such commodities as in favorable market conditions.

Thus the combination of fluctuating market prices and prices of production, not a static system of prices, appears here as a necessary mechanism for the working of the law of value through capitalist competition, so equalising the rate of profit across industries for capitals existing in both production and circulation. The costs of circulation which attend circulation capital would also be subject to normalisation through the incessant anarchical fluctuation along with circulation capital.[25]

How about the possible difference in the period of circulation and the costs of circulation among competing capitals within each industrial branch? There seems to be many accidental differences in the length of period of circulation and the attendant costs of circulation among capitals in any industry. Especially when exactly same price is assumed for the same commodity from an industry, then the purchasers of the commodity would go quite accidentally to any of the various capitalists, possibly diversifying the length of their selling period. This might happen even within the constraint of technologically determinant conditions of circulation for the industry as a whole. However, individual differences in the period of circulation and the attendant costs can be substantially reduced, so far as commercial capitals take over the selling processes collectively from various industrial capitals. We shall come back to this social function of commercial capital in Chapter 8. In addition, the movements, of price of the same commodity product would not simply fluctuate as a completely unified level around the price of production, but will also involve an incessant anarchic and individual deviation from it. Unlike a socialist planned economy with social price control, such individual deviations of pricing are inevitable in an anarchic commodity economy. Besides the always imperfect information of the whole market situation, the individual capitalist can actively use pricing as a weapon to promote his selling, speculating as to the future, especially when his period of circulation becomes unsatisfactorily longer than others in the same industry. Such a way of promoting the individual period of circulation will not eliminate differences in it, but will tend to trim off any anomalous prolongation. The law of indifference of prices for the same commodity asserts itself as a composite of such anarchical pricings by individual capitals in the form of fluctuating market prices. In the process of the tendential normalisation of the period of sale through individual pricing among competitive capitals, the law of price indifference would always approximately equalise the rate of profit in an industry among capitals with similar prevailing conditions of production.

In the case of different conditions of production among capitals in an industry, the law of price indifference causes differentiation of their rate of profit. The different conditions of production, due to the difference either in technological equipment, in the scale of production or in the natural conditions of land, are surely variable, but cannot be tendentially equalised through fluctuating market prices. Competition among capitals with representative conditions of production would tendentially equalise their rate of profit across industries by forming prices of production as a gravitational centre of fluctuating market prices. The same process of competition must then create various rates of profit according to the different conditions of production within each industrial branch. Here appears then a problem of how to define the price of production or the basic production conditions in each industry with varying conditions of production among many capitals.

Marx's theory of market value in its essence concerns this problem. Despite its being located after the theory of prices of production, chapter 10 of the third volume of *Capital* treats the problem in the main in terms of market *value*. A probable reason is that the problem seems analysable without referring to competition among capitals *across* industrial branches. However, as Marx notices (III, p. 300), the analyses of market value can apply with the necessary limitations to prices of production, or to 'market price of production'. The notion of market prices of production appears as a concretisation of prices of production in the light of competition among capitals within each branch of production. From our position that the prices of production are the developed form of value, and not a separable correction of the value concept, the market prices of production should not be seen as a separated correction of market value either, but rather, could be treated directly after the theory of prices of production without an intermediary notion of market value. At least some difficulties in Marx's theory of market value would be solved in this way.

There are two or three discernibly different notions of market value in Marx's treatment. He assumes three different conditions of production, better, average and worse, in an industrial sphere producing the same sort of commodity. The individual value of the commodity produced by better conditions is smaller, and that by worse conditions is larger than average. The first notion of market value that Marx has can be called the 'technical average' theory, where market value is defined as 'the average value of commodities produced in a single sphere' (III, p. 279). In this notion, market value which is the weighted average of individual values in a sphere of production may not coincide with any actually existing individual value. In Marx's second notion, which can be called the 'dominant mass' theory, market value is viewed as the actual 'individual value of commodities produced under average conditions in the sphere in question, and forming the great mass of its commodities' (III, p. 279). In contrast with these two notions, where technical conditions of production define market value in one way or the other without referring to the situation of demand and supply in the market, Marx's third notion gives demand a decisive role in determining the market value, and can be called the 'demand and supply' theory. For instance this type of notion is expressed as follows: 'If the demand is so strong that it does not contract when price is determined by the value of commodities produced in the worst conditions, then it is these that determine the market value. . . . If the mass of commodities is too great to find a complete outlet at the market value, market value is determined by the commodities produced under the best conditions.' (III, pp. 279–80).

No one can deny that these three types of notions are not easily made consistent. At first sight the first type of notion seems the most proper application of the embodied labour theory of value, since it defines market value as the exact social average of labour embodied in a commodity in the sphere of production in question. In this notion the extra surplus-value acquired by producers with better technical conditions, who can sell their commodity products dearer than those individual values, can be regarded as a transfer of labour value from other producers in the same sphere operating under worse than average conditions. However, this notion lacks any internal relation with the dynamism of the market in determining market value. It is clear that Marx intended here to introduce such a role for the market into his value theory, as suggested in the third type of notion. Actually the technical average of individual values in the first notion may not serve as a gravitational centre for fluctuating market prices, in so far as the mathematical average may not represent any concrete individual value defined by real conditions of production. For instance, in the case that the individual value of commodities produced by the dominant great mass of producers in the sphere is smaller than the technical average value, then the market price coinciding with the average value would not stabilise demand and supply in the market, but tend to be reduced by a relatively rapid increase of supply by the dominant producers. Marx's second type of notion of market value seems immune from such a problem in most cases. However, the market value of a commodity produced by utilising the different and restricted natural conditions represented by land cannot be regulated by the dominant mass of conditions, but by the marginal condition of land as we shall see in more detail in the theory of differential rent.

The basis of ground-rent theory might be somewhat closer to the third type of notion of market value in Marx. However, this 'demand and supply' theory tends to emphasise one-sidedly the role of demand as the determinant of market value without much examining the reaction of supply in regulating prices. As a result, the theoretical distinction between the market value or market price of production and market price becomes obscured. This theory could easily be connected with the Rubin School, where the social evaluation of labour value in a market is made much of. Although the role of the market must surely be taken into consideration here in the theory of market value, the more basic role of objective technical conditions of production to regulate values should not be disregarded, but rather concretely clarified through the motion of market. From this view point, the one-sidedly demand-oriented notion, as well as the statically technological notions, of market value in Marx must be corrected together with their inconsistency.

The market value appears as the gravitational center of market prices. The conceptual separation and relation between market value and market price as concretely developed forms of value are essential to reach a proper understanding here again. Since there is no direct social means of defining representative conditions of production in various spheres in a commodity economy, the market value corresponding to the representative conditions of production must be sought through the anarchical fluctuations of market price. Market value is thus social value determined through the mediation of the market and 'depends upon the condition of production under which the supply of the commodity is capable of being adjusted to the fluctuating demand for it', as K. Uno defines it.[26] Actually price pushed up by a strong demand would be regulated by the value of commodities produced in the worst conditions in so far as the fluctuating demand is adjusted in the main by such conditions of production. This would apply to the restricted natural conditions of land as in the theory of differential rent. Otherwise, price pulled up by strong demand would eventually be pulled down by increased supply from dominant and better conditions of production. Market value thus regulates market price, normally depending upon the dominant mass of conditions of production so far as technically improvable methods of production and the related scales of capital are concerned. It is conceivable in the very process of innovation of methods of production that the dominant conditions of production regulating market value are indeterminate for a while, with an unstable downward motion of price. The resultant shift of market value, which appears with the settlement of any newly dominant method of production, cannot be directly identified, but must be sought out again through the fluctuating market price.

Thus, what Marx intended to signify in his different notions of market value can be integrated, in my view, into a single notion as social value determined through the mediation of the market, reflecting the dominant conditions of production to meet fluctuating demand. In this reformulation the theory of differential rent could be an extended development, and not a revision, of the theory of market value. The reformulated notion of market value is straightforwardly identifiable with the notion of market price of production, particularly being freed from the definition of market value as technical average of individual labour values embodied in the sphere of production in question. So long as market value appears as the gravitational centre of market price through fluctuating demand, it consequently shows the representative conditions of production for capitalist competition across many branches of production. The cost-price and the average profit making up the price of production must be based upon such representative conditions of production dominating each sphere to meet fluctuating demand in the market. The market price of production defined above is nothing but a concrete feature of market value in the light of capitalist competition across industrial spheres. When the market price of a commodity is higher than the market price of production determined by such representative conditions, then a higher rate of profit than the general rate must be given to capitalists with such conditions, and it therefore promotes the rapid expansion of supply of the commodity in the market so as to pull down both its market price and the rate of profit for its producers. The motion of market price gravitating around the market price of production thus forms a concrete adjustment mechanism for the distribution of socially necessary labour in accordance with a social system of needs for various commodity products, and it simultaneously reveals through the market the socially standard conditions of production in each sphere as the basis of capitalist competition which tendentially equalises the rate of profit between industrial spheres.

The same capitalist competition which equalises the rate of profit across industrial spheres must, contrastingly, always leave differences in the rate of profit among capitals having different conditions of production within each sphere. Extra profit due to a higher rate of profit than the general rate accrues to capitals with conditions of production better than the representative ones which regulate the market price of production. Conversely, capitals with conditions of production worse than the representative ones must obtain less than the general rate of profit so long as the market price of production prevails in the fluctuating market. Therefore, capitalist competition which seeks to obtain a higher rate of profit as far as possible, tends to shift the technologically mobile conditions of production from the worse to better. The market-regulating conditions of production would eventually be altered in the process of such competition among capitals. Certainly there are inertia or frictions for capitals in altering their methods of production for some periods of time, such as the restriction of existing fixed capital still much to be depreciated. Otherwise better conditions of production would be so easily and rapidly imitated and spread that those cannot be structually stable basis for extra profit even for a short period of time. Nevertheless, so long as the differences in conditions of production such as technological methods or scales of production are transferable and imitable in their nature by capitals, extra profit due to the difference has a transient character, appearing and disappearing in the course of time. This type of extra profit, therefore, cannot form a fundamental obstacle against the process of capitalist competition equalising the rate of profit, and it is actually obtained by capitalists with better conditions of production.

In contrast to the case of the 'technical average' theory of market value, we need not limit the substantial source of extra profit gained by individual capitals with better conditions of production to the surplus-labour extracted in the *same* industrial sphere. Such extra profit is logically conceivable even in a case where capital of worse than the standard condition of production does not exist, and therefore where there is no countervailing transfer of the substance of value within the *same* sphere. The substance of this type of extra profit can also be the transfer of surplus-labour extracted in other industrial spheres just as the substance of some portion of average profit, as we have already argued in Chapter 5, Section 5.2 concerning the extra surplus-value obtained by capitals with improved methods of production. In its nature the substance of extra profit obtained by technologically superior conditions of production contains a role for the socially necessary labour cost of improving and renewing production methods, a cost which is more or less common to all forms of society, and also to a socialist society. There is no doubt, however, that capitalism would never consciously intend to develop production methods in favour of workers' own well-being or in ecological harmony with wider nature, as far as it copes with the labour costs of improving production methods subject to the individualistic chrematistic form of extra profit.

## 7.3 GROUND-RENT AND LANDED PROPERTY

### The Capitalistic Form of Landed Property

In contrast with the extra profit obtained from better technological conditions of production, the extra profit gained on the basis of the monopolisable natural conditions of the land is not subject to an equalisation of the rate of profit through the process of competition confined only to that between capitals.[27] It is because the differences in the conditions of production concerning the monopolisable natural conditions of land, unlike the differences due to technological conditions, are not easily changeable or transferable by capitals through the process of their competition. Certainly the better condition of land is not absolutely unchangeable, but shifts in the process of technological development. The utilisation of chemical fertilisers or the development of the transport system, for example, have much affected the difference in grades of land or in the relative costs of capital invested in land. However, changes in the grades of land often occur from external causes beyond the control of the capital directly using it, and usually take a longer time to become effective in comparison with changes in the technological methods of production. The difference in the monopolisable natural conditions of land therefore must appear as a solid and definite external precondition for competition among capitals at least for a certain period of time. The extra profit due to such differences in the natural conditions of land should in principle be excluded from capitalist competition so as to equalise the rate of profit between themselves, and must be transformed into differential rent. This defines the basic position and the economic form of landed property under a capitalist order of production.

In precapitalist class societies, landed property is one form or the other was always central to the relation of production, and served as the social basis for the dominant landlord class to appropriate effectively the whole surplus product or surplus-labour of the direct producers. In contrast, landed property can no longer be central to the relations of production in a capitalist society. Its economic realisation becomes limited in principle to the appropriation of a portion of the social surplus-product, and in the form of a secondary redistribution of surplus value initially obtained by capital. Nevertheless, the monopoly of landed property in the form of private ownership is 'a historical precondition for the capitalist mode of production and remains its permanent foundation' (III, p. 754). As Marx reminds us in his analysis of 'The Primitive Accumulation of Capital,' the capitalist mode of production 'presupposes on the one hand that the direct producers are freed from the position of a mere appendage of the soil (in the form of bondsmen, serfs, slaves, etc.) and on the other hand the expropriation of the mass of the people from the land.' (III, pp. 753–4). Modern private ownership of land is thus a historically given precondition for the development of capitalist production. It is, coupled with the formation of a class of modern wage-workers being 'free in the double sense' (I, p. 272) that they can dispose of their labour-power freely as a commodity, and also that they have no other commodity for sale being free of all the means of production needed for the realisation of their labour-power. Just as we cannot deduce the existence and the formation of a class of modern wage-workers from the logic of the development of a commodity economy in general, we cannot theoretically deduce the private monopolisation of land internally from the logic of the motion of capital itself. The historical process of the dissolution and transformation of the preceding feudal ownership of land into modern private ownership must here be taken as a given precondition. Thus, capitals cannot utilise land freely without the permission of the landowners by offering some payment called rent, just as workers do no longer have any right to utilise land freely or in the name of preceding feudal traditions or customs. Thus what capitals can really achieve in principle is not the creation of the form of rent or landed property. They rather restrict the level of rent, and therefore the economic value of landed property, so as to suit their own laws of motion in the process of mutual competition.

The position of landed property, which is subject to the law of motion of capital, is basically shown in the principles of differential rent. The transformation of a portion of surplus-value into ground-rent in the form of differential rent is explained as an extension of, not a deviation from, the law of market prices of production to give rise to extra profit for capitals with better than representative conditions of production in each industrial sphere. Absolute rent, which is in a sense a concession by capital to landed property, appears on the basis of differential rent and is restricted by the motion of differential rent as we shall shortly discuss. By restricting the range of rent, in the forms of both differential and absolute rent, to its law of motion, capital turns the modern form of private ownership of land more concretely into capitalist landed property.[28] The basic theory of rent for capitalistic landed property would surely serve as a frame of reference for analyses of the economic roles of other types of modern landed property, in relation to small peasants or urban tenants, as well as for the analyses of precapitalist historical forms of landed property, in more concrete levels of researches.

## Differential Rent

Marx explains differential rent in general illustrating how the surplus profit of capitalist factories powered by natural waterfalls instead of steam-engines is transformed into ground-rent. According to the example the factories in a country are powered predominantly by steam-engines. The market price of production for a quantity of a commodity, which requires a capital of 100, is given as 115 with a general rate of profit of 15 per cent in the general and representative conditions of production using steam-engines in an industrial sphere, say of cotton-spinning. If the capital cost for the same quantity of same commodity is 90 for a capital using the natural waterfall on a certain piece of land, then the individual price of production for the capital would be 103.5 ($90 + 90 \times 0.15$). An extra profit of 11.5 above the average profit is gained on the quantity of the commodity, so far as the commodity is also sold at the market price of production of 115 by the capital using the waterfall. The market price of production as the gravitational centre of the market price must remain at 115, when the monopolisable natural condition of land with waterfalls is too limited to satisfy the social need for the commodity, and assuming that the factories driven by steam-engines can adjust their output in correspondence with the fluctuating social demand.

Under these circumstances, an extra profit of 11.5 per quantity of commodity must be transformed into differential rent through competition among capitals. Capital which makes use of the land with the waterfall would retain some surplus profit beyond the general rate of profit, if a level of rent lower than 11.5 per quantity of the commodity is being paid. Then, competitive bids, offering a higher rent to the landowner must push the level of rent up. On the contrary, if the landowner insists on charging a rent higher than that level of 11.5, then no capitalist would come to rent the land. The landowner would thus be forced to reduce the proposed level of rent. It is thus clearly the competition of capitals, and not the demand of landowners, which determines the level of differential rent. The landowner is placed in a passive position, just receiving a level of rent determined by the law of motion of capital.

Extra profit, and therefore the differential rent, due to the waterfall in the example above may decrease and finally disappear in the process of improving the efficiency of steam-engines. The land with the waterfall may thus fall out of use. However, the difference between the natural conditions of fertility and location of the land must generally remain in one way or the other, bringing about extra profit to be transformed into differential rent. Just as extra profit accrues to capital using land with the waterfall in the example above, extra profit gained by capitals using superior monopolisable natural conditions of land, turns into differential rent through competition between capitals. The notion of differential rent can further be broken into two forms, i.e. differential rent I and II, according to Marx.

Differential rent I shows how extra profit is gained and transformed into rent by equal quantities of capital being invested on different grades of land, whereas differential rent II relates to the difference in productivity of equal quantities of capital invested successively and intensively on the same land. The basic logic of differential rent is shown in Marx's numerical examples concerning the agricultural production of wheat on land of different grades of fertility. Since the logic is easily applicable to the land graded by location, differentiating the costs of operation for industrial and commercial, as well as agricultural, capitals, let us follow Marx's simple example.[29] Different harvests for the same amount of capital investment of 50 shillings are assumed. By excluding different costs of production due to the techniques of production in use, the same amount of capital would be invested on approximately equal areas of land. The results in the four grades of land is used by Marx as a starting-point to show the logic of differential rent I (III, p. 791).

*Table* 7.7

| *Type of soil* | *Product* | | *Capital advanced* | *Profit* | *Rent* |
|---|---|---|---|---|---|
| | *Quarters* | *Shillings* | | *Shillings* | *Shillings* |
| *A* | 1 | 60 | 50 | 10 | — |
| *B* | 2 | 120 | 50 | 70 | 60 |
| *C* | 3 | 180 | 50 | 130 | 120 |
| *D* | 4 | 240 | 50 | 190 | 180 |
| Total | 10 qrs | 600 sh. | 200 sh. | 400 sh. | 360 sh. |

It is assumed in an economy represented by Table 7.7, the general rate of profit is 20 per cent giving 10 sh. of average profit for 50 sh. of capital advanced. So far as the soil type *A* is now the regulative natural condition determining the market price of production of wheat in the table, then capitals invested in the types of soil *B*, *C* and *D* would each obtain 60 sh., 120 sh., and 180 sh. of extra profit beyond 10 sh. of average profit. These amounts of extra profit must be transformed into differential rent, as was the extra profit for capital utilising the favourable land with a waterfall in the previous case.

As Marx criticised, Ricardo erroneously believed that cultivation of land had always started from the best grade of soil down to the worse grades along with the law of decreasing returns. The order of the soil grades was conceivable historically and actually to be made up in either descending, ascending or a mixed order. Development of technologies and transportation, as well as the changes of the social attitudes of landowners, has often altered the accessible grades of land. However, as a result of such development, the following social conditions must now exist for the time being in support of Table 7.7:

(i) –The supply of wheat from the worst soil, type *A* of the four types, is indispensable to satisfy the social need of wheat under the given technological conditions of capital.
(ii) –The soil type *A* represents the natural conditions of reproduction of wheat which allows the flexibility to adjust the supply to meet fluctuating demand. In other words, the supply can be increased or decreased in about the same soil type *A* when the social demand for wheat increases or decreases for the moment.
(iii) –In contrast, the better soil types *B*, *C*, *D* are now restricted and capitals are unable to expand cultivation on these types of soil. Otherwise, the conditions (i) and (ii) above could not be assured.

In so far as the soil type *A* represents for the present the natural conditions of supply to meet the fluctuating demand for wheat under these social conditions, the governing market price of production of wheat is determined by the conditions of production on this type of soil. Upon the basis of such a determination of the market price of production the extra profit for capitals invested on the better soil types *B*, *C*, *D* must necessarily be obtained by selling their products at the governing market price of production, and it must be transformed into differential rent as shown in Table 7.7

There seem to be two related problems here in the theory of differential rent, which have been favoured targets of anti-Marxian critiques, especially in view of the 'technological average' theory of market value, along with a one-sidedly technological approach to the labour theory of value. In the conventional Marxian 'technological average' theory of market value, it is believed to be the socially average quantity of labour embodied in commodities produced in an industrial sphere which determines their market value. The extra surplus value obtained by capitals with better than average technical conditions of production is then regarded as a transfer of surplus-labour from capitals with inferior technical conditions in the same sphere. The theory of differential rent seems to contradict these general notions in two points: first in its definition of the market value or market price of production by the worst 'marginal' productive conditions of land in use, and second in its notion of extra profit without a countervailing transfer of surplus-labour from capitals in the same sphere with inferior productive conditions.

From what we argued in the previous section, the first point can no longer be a serious problem. The notion of market value or market price of production must be, not a mechanical average of individual labour values of one type of commodity, but the centre of gravitation of market price, anarchically revealing under what conditions of production the current necessary amount of commodities for a changing social demand is elastically supplied. The motion of the size of the social demand for a kind of commodity may affect a shift in the regulative conditions of production, but not always. Generally in the short run the conditions of production regulating the market price of production through the fluctuation of the market can be regarded as independent from marginal changes in social demand for the time being. The determination of the market price of production of wheat by the natural conditions of the soil type *A* above is thus not at all inconsistent or a substantial revision of the theory of market price of production in general when reformulated in this way.

Further how can we solve, then the second point? Let us confirm exactly where the problem is. Marx introduces here a concept of 'real production price', which is 240 sh. for 10 qrs or 24 sh. per qr in the case of Table 7.7. It signifies that 10 qrs of wheat are actually produced by 200 sh. of capital invested in total on the four soil types with a 20 per cent general rate of profit. These 10 qrs are sold for 600 sh. instead of 240 sh. since the market price of production is determined by the production price of *A*, which is 60 sh. per qr. According to Marx, 'this is determination by a market value brought about by competition on the basis of the capitalist mode of production; it is competition that produces a false social value' (III, p. 799). This concept of 'false social value' seems self-contradictory. In Marx's basic position, competition among capitals cannot produce any substantial value, and generally social value cannot be false. The Rubin School might argue that the market value of 600 sh. in this case represents so much labour value estimated in the market. Another seemingly opposite view is that 'false social value' is created in the production process by intensified labour under better conditions of production just like the extra surplus value due to improved technical method of production realised in the process of producing relative surplus-value.[30] In my opinion, both of these positions interpret labour value fictitiously, as something remote from real labour-time embodied in commodities and are unpersuasive.

Marx himself also recognises that 'false social value' does not represent the real amount of labour-time embodied in products, when he argues as follows: 'If we imagine that the capitalist form of society has been abolished and that society has been organised as a conscious association working according to a plan, the 10 qrs. represent a quantity of autonomous labour-time equal to that contained in 240 sh. Society would therefore not purchase this product at $2\frac{1}{2}$ times the actual labour-time contained in it; the basis for a class of landowners would thereby disappear.' (III, p. 799). The source of 'false social value' to be transformed into differential rent then, still remains to be explained. Marx suggests that: 'Where society, considered as a consumer, pays too much for agricultural products, this is a minus for the realisation of its labour-time in agricultural production, but it forms a plus for one portion of society, the landowners'. (III, p. 800).

Suppose that a quantity of labour-time contained in 10 qrs of wheat is 480 hours, or that the price–labour coefficient is $\frac{1}{2}$ (i.e. $y = \frac{1}{2}$ in our three tables [Tables 7.4–7.6] approach to the transformation problem in the last part of Section 7.1 of this chapter, assuming that wheat production is in the department II) in terms of real production price of 240 sh. In case these 10 qrs of wheat is a part of the necessary means of consumption sustaining the reproduction of labour-power, the wages as a form of value of labour-power must contain 600 sh., not just 240 sh., as a portion to purchase this quantity of wheat at the market price of production in a capitalist economy. Through this portion of the value-form of labour-power, workers get back 480 hours, not 1200 hours, of their necessary labour-time. The gap between 600 sh. being paid back by the workers as consumers and 240 sh. as the 'real price of production' forms the extra profit to be transformed into differential rent. Thus from the view of the forms of value, the wage-workers as consumers seem to pay 360 sh. of differential rent in this case. However, underneath the forms of value, the workers must obtain the necessary means of subsistence including the necessary labour-time equal to the substance of value of labour-power, which cannot in principle be cut off by differential rent.[31] Therefore, in the light of our theoretical distinction between the forms and the substance of value, we can be sure that the substance of the differential rent is to be regarded not as a share-out from the substance of value of labour-power, but as a transfer of social surplus-labour through the social transactions of the commodity labour-power, wheat and payment of rent beneath the forms of value.

Since Ricardo did not distinguish the forms and the substance of value he would straightforwardly define the value of wheat and then the value of labour (-power) on the worst condition of land. The form of market value, 600 sh. in the above instance, could not theoretically be distinguished from the real substance of value or the quantity of labour-time actually embodied in wheat. Marx was conscious of the point, but he did not thoroughly solve the problem with his clumsy concept of 'false social value'. The conventional Marxian 'technical average' theory of market value was unable to solve the problem. Uno's reformulation of the theory of market value, as well as his thorough distinction between the forms and the substance of value found the way forward.[32] From the view of the form of market value in our reformulation, the governing price of production of wheat which is determined by the production conditions of the soil type *A* can no longer be exceptional. The general notion of market value or market price of production as the gravitational centre of fluctuating market price, revealing the conditions of production which can meet social demand elastically, is exactly applicable to the governing price of wheat. From the view of the substance of value, however, the difference in the conditions of production based upon the monopolisable natural conditions of land must be treated separately. In case of technical conditions of production, the representative conditions in a sphere of production, which are revealed through a fluctuating market, must be a standard basis on which to define the substance of value or the quantity of labour-time embodied in a commodity product of the sphere. Such representative technical conditions of production are socially to be confirmed even among capitals cultivating the same soil type *A*, as well as on the other soil types. Apart from such representativeness of technical conditions of production, we should not just take the natural conditions of the soil type *A* for the social standard basis or which to define the substance of value embodied in the product of the soil, even though the soil type *A* would serve here as the regulative condition of land for the market price of production. Thus, in contrast with the conventional notion of the value of land-products since Ricardo, the substance, not the form, of value of the land-products must be determined by the total or average conditions of land, and not by the worst marginal condition.

Upon the basis of differential rent I as we have seen, differential rent II appears when sums of capital are invested successively on the same piece of land with varying productivity. Each unit of successive investment must be mutually separable and independent so as to form extra profit due to the various productivities to be transformed into differential rent II. For instance, an additional unit of seeds, fertiliser and labour-power as in double-cropping would easily be separable from the preceding units of investment on the same piece of land. In contrast, developments in the method of production often brings with them increases in the unit of capital investment, which cannot be partially divided. The effect of increased units of investment in such a case of developed technologies must be counted only as a whole in the form of differential rent I.

The simplest case for differential rent II can be illustrated as follows (cf. III, p. 816). The case of differential rent I in Table 7.7 is assumed, where the soil type *A* regulates the market price of production at 60 sh. including 10 sh. of average profit. If 4 units, instead of 1 unit, of independent capitals of 50 sh. were successively invested on the same 1 acre of the soil type *D*, so that the first investment yielded 4 qrs. the second 3 qrs. the third 2 qrs. and the fourth 1 qr. with the same regulating market price of production of 60 sh., then the first investment would yield extra profit of 180 sh., the second that of 120 sh., and the third that of 60 sh. These extra profits, 360 sh. in total, must be transformed into differential rent through competition among capitals, just as the extra profit yielded by capital investment on the soil types *D*, *C*, *B* in Table 7.7.

The possibility of such successive capital investments on the same piece of land yielding differential rent II is a means by which capital gets around the natural restrictions of land to certain extent. Capital can increase the supply of agricultural products even within the old lease holds of better soil types by additional investment. When such increases of the supply of wheat by successive investments is great enough in comparison with social demand, then the least-fertile soil type *A* in table 7.7 may become unnecessary and driven out of cultivation. If the soil type *A*, and therefore the fourth investment on the soil type *D*, was actually thus driven out so that the soil type *B* become the regulative condition for the market price of production of wheat, then the structure of extra profit to be transformed into differential rent would alter as shown in Table 7.8.

The amount of surplus-value to be transmitted to landowners in the form of differential rent can usually be reduced by elevating the level of the worst grade of cultivated land (from *A* to *B* in this case) with a lowered market price of production. Conversely the differential rent would normally increase when the level of the worst grade of cultivated land is lowered (from *B* to *A* for example) in the process of capital accumulation which increases social demand and supply.

Thus the landowner class may become better off just by passively

Table 7.8

| *Type of soil or successive investment on D* | *Product* | | *Capital advanced* | *Profit* | *Rent* |
|---|---|---|---|---|---|
| | *Quarters* | *Shillings* | | *Shil-lings* | *Shil-lings* |
| *B III* | 2 | 60 | 50 | 10 | – |
| *C II* | 3 | 90 | 50 | 40 | 30 |
| *D I* | 4 | 120 | 50 | 70 | 60 |
| Total | 9 qrs | 270 sh. | 150 sh. | 120 sh. | 90 sh. |

reflecting the result of the social process of capital accumulation. Furthermore the landowners can often get back their land with the incorporated effects of capital investment, such as improvement of soil, irrigation or farm buildings, as well as the remaining value of capital incorporated into the earth or '*la terre-capital*' (III, p. 756), when the lease periods are over. On the other side, by the successive additional investment on lease land, capitalists may obtain extra profit for themselves, which would be transformed into differential rent only after the lease period. Therefore, the landowners tend to attempt to shorten the term of the leases as far as possible, while capitalists resist it and attempt to prolong the term. At the same time capitalists tend to avoid long-term investments on land, preferring investment to get extra profit for themselves in shorter turnover periods. This effect of the lease period is a source of distortion in agricultural production, and a threat to the ecological conditions of soil and land under capitalism.

So far, it was assumed that the least-fertile grade of land in cultivation would not yield any extra profit to be transformed into differential rent. However, in cases where successive investments with varying productivity on the least-fertile grade of land become socially necessary to satisfy the demand, then differential rent II can appear even on the worst grades of cultivated land. For instance, if the first investment on the soil type *A* in Table 7.7 no longer suffices in order to meet the social demand for wheat, the second investment with a smaller productivity producing just 0.8 qr. on 1 acre of land *A* with the same 50 sh. of capital would become the regulative condition for the market price of production of wheat. Then the market price of production must rise to 75 sh. (60 sh./0.8 qr.) so as to yield 15 sh. of extra profit to be transformed into differential rent II on the least-fertile type of land *A*. An investment to regulate the market price of production at a lower level than the first investment on *A* may also be performed not on *A*, but somewhere on the upper grade of soil *B* or *C* or *D*. Anyway, through the motion of differential rent II, even the least-fertile land in cultivation is given the possibility of yielding differential rent. It means that all types of cultivated land possibly yield differential rent. However, so far as we observe with Ricardo only the logic of differential rent, there is no theoretical guarantee that the least-fertile land will yield extra profit to be converted into rent. Since without exception landowners would not lend capitalists their land free in any case, we have to see another possible form of rent beyond Ricardo's theoretical limits, following Marx's analyses of absolute rent.

**Absolute Rent**

Concerning differential rent as we have seen, 'landed property simply causes the transfer of a portion of the commodity price that arises without any effort on its part (rather as a result of the determination by competition of the production price governing the market)'. 'Landed property is not in this case a cause that *creates* this component of price or the rise in price that it presupposses. But if the worst type *A* land cannot be cultivated – even though its cultivation would yield the price of production – until it yields a surplus over and above this production price, a rent, then landed property is the creative basis of this rise in price. *Landed property has produced this rent itself.*' (III, p. 889). Absolute rent thus appears as transformation of extra profit which springs from rejection by landowners to lending their land free, even of the least-fertile type.

For instance, if the landowners of the soil type *A* in the previous Table 7.7 would not lend their land without getting at least 5 sh. an acre as ground-rent, the governing market price assuring that supply meets the demand of wheat must go up to 65 sh. from 60 sh.. Extra profit of 5 sh. an acre is now available for capitalist farmers operating on the worst-type *A* land, and is converted into rent. This may appear as if it were differential rent II in the worst type of cultivated land, when additional investment on the old leaseholds in the upper grades of land produces wheat at the production price of 65 sh. a quarter without yielding rent. It is apparent, however, that such additional investment is enabled here only by restriction by landwowners of the worst-type *A* land so as to raise the governing price to 65 sh. When the governing price of wheat thus becomes 65 sh. the extra profit to be transformed into rent in Table 7.7 must increase from 60 sh. to 70 sh. in *B*, from 120 sh. to 135 sh. in *C*, and from 180 sh. to 200 sh. in *D*. In total it would go up from 360 sh. to 410 sh. including the newly created 5 sh. in *A*. The structure of rent in *B*, *C* and *D* is quite similar to that of differential rent in Table 7.7. The increase of rent, 50 sh. in this case, has a character of absolute rent, produced by landed property. Certainly what is 'produced' by landed property cannot be the substance of value or embodied labour-time obtained in the form of absolute rent, but must be just the form of value or a portion of a raised price enabling the yield of extra profit to be converted into absolute rent.

The restriction of landowners on cultivation of their land in some circumstances exists not merely on the worst type of soil, but also on the better types of land. The reasons for landowners to reject cultivation can be various. For instance they may avoid the leasehold conditions which are available under the current situation of market, and prefer to wait better possible conditions in the near future, especially when the terms of the lease are usually fixed for a period of many years. Owners of land, particularly on a large scale, need not be such money-grubbers as capitalists, and may keep some part of their land, even of the better soil types, for luxurious purposes such as the maintainance of vast residential parks of deer forests. In so far as some portions of the better types of land are thus kept out of cultivation by landowners' own wishes, the market regulating price of the land-products would be so much enhanced, and so become regulated by worse soil types than otherwise. This effect, in addition to the landowners' demand for some rent even on the worst type of land for cultivation, increases ground-rent for the land in use. The portion of rent thus increased is absolute rent in its character, being 'produced' by landed property, although it is obtained from the form of extra profit arising between the market regulative price and the individual prices of production just as in the case of differential rent.

Absolute rent is essentially a concession by capital to landed property in transferring a part of surplus-value as a burdensome social payment against the private right of landowners to be able to refuse to allow investment on their land. It is an indispensable burden on capitals so long as capitalist production must maintain the private ownership of land as a vital historical precondition of its own existence.

However, capitals deal with the burden of absolute rent socially as a category annexed to differential rent converted from exactly the same form of extra profit. Furthermore, capitals will not accept the concession or the burden of absolute rent without limit.

Marx defined a theoretical limit to absolute rent within the range of 'the excess value over and above the price of production' (III, p. 898), assuming that the value (or the value-price) of agricultural products is higher than their price of production because the organic composition of agricultural capital is generally lower than social average. In other words, the substance of absolute rent is conceived by Marx as 'simply a part of the agricultural surplus-value, the transformation of this surplus-value into rent, its seizure by landowners' (III, p. 898). Marx was inclined to combine in this context his critiques of Ricardo's theoretical failure to distinguish value and price of production on the one hand, and to discern absolute rent from differential rent on the other. Though Marx's progress beyond Ricardo is clear in presenting the theories of both the price of production and absolute rent, his combination of these theories in defining the limit to, or the source of absolute rent, is not very persuasive.[33] For one thing, absolute rent according to Marx's definition cannot exist when the organic composition of agricultural capital becomes higher than social average (a case easily conceivable for the recent development in the advanced capitalist countries). Neither can it exist generally for the lease of land for capital investment in various industrial spheres, whereas landed property would surely demand and manage to obtain some rent absolutely beyond mere differential rent in any industrial sphere. For another, the value or the value-price cannot serve in itself as a standard or an upper limit for the pricing of capitalist commodity products, and there is no reason why the range of absolute rent should remain within the labour-substance of surplus-value embodied on the land concerned. Neither does it much matter in our theoretical view of value and prices of production whether the absolute rent is substantially a part of the surplus labour of workers employed on the land concerned or not.

Where then is the upper limit of absolute rent apart from the labour-value of the landed products? In my view, the possible increase in the supply of landed products by additional capital investment on the old leaseholds would give an upper limit for absolute rent. Additional capital investments with lower productivity are made possible on the old leaseholds by the increased price of land-products, say wheat in our example, due to a restriction of investment, and they would not yield absolute rent. On the other side, the possibility of increasing the supply of land-products on the old leaseholds without paying additional rent for the time being must limit the claim of landowners to ever larger amounts of absolute rent. For instance, additional investments on the better soil type *B*, or *C*, or *D* with a lower productivity in producing wheat at the price of production of 65 sh. a quarter was made possible in our previous example by the restriction of landowners of the worst type *A* land which raised the governing price up to that level. On the other side, however, the landowners of the type *A* land cannot demand more than 5 sh. an acre as absolute rent by pulling up the governing price further, in so far as additional investment with such a productivity can still be expanded on the old leaseholds of better soil types.

Thus, absolute rent is generally subject to the motion of differential rent both in its qualitative form of appearance and its quantitative limitation. In this regard, absolute rent is theoretically separable from monopoly rent, which is not subject to such a general limitation and is determined 'rather by the demand of the purchasers and their ability to pay' (III, p. 898) as in the case of some vineyards suitable for producing special kinds of wine. Monopoly rent as such can be put outside of the principles of ground rent in a capitalist economy, so as to be analysed in more concrete levels of research. In principle, capitals determine by their own motion the form and the limitation of the concessionary transfers of certain parts of surplus-value to landed property, as we have seen in the two 'normal' forms (ibid.) of both differential and absolute rent. The basic logic of competition among capitals centring around a general rate of profit is not at all distorted by payment of these forms of ground-rent, but rather carried out through them.

# 8 The Mobilisation of Capitals

Competition among capitals which forms a general rate of profit and the market prices of production across industrial spheres, through the process of fluctuating market prices, demonstrates the concretely developed forms of the law of value as the law of motion of a capitalist economy. An anarchical capitalist market economy must incessantly misallocate dead and living labour in various spheres, bringing about either an excessive or short supply of commodities. Such misallocation of labour is not generally insolvable. It is usually repeatedly readjusted in the process of the expansion of capitalist production, guided by the movement of market prices. A short supply of commodity products in relation to social demand is indicated when extra profit is obtained by some spheres by selling their products at market prices higher than the market prices of production. Then the expansion of production in such spheres is speeded up basically by reinvesting the extra in addition to the average profit. An excessive supply of commodity products would cause the reverse effects. The shortening of the selling-time of commodity products reflecting favourable market conditions would usually go along with the rise in market prices, having similar effects, and the prolongation of selling-time would have the opposite effects.[1]

The general economic rule common to all social formations, which is to adjust the allocation of labour so as to suit the social system of needs, on the basis of given technical conditions of production, is thus carried through by an anarchical market mechanism in the process of competition among capitals. Capitalism is not one-sidedly a destructive or unbalancing economic order, but in a peculiar way it is also an efficient order in that it expands production by readjusting its own misallocation of labour. Competition among capitals to get higher individual rates of profit, resultingly equalising the rate of profit across industries, serves as the basic mechanism for capitals to adjust the allocation of labour in the process of the expansion of production.

Such a process of competition among capitals along with their expansion of production cannot be as smooth and efficient as it could be, if capital remains just individual industrial capitals. Individual industrial capitals with lower rates of profit, cannot rapidly escape from their own industrial spheres so as to move into other spheres with higher profit rates, especially because they usually have fixed capitals to be depreciated. Possible capital loss due to abandonment of existing fixed capitals, besides the necessity of accumulating considerable funds to install new plant and equipment, would usually slow down the mobility of individual industrial capitals across industries. Other forms of capitals are required, therefore, in particular to mobilise the idle funds of capitals into the process of the competitive expansion of capitals, as the higher mechanism of the motion of capital in equalising the rate of profit and expanding their production more efficiently. The basic forms and positive functions of commercial capital, loan capital, bank capital and joint-stock capital can be fundamentally understood in this context.

## 8.1 COMMERCIAL CAPITAL

Commercial capital appears as a particular species of capital which concentrates its activity in commodity-dealing in the sphere of circulation without involving the process of production.[2] The distinct form and functions of commercial capital must theoretically be separated from its functions of transport and storage which can be regarded as production processes continuing within the process of circulation (III, p. 379), although commercial capital often carry out these functions as well.[3] In its pure main form the motion of commercial capital appears in the form $M - C - M'$, or the purchase of commodities in order to sell them dearer. So far it has the same circulating form as the formula for merchants' capital, which has existed from ancient periods broadly in commodity circulation, as we discussed in the theory of the transformation of money into capital (in Chapter 4, Section 4.3). Its social basis of existence, however, is different from merchants' capital, and depends on the acquisition of a part of the surplus-value produced in the process of capitalist production by promoting the motion of industrial capitals. There are two interrelated aspects of the social functions of commercial capital in promoting the motion of industrial capitals.

First, commercial capital promotes the expansion of production of capitals by accelerating the turnover of capitals and reducing the period and the costs of circulation of capitals. Since capital does not produce surplus-value in the process of circulation, economising on the costs and the period of circulation would so much enable an increase in the efficiency of the valorisation of capital as a whole. In Marx's words, 'As a result of division of labour, the capital that is exclusively concerned with buying and selling is smaller than it would be if the industrial capitalist had to conduct the entire commercial part of his business himself.' (III, p. 388). The capital to be allotted for the costs of circulation such as the costs of book-keeping of transactions, maintenance of warehouses, shops, or the costs of advertisement, and of transport, can be substantially reduced by being concentrated into the hands of commercial capitals. Even in case the absolute amount of such costs of circulation increase in the activity of commercial capitals, efficiency of the valorisation of capital as a whole would still be elevated by a relative reduction of unproductive circulation capital. So far as the total amount of circulation capital and the costs of circulation are socially reduced by the investment of commercial capital in them, a positive effect for the general rate of profit would remain.[4]

Why and how can commercial capital socially accelerate the period of circulation so as to make the circulation capital smaller as a whole by its activity? In a purely capitalist society where little saving if any on the part of workers or capitalists as consumers is assumed, there seems to be little room for commercial capital to speed up and expand total sales. So long as the size of social reproduction and the total income induced are given, acceleration of sales of some commodities by commercial capitals must retard sales of other commodities. Even in a society where a substantial part of income tends to be saved, the effect of the sales efforts of commercial capital in reducing the rate of saving as a whole cannot be certain.[5] 'Division of labour' between industrial and commercial capital would not be very effective in a condition of well-balanced static social reproduction. However, a well-balanced static situation cannot exist in a capitalist social reproduction but only as a mere abstruction.

In an actual capitalist society with all its dynamism, the anarchical misallocation of labour and the resulting imbalance between demand and supply, or social needs and production, are both incessant and inevitable in one way or another across various industries. Inefficiency as a result of such misallocation of labour and resources, having excess supplies of one group of commodities as well as shortages of another, is obvious in view of the possiby realisable expansion of production. While industrial capitals with fixed capitals generally cannot move so swiftly away from industries in excess production into other industries to increase the production of commodities in short supply, commercial capitals without production process can move around much more easily. Commercial capitals tend to increase their purchase of commodity products which happen to be in relative short supply against social demand and therefore also easily saleable in a market. Such activity accelerates the turnover of industrial capitals in the spheres producing those commodities, and clearly promotes the expansion of production more smoothly than would be the case where all capitals just took the form of industrial capitals. By accelerating the expansion of production in the industrial spheres which fail to meet demand, commercial capitals also indirectly promote the sales of spheres in excess supply through contributing to the readjustment of misallocated labour and so prompting an increase in social demand.

Second, in close relation to its first function discussed above, commercial capital also promotes the process of equalising the rate of profit across industrial spheres by its selective purchase of commodity products. As the expansion of production of commodities in short supply is accelerated by their increased purchase, excess demand for those products will eventually disappear and faster than it might otherwise. The elevated market prices of those products due to excess demand and the extra profit obtained by such prices will then also disappear faster. Commercial capitals also serve to solve excess supply in other industries, indirectly through prompting the expansion of production and derivative social demand as a whole. Depressed market prices and the attendant lower than general profit rate would be pulled up so much faster in the process of expanded reproduction. Thus, commercial capital forms a portion of the capitalistic mechanism which anarchically adjusts the social allocation of labour through competition among capitals across industries, guided by fluctuating profit rates which centre on the general rate of profit. Within each sphere of production, commercial capital reduces the random differences in the costs of circulation or the periods of sale among individual producers, by taking over such costs or the responsibility for such periods, collectively and thus makes the basis of competition for the rate of profit among industrial capitals so much more objective.

Commercial capitals themselves also participate in competition, pivoting around the general rate of profit. Individual, accidental, random differences in the costs of circulation or the periods of sale for the individual commodity are apt to be more or less cancelled out in the hands of commercial capitals by concentrating the process of the sales of many industrial capitals and particularly those in various spheres of production. Therefore, the basis on which commercial capitals compete for profit cannot be one-sidedly accidentally random. Furthermore, competition is pursued not merely among commercial capitals but also between commercial capitals and industrial capitals which have solid technical bases for competition to equalise the rate of profit. There is no fundamental obstacle to transferring capitals from commerce into industry or contrariwise, guided by prospect of a higher rate of profit, except such impediments as existing fixed capital in the short run. The rate of profit of commercial capital is thus also subject to the law of competition among capitals which forms the general average rate of profit.

A capitalistic rationale for industrial capital to share out a portion of surplus-value to unproductive commercial capital is in the social function of commercial capital which economises the costs of circulation and circulation capital as a whole, so as to enable the extension of the scale of production of surplus-value. Individual industrial capitals can certainly carry out the process of selling by themselves. Individually they sell their commodity products to commercial capitals at wholesale prices, which are lower than finally saleable prices with room for commercial profits, only in so far as they conceive such wholesale as being more profitable than their own retailing. The final sales prices can generally be assumed here to be the market prices of production. The wholesale price of a commodity to commercial from industrial capital must be lower than the market price of production so as to enable commercial capital to obtain average profits and to replenish the costs of circulation on the average calculation for an individual commodity. In other words, commercial capital must get an average profit and replenish the necessary costs of circulation as an average calculation, from the difference between the wholesale price which it pays and the market price of production which it receives. By selling its commodity products so much cheaper, industrial capital can still get a higher, not lower, rate of profit, as its turnover is accelerated or the costs of circulation become much reduced or exempted. Or rather in so far as industrial capital expects such an effect, it wholesales its products to commercial capital.

There are some theoretical complications or confusions in Marx's treatment of commercial capital including his numerical examples concerning the conception of the wholesale price charged by industrial capital to commercial capital. They have been sources of trouble for Marxian researchers as well.

First, Marx constructs numerical examples as if the general rate of profit were reduced by the participation of commercial capital. He starts with assuming that the total industrial capital advanced during the year is $720c + 180v = 900$ and that the rate of surplus-value $s' =$ 100 per cent. Then the value or the total price of production of the commodity products must be $1080 = 720c + 180v + 180s$, and the rate of profit would be 20 per cent. When a commercial capital of 100 comes in, moving only in the sphere of circulation without producing any surplus-value, the rate of profit must be reduced to 18 per cent on the total social capital of 1000. Industrial capital now wholesales its products at the price of $1062 = 720c + 180v + 162s$, getting the average profit of 18 per cent on its own capital of 900. Commercial capital purchases these products at this price and sells them at their value or the price of production of 1080 in the market, and obtains the average profit of 18 per cent against its capital of 100, by making 10.62 times turnover of trading in a year. This example obviously contradicts Marx's own correct observation that commercial capital 'increases the ratio of surplus-value to the capital advanced, i.e. the rate of profit' by cutting down the turnover time (III, p. 393). The problem was in the initial assumption. As Marx revises it, 'the additional capital needed [as circulation capital – M. I.] to do without the independent operation of commercial capital might perhaps be 200, and we would then have a total advance of 1100 by the industrial capitalist instead of 900' (III, p. 405). Then the rate of profit would rather go up from 16.36 per cent to 18 per cent, not decline from 20 per cent, through the independent operation of commercial capital.

Second, Marx writes as if the value or the total price of production of the commodity products could be increased by adding the costs of circulation advanced by commercial capital. He presents a case where an additional commercial capital of 50 was further advanced for the costs of circulation, besides the commercial capital of 100 for purchasing commodities from industrial capital. Then, 'the total surplus-value of 180 would now be distributed between a productive capital of 900 and a commercial capital of 150, making a total of 1050. The average rate of profit would thus fall to $17\frac{1}{7}$ per cent. The industrial capitalist sells the commodities to the merchants at $900 + 154\frac{2}{7} = 1054\frac{2}{7}$ and the merchant sells them for 1130 (1080 + 50 for expenses that he has to recover).' (III, p. 406). In this context C. Panico interprets this to mean that Marx's notion of the selling price would become not equal value but be elevated by *B* units of capital advanced 'to perform the necessary acts of circulation'.[6] Although B.

Fine should have recognised Marx's own incompleteness in this regard when opposing Panico's interpretation, Fine is correct in pointing out that the costs of circulation must not merely be added to the denominator for the rate of profit as an additional capital advanced, but also be deducted from surplus-value as the numerator, so as to maintain the selling price by commercial capital at the value of commodities.[7] The average rate of profit would be (180 – 50) ÷ (900 + 100 + 50) = 12.38 per cent instead of $17\frac{1}{7}$. Industrial capital would wholesale the commodities at 900 + 111.42 = 1011.42, and commercial capital sells them for 1080, expending 50 on the costs of circulation and getting the average profit of 18.58 (12.38 per cent of 150) by the difference between the selling price and the purchasing price (1080 – 1011.42 = 50 + 18.58). We should notice here also that industrial capital would have to spend more than 50 as the circulation costs without commercial capital, and that the profit rate of 12.38 per cent is therefore not reduced but raised by the role of commercial capital just as discussed in the first point above.

Third, there is a further source of theoretical complication in Marx's treatment of the variable capital of commercial capital in the latter part of chapter 17 of the third volume of *Capital*. Marx says for instance. 'Since the labour-time and labour of merchant himself is not value-creating labour, even though it procures him a share in the surplus-value already produced, what is the situation with the variable capital that he lays out on the purchase of commercial labour-power? Should this variable capital be included as part of the cost of the outlay of the commercial capital the merchant has advanced?' (III, p. 408). K. Uno reformulated this problem as a particular fetish feature of commercial capital. According to Uno, 'commercial labour is the only labour that "capitalist" may perform',[8] and its costs together with other pure costs of circulation individualy would vary so that its costs, unlike other costs of production, would not be an objective capital advance requiring an average profit in the hands of industrial capitalists, but simply be a deduction from surplus-value. The pure costs of ciculation then, especially of commercial labour, are turned into capital to procure an average profit only through the fetish form of capital as commercial capital. Although there may be a real complication in the distinction between capital investment in commercial wage labour and managerial salaries, including profit-sharing for middle and upper business men and managers, this cannot properly analysed in any detail in the basic theory. Apart from this actual complication, it must be recognised in my view that industrial capital, not confined to the commercial, would already basically deal, with a certain degree of objectivity, with the pure costs of circulation as both a portion of capital and a deduction from surplus-value, as we have argued in the Section 7.2 of Chapter 7.

Having done with these theoretical problems in Marx, it must now be obvious that there are social functions of commercial capitals which economise the costs of circulation and the circulation capital in combination, by elevating the mobility of capital as a whole. The positive functions of commercial capitals in promoting the expansion of production and competition among capitals so equalising the rate of profit, however, have certain limitations. They are effective only so long as the extensive process of accumulation of industrial capital as a whole can go on without serious difficulties. When capital accumulation becomes excessive and smooth expansion difficult to continue, the functions of commercial capital turn rather to the speculative, disturbing and even destructive operations for social reproduction, as we shall see in Chapter 9. Even putting asside such a reversal in its manner of working, the functions of commercial capital which promote the motion of industrial capitals in their process of expansion, by mobilising and economising the costs of and the mass of capitals in circulation are yet far from complete. For one thing commercial capitals cannot take over the total process of the selling of commodities from industrial capitals. Industrial capitals often perform direct transactions among themselves, if not so often against the many final consumers. Commercial capitals also tend to avoid trading commodities which are becoming excessive in a market. For another thing commercial capitals cannot mobilise idle-money capital existing in the turnover of industrial capitals for the expansion of production.

The credit system is a higher more comprehensive mechanism for the mobilisation of capitals over such limitations in the functions of commercial capital.

## 8.2 THE CREDIT SYSTEM

### *How to Approach It*

There are methodological problems in constructing a basic theory of the credit system and interest. First, the credit system including the major forms and functions of bank credit has very much changed along with the stages of capitalist development. If we try to deduce the nature and function of the credit system common to all historical stages of capitalism, the theory would become too formal and abstract to clarify the basic workings of the credit system for capitalist production. We are in a sense forced to be conscious of the actual basis of abstraction in analysing such concrete mechanisms of capitalism as the credit system. Thus if we ever choose a stage of capitalism in this regard, we must take the stage of liberalism in the mid-nineteenth century. It is because the British credit system at that stage was constructed and worked most typically as an inner mechanism of competition among individual capitals. Giant monopolistic corporations were not yet significant either in industries or in banking at that time.[9] Typical business cycles and crises regularly occurred there through the working of the credit system. Therefore, Marx's attempt to build up a basic theory of the credit system based upon his own experience of British capitalism must not be taken as outdated even today.

Second, prior to dealing with the credit system, Marx presents the form of interest-bearing capital and the division of profit into interest and profit of enterprise in the first four chapters of part v of the third volume of *Capital*. Just as the form of profit, the form of interest and interest-bearing capital were, however, not newly created by a capitalist economy, as Marx himself made sufficiently clear in the last chapter of the same part. It was a historical fact in precapitalist societies. Therefore, we had better define the form of interest-bearing capital in the theory of the transformation of money into capital in a commodity economy in general, prior to the analysis of capitalist production, as we have discussed in Section 4.3 of Chapter 4 in this volume. Then we can dispense with the theory of the form of interest-bearing capital here anew. Besides, the theory of the division of profit into interest and profit of enterprise in the first four chapters of part v has left us some substantial difficulties, in spite of their stylistic completeness compared with the later chapters in the part. For instance, interest is presented there first as a relation between 'money capitalists' without functioning as either industrial or commercial capitalists and 'functioning capitalists' without having any capital. Although the classical school used to define interest as a separate economic basis for a certain social class called 'moneyed interest' or 'money capitalists'; interest unlike wages, profit or rent cannot be a definite form of surplus-value exclusively confined to the income of a certain social class such as the rentier type of money capitalist, but basically tends rather to function as a form of internal redistribution of surplus-value among industrial and commercial capitalists through the credit system. A mere 'functioning capitalist' without his own capital is also theoretically too abstract to be real. Furthermore, the qualitative division of profit into interest and profit of enterprise, which wipes out the notion of profit upon advanced capital, would also be too abstract to be theorised on the basis of some actual form or mechanism of the movement of capital. (An idea though that capital naturally brings about interest, and the rest of profit is obtained as a sort of wage or remuneration for entrepreneurship is to some degree common to vulgar fetish notions in bourgeois society.[10]) Therefore the basic theory of interest as a form of surplus-value had better be analysed directly within the form and functions of the credit system, not in the abstract theory of interest-bearing capital.[11]

Third, in relation with the point above, Marx tends to observe the role of banks in the credit system as intermediaries for various external money-lenders like 'money capitalists' and borrowers as industrial and commercial capitalists. As a result the credit system could not be theorised as a thoroughly internal mechanism of capitalist production, or among industrial and commercial capitals, nor could the basic motion of interest be explained as thoroughly internally determined on the basis of capitalist production. On the other side, in the second volume of *Capital*, Marx showed that idle-money capital such as depreciation funds, reserves for accumulation or to guard against price fluctuations, and a fund to maintain continuity in the process of production during the circulation periods, must more or less accompany the turnover of capital, and noted that such idle-money capital would serve as a basis for the credit system. Commercial credit and bank credit mobilise this idle-money capital formed from within the motion of industrial capital. Although banks actually utilise external deposits from the middle and rentier class, their loanable money capital becomes in a sense internalised and subject to the motion of industrial capitals and annexed commercial capitals, so far as it is lent out and so added to these capitals, and must be re-created as idle money in the turnover of capital as it flows back into the banks together with other idle-money capital. Such an internal creation and re-creation of a loanable money fund from the turnover of capital is also decisive for the motion of the money market in the process of business cycles. Therefore, the basic theory of the credit system had better be clarified as an internal mechanism of capital mobilising idle capital among industrial and commercial capitalists.

Bearing these methodological clarifications in mind, 'we shall simply be dealing with commercial and bank credit' (III, p. 525) as basic major forms of the capitalist credit system. The simplified or purified basic theory would then surely serve as a standard frame of reference for the analyses of capitalist credit including various other economic forms of social relations such as state debt or consumer credit in upper, more concrete, levels of researhes.

**Commercial Credit**

Commercial credit is 'the credit that capitalists involved in the reproduction process give one another. This forms the basis of the credit system. Its representative is the bill of exchange, a promisory note with a fixed date of payment, i.e. "a document of deferred payment".' (III, p. 610). As Marx notices, the spontaneous basis for the credit system is in the function of money as a means of payment in simple commodity circulation and the corresponding relationship of creditor and debtor, but it is 'expanded, generalized and elaborated' with the development of the capitalist mode of production (III, p. 525).

Let us assume four capitalists who are directly or indirectly involved in a series of reproduction process, i.e. a cotton textile manufacturer (*A*), a spinner (*B*), a trader of raw cotton (*C*) and a raw-cotton grower (*D*). A simple type of commercial credit can be formed when *A*, without having enough amount of cash, wants to purchase a certain quantity of cotton thread from *B* by drawing up a promissory note to *B*. *B* may transfer this note to C with his endorsement in order to purchase raw cotton instead of waiting for the deferred payment from *A* on the due date, say in three months' time. In such a case, however, a bill of exchange is utilised as a more typical and general form of commercial credit. As illustrated in Figure 8.1 below, a bill of exchange in this case is drawn by *B*, commanding *A* to pay *C* a certain amount of money after three months on a due date. When accepted by *A*, *B* passes the bill to *C* and thus cancels out his credit and debt. *C* receives the bill as a changeover of his credit from *B* to *A*. However, if *A* is insolvent on the due date, *C* can instantly demand payment of *B* as a surety jointly liable. Cancellation of debt and credit on the part of *B* thus still leaves him the responsibility of joint liability. The trader *C* would use the bill with his endorsement to signify the same joint liability if the cotton-grower $D$ receives it in wholesaling raw cotton. Then, $A$'s debt to $C$ would further be changed to a debt to $D$.

*Figure* 8.1

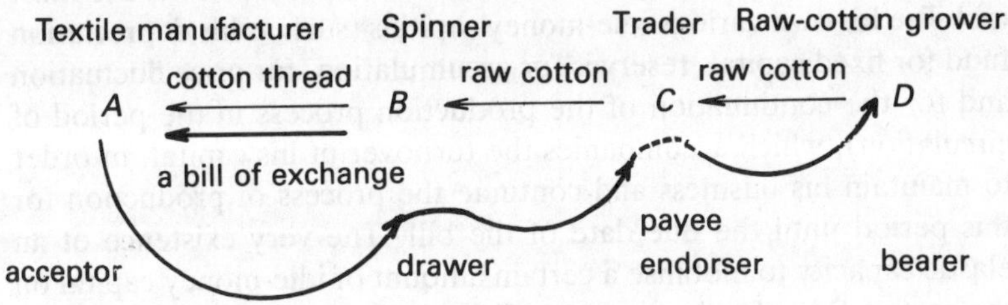


Thus, a bill of exchange would circulate as basic capitalistic credit money utilised in the transactions of commodities among industrial and commercial capitalists. Though it is a private document of promise to pay, its circulation is facilitated by the joint liability of a drawer and endorsers in addition to the acceptor. And since it is a private promise to pay issued and received among actual capitalists according to their own will and necessity, it can elastically expand transactions among them relatively independently of the external circumstances or regulations like those effecting the quantity of the money-supply.[12]

Commercial credit enables a co-operative economy of circulation capital and so facilitates the expansion of reproduction. It is apparent in the above case that the commodity capitals in circulation, cotton thread and raw cotton, are mobilised for the extension of the reproduction of manufacturing capitalists $A$ and $B$ faster than would be the case without commercial credit. On the part of such capitalists as $A$ and $B$, a portion of idle-money capital which must be prepared in order to continue the process of production during the period of selling their commodity products, can also be spared by the repetition of transactions through commercial credit. A capitalist selling by use of a bill of exchange would gain as well since he can economise on the costs of circulation such as storage or on the money reserve to guard against price fluctuations. Moreover, he may be able to use the bill, just as $C$ does in the above case, in purchasing the necessary commodity from other capitalist, further extending the chain of commercial credit.

Such an extension of the chain of commercial credit is in its nature not without limit. It has inner logical limitations as we shall shortly see, and therefore must always leave a terminal capitalist in the chain who acts as the final bearer of the bill until the due date. Suppose *D* in the above becomes the final bearer of the bill for three months until due. This raw-cotton grower, *D*, cannot then get back the money for the commodity sold by the bill in the meantime. He must mobilise his own various idle-money capitals (such as his depreciation fund for fixed capital, reserves for accumulation, for price fluctuation and for the continuation of the production process in the period of circulation), which accompanies the turnover of his capital, in order to maintain his business and continue the process of production for this period until the due date of the bill. The very existence of an elastic capacity to mobilise a certain amount of idle-money capital on the part of *D* is a fundamental condition to form and maintain a chain of transactions through the bill of exchange between the four capitalists above. In this regard the idle capital of *D* is mobilised not merely for his own sake, but simultaneously also accomodates in fact the acceleration of transactions and the extension of reproduction of the other capitalists *A*, *B* and *C* as well.

Extension of reproduction by means of commercial credit would usually work in the direction of adjusting the anarchical imbalance between industrial spheres, and thus also to equalise the rate of profit among them. In particular, the spheres in which commodity products are in short supply would expand their purchase of means of production more positively than others depending on the elastic extension of commercial credit. Their production would thereby be accelerated more than others, and therefore the surplus-profit due to the excess of the market prices of their products over their prices of production would eventually disappear. On the contrary, the spheres in excessive production would attempt to promote sales of their products positively by giving credit, and would reduce their own purchases by credit. Thus, commercial credit usually works both ways simultaneously. While it fosters the extension of reproduction and elevates the general rate of profit by mobilising idle-money capitals in order to economise on the size of circulation capital through private transactions on credit among actual capitals, it also functions to promote the equalisation of the rate of profit across industrial spheres.

Since individual capitalists can usually elevate their rate of profit and obtain additional profit by purchase on commercial credit, they have a reason to share out a portion of their increased profit by paying interest for their debts. On the other side, a capitalist who gives credit by selling his commodities against deferred payment does not directly hand out his money as a loan. The practical use of his idle money, as in the case of the raw-cotton grower *D* above, is necessary to maintain the chain of commercial credit by allowing him to give credit for a certain period of time. But the substantial amount of money mobilised to sustain his own process of production would not always coincide with the amount of credit given in selling his commodities. Nevertheless credit and debt here are not in terms of commodities transferred, but definitely in terms of money. A buyer on commercial credit cannot return the commodities on the due date, and has to pay the money promised by all means, while he gets complete property-rights over the commodities immediately on the date of purchase even on credit. Given the form of interest-bearing capital in a commodity economy in general, credit and debt in terms of money among capitals are naturally regarded as reasonable grounds on which to claim interest from the view of creditor, even if the creditor did not have an opportunity cost since he was just mobilising his *idle* money and commodity capital.[13] Thus, the reason for claiming interest payments would arise from the fact that the form of interest exist generally in a commodity economy and not from the substantial capitalistic production relation. On the other side, the capitalistically reasonable grounds for paying interest by the debtor lies clearly in the additional profit or surplus-value obtainable through the use of credit.

Interest in commercial credit is claimed and transmitted as a difference between the cash price and credit price of commodities. It does not yet appear in a form independent of commodity prices and commodity transactions. Ther rate of interest is still in a sense buried in credit prices, and it cannot therefore be generalised, so leaving various individual divergences. For instance, the credit price of a commodity whose social demand seems to be increasing more than its supply would for the time being be heightened in comparison with the cash price more than otherwise, reflecting the anticipated increase in its market price in the near future. A gap between the cash price and the credit price would be less than average in the opposite case. Divergency of the rate of interest accords with the nature of commercial credit which is formed as a private relation of credit between individual capitalists in their transactions of commodities.

Commercial credit must be subject to certain limit originating in its basic nature. First, it cannot come into the transactions between capitalists and workers or consumers. Second, even among capitalists, it cannot be a socially universal organisation of credit, but is basically confined to the relations among capitalists possibly being linked in the line of manufacturing processes. It cannot form a credit relation between capitalists in the unrelated processes such as baking and spinning. Third, the amount of money, or the terms for payment of a bill, would not be suitable for successive transactions after a certain length in the chain, say possibly after the raw-cotton grower *D* in the example above. Fourth, even with the joint liability of capitalists written on the bill, its credibility cannot yet be of a social character in any sense, and may not be of sufficient quality to be accepted by some capitalists, say possibly a trader *E* to sell fertiliser to *D*. Therefore, the chain of commercial credit formed through a bill of exchange cannot be very long, and must always leave a simple debtor and a simple creditor at both ends, as we have suggested.

Corresponding to such limitations, the functions of commercial credit in economising on circulation capital and facilitating the equalisation of the rate of profit are also restricted and cannot be thorough. Bank credit is formed as an higher organisation of the capitalist credit system which dissolves, if not absolutely, the limitations of commercial credit.

## Bank Credit

Typical bank credit in the basic theory of the credit system appears on the basis of commercial credit. It is a capitalistic social organisation mediating the mutual accommodation of idle capitals on a broader scale than commercial credit. Banks form capitalist social relations of debt and credit with many and unspecified industrial and commercial capitalists. Their debt is basically in the form of issued bank notes and received deposit. They give credit typically in the form of the discount of bills of exchange.

Bank notes appear as bank's promissory notes to pay on sight a quantity of the money commodity, e.g. a quarter-pound of gold coined as a pound sterling. It can obtain a broader circulation as a higher grade of credit money beyond the restrictions on bills of exchange in commercial credit. A capitalist like *D* above, who cannot purchase the necessary commodities by a bill of exchange received, because of the restrictions of time, amount or creditability, would be able to go on with the necessary transactions if he could get bank notes at a bank in exchange for the bill. The bank would thereby obtain money credit in the form of the bill upon a certain debtor (like

*A* above) until the due date, but also stand in money debt in the form of the bank notes issued when it discounted the bill for *D*. The cash reserve of a bank to pay its money debt when requested, is formed not merely by a portion of the banker's own capital, but also by an inflow of cash as deposits, and payment for the bills of exchange held by it at their redemption dates. The proportion of a banker's own capital in the cash reserve can be substantially reduced and may even become zero when the bank becomes consolidated and is able to depend sufficiently on its cash inflow through return payments and deposits for, reserve. Practically, the extension of bank credit relies on the trend of deposits and return payments. When bank notes issued by a bank are brought back into the same bank in the form of a deposit or return payment, it reduces the bank's money debt, especially as a ratio to its cash reserve so as to facilitate the potential extension of bank credit. Its effect is similar to a cash inflow which increases the bank's reserve against its money debt.

So far as bank credit is extendible on the basis of the growth of capitalist production, banks would receive deposits by accepting and mobilising various idle-money capitals in the hands of industrial and commercial capitalists, so that the banks can increase their own bases of business. Industrial and commercial capitals would also regard it as convenient to have deposits at banks in order to economise on the cost of storing, paying and receiving money, as well as the costs of clearing credit transactions. Banks act in this function as a modernised form of money-dealing capital (see note 2 of this chapter). In the case that a bank receives deposits easily and plentifully, it need not issue bank notes for its business, though it may occasionally issue some forms of bank cheque or bank draft to make its business elastic.

When a bank exchanges cash or bank notes for a commercial bill of exchange upon the request of capitalist, say the raw-cotton grower *D*, it does not pay the same amount of cash or bank notes as the nominal price given on the bill. A certain amount, according to the period remaining until the redemption date of the bill, is discounted from the nominal price. The discount is actually a form of interest. For instance, if the general rate of interest is 8 per cent a year, about £200 would be discounted from the bill of £10 000 on surface with 3 months' time of due, and £9800 of cash or bank notes are given in exchange with the bill. Suppose the bill is from capitalist *D* in the illustration above. The bank which discounts the bill will actually obtain interest of £200 together with the principal sum of the money credit of £9800, when the return payment of £10 000 is paid from *A* on the due date of the bill.

Capitalists who get cash or bank notes in exchange for commercial bills can accelerate the turnover of their capital, economise their idle funds, and thus obtain additional profit.[14] They would not mind sharing out a portion of the available additional profit as interest in the form of discount on bills. However, the capitalist like *D* who asks a bank to discount a commercial bill of exchange is not really a sole bearer of the discount interest for the bill. The raw-cotton grower *D* has already sold his commodity product raw cotton, for the commercial bill with a 3 months' life, at a credit price of £10 000, higher than the cash price of about £9800. The nominal price of a commercial bill thus contains a portion of interest from the date of its issue, and its transfer must always accompany the credit price being more or less higher than a cash price. Therefore, the discount interest obtained by a bank for the bill was actually born by the initial debtor capitalist *A*, and possibly also by the series of capitalists *B*, *C* and *D*, who subsequently used and passed the bill before it was discounted by the bank. Distribution of the costs of interest contained in the nominal price of the bill, which is finally discounted by the bank, would vary among the four capitalists concerned, depending on the different rates of interest contained in the credit prices of each individual transaction, as well as on the different length of time in which the bill remains in a hands of each capitalist.

Anyway, interest obtained by banks through the discount and redemption of the commercial bill is no longer buried in the credit price of commodities transacted by commercial credit. It now appears clearly as interest on a money loan taking the form of discount, and is obviously separated from the transactions of commodities in the case of bank credit. This must react on commercial credit in making capitalists more conscious of the interest contained by the credit prices of commodities, though individual divergence in its rate would still remain. As banks can extend their basis of loan to earn interest by gathering more deposits, they pay interest to depositors to encourage it, and thus further generalise interest or the form of interest-bearing capital in a capitalist economy. Against loan capital in the form of interest-bearing capital, industrial and commercial capitals are contrasted as *real capital* invested in profit-making enterprises.

Although banks have the capitalistic social function of mobilising idle capitals, they appear in principle as profit-making enterprises attracting individual capital investment just as industrial and commercial capitals. A portion of bank capital or the banker's own capital is used as cash reserves against the balance of received deposits and issued bank notes. However, its proportion decreases as the cash reserve becomes more easily secured through return payments and deposits in the process of the establishment and development of bank business. Anyway, unlike a money-lender or a usurer, a modern bank would not use its own capital directly for lending purposes. A major portion of bank capital is advanced on the costs of circulation related to monetary phenomena such as the costs of storage and transaction of money, or the costs of intermediation and the clearance of credit transactions. More concretely it is invested in the costs of office building, book-keeping, credit inquiries, collection of money on the matured bills, storage of money and bills, and salaries or wages of clerks neccesary for its business. These costs are basically the pure costs of circulation and *faux frais* of production from the social point of view of the general economic rule common to all forms of societies. They cannot add to the substance of value or surplus-value, and therefore they must be deducted and replenished together with profit on capitals invested in them, from the substance of yearly surplus-value, just as in the case of pure circulation costs advanced by commercial capitalists. A capitalistic rationale for allowing such deductions from surplus-value is in the function of bank credit in economising these circulation costs for industrial and commercial capitals, and in increasing the efficiency of the production of surplus-value as a whole, by mobilising idle capital. In general individual industrial and commercial capitalists would not use a bank without seeing a positive benefit for their own rate of profit in one way or the other. Again, investment by banks in an unproductive, negative area, from the standpoint of the direct production of surplus-value, usually brings about positive effects on the efficiency of the production of total social surplus-value, and adds to individual profit by reducing unproductive costs and idle capitals on the part of real industrial and commercial capitals. We must be sure not to confuse these intricate reverse effects of bank investment, compared to the vulgar view which defines it a directly productive of value and surplus-value.

Generally, a portion of additional profit available by an additional expansion of the business of industrial or commercial capitals which depends on bank credit, is shared out and given to banks as interest, typically in the form of discount on commercial bills. In the case that a bank pays interest on deposits to induce their growth, the bank behaves as a sort of commercial capital in the business of purchasing cheap the use of money as a commodity in order to sell it dearer. Interest and its rates signify prices for this particular commodity, the use of money for certain period as a fund. Interest obtained by a bank in a year through lending or selling available funds must thus be divided into three basic parts. A portion should be paid out to depositors as deposit interest. The rest is divided into a portion necessary to replenish bank capital invested and consumed in a year while a third portion remains as bank profit for the total bank capital invested. There is no obvious technically definite standard for the size of bank capitals in a certain area or in the banking business as a whole. However, excessive investment in banks beyond capitalistically rational amounts, either in a certain area or in the business as a whole, at a certain time period must be ascertained and checked by comparing the lowered rate of bank profit with the general rate of profit which is objectively determined on the basis of the technical and physical data of production. There are no fundamental obstacles for bank capitals to be converted into industrial capital or commercial capital, excepting some constraints such as existing fixed capital. In the opposite case, when the rate of bank profit becomes higher than the general rate, industrial and commercial capitals would move into the banking business, eventually causing a reduction in the rate of bank profit. Thus, in competitive social relations with industrial and commercial capitals, the rate of bank profit must also be subject to the law of the equalisation of the profit rate centering around its general rate. In this respect bank capital also appears as a sort of real capital in distinction from loan capital.

Since banking is a sphere of private business for capital investment in parallel with manufacture and commerce, an individual bank cannot be so large-scale as directly to organise the whole of social credit. Each capital with more or less limited capital of its own would concentrate primarily on the discount of commercial bills from capitalists in certain regional areas or spheres of commerce and industry, while it receives credence on its bank notes or on deposits primarily also from those capitalists within its business territory. Accordingly the demand and supply of credit or loanable capital organised by individual banks must have a speciality based upon its particular business territory. For instance a bank in an agricultural area would generally tend to have excessive loanable money capital except in busy farming seasons, while a bank in an area with rapidly growing industries would conversely be short of loanable money capital.

The trend and movement in the balance of demand and supply of loanable capital for a bank is reflected in the cash reserve ratio, i.e. the ratio between its cash reserve and its total liabilities in the form of deposit received or bank notes issued. Cash reserves can be replenished and increased by receiving return payments and deposits. Return payments and deposits in the form of its own bank notes reduce the balance of liability of the bank. Anyway, when demand for the discount of bills at a bank is greater than the supply of loanable capital resulting from deposits and repayments, the bank must reduce its cash reserve or increase its liabilities in the balance of its own bank notes issued in order to meet demand. The cash-reserve ratio must thus decline.

Although a minimum cash-reserve ratio cannot be defined on technological grounds and always allows an elasticity for bankers operations, there is a self-regulative minimum level in the ratio to guard cash reserves, and a bank with a declining cash-reserve ratio in meeting an excessive demand for loans in its business, would ask other banks for loans. Conversely a bank which has a relative plenty of loanable capital, and a higher cash reserve ratio would positively and easily respond to such requests from other banks, and rediscount the commercial bills endorsed by other banks or discount other banker's bills. Thus a mutual accommodation among banks is formed and concentrated in a money market. A major part of the money market is concretely concentrated into a certain area in a commercial centre, like the City. It works as a rediscount market in commercial bills between banks, as well as an efficient place to settle up and clear the matured commercial bills every day.

The rate of interest initially discounted by individual banks would differ, reflecting to a greater or lesser degree the speciality of the territory of each bank, the differing degree of credence or acceptability of each commercial bill and so on. Such differences in the discount rate would mostly disappear in a money market among banks, as the degree of acceptability of the bills endorsed or accepted by banks would become similar, and as the relation between the demand and supply of loanable money capital is concentrated into a single balance getting rid of local speciality. A general market rate of interest thus clearly appears in a money market. Marx's characterisation of the money market should be understood in this context, upon the basis of the functions of credit system, although it is given in chapter 22 of the third volume of *Capital* in an abstract formal theory of interest-bearing capital prior to the analysis of the credit system beginning from chapter 25.

> As far as the permanently fluctuating market rate of interest is concerned, this is a fixed magnitude at any given moment, just like the market price of commodities, because on the money market all capital for loan confronts the functioning capital as an overall mass; i.e. the relationship between the supply of loan capital on the one hand, and the demand for it on the other, is what determines the market level of interest at any given time. This is all the more true, the more the development and associated concentration of the credit system gives loan capital a general social character, and puts it on the money market all at once, simultaneously. (III, p. 488).

Loanable money is treated as a homogenous commodity transacted at the same price, which is the market rate of interest, according to the law of indifference in such a money market. Depending on a money market, individual banks can so much more easily extend their business as mediators of credit transactions. However, in the concrete structure of commercial credit and bank credit, the inter-bank money market cannot gather together all the loanable money and so the social relations of credit. Just as bank credit, facilitating the expansion of commercial credit as its basis, concentrates some portion of the commercial bills and the credit relations expressed in the bills, the money market facilitating the expansion of individual bank credit, concentrates the central portion of loanable capital and credit relations among individual banks. This means that there is room for basic commercial credit and individual bank credit to move relatively independently of the balance of demand and supply in the money market.[15] Correspondingly, divergences would more or less remain in both the rate of interest in commercial credit and in individual banker's discount rates, in spite of the formation of a unified market rate of interest in the money market. The market rate of interest is regulated from below by the degree of ease or difficulty in the extension in commercial credit and basic bank credit. On the other side, however, in so far as the degree of ease and difficulty in extending commercial credit depends on bank credit, and also as the responses of individual banks depend on the situation in the money market, the unified money market rate of interest must serve as a standard, and so more or less regulate the movement of the divergent rates of interest charged in commercial credit and individual bank credit.

There is a problem as to whether and how we can conceive of a central bank in a basic theory of a capitalist economy. In relation to the function of a bank in giving credit in the form of bank notes, Marx explains the following:

> This last form of credit seems especially striking and important to the layman, firstly because this kind of credit money emerges from commercial circulation into general circulation and functions here as money; also because in most countries the major banks that issue notes are a peculiar mishmash between national banks and private banks and actually have the government's credit behind them, their notes being more or less legal tender; and because it is evident here that what the banker is dealing in is credit itself, since the banknote merely represents a circulating token of credit. (III, p. 529).

Since the role of government or state must be abstracted from the basic theory of a capitalist economy, we have to put aside the role of the central bank as a government's cashier with a privileged monopolistic position in issuing notes as legal tender. Then, a bank of issue would not be confined to a single central bank, and the position of the central bank itself may seem difficult to define among anarchically competitive capitals themselves lacking any political and legal privileges. However, in my opinion, the position of a central bank of issue is deducible from the nature of the credit system which constructs a pyramid making credit transactions more and more efficient and flexible, although it cannot exclude the existence or emergence of other banks of issue in principle. Especially, banks in the central money market need not adhere much to issuing their own bank notes in order that their business extends, as they are in a good position to receive many deposits and repayments from capitalists who trade at the commercial centre, as well as money funds from other local banks for purposes of settlement and for their own reserves. Those banks in the centre can also, in general, easily rely on the money market to raise their cash reserve if necessary. Further, those banks acting in the central money market would increase their efficiency and flexibility in credit transaction and in making settlements between themselves by depositing some portion of their money funds with a single central bank and using its bank notes in common. Thus logically chosen, the central bank retains the common cash reserve, upon which the flexible rediscounting of bills can take place. It is just like the basic case where individual industrial capitals mutually economise their reserve funds by utilising a common local bank.

The central bank appears thus as the bank for banks especially in the central money market. The bank notes issued by such a central bank are used as a common means of settlement, not merely among the banks in the central money market, but also in commercial transactions in the commercial centre as 'the coin of wholesale trade' (III, p. 529). The range of circulation of the central bank notes would further be extended into commercial and credit transactions with and within local areas which have close relations with the commercial centre. However, in so far as a central bank in our basic theory is still private bank capital with a limited amount of capital investment and acceptability, the central bank notes would not come unlimitedly 'into general circulation' outside of central commercial and credit circulation. The central bank and the central money market cannot form equally close relations with all the local areas. Banks of issue independent from the central bank would continue to operate mostly in such areas as relatively alienated from the commercial centre or having their own special needs for credit expansion, like the agricultural country banks or the Scottish banks of issue coexisting with the Bank of England in UK in the nineteenth century.[16] Specie payment is necessary for the settlement of commercial and credit transactions with such areas. The central bank note as the 'the coin of wholesale trade' would not be completely substituted for by real coins, particularly in the small amounts of payment for wages and retail trade, as the bank would regard it unprofitable to issue and handle bank notes of small face value in view of its basic position as the bank of banks.[17] Therefore the general need for specie and hard coins as the means of circulation and of payment remain along with the circulation of the central bank notes. Correspondingly the cash reserve of the central bank against its liability in the form of both its bank notes issued and deposits accepted must be in the form of specie or hard coins as the gold reserve.

The flexible extensibility of bank credit which is generalised by the money market between banks is thus further increased by the formation of a central bank as the bank of banks. The relative independence of credit expansion in local areas, as well as in individual banks at the commercial centre, would not disappear with the formation of the central bank. However, the social balance of the demand and supply of loanable money capital in the whole credit system is reflected and summarised not merely in the situation of the central money market, but also in the gold reserve ratio of the central bank at the peak of the pyramid, which is actually influenced by the trends in demand for rediscounting of commercial bills and inflows of repayments and deposits from other banks. The movement of the rediscount rate of the central bank, reflecting its gold reserve ratio, thus serves as the most obvious single indicator for the general market rate of interest.

**The Rate of Interest**

Marx clearly noticed the different characters of the general rate of profit and that of interest. 'Average profit does not appear as a directly given fact, but rather as the end-product of an equalisation of opposing tendencies that can only be established by investigation.' Thus 'the general rate of profit presents a blurred and hazy picture compared with the sharply defined rate of interest, which although its level fluctuates always confronts the borrowers as fixed and given, because it fluctuates in the same way for them all' (III, pp. 490–1). This characteristic of interest is distinct especially in the general rate of interest in the money market. Having an obvious single indicator in the rediscount rate of the central bank, the general rate of interest in the money market works as a summary reflector and a regulating standard for the relatively independent and divergent interest rates of individual bank credit and commercial credit in the hierarchy of the credit sytem. In the money market the loanable money fund appears as a homogenous commodity transacted at the same price, the general market rate of interest. Money which originates in commodities is thus reduced to an ordinary commodity transacted in a market though in a sophisticated form. In the transaction of money in the money market, the form of interest-bearing capital appears as an ideal type of capital with a homogenous rate of valorisation in comparison with real capitals with their heterogenous rates of profit.

Actually the general rate of interest serves as an external measure for the individual rates of profit of industrial and commercial capitals. As the general rate of interest tends to more or less regulate somewhat divergent rates of interest of private bank credit and commercial credit, individual real capitals in industry and commerce with a prospect of a total or marginal profit rate higher than the general rate of interest in the money market will be encouraged to utilise more loans to expand their business. On the contrary, real capitals with a prospect of a total or marginal profit rate lower than the general rate of interest will be forced to reduce their debt and business. For instance, the expansion of production in the spheres of production is accelerated by a margin between a higher rate of profit including extra profit and the general rate of interest where commodity products are in short supply so elevating their market prices above the prices of production. As a result a relatively rapid increase in supply of the commodity products would eventually lower their market prices so as to decrease and then remove extra profit, and vice versa. Thus, the money market together with the whole substructure of the credit system works as a concrete mechanism for 'the equalisation of the profit rate or the movement of this equalisation, on which the whole of capitalist production depends' (III, p. 566). This working is substantially realised in combination with another function of the credit system in reducing circulation costs and idle circulation capitals (similar to, but more broadly than, commercial capitals) by accelerating 'the velocity of the metamorphosis of commodities, and with this the velocity of monetary circulation' (III, p. 567).

In the neo-classical school, the rate of interest and the general rate of profit are considered equal in equilibrium analyses. This assumes on the one hand the perfect mobility and convertibility of capital values between loan capital in the money market and real capital in industry and commerce, and on the other hand determination of the rate of profit as well as that of interest in the sphere of the market. These assumptions and the resulting identity between both rates are not in the tradition of the classical or the Marxian schools. This must be regarded as an important watershed, dividing the major theoretical currents in economics.

In the Marxian school, which critically developed classical economics, the general rate of profit is determined by the physical conditions of reproduction as we have seen. In contrast, the general rate of interest is not determinable directly by the physical and technical conditions, but substantially dependent upon the balance of supply and demand of loan capital in the money market. The determinants of both rates are quite separate. Perfect mobility and convertibility between loanable money capital and real (industrial and commercial) capital is indeed too abstract and formalistic an assumption to be actual. Industrial and commercial capitals with more or less fixed capital, cannot actually be formed by converting loanable money capital of any size and length of term, nor can they easily be converted into loanable capital as a whole. As we have analysed, only the portions of idle-money capital in the hands of their owners, which cannot be invested as real profit-making capitals for the time being, are mobilised as loanable capital through the credit system. Therefore, the general rate of interest is determined and moves relatively independently of the motion of the general rate of profit. Having such an independent character in its motion, the general rate of interest serves as a common external measure or standard for individual rates of profit. The fluctuation of the general rate of interest actually serves such a measure in the concrete process of business cycles. How the general rate of interest is related with the general rate of profit in the process of business cycles is an important problem formulated in Marx's credit theory, which we shall reserve for the next chapter.

It is interesting and noteworthy that Marx was well aware of the technologically indeterminateness of the average rate of interest as a gravitational centre of the fluctuating market rate of interest, and did not present a strong theory on it, in sharp distinction to his theories of wages, profit, and ground rent. He says, for example; 'The prevailing average rate of interest in a country, as distinct from the constantly fluctuating market rate, cannot be determined by any law. There is no natural rate of interest, therefore, in the sense that economists speak of a natural rate of profit and a natural rate of wages.' (III, p. 484). The average rate of interest in this context is conceptually different from the general rate of interest, which is again distinct from divergent interest rates in individual transactions in commercial and bank credit, but fluctuating daily in the money market. Although the average rate of interest is technologically indeterminate unlike the general rate of profit, it is not totally independent of the general rate of profit.

Under a gold-standard system without the inflationary nominal movement in prices, profit and interest, it would be observable that 'in any given country, the average rate of interest is constant over long periods, because the general rate of profit changes only in the long run. . . . And the relative constancy of the profit rate is precisely reflected in this more or less constant character of the average or common rate of interest.' (III, p. 488). Marx seems to have overplayed this point and is inconsistent when he says: 'The rate of interest is related to the profit rate in a similar way as the market price of commodity is to its value.' (III, p. 487). It is because the average rate of interest is not so strictly regulated by the general rate of profit, and quantitatively it is 'not a pure or reliable expression of the general rate of profit' (ibid.), as Marx himself points out. 'At all events, the average rate of profit should be regarded as ultimately determining the maximum limit of the interest' (III, p. 482) as a long-run phenomenon, since no capitalist would continue borrowing with a net loss after paying interest. Whereas, 'the minimum limit of interest is completely indeterminate' (III, p. 480).

According to Marx's law of the tendential fall in the rate of profit due to the rising organic composition of capital, the maximum limit and resultantly the average level, of interest must tendentially decline in the long run (III, p. 481), although this law does not seem to have worked so decisively, often being counteracted by the destruction of capital in crises and especially by technological innovations which reduce unit values of constant capitals. Apart from the movement of the rate of profit Marx points to two more 'major reasons' for the rate of interest to fall tendentially (III, pp. 483–4). (1) As a nation advances in accumulation of wealth the population in the class of rentiers as mere lenders of capital would increase. (2) Through the development of the credit system the savings of all classes would be more and more concentrated in banks as utilisable money capital. It is hard to treat these factors, which are more or less external to the motion of real capitals, in the basic principles of a capitalist economy, and then must be subject to more concrete analyses at separate levels of research. Actually the balance between these and the countervailing factors such as the growth of new and promising industries rapidly absorbing loanable capital, the outflow of loanable capital to foreign investment, the growth of state debt as well as of the debt of consumers cannot be predicted abstractly without concrete analyses.[18]

Thus Marx seems decisive in *not* presenting a positive and strong theory to determine the average rate of interest, simply clarifying a few essential points. He clearly states, properly in my opinion, first, that the average rate of interest is not identical with the level of the average rate of profit: second, that it must be somewhere between the average rate of profit as the maximum limit and zero, and, third, that it depends on the whole balance of the supply against the demand of loanable money capital. A series of intricate structural balances are presumably reflected in the third point, such as the average social quantity of idle-money capital reproduced in the turnover of capitals, the tendential imbalances in the demand and supply for commodities among the various industrial spheres to be adjusted, along with the divergent profit rates among them, or the total imbalance and the size of gap between stagnant industries and the rapidly growing ones.

Anyway, it is both the height of the average rate of interest and the social quantity of mobilisable money capital available for banks to handle, though these are technologically somewhat indeterminate, that logically define the social magnitude of investible bank capital to be maintained with the average rate of profit. The higher the average rate of interest the greater amount of it would remain per unit of loanable capital for banks to replenish their own capital and to be taken as profit even after paying correspondingly a bit higher interest to depositors. As I have already suggested, when the rate of profit on bank capital is higher than the general rate, some industrial and commercial capitals would be converted into bank capital eventually to equalise the rate of profit. And the reverse would take place in the opposite case. Technologically, there must be a great flexibility in the amount of loanable money capital to be dealt with by a certain size of bank capital which is invested in cash reserves and the costs of circulation related to monetary and credit transactions. Therefore, it must be an incorrect standpoint, tied to appearances, to argue that there is a technological relationship between the amount of bank capital and the level of activity of banks by analogy with a representative technological relations between the amount of capital and the level of productive activity in a sphere of industry. A Sraffian use of simultaneous equations based on such a standpoint, viewing the relationship between the total amount of bank capital and that of loans as technologically rigid, induces C. Panico's conclusion that 'once the wage rate is taken as an independent variable the rate of interest is determined within the material conditions of reproduction' in parallel with the general rate of profit and the prices of production.[19] Though Panico's argument seems in a sense attractive and is worth careful examination, it is not acceptable in my view even apart from its deviation from Marx's position on the average rate of interest and its neglect of Marx's theoretical concern with the fluctuation of the market rate of interest. Contrary to the implications of Panico's analysis, the average rate of interest is not technologically determinable; together with the social quantity of mobilisable money capital, it regulates, with some elasticity, the total investible amount of bank capital, and not vice versa.

The positive role of both credit and interest in promoting the equalisation of the profit rate and the expansion of production by mobilising or reducing idle circulation capital and costs is not always guaranteed. The accumulation of loanable money capital through bank credit, proceeding separately but alongside the accumulation of real capitals, will not always be harmonious. In a special phase, over-accumulation of real capital causes shortage of loanable capital. Then, the market rate of interest cannot remain within the maximum limit of the general rate of profit, but rises in conflict with the falling rate of profit. The whole credit system and interest movements work then as a disturbing and destructive mechanism for a capitalist economy. In the depression which follows, the credit system would neither be so destructive nor positive for the accumulation of real capital. The functions of the credit system in promoting competition and the accumulation of real capitals must be clarified more concretely through such changing phases in the process of capital accumulation. This is a problem for the theory of business cycles in Chapter 9, a theme which Marx, unlike the classical or the neoclassical school, so emphatically attempted to pursue throughout his analyses of the credit system, especially in the chapters on 'Money Capital and Real Capital' in the third volume of *Capital*.

## 8.3 JOINT-STOCK CAPITAL

In his initial plan for his lifework Marx intended to present 'joint-stock capital' as the highest complete form of 'capital' in the fourth and last part of the volume on capital after the parts on 'capital in general', 'competition' and 'credit', as we have seen in Chapter 3, Section 3.2 of this volume. Although Marx much expanded the theoretical system of 'capital in general' in the *Grundrisse*, and reformed it so as to include basic theories not merely on competition and credit among capitals, but also on the positions of landed property and wage-labour, presenting the principles of a capitalist economy as a whole in *Capital*, he did not develop a theoretical chapter or part on joint-stock capital, except for some theoretical notes annexed to the working of the credit system. It seems clear that the actual position of joint-stock capital especially in the industrial spheres was so marginal in Marx's age as to have restricted him in giving a full treatment of its form and functions. It was R. Hilferding in *Finance Capital* (1910) who initiated a Marxian theory of joint-stock capital more fully on the basis of the historical development of industrial joint-stock corporations in heavy industries from the last quarter of nineteenth century. Thus, just as we had to specify our basis of abstraction for the basic theory of the credit system in accord with Marx's own age, we must shift our basis of abstraction for the full-scale basic theory of joint-stock capital into the later period of capitalism. At the same time we should avoid Hilferding's tendency abstractly to generalise those special features of German joint-stock corporations in relation to the banks in his age, and to mix up the different levels of researches, the basis principles of the capitalist economy and the more concrete studies of the stages of capitalist development with its international relations in the world market.[20] Bearing these methodological points in mind, let us try to formulate the theory of joint-stock capital as the highest and the last form of capital at the level of basic principles.

The functions of the credit system and the money market centre on short-term mutual accomodations of idle-money funds through the representative form of bills of exchange. The forms and mechanisms of the credit system in the basic theory are grounded in the process of commodity circulation among industrial and commercial capitals mobilising their own more or less short-term idle-money capital. A longer-term loan for fixed capitals was outside of the usual business of commercial banks, and it usually entailed a special tie or control similar to the case of joint enterprises as we saw in the activity of German investment banks. Hilferding presupposed such a long-term loan for fixed capital in his notion of 'capital (or investment) credit', as if it were a part of a general theory of bank credit, and then deduced the necessity of the formation of joint-stock capital so that the banks could restore their liquidity by selling the share of industrial capitals. However, the logic of the formation and the functions of joint-stock capital are not generally confined to those indicated in Hilferding's theory which reflected rather the specific German historical experience of his age. Apart from such specifically German experience, joint-stock capital is generally a form of capital which is definitely suitable for mobilising idle-money capital into the construction of huge sums of fixed capital beyond the limits of bank credit grounded on short-term commercial credit.

Joint-stock capital takes the form of dividing property into many shares or stocks. Each stock normally represents a share of the equally divided principal capital invested in a corporation. When an industrial enterprise is converted into a joint-stock corporation, the ownership of capital becomes in a sense doubled: on one hand the ownership of the real capital active in the process of production and circulation centrally controlled by the corporation itself, and on the other hand ownership of the corporation by the shareholders. Correspondingly, the acquisition of profit from the motion of real capital also takes two steps and is divided into the acquisition of actual profit by the corporation, and then the secondary acquisition of profit mainly as share dividend among shareholders. Dividends on profit, after the deduction of managerial costs are normally declared to shareholders in proportion to the numbers of stocks they have. Thus by dualising both ownership of capital and acquisition of profit, the form of joint-stock corporation assures that on the one side their is unity of managerial control over real capital, and on the other co-propriatorship of the same capital among many capitalists. The managerial operation of real capital in motion is not usually impeded by changes in shareholdings or by any increase of them. Therefore, the stocks representing the shares of ownership of corporation are generally freely saleable.

Joint-stock corporations with their negotiable stocks appear as the most suitable form of capitalist organisation for expanding the number and the range of joint investment for a certain enterprise. It facilitates the joint investment in large-scale fixed capital, which cannot easily be undertaken by an individual capitalist. Bank credit based upon commercial credit cannot generally finance the construction of such fixed capitals as we have seen. Since the basic principle of a capitalist economy lies in the individual pursuit of private profit based upon a commodity economy, sharing investment and profit with other capitalists would not usually be done in the spheres where the expansion of production can be carried out by individual capitalists. There have actually always been many industrial spheres (as well as spheres in commerce and services) technologically suitable for small individually owned enterprise in the process of uneven development, even in the most advanced capitalist countries with giant joint-stock corporations at their centre.[21] However, in the spheres where the size of fixed capital becomes so massive that it is difficult for individual capitalists to provide, joint investment to a large extent in the form of joint-stock corporations must be introduced. Money gathered in exchange for stocks issued by founding a joint-stock corporation or by increasing the stocks of an existing corporation, can jointly be invested in the motion of real capital including massive fixed capital. Idle money is thus concentrated and mobilised into the motion of real capital to earn profit in the form of joint-stock capital. In this way, as Marx pointed out, the 'formation of joint-stock companies' involves a 'tremendous expansion in the scale of production, and enterprise which would be impossible for individual capitals' (III, p. 567).

In the process of the uneven development and increasing number of industrial spheres, joint-stock companies were formed initially rather in peripheral spheres like transportation, mining or some part of banking, but later on it extended to the more central spheres along with the development of heavy industries. When industries with massive fixed capital become dominant in determining business fluctuations, the typical business cycles become metamorphosed into more irregular fluctuations often with prolonged depressions. While social demand is one-sidedly increased in the gestation period necessary to build up huge plants and equip them, this creates a speculative boom in some industries in the phase of prosperity. Excessive large-scale fixed capitals, often completed after the beginning of depression, tend to impede and prolong the process of restructuring. Equalisation of the rate of profit across industries and its social function of readjusting the imbalance of investment among industries would also be so much obstructed in a prolonged depression as well as in the speculative boom, as we shall see in more detail in Chapter 9.

The form of joint-stock capital thus functions as a means to facilitate the construction of massive fixed capitals, and resultingly brings about the metamorphosis of business cycles. Prolonged depression and a chronic continuance of excessive capitals, in the form of idle-capacity and idle-money funds, tend to prevail in a certain number of industrial spheres, even in speculative boom periods. Idle-money capital in those depressed industries, such as depreciation funds and accumulation funds, would look for other channels for investment outside of both its original individual process of production and the short-term money market. The form of joint-stock capital is utilised to absorb and channel various money funds, including such idle-money capital, into the construction of larger-scale fixed capitals with new technologies or in new industries expecting to get extra profit. In this regard joint-stock capital can mobilise and shift idle- money capital from depressed spheres to other industries where commodity products are still in short of supply. In contrast, the difficulty in the depressed industries with excessive fixed capitals cannot directly be solved through the functions of joint-stock capital.

In fact, the difficulty may be deepened by joint-stock capital which may add a greater and more modern capacity even to the depressed industries. Excessive fixed capitals cannot but be gradually depreciated and withdrawn, so far as they are not scrapped and destroyed as capital values.

The form of joint-stock capital is then utilised not merely in mobilising idle-money capital for use as real capital, but also in combining existing industrial capitals together in order to mitigate the difficulty of accumulation in the depressed industries. It is easy to combine multiple industrial capitals into a single capital in the form of joint-stock capital. The merger of multiple industrial capitals by founding a joint-stock corporation is realised without impeding or altering the motion of real capitals. In this case the stocks of a new corporation are distributed among the owners of old capitals in proportion to their estimated assets. Merger is also possible by increasing the capital stocks of an existing corporation so as to merge the capital assets of others in exchange for the newly issued stocks. Rationalisation by technological unity of the processes of production, utilisation of by-products, economy in the costs of circulation, etc., are usually expected to improve profitability in a vertical merger of capitals across related industrial spheres. Instability of profit due to fluctuations of prices of raw materials, semi-products and finished products may also be expected to be mitigated. Horizontal merger of capitals within the same industry is often aimed at avoiding or mitigating severe price competition, besides economy in the costs of management and circulation. As the number of industrial capitals in the same sphere decreases with their increased size, competition to reduce the price of commodity products may become cut-throat without easily driving out competitors, and it therefore tends to be avoided, or ended by such horizontal mergers.[22]

The basic function of joint-stock capital of extending the range of joint investors is further scaled up through the centralisation of capitals by merger creating bigger corporations. Giant joint-stock corporations are thus formed. Stocks of giant corporations become so numerous and shared among so many holders that they are dealt with as a perfect commodity and daily transacted on stock exchanges. Each stock represents a share of ownership in real capital invested in a corporation, and fundamentally differs from a negotiable instrument giving the right to regular money income such as a state bond. However, daily transactions of stocks on the exchange would not usually cause an alteration in the persons having substantial control over the real capital of corporations. As the stocks of giant corporations are much increased in number and scattered among numerous share holders, those small shareholders who cannot in practice participate in the substantial control or management of the corporation must increase in number. Purchase of stocks by such small shareholders in practice means nothing but the purchase of negotiable certificates of title for a share in the profit of a corporation. Just as the democratic right to vote in a bourgeois general election by no means guarantees the people substantial participation in real political decisions, a formal democratic right to vote at a general meeting of stockholders in proportion to their number of stocks substantially excludes a large number of small shareholders from real decisions over the managerial policies of a corporation. The centralisation of control in a corporation into the hands of a small number of big shareholders is thus so much strengthened. The more dispersed and widespread the owners of a giant corporation become, the more easily a small number of big shareholders can maintain their control over the management of the corporation, including the capitals of other persons, by safely reducing their holding ratio of stocks.

Big shareholders are enabled thus to withdraw a portion of their capital from their own firm, and can mobilise a portion of their capital back into its money-form by selling a part of their stock without abandoning their control over the firm. According to Hilferding: 'In practice, the amount of capital necessary to ensure control of a corporation is usually less than a half, amounting to a third or a quarter, or even less.'[23] It is not rare nowadays to see the ratio of the biggest shareholder of a giant corporation even less than 10 per cent. As Hilferding points out: 'The large capital dominating a corporation has even greater impact when it is no longer a question of a single corporation, but a system of interdependent companies.'[24] Besides the vertical system of holding stocks of subordinate companies, the horizontal relation of the mutual holding of stocks between companies in the different spheres is also conspicuous. Through such developments even the big shareholders would not commonly participate in the daily practice of the management of real capital, leaving it more to hired directors and managers. In Marx's words the formation of joint-stock companies involves the 'transformation of the actual functioning capitalist into a mere manager, in charge of other people's capital, and of the capital owner into a mere owner, a mere money capitalist' (III, p. 567). In my view, however, Marx's statement appears to separate ownership and the function of capital far too completely. It must be noted that the big shareholders are in a position to decide crucial managerial policies, including the employment of directors. Actually a shift of control over a corporation from certain shareholders to others is possible as in a case of a take-over bid through the purchase of stocks of the corporation.

Stocks which are transacted at a market signify therefore a title, not merely to the proportional share of profit as dividend. The situation, which appears as a thorough separation of control from ownership of capital in the eyes of small shareholders, conceals the centralisation of managerial control into the hands of big shareholders on the basis of their ownership of stocks, as well as the vertical and horizontal system of holding stocks among companies. Transactions in the stock exchange sustain this centralisation of substantial control over real capital, and may even actually shift it from certain holders to others. The title of a stock to dividend as a share of profit, and not for interest, also signifies that a stock is in its essence a title to a share of the ownership of actual capital in the form of corporation itself. In these regards the transactions of stocks at the exchange form transactions of industrial or actual capitals in motion as a commodity, not merely in a legalistic sense, but also in their economic nature as well. The stock exchange is thus essentially a capital market.

In a capital market the stocks of giant corporations are daily traded, and the units traded can be of relatively small amounts. Some of idle-money funds which would otherwise flow into banks as deposits earning interest, may enter the capital market and purchase stocks despite the speculative risk of loss as well as gain, through fluctuations in stock prices. Contrarily, money funds withdrawn from the capital market by the selling of stocks in some periods often flow back into the money market through the banks. A fluid interrelation is thus formed between the money market and the capital market. Then the owners of idle-money funds would certainly compare the ratio of dividends from profit per stock against the price of a stock in the market as the dividend yield, with the rate of interest in the money market when they consider the profitability of the investment of their funds in stocks in the capital market . Therefore, the rate of interest in the money market serves as a standard of judgement for the possible investment of idle money in the capital market. As a result demand and supply in the capital market determining the overall level of stock prices, is regulated by the rate of interest ($i$), so as to equalise the dividend yield ($y = d/Ps$, i.e. dividend $d$ per stock, divided by the price of a stock, *Ps*) and the rate of interest. In other words, the price of a stock is tendentially determined around the standard price, being the capitalised amount of dividend per stock, or the price calculated by dividing the dividend per stock by the rate of interest ($Ps = d/i$).

In practice the dividend does not precisely represent the actual profit earned by a corporation. A part of profit must be subtracted for the remuneration of directors and managers. Internal reserves and a disguised form of profit through accelerated depreciation funds, etc., are often also subtracted (although stock investors use indices that compensate for such manoeuvers). Contrariwise, a portion of internal reserves are sometimes added to the dividend in order to stabilise the stock price against a decline in actual profit. In addition, transactions of stocks in the capital market always involve anarchic speculation as to prospects of individual companies, the motion of interest, and business activities in specific spheres and in general. Consequently, the actual stock price commonly deviates above and below the theoretical standard level of the capitalised dividend from profit per stock. However, the stock price of a corporation must increase tendentially as its actual profit per stock rises, reflecting actual profitability, and would generally decline as the rate of interest rises, so as to fluctuate if widely around the theoretical standard defined above.

Even though the dividend yield ($y$) thus tends to be equalised with the rate of interest ($i$), giving profit the form of interest, it does not mean that the real rate of profit ($p'$) against a corporation's own principal capital actually invested, and not against the stock price, also becomes identical to the interest rate. Competition among capitals for higher rates of profit on actually invested capital must effect even giant corporations and consequently works as a means of equalising the rate of profit in the long run by shifting capitals from spheres with a profit rate lower than average to other spheres with a higher profit rate. Marx seems to neglect this when he says: 'Since profit here simply assumes the form of interest, enterprises that merely yield an interest are possible, and this is one of the reasons that hold up the fall in the general rate of profit, since these enterprises, where the constant capital stands in such a tremendous ratio to the variable, do not necessarily go into the equalization of the general rate of profit.' (III, p. 568). Hilferding criticises Marx's statement here by saying: 'Marx was thinking of the railway corporations of his day', . . . . 'it is clear that with the spread of the corporation its profit, just like that of an individually owned enterprise, must contribute to the equalization of the general rate of profit.'[25] Hilferding must be relatively correct here, though we have to admit also that the equalisation of the rate of profit is obstructed and retarded in case of giant corporations because of the immobility of huge masses of fixed capital and to some extent also by the splits in the mutual interest between small shareholders , hired managers and big shareholders.

In so far as the average rate of profit is usually higher than the rate of interest, the capitalised amount of the dividend from profit would generally be greater than the amount of capital actually invested as profit-bearing. The gap is defined by Hilferding as 'promoter's profit' (*Gründergewinn*) which is 'an economic category *sui generis*'.[26] According to Hilferding's numerical example, an industrial enterprise with a capital of 1 000 000 marks makes profit of 150 000 marks with the average profit rate of 15 per cent. When the interest rate is 5 per cent, straight capitalisation of annual income of 150 000 marks will have an estimated price of 3 000 000 marks. A deduction of 20 000 marks for various costs of administration and directors' fees, etc., would make actual dividend for shareholders 130 000 marks out of 150 000 marks. A risk premium of 2 per cent would be added to a fixed safe rate of interest of 5 per cent in estimating the actual stock price. Then the stock price of the enterprise would be 1 857 143 (130 000 ÷ 0.07) marks, or in round figures, 1 900 000 marks, which leaves 900 000 marks free after deducting the actual initial investment of 1 000 000 marks. This balance of 900 000 marks appears as 'promoter's profit', which 'arises from the conversion of profit-bearing capital into interest-(or dividend-)bearing capital'.[27] The founders of the enterprise, or the promoter (mostly assumed to be a bank in Hilferding's analyses) who promotes the conversion of the enterprise into a joint-stock company, can earn the promoter's profit by selling the stocks of the enteprise on a capital market.

Where does the promoter's profit come from? Who bears or pays this profit to the founder or the promoter? Hilferding attempts to explain this, following Marx's theory of the qualitative division of profit into interest and profit of enterprise (or entrepreneurial profit), upon the assumption that the promoter is a bank.

> While the money capitalist receives interest on the money he lends, the bank which issues shares lends nothing and therefore does not receive interest. Instead, the interest goes to the shareholders in the form of dividends. The bank receives a flow of entrepreneurial

> profit, not in the form of an annual revenue, but as capitalized promoter's profit. Entrepreneurial profit is a continuous stream of income, but it is paid to the bank as a lump sum in the form of promoter's profit.[28]

This explanation is theoretically confusing and incorrect, though it might to some extent well suit the capitalists' superficial conception and their way of calculation. In reality, acquisition of the promoter's profit does not eliminate an annual inflow of total profit which contains, in the conception of the qualitative division of profit, both the portion of entrepreneurial profit and the portion of interest. Actually the annual total profit of the company as such would continuously be shared through dividends. In other words, dividends as a whole cannot be limited to the portion of interest in a notion of the qualitative division of profit, but must represent in principle the distribution from the total profit of the enterprise. Therefore, the substantial source of the promoter's profit is not from the profit of the enterprise as Hilferding tries to show, but rather from outside of it in the idle-money funds of capitalists, landowners and so forth who purchase the stocks issued mostly as small shareholders comparing expected yields with the interest rate at the money market. Thus, in my view, the promoter's profit represents a redistribution of the already existing monetary assets through the transactions of stocks of companies newly founded or reorganised. It is obtained also in the case of an increase in capital by the issue of new stocks from existing companies. It must additionally be noted that the promoter's profit is not totally realised, but remains an imaginary calculation in respect to the portion of shares continuously kept in the hands of founders as big shareholders.

Anyway, capitals organised in the form of joint-stock capital are given the complete form of a commodity transacted daily in a capital market, besides their actual motion as accumulating and self-expanding value through the processes of production and circulation. Capitals as the movement of self-increasing value are thus traded as a perfect commodity at stock prices. In so far as stock prices tends to equalise the yield rate of dividends and the interest rate in the money market, industrial capitals, or profit-earning real capitals including commercial and bank capitals, organised as joint-stock companies are given a form of expression as an indifferent part of total social money capital. Thus, joint-stock capitals which in fact have uneven rates of profit appear in the form if fictitious money capitals with equal yields on their stock prices. The actual inequality of the rates of profit is thus hidden and buried in the tendential equality of the rates of dividend yield in the form of joint-stock capital. Similarly, any regular annual income such as ground-rent or fixed interest on state bonds is given the fictitious form of money capital as the capitalised amount of the annual income estimated on the current rate of interest. In principle this is the way to determine the standard price of land on the basis of the preceding theory of ground-rent.[29]

Capitalism is a specific socio-economic formation grounded on the commodity form. It systematically embraces into that form all the elements of economic life under the dominant motion of capital. The commodity form of labour-power, besides that of the means of production and consumption, was an essential precondition for the formation of a thorough commodity economy as capitalism. In the mechanisms of the motion of capitalism, the commodity form is further given to money funds in a money market, and finally to capital itself, which is the central subject of the whole system. The logical process of the development of the forms of commoditisation in a capitalist economy then reaches in principle its final and highest form in joint-stock capital. As Marx suggested in his initial plan, joint-stock capital must thus be really presented as the most developed final form of capital. In fact capitalism has not created any further forms of capital beyond this. For instance, finance capital or monopoly capital is a concrete organisation of giant joint-stock corporations each with its national characteristics,[30] and multinational corporations are the more developed organisation of such finance capital across international spheres of activity. Development of both of these types of capital does not contain a fundamentally new form, but are rather related to the more concrete national or international economic conditions faced, which must be studied along with their actual historical significance at separate, more concrete levels of researches founded on the basic principles of capitalism.

In its highest complete form of joint-stock capital, however, capital cannot effectively make up a completely unified system of reproduction. The creation of giant joint-stock capitals partially mitigate the difficulty of accumulation and profitability for themselves, but does not solve and may indeed deepen the difficulties for other capitals as well as of the economy as a whole. The movement of capitals in readjusting the anarchical imbalances between industrial spheres, through competition among capitals equalising the rate of profit, are constantly obstructed and retarded by the relative immobility of giant joint-stock corporations with huge fixed capitals. Though a shift of capital into a new and promising industrial sphere is facilitated by joint-stock capital, the difficulty in coping with excessive capital in the production processes of existing industries tends to be prolonged. Such a difficulty is not only found in the horizontal relations across industrial spheres, but it also slows down the vertical resolution of the social contradiction between the growth of productive power and the production relations, prolonging the depression with its conspicuous and hidden unemployment. The law of value is thus impeded in its work, and many imbalances in the economic processes tend to remain both horizontally and vertically.

The formation of the final and highest form of capital in joint-stock capital, therefore, does not substantially remove the difficulties or imbalances in capitalist reproduction as a whole, but remains an individualistic form of organisation only partially mitigating difficulties in profitability. The stock price form, which expresses the equalisation of the rate of dividend yield compared to the rate of interest, is in a sense an inverted expression of the real difficulty in equalising the rate of profit, with all the difficulties in readjusting the imbalances in the whole economy. Thus, even in its highest form of development, the organisation of production by capitals must remain partial, and cannot be directly socially comprehensive and harmonious. This corresponds to the historically specific character of capitalism, based on the forms of a commodity economy which originate outside of social production. Joint-stock capital as the highest form of the development of capital thus clarifies in its ultimate form the historically restrictive nature of capital as the subject for organising social production.

This historical restrictive character of capitalism is more concretely to be seen in the dynamics of capital accumulation, in its business cycles and crises, which are now ready to be analysed.

# 9 Business Cycles and Crises

## 9.1 THREE SOURCES OF CONFUSION TO BE CLEARED UP

Capitalism as a historically specific social formation contains inner contradictions which appear most obviously in those periodical self-destructive crises, in the process of business cycles. The classical school and the neo-classical school treated capitalism one-sidedly as a harmonious economic order and disregarded both its historical character and its inner contradictions. A natural result was a lack of crisis theories in these schools. A great advantage of Marx's *Capital* as compared to these schools is its comprehensive attempt to clarify the logical inevitability of periodic business cycles and crises from the basic contradictions in capitalism. However, *Capital* was left incomplete, especially in this field, and theoretical positions among Marxians have been diverse here. In my opinion, there are initially three major sources of confusion to be established and then cleared up as far as possible.

*First: the historical basis of abstraction*. Just as in the case of the theory of the credit system and joint-stock capital, the basic theory of business cycles and crises requires conscious clarification of the historical basis of abstraction. The theory of regular periodical business cycles and crises must be abstracted from the stage of economic liberalism, because in this period capitalism repeated its most typical cycle of prosperity, crisis and depression around every ten years, following a similar course and with the least state intervention. At the same time various causal factors and incidents which characterise each individual cycle, even within the same stage of liberalism, must certainly be excluded from the basic theory and studied at more concrete levels of research. If we directly take into consideration different historical periods and individual processes from the start of our process of analysis, then we probably have to be satisfied, as G. Haberler suggests,[1] with a typology of the various causal factors as associated with business cycles, so denying a coherent logical explanation of regular cycles with sharp inevitable crises. Or, some theorists might happily agree with R. Hilferding in asserting that 'it is the alternation of prosperity and depression which is crucial for the wave-like character of the business cycle, and the suddenness of the change is a secondary matter',[2] retreating somewhat from Marx's position on crisis theory, by generalising from the historical experience of the later stage of capitalism. However, the description of the alternation between prosperity and depression itself cannot be either a solid or unified theory without a central concept of regular crises based on the typical business cycle of the liberalist stage, since the metamorphoses of business cycles since the imperialist stage have actually shown indeterminate and unstable changes which are difficult to theorise into a positive explanation of regular cycles, as we shall discuss later.

Once a coherent basic theory of regular cycles and crises is obtained upon the historical ground as argued above, it can serve as a solid and not an arbitrary frame of reference for studies of the metamorphoses of cycles at various levels of research as well as for the specificities of each individual cycle. Certainly, since it is consciously abstracted from the liberalist stage, the basic theory of regular cycles and crises cannot be directly or simply applicable to any other stage in the same causal manner. The historical metamorphoses of business cycles, as well as their individual characteristics can, however, be analysed more objectively and assessed in accord with actual changes, once we have thus confirmed the specific stage of capitalism as the basis for the abstraction of the theory of regular cycles and crises. At the same time we can still avoid the arbitrary act of either making abstract generalisation of each special historical period in turn, or in the application of a randomly constructed model using various causal propositions put in a typological order at best.

*Second: different theories in Marx.* There are two major different theories of crisis in Marx, each of them containing a further two separate variants. In the third part of the third volume of *Capital*, Marx attempts to show that excessive capital accumulation causes a fall in the rate of profit, either tendentially due to the rising organic composition of capital, or suddenly, due to labour shortage and a rise in wages, which threaten capital and generate crises (cf. III, p. 350, pp.360–8). In these types of theories, over-supply of commodities in a market in relation to demand appears as a result of the over-accumulation of capital which is expressed in a fall in the profit rate. At the same time Marx also says in the same third part that 'The conditions for immediate exploitation and for the realization of that exploitation are not identical. . . . The former is restricted only by the society's productive forces, the latter by the proportionality between the different branches of production and by the society's power of consumption.' (III, p. 352. See also p. 615 in the fifth part.) The excess commodity theories of crisis are presented here. In these, the excess of commodities which are difficult to sell, either due to the disproportionality of production in various branches or the narrowly restricted consumption of the masses, are conceived to be the ultimate reason of crises.[3] Excessive capital and a fall in the profit rate are seen, unlike in the excess capital theories, as results of overproduction of commodities beyond effective demand causing crises.

A source of confusion among Marxian crisis theorists has been in the tendency to interpret Marx's theory of crisis as complete and unique, choosing one of four variants and accusing other theories of not being founded in Marx's work and so not really Marxian.[4] As an interpretation there is no doubt that different crisis theories have been left unfinished in *Capital*. We should confirm this as a fact and should discuss how to complete a basic theory of crisis from the theoretical material left us by Marx. A typological approach might enable us to hold all the four theories together in a tool box. Practically, too, in the concrete analyses of the historical metamorphoses and the individual features of crises, different causal factors must actually and flexibly be taken into consideration. A consistent theory of regular business cycles and crises required at the level of basic principles, however, cannot be contructed through a typology of different possible causal factors. What then are the requisites for the basic theory of the business cycle and crisis? In my view they can be summarised into three points: (i) a Marxian theory of crisis must show the logical inevitability, not the mere possibility, of sharp, generalised crises as an expression (even if not an absolutely indispensable expression) of the inner contradictions of capitalist production. (ii) It must also show the cyclical character of crises together with the regular alternation of prosperity and depression as a form of capitalist development, since economic crises themselves can neither be so chronic nor so completely destructive, especially in the form of regular cycles. (iii) It should be consistent with the working of the law of value. This final point combined with the other two needs some further clarification so as to assist us in selecting an appropriate type of crisis theory to act as the basic principle.

*Third: the relation with the law of value.* As the excess-commodity theory of crisis originates from the anti-classical school, e.g. J.-C.-L.

S. de Sismondi and T. R. Malthus, its logical relation with the labour theory of value has been a difficult problem to overcome for Marx and his followers.[5] According to the labour theory of value the varying amounts of labour required to produce commodities regulate prices. When some commodities, say the means of consumption, are produced well beyond the effective demand for them, their prices will decline below the prices of production so as to act as a brake on the expansion of their production. This may not necessarily generate a crisis. So far as capital accumulation proceeds as a whole, effective demand for the means of consumption, especially in the spheres producing the means of production, will continue to increase, while their production is slowed down. Then the prices of the means of consumption should be restored as the imbalance between demand for and supply of them is solved. Thus, the supply of and demand for the commodity products, and the allocation of labour socially necessary to produce them can repeatedly be readjusted as an effect of the operation of the law of value, as long as capital accumulation goes on. All that the excess commodity theory of crisis, either of an under-consumption type or of disproportionality type, can show is the possibility, and not the logical inevitability of general crises, in relation to such an operation of the law of value. Crisis theory must clarify how the working of the law of value becomes distorted, destroyed and restored in the course of business cycles. So long as the under-consumption or the disproportionality types of excess commodity theory of crisis are argued as the logic of a cumulative process of an increasing imbalance between supply and demand, neglecting the working of the law of value, it then becomes quite difficult to explain why an imbalance should suddenly become so severe as to cause a general crises, yet of a periodic character and after a certain length of prosperity.[6] In the phase of prosperity, it is relatively easy for capitals generally to readjust an imbalance between supply and demand in a commodity market. Say's law *seems* operative in the process of prosperity. Explanation of this sort of prosperity must remain a difficulty for the excess commodity theories. The difficulties in the excess commodity theories seem to me to come from the fact that this position does not present a more basic difficulty for capital accumulation prior to an over-supply of commodity products.

Excess-capital theories of crisis can fall more in the Ricardo–Marx tradition, and are easier to make consistent with the law of value. In the excess-capital theories the rising organic composition variant arises from Marx's explanation of the law of tendential fall in the profit rate. This law is presented exactly in terms of labour value without referring to the realisation problem in the market. Its essence is as follows: In the process of capital accumulation the organic composition of capital expressed in the ratio between the amount of living labour $(v + s)$ and that of dead labour $(c)$ embodied in the means of production, i.e. $q = (v + s)/c$, would decline without limit in the long run. The same amount of living labour, expressing rising productivity, will use more and more of the means of production not merely physically but also in terms of labour-substance. Then the rate of profit, $p' = s/(c + v)$, must also tendentially fall as its upper limit $(q > p')$ declines. This logic holds indifferently of the movement of the rate of surplus-value $(s' = s/v)$ upwards, reflecting the production of relative surplus-value as a result of rising productivity. Nevertheless, the working of the law of the tendency of the rate of profit to fall cannot, if ever, be very suitable for explaining periodical crises. For one thing, its working may not be so conspicuous within a period of prosperity, where capital accumulation may take rather a widening native with a relatively constant composition. Besides, the increase of the physical amount of the means of production against the same amount of living labour tends to be counteracted by the reduction of labour-value per unit through the process of rising productivity. For another, the working of the law of the tendency of the rate of profit to fall does not exclude a continuous increase in the absolute amount of surplus-value and capital in the process of accumulation even if at a reduced pace, and therefore the law cannot show in itself at what point of the process a clear limit to capital accumulation causes a periodical crisis to appear. Three options remain: either to rely on some particular arbitary specific premises (as in the case of H. Grossmann), to combine some other crisis theories (E. Preiser, M. Dobb and E. Mandel), or to show only an abstract need for capitalism to mitigate the law of the tendency of the rate of profit to fall through the process of crises (P. Bullock and D. Yaffe).[7] Neither of them is satisfactory in showing the logical inevitability of periodical crises in a coherent way.

The labour-power shortage variant of excess-capital theory might be considered to be able to overcome such defects and to present logical inevitability more consistently in relation to the law of value. It can fully agree that it is the operation of the law of value which adjusts the incessant anarchic imbalance between the supply of and demand for commodity products in the process of prosperity, and can further explain how the working of the law of value becomes distorted and then breaks down as a shortage of labour-power obstructs capital accumulation by pulling down the profit rate. We shall see in more detail a little later, how excessive capital accumulation in relation to the labouring population would reverse the social functions of the credit system and generate an acute crisis, and then how excessive capitals are destroyed and capitalism is restructured through the period of depression, so as to prepare for the next periodical prosperity. It must be one of conspicuous contributions of K. Uno and his followers to have remoulded Marx's more or less fragmentary theories into a coherent basic theory of regular periodical business cycles and crises on this variant of the excess-capital theory.[8] Before coming to its contents, however, we have to discuss Marx's 'General Law of Capitalist Accumulation' and the capitalist law of population in chapter 25 (English version) of the first volume of *Capital* as a necessary preparation.

## 9.2 THE LAW OF CAPITALIST ACCUMULATION

It is often believed that Marx's law of capital accumulation demonstrates the continuous progressive production of a relative surplus-population through an incessant process of the rising organic composition of capital. If capital accumulation as a whole always provides, by itself, an excessive supply of labour-power in the form of a relative surplus-population or an industrial reserve army independent of the size or growth of the labouring population, the labour-power shortage variant of the excess capital theory of crisis would lose any validity. It might be a reason why Marx presented the notion of 'an absolute overproduction of capital' in relation to the labouring population (III, p. 360) in the subjunctive mood and further reviewed it as occurring 'under the most extreme assumption' (III, p. 364). Such an interpretation of Marx's law of capital accumulation has certainly been stressed by advocates of other variants, especially the underconsumptionist variant of crisis theory.[9] As an interpretation, it is not totally wrong, but clearly neither comprehensive nor complete if studied a little more carefully. Marx's formulation of the general law of capitalist accumulation and the capitalist law of population in chapter 25 of the first volume of *Capital* is actually composed of three somewhat different arguments, which are somewhat independent and not yet organically unified. Let me first summarise those arguments:[10]

(i) The first section of chapter 25 is titled 'A Growing Demand for

Labour-Power Accompanies Accumulation if the Composition of Capital Remains the Same'. Under this assumption, the demand for labour-power increases in the same proportion as capital and must eventually exceed the supply making wages rise. 'This must indeed ultimately be the case if the conditions assumed above continue to prevail', as the increment of the capital itself 'grows every year along with the augmentation of the capital already functioning' (I, p. 763). When wages rise, 'all other circumstances remaining equal, the unpaid labour diminishes in proportion' (I, p. 771).

Marx assumes here that as a consequence of the rise in the price of labour-power 'the rate of accumulation lessens; but this means that the primary cause of that lessening itself vanishes, i.e. the disproportion between capital and exploitable labour-power' (I, p. 770). Thus, Marx presents a complete cycle of the capitalist law of population already in this first section,[11] and expresses it also mathematically in the famous phrase that 'the rate of accumulation is the independent, not the dependent variable; the rate of wages is the dependent, not the independent variable' (I, p. 770).

(ii) In contrast to the first section, where the organic composition of capital is assumed to be constant, the subsequent sections in the same chapter of *Capital* shows the different position where the rising composition of capital results in a 'progressive production of a relative surplus population or industrial reserve army'. Assuming the continuous increase in the organic composition of capital in the process of accumulation Marx states: 'it is capitalist accumulation itself that constantly produces, and produces indeed in direct relation with its own energy and extent, a relatively redundant working population , i.e. a population which is superfluous to capital's average requirements for its own valorization, and is therefore a surplus-population' (I, p. 782).

This formulation of the capitalist law of population is combined with the analysis of different forms of the relative surplus-population and the illustrations of those forms in the fourth and fifth sections, based on concrete studies of the dire conditions of the labouring class in England at that time. Observing the floating (in the centres of modern industry), the latent (in agriculture) and the stagnant (in domestic industry, etc.) forms of industrial reserve army, and further the sphere of pauperism at the bottom, Marx locates them as the forms of relative surplus-population created and increased by the process of capital accumulation. In this context he concludes as follows:

> The relative mass of the industrial reserve army thus increases with the potential energy of wealth. But the greater this reserve army in proportion to the active labour-army, the greater is the mass of a consolidated surplus population, whose misery is in inverse ratio to the amount of torture it has to undergo in the form of labour. The more extensive, finally, the pauperized sections of the working class and the industrial reserve army, the greater is official pauperism. This is the absolute general law of capitalist accumulation. (I, p. 798).

This statement has often quoted by critics of Marx as evidence of Marx's assertion of the law of increasing misery, and by some Marxians as well. It seems clear that Marx formulated here the general law of capitalist accumulation as progressive increase of the industrial reserve army. If this law thus formulated were valid and effective, a rise in wages due to the absorption of wage-labourers could not occur except in extremely rare cases. And labour-power shortage would not be related to the regular movement of business cycles. This is exactly the case for the advocates of under-consumptionism and for their critique of the labour-power-shortage theory of crisis.

(iii) However, there is also another argument in the same sections. According to this, the cyclical process of the absorption and reformation of the relative surplus population is regarded as a basis of a decennial business cycle. Marx says for instance: 'The path characteristically described by modern industry, which takes the form of a decennial cycle (interrupted by smaller oscillations) of periods of average activity, production at high pressure, crisis and stagnation, depends on the constant formation, the greater or less absorption, and reformation of the industrial reserve army or surplus population.' (I, p. 785). In the same context we read:

> The appropriate law for modern industry . . . is the law of the regulation of the demand and supply of labour by the alternative expansion and contraction of capital, i.e. by the level of capital's valorization requirements at the relevant moment, the labour-market sometimes appearing relatively under-supplied because capital is expanding, and sometimes relatively over-supplied because it is contracting. (I, p. 790).

Then wages cannot be one-sidedly under the pressure of the

progressively increasing industrial reserve army. They must be subject to fluctuations in the process of the alternate phases of business cycles. In Marx's words, 'the general movement of wages are exclusively regulated by the expansion and contraction of the industrial reserve army, and this in turn corresponds to the periodic alterations of the industrial cycle' (I, p, 790). Thus, on a different presupposition from the first section, where the composition of capital was assumed to remain constant, a similar complete cycle of the capitalist law of population including the law of motion of wages is presented. This is the case which P. Sweezy once underlined, when he noticed 'a well-articulated theory of crises' in the combination of the notion of 'the absolute overproduction of capital' in the third volume of *Capital* and the theory of capital accumulation in its first volume.[12]

In all these three arguments Marx makes it clear that the capitalist law of population, the generation of an excessive working population, is a result of the motion of capital accumulation, and not at all a natural phenomenon as described by T. R. Malthus. In this regard the theory of a relative surplus-population produced by a rising organic composition of capital is doubtless one of Marx's great discoveries. It is also true that Marx tended to emphasise the second argument among the three above, or the progressive production of a relative surplus-population, for two reasons.

First, the logic fits with one of Marx's fundamental theoretical views that a capitalist society polarises a larger and larger number of poor workers and a decreasing number of rich capitalists through the appropriation and centralisation of the means of production. This view originated from Marx's early writings such as the *Manifesto of the Communist Party*, as we saw in Chapter 3, Section 3.1, and was also maintained in *Capital*, especially in the related sections of chapter 25 and chapter 32 'The Historical Tendency of Capitalist Accumulation', as a source for the debates on the law of increasing misery. However, from this view an increase of employment, in the process of prosperity, cannot be properly explained and the possibility for capitalist production to grow as a social formation must be unduly neglected.

Secondly, while observing the concrete forms of the relative surplus-population in England in his time, Marx tended to regard all of the industrial reserve army which actually existed outside of the central capitalist industries as a relative surplus-population expelled from capitalist production. As a result, it seems that capitalist production is an extremely powerful mechanism for generating an excess population. However, a large number of people, especially classified in the latent and the stagnant forms of the reserve army were in these positions through the process of social decomposition induced by capitalist development at the centre, and not through being expelled from the inside of capitalist production. Although they surely play the role of a reserve army for capitalist production, the process and the result of their formation should be categorically distinguished from the production of a relative surplus-population as the result of capitalist accumulation itself. In this respect Marx was in fact not analysing pure capitalism even in the first volume of *Capital*. However, in so far as the basic theory of capitalism concentrates on the internal law of motion of capital, the external decomposition process of other modes of production and its consequences should be studied at more concrete levels of research. In this case the concept of a relative surplus-population being created from within the capitalist process of accumulation may be said roughly to correspond only to the periodically recurring and floating form of the reserve army in reality. The relative surplus-population in this form is certainly absorbed, exhausted and re-created recurrently through business cycles.

Thus, despite Marx's inclination, followed by most of his underconsumptionist successors, to emphasise the logic of the progressive production of relative surplus-population, his other two arguments which recognise the expansion of employment and the absorption of surplus working population, particularly in the phase of prosperity, should be seriously taken into consideration. Is it not possible then to unify those arguments in Marx more organically? Following Uno's lead, I maintain that a growing demand for labour-power accompanying capital accumulation with a relatively constant composition of capital characterises the phase of prosperity, whereas the production of the relative surplus-population with a rising composition of capital appears intensively in the phase of depression in the process of regular business cycles. Thus, Marx's first and second arguments can be understood as the alternate processess, which form the cyclical movement of the absorption and reformation of relative surplus-population in the more contrasting third argument. There are reasons for such an understanding.

It is often believed among Marxians that capitalist accumulation, motivated by the possibility of obtaining extra surplus-value as well as by the pressure of mutual competition, incessantly revolutionises labour productivity, and thus tends continuously to expel living labour from the production process. Though such motivation does always exist abstractly, there are also circumstances which would constrain differently its working through the alternate phases of the business cycle. The pressure of competition, for example, would work differently in the phases of prosperity and depression. Marx notices this, and refers to the intensified severity of competition as a result of 'absolute overproduction of capital' in the phase of depression, and further to the effect of such a severe competitive struggle for the improvement of productivity:

> As long as every thing goes well, competition acts, as is always the case when the general rate of profit is settled, as a practical freemasonry of the capitalist class, so that they all share in the common booty in proportion to the size of the portion that each puts in. But as soon as it is no longer a question of division of profit, but rather of loss, each seeks as far as he can to restrict his share of this loss and pass it to someone else . . . and competition now becomes a struggle of enemy brothers. (III, pp. 361–2). The fall in prices and the competitive struggle impel each capitalist to reduce the individual value of his total product below its general value by employing new machinery, new and improved methods of labour and new forms of combination. That is, they impel him to raise the productivity of a given quantity of labour, to reduce the portion of variable capital to constant and thereby to dismiss workers, in short to create an artificial surplus population. (III, p. 363).

This implies that the capitalist motivation for the improvement of productivity and rationalisation is milder and not so severe in the phase of prosperity. In addition, the specific restrictions of existing fixed capital on the changes in the method of production must be taken into account. The relative 'freemasonry' in competition during the phase of prosperity would generally allow the existing fixed capitals to keep on working profitably. Prosperity spreads certain sets of technologies in an extensive way and is thus characterised by the quantitative expansion of production. Accumulation with an absolutely constant organic composition of capital, as formulated in Marx's first argument above, is certainly too strict a notion for the phase of prosperity, if taken literally. New investment from profit can make possible investment in new methods of production and a rise in the technical composition of capital. However, so long as the existing fixed capitals continue to work, the competitive introduction of new methods of production has to be partial and limited, particularly in the case where new machines are added to existing plant. Even the equipment already fully depreciated tend to be utilised as a sort of free asset being more profitable than otherwise. In this respect, as Marx points out, 'machinery is most valuable for capital when its value = 0.'[13] In so far as the existing fixed capitals are thus not easily abandoned in the prosperity phase, the demand for labour-power must increase absolutely, even if not strictly proportionally to the accumulation of capital.[14] Therefore, accumulation of capital during prosperity, which goes on with a relatively constant composition, absorbing progressively larger number of workers into the production process, must sooner or later cause an over-accumulation in relation to the labouring population.

In contrast, while the intensified competition, the 'struggle of enemy brothers' impels capitalist rationalisation of the process of production by the employment of new methods, as Marx notices, the restriction of existing fixed capitals on radical changes in methods of production are much lessened. Since the existing fixed capitals are no longer profitable, there appears a general pressure for capitalists to renew them in order to restore profitability of the total capitals. Before being replaced, most of the value invested in fixed capitals must be converted to the money form, in an amortisation or sinking fund, so as to reduce the loss from abandoning the remaining capital value and also to amass the necessary amount of money capital for new equipment. So long as profitable expansion is impossible on the basis of old equipment, profit, and some of the circulating capitals are also collected in money-form, as a preparation for completely new investment. Thus, the introduction of completely new methods of production accompanied by renewal of fixed capital is generally prepared and enforced during the depression and realised mostly towards the end of depression as a decisive moment for changing the phase back into prosperity – this is a typical case, of course, at the level of the basic principle in the theory of regular business cycles.

The irrational character of capitalism from the view of human welfare is clearly shown in very severe 'rationalization' of the production processes so producing a relative surplus-population in the phase of depression, adding to the already existing unemployed from the destructive phase of the crisis. The additional relative surplus-population produced by a rise of the organic composition of capital serves as grounds for capital possibly to achieve a level of accumulation in the next period of prosperity higher than the previous peak, independently of the growth of the absolute number of the active population. In the long run capital accumulation can proceed without being restricted by the 'natural' growth rate of population, on the grounds of the mechanism which produces relative surplus-population through a rising organic composition of capital. This long-run process can not always be harmonious or one-sidedly and progressively devastating in reducing employment and increasing the relative surplus-population. It contains alternate processes of absorption and reformation of the relative surplus-population as the capitalist law of population, which appears as a foundation for the regular business cycle. If one believed simply in Marx's second argument above, that capital can always avoid the shortage of labour-power by raising the composition of capital without causing the serious difficulty of excessive accumulation, one would surely rely too much on the malleability of capital, and neglect the restrictions imposed by fixed capitals, just as the neo-classical growth theories do. If one held that even the expansive accumulation of capital in the phase of prosperity does not therefore decrease, but increase the absolute size of the industrial reserve army, one would be to blame for neglecting not merely the non-malleability of capital, but also the positive ability of capitalism to increase the number of workers employed in the long run as a growing social formation through the repetition of industrial cycles.

A theory of capital accumulation which clarifies the capitalist law of population in the form of alternate processes of the absorption and reformation of a relative surplus-population however, cannot be by itself a complete theory of business cycles and crises. In addition to the basic theory of accumulation and the capitalist law of population, the concrete mechanisms of motion of capitals through competition and credit must be taken into consideration. In particular it is not yet certain or clear what happens as a result of over-accumulation of capital in relation to the labouring population, if it causes a destructive crisis and alters the phase into depression. For instance, Marx states as follows in the first section of chapter 25 in the first volume of *Capital*:

> Either the price of labour keeps on rising, because its rise does not interfere with the process of accumulation. . . . Or, the other alternative, accumulation slackens as a result of the rise in the price of labour, because the stimulus of gain is blunted. The rate of

> accumulation lessens; but this means that the primary cause of that lessening vanishes, i.e. the disproportion between capital and exploitable labour-power. The mechanism of the capitalist production process removes the very obstacles it temporarily creates. The price of labour falls again to a level corresponding with capital's requirements for self-valorization. (I, p. 770).

In this statement, we cannot see on the one hand a logical limitation to the process of the rising price of labour-power, or on the other hand the reason why capital accumulation would not slacken and just pass into a mild stagnation with a relatively high level of employment, rather than cause an acute crisis making both the level of employment and wages fall radically in the process of regular business cycle. In order to solve these problems among others, we must now consider the contents of the theory of regular business cycles on the basis of the law of capital accumulation as put into order above.

## 9.3 REGULAR BUSINESS CYCLES AND CRISES

Regular business cycles are composed of three dintinct phases; i.e. prosperity, crisis and depression. There seems to be a problem about which phase we should begin our analysis, since each phase in turn appears as a result of the preceding phase. In contrast with other phases, however, the phase of prosperity represents a positive and general process of capital accumulation. A capitalist economy must generate an expansive process of production from its own essential nature even apart from the causal effects of the preceding depression or crisis. Therefore, the phase of prosperity as a general expansive process of production under capital is initially taken up here, although the final stage of its phase containing the over-accumulation of capital with all its distortions must be treated within it though separately as an inevitable result of its own process.

### Prosperity

When capital accumulation can proceed as positively expanding reproduction, capitals generally maintain and valorise existing fixed capitals by yearly adding surplus-value to them. As a result, the composition of capital in the process of accumulation would remain relatively constant as we have discussed. As accumulation proceeds, in such a form, the demand for labour-power or the size of employment would grow, if not literally proportionally to capital accumulation. In so far as the absorbable relative surplus-population exists, enabling capitals to increase employment at about the existing level of wages, capital accumulation would then take the form of a widening process, quantitatively expanding its productive power within stable existing relations of production between capital and labourers, expressed in a stable rate of surplus-value. Upon the basis of relatively stable productivity and wages as well as the rate of surplus-value, capital accumulation would also retain relatively stable value relations in commodity products. The motion of the market prices of commodity products in the various spheres of production would then be subject to an easy adjustment process, gravitating around the relatively stable market prices of production.

The anarchical imbalance between the demand and supply of commodity products is certainly unavoidable in a capitalist economy. The imbalance being expressed in the deviation of market prices from the prices of production, however, can be readjusted relatively smoothly and rapidly within a comparatively narrow range of price fluctuations, as capitalist reproduction extends as a whole, with stable conditions in the labour market. In such a process the equalisation of the rate of profit across industrial spheres must also work relatively smoothly. The roles of commercial capital and the credit system in promoting both the expansion of capitalist reproduction and the equalisation of the profit rate are effective under such conditions favourable to capital accumulation, particularly in relation to an absorbable relative surplus-population.

The process of prosperity in a regular business cycle is thus basically characterised, so to speak, as a quantitative boom. For production is expanded mainly quantitatively with relatively stable prices of commodity products based on relatively constant technical conditions of production and wages which correspond to the value of labour-power. In such a process the total amount of profit increases as capital accumulates with a stable general rate of profit determined by the dominant technical conditions of production and real wages. The rate of interest would also be maintained at a stable level favourable to the promotion of real capital accumulation through the use of the credit system. Marx notices a relatively low rate of interest in comparison with the level of the profit rate in the phase of prosperity, for instance in the following statement:

> If the production process has reached the flourishing stage that precedes that of over-exertion, commercial credit undergoes a very great expansion, this in turn actually forming the 'healthy' basis for a ready flow of returns and an expansion of production. In this situation, the rate of interest is still low, even if it has risen above its minimum. This is actually the only point in time at which it may be said that a low rate of interest, and hence a relative abundance of loanable capital, coincides with an actual expansion of industrial capital. The ease and regularity of returns, combined with an expanded commercial credit, ensures the supply of loan capital despite the increased demand and prevents the interest level from rising. (III, p. 619).

As the reproduction process extends, the demand for loanable capital at banks in the form of request for discounting commercial bills certainly increases. Nevertheless the rate of interest is prevented from rising, as Marx notices, for two reasons. For one thing, the supply of loanable capital from idle-money capital formed in the turnover of capitals (such as depreciation and accumulation funds, money reserves for price fluctuations or the necessary funds to maintain production process during the periods of circulation of capitals) would also increase as the scale of reproduction extends. Such idle-capital flows into banks directly in the form of deposits. In addition the ease and regularity of return payments for discounted bills ensures the reformation and increase of cash reserves at banks as an actual concrete basis of loanable money capital. For another thing the demand for loanable money capital in the form of request for discounting bills must be comparatively restricted because of 'the relative independence of commercial credit from bank credit' (III, pp. 626–7). Actually, in the phase of prosperity commercial credit among industrial and commercial capitalists greatly expands by itself, forming longer chains of circulation of commercial bills with much confidence and optimism. This is not a mere social psychological phenomenon, but is actually based upon the relatively smooth process of reproduction as a whole. Thus, both the easy supply of loanable money capital in bank credit, and the comparatively restricted demand for it, have a common basis in the easily expanding process of real capital[15] accumulation with a flexibly absorbable relative surplus-population. So far, the credit relations among banks can also easily be expanded, and the central bank in a central money market would not have any difficulty in maintaining its cash reserve by accepting both deposits and return payments sufficiently, while the demand for rediscounting would remain relatively low.

Therefore, the interest rate in the money market between banks would also be comparatively low, reflecting a relative abundance of loanable money capital. It easily facilitates industrial and commercial capitals expanding their commercial credit at a low rate of interest and their business activity in general. However, the relative abundance of loanable money capital must not be taken for a basic cause of the prosperity. The easy money market in this phase expresses rather, the prosperous expansive accumulation of real capitals with a relatively stable and satisfactory rate of profit. Though such a rate of profit and a comparatively low rate of interest appear logically interrelated in the phase of prosperity, the determinants of both rates must be conceived separately as we have argued in Chapter 8, Section 8.2; the former rate is regulated basically by the system of the technical conditions of production and the level of real wages in physical terms, whereas the latter rate is determined by the balance between the demand for and the supply of loanable money capital. Therefore, it is no surprise to observe a divergence between the general rate of profit and the comparatively lower rate of interest in the process of prosperity, despite a traditional tendency in neo-classicists to identify them. This is not to deny that real capitalists would usually consider the interest rate as a minimum standard for their marginal rate of profit for additional investment.

Since the process of capital accumulation with a relatively stable and satisfactory rate of profit continues in a expensive fashion as a quantitative boom, it one-sidedly absorbs the labouring population into the capitalist process of production, if not literally proportionally to the increase of the total value of capital. So far as the ratio of capital yearly accumulated, as a dependant function of the rate of profit, generally surpasses the rate of growth of population in the phase of prosperity, the relative surplus-population would decrease further and further, and the labour market would become tightened sooner or later. Then, towards the end of prosperity wages must rise. Unlike in case of commodity products, capital cannot increase the absolute amount of the supply of labour-power even when its price rises. Because of this inelasticity in the supply of labour-power, the rise of its price, the nominal wage-rate, in the labour market cannot be generally counterbalanced by the possible rises of other commodity prices here in our basic principles.

In contrast, it is assumed in the Kalecki–Okishio type of business-cycle theory, that investment demand would pull up the prices of commodity products more than the nominal wage-rate, resulting in both the reduction of the real wage-rate and the realisation problem for commodity products towards the end of prosperity. In my opinion this type of theory depends on the three following presuppositions, which may occassionally become effective in the later stage of capitalism, but are somewhat remote from Marx's basic position as well as ours here: (i) The investment demand is supposed to increase very much independently from the social surplus-value annually produced. (ii) The supply of commodity products cannot increase in accord with the investment, because the supply is delayed or restricted by either the production period, full-capacity utilisation or monopoly. (iii) The supply of credit necessary to support the explosive investment boom can be available elastically and effective in generating an inflationary rise in prices of commodity products. Whereas our basic position assumes that according to Marx: (i) Investment is fundamentally the transformation of surplus-value into capital, and cannot be independent from the movement of the social surplus-value produced and acquired by capital. (ii) Investment would bring about both demand for and supply of commodity products more or less simultaneously as described in the extended reproduction schemes. (iii) In the competitive capitalist market, under the gold-standard monetary system, explosive hyperinflation is not likely to occur even when the nominal wage-rate rises. It is also assumed that despite the limitation of the absolute number of the working population, the marginal increase of the labour input necessary for capital investment, maintaining the relative elasticity of supply of commodity products, is still available, though with a further increase in wage rates.

In our position, upon these assumptions therefore, with a rise in the nominal wage-rates the real-wage rate would also rise, and as a result the rate of surplus-value as well as the rate of profit must continually fall. (Actually, the bargaining power of trade unions, if existent, must be very much strengthened, and will intensify the rise in wages,[16] although the favourable market condition for workers is the basis for such a change.) The process of such a falling rate of profit due to a rise in wages must result in 'an absolute overproduction of capital' as defined by Marx as follows:

As soon as capital has grown in such proportion to the working population that neither the absolute labour-time that this working population supplies nor its relative surplus labour-time can be extended (the latter would not be possible in any case in a situation where the demand for labour was so strong, and there was thus a tendency for wages to rise); where, therefore, the expanded capital produces only the same mass of surplus-value as before, there will be an absolute overproduction of capital; i.e. the expanded $C + \Delta C$ will not produce any more profit, or will even produce less profit, than the capital $C$ did before its increase by $\Delta C$ (III, p. 360).

The purpose of capitalist production, the valorisation of capital, cannot be achieved in such a situation. Even though Marx infers that 'in actual fact, the situation would take the form that one portion of the capital would lie completely or partially idle (since it would first have to expel the capital already functioning from its position, to be valorized at all)' (ibid.), capitals in competition would not so easily mitigate the difficulty of the overaccumulation of capital by making a portion idle. A capitalist who would make a portion of his capital idle in view of the falling rate of profit would lose his share in the market and experience a more rapid fall in both the mass of and the individual rate of profit, without being able individually to reduce the pressure of the over-accumulation of total capital and the resulting rise in wages. Therefore, individual capitals must rather continue to attempt to maintain or increase the amount of profit by increasing their active capital further in the face of the falling rate of profit due to rising wages. Thus, even in the last phase of prosperity which begins with excessive capital accumulation in relation to the labouring population, the social process of expanded reproduction would still continue in spite of a falling rate of profit.

The social functions of the motion of capital in the expanding process of reproduction must, however, become much altered, reflecting the difficulty due to over-accumulated capital. The process of capital accumulation intensifies its character of speculative and uneven development. As the pace of expansion of reproduction slows down with a fall in the profit rate, the process of adjustment of the anarchical imbalance between various spheres of production is retarded. The fluctuations in prices of commodity products are then widened. In addition, a rise in wages must cause a disturbance in the system of market prices of production from both costs of and demand for commodity products. The cost-prices would be affected by a rise in wages in different proportions according to the different compositions of capital in various spheres of production. Roughly speaking, for instance, if the composition of capital producing the money commodity gold is about the social average, the market prices of production of commodities produced in the spheres with the composition of capital lower than average must rise, whereas the market prices of commodities produced in the spheres with the higher composition of capital must fall, so long as equalisation of profit rate still works across the various spheres, including the gold industry.[17] Similarly, the market prices of production of commodities produced in the spheres with greater speeds of turnover of capital, whose composition is about the social average, must also rise as a result of a rise in wages in the process of the equalisation of the profit rate. Thus, there must appear certain commodities whose prices rise tendentially as their wage costs increase more than average per unit of capital. Besides, with a rise in wages, the demand for some means of consumption or their raw materials would suddenly increase, whereas the supply of these cannot be so quickly expanded in the short run, as in the case of agricultural products. The market prices of such commodity products must rise as the demand surpasses the supply as a result of a rise in wages.

In the last phase of prosperity therefore, where excessive capital accumulation causes a rise in wages, the fluctuation of commodity products would not merely be distorted and widened, but also contain a tendency to rise in the case of some commodities which experience a more than social average increase in their costs or in demand or in both. Speculative trading in order to gain by utilising such fluctuations in commodity prices never then fails to develop. Large-scale stockpiling of those commodities whose prices tend to rise subsequently takes place among capitals, especially by commercial capitals depending on commercial and bank credit. This reduces the actual supply of those commodities in the market, and artificially adds to the rising momentum of their prices. Such speculative trading must intensify the uneven development and imbalances across the various spheres of production. Marx pointed to the fact that speculative 'operations are conducted largely with credit capital' (III, p. 645), utilising a relative low rate of interest, and also that speculation artificially intensifies a rise in prices of some commodities when there is an unusual reduction of supply, as with a harvest failure (III, p. 647). From what we have discussed, the development of such speculative operations are by no means accidental, but a corollary of the last phase of prosperity where real capital is over-accumulated with a rise in wages.[18] Such a process of over-accumulation and the resulting speculative development finds its restriction not merely in the falling profit rate, but also particularly in the rise of interest together with the reversed functions of the credit system.

The basis of credit expansion in the process of prosperity is in the formation and re-formation of idle-money capital in the turnover of capital. This basis becomes much narrowed with the over-accumulation of capital in three ways. First, since wages must always be paid in cash, capitals have to mobilise their own idle-money capital for wage-payments as wages rise. Second, the formation of an idle-money fund saved out of surplus-value or profit, such as the accumulation fund, must be reduced as the rate of profit falls. Third, capitals which increase their commodity stocks in the process of speculative development would mobilise their idle-money capital for speculative operations, and as a result would reduce their idle funds.

On the other hand, the demand for the expansion of credit, especially of bank credit, continues to increase in this phase of prosperity as capitalist extension of reproduction with its explosive speculative stockpiling is carried on. However, idle-money capital, as a necessary basis for the extension of commercial credit, cannot now be plentifully formed in the desired hands among industrial and commercial capitalists. Therefore, while commercial credit among capitalists is still called for causing an actual increase in the number of commercial bills, its smooth expansion is substantially restricted. The increased number of commercial bills cannot now circulate in long chains of transactions. They tend to be brought into banks relatively shortly after being drawn up. 'The relative independence of commercial credit from bank credit' which characterised most of the course of prosperity now disappears. The demand for bank credit in the form of discounting bills of exchange must thus greatly increases.

Against such an increase in the demand for bank credit, the expansion of the supply of loanable money funds for use as bank credit is contrarily increasingly restricted. In banks of issue, while the balance of issued bank notes for cash payments increases with an increase in the demand for the discounting of bills of exchange, the formation of cash reserves is slowed down and even reduced by the practical slow down in return payments for discounted bills. The due periods of the bills tend to become longer, and a formal return payment will often depend upon money being obtained by discounting other bills. In deposit banks, the cash reserve against their social debt in the form of the accepted amount of deposits tends to be reduced, as a result of both an increase of the demand for discount and the substantial slowdown of return payments as well as decreasing cash deposits. Mutual accommodation amongst banks in the money market then increases. But this can only equalise the balance between the demand for and the supply of loanable money funds among banks to a certain degree, and cannot remove the fall in the total ratio of the cash reserves against the total social debt of banks. The demand in the money market has thus to surpass the supply, pulling up the interest rate.

Marx, noting that 'a rise in interest comes between prosperity and its collapse' (III, p. 482), pays attention to speculative stockpiling and a rise in wages as the factors pulling up the interest rate. For instance he has this to say:

> In order to pay for the commodities bought without selling them, gold is obtained by way of commercial 'bill of exchange operations'. In this case the demand for loan capital grows, and the rate of interest may rise as a result of this attempt to block the supply of commodities to the market artificially. The higher rate of interest then expresses an artificial reduction in the supply of commodity capital. (III, p. 647).
>
> An increased demand for labour-power raises the price of this commodity just like any other, without raising profits, which depend principally on the relative cheapness of this particular commodity. At the same time, under the conditions we have assumed, this demand raises the rate of interest, by increasing the demand for money capital. . . . If wages rise for whatever reason, in otherwise unfavourable conjunctures, the rise in wages causes the profit rate to fall, although the rate of interest rises to the extent that the wage rise increases the demand for money capital. (III, p. 646).

It must be recognised that Marx did not manage to combine organically these notes with his notion of the 'absolute overproduction of capital' so as to formulate a very coherent crisis theory. However, it also seems clear that he was thus virtually presenting or suggesting to us a well-articulated excess capital theory of crisis of a labour shortage type throughout his theories of capital accumulation, profit and interest. What is worth emphasising is Marx's serious attempt to clarify the social functions of credit and interest in the process of causing periodical crises.[19]

Anyhow, a rise in the interest rate in the face of the falling rate of profit must form an important restriction on the motion of capitals which have so much depended upon an extensive credit system for their reproduction. The process of a tightening money market becomes more clearly decisive when the gold reserve of the central bank begins to drain away. In the basic theory of capitalism the central bank must be conceived as a private central bank of issue, and its bank notes cannot be totally substituted for gold money, particularly in transactions with places well outside of the central trading area as well as for use in wage payments, as we discussed in Chapter 8, Section 8.2. As the special fluctuations in commodity prices and the speculative trades develop with the process of the over-accumulation of capital, the balance of payments among increasing commercial bills between various trading areas would be very much distorted. The necessary amount of specie payment to settle the balance of credit between various areas would thus increase along with an increase of cash payment for wages. Capitals and banks have now to hold more gold money as reserve for payment. Therefore, an inflow of gold to the central bank through return payments and deposits would become smaller than before, whereas the outflow of gold in the forms of withdrawals of deposits or conversions of bank notes increases. The gold reserve of the central bank which is a central indicator of the money market must then absolutely decrease.[20] Since the central bank cannot use the other bankers' notes or bills as its reserve for payment, it must raise its discount rate so as to reduce the absolute amount of discount and attempt to control the daily quantity of discount business when such an absolute decrease in the gold reserve occurs. All other banks then find it difficult to continue their expansion of credit by relying upon rediscounting commercial bills in the money market or with the central bank, while carefully securing their cash reserves. A sharp rise in the interest rate therefore generally appears with a quantitative restriction on the credit supply.

The speculative stockpile of various commodities, which has been increased and maintained upon a basis of expandable credit and in expectation of a rise in prices, must lose its rationale, eroded from two sides; the slowing down of the total demand in the commodity market due to a falling rate of profit, and a sharp rise in the rate of interest in the money market towards the very end of the prosperity. When the expected rate of rise in the price of a commodity becomes lower than the increasing rate of interest, it must be seen that to carry on holding the stockpile on the basis of credit (alone increasing it) will make a loss. In particular, the capitals which have formed speculative stockpiles on a large-scale utilising credit are forced to sell at a sacrifice sooner or later in the process of a sharp rise in interest rates in order to avoid increases of losses as well as to secure the necessary cash to pay off both principal and interest on their debts.

Thus, the credit system, which promotes capital accumulation and the equalisation of the rate of profit, adjusting the incessant imbalances among various industrial spheres in the positive phase of prosperity, completely changes its social functions as the over-accumulation of capital in relation to the labouring population appears. It then promotes a speculative uneven development which is characteristic of the last phase of prosperity. The distortions and fluctuations in prices due to the over-accumulation of capital with a rise in wages are wildly exaggerated by speculative trading and stockpiling, utilising the extendible nature of the credit system. A rise in commodity prices thus exaggerated by the speculative use of credit might substantially mitigate the pressure of a rise in wages on the rate of profit in certain industrial spheres producing the commodities concerned. However, it would not remove the absolute difficulty of the general fall in the rate of profit in the process of the over-accumulation of capital, and often unevenly intensifies the difficulties in other industries by adding to the rising costs of production. The substantial disequilibrium among industrial spheres must deepen beneath the surface of a speculative boom based on credit expansion. Over-accumulation of real capital finally causes a clash between a fall in the profit rate and a sharp rise in the interest rate, with a quantitative restriction on the expansion of credit, occuring through a speculative and uneven process towards the end of prosperity, and thus turns this phase of the business cycle into an acute crisis.

**Crisis**

The beginning of a crisis is given ordinarily by the breakdown of large-scale speculative operations by commercial capitals mostly in the field of wholesale trade. For at the end of prosperity, speculative stockpiling utilising credit has been developed most intensively and on a large scale of this field, and the shock of tightened credit and a rising rate of interest is therefore also most serious here. On the other hand, the collapse of speculative activity by these commercial capitals in large-scale trading results in a destructive shock to both the commodity market and the money market. As Marx points out: 'This explains the phenomenon that crises do not first break out and are not first apparent in the retail trade, which bears on immediate consumption, but rather in the sphere of wholesale trade, as well as banking, which places the money capital of the entire society at the wholesalers' disposal.' (III, p. 419).

Since speculative overtrading is an appearance of the inner difficulty of excessive capital accumulation, generally involving industrial capitals as well, the resulting collapse in speculation by wholesalers cannot be an isolated phenomenon. With the breakdown of large-scale speculative operations in wholesale trade, the prices of commodities which have been elevated to higher levels by such operations must collapse. The basis of credit relations, which are extended assuming certain relations of prices, is then destroyed. The difficulty of finding the necessary amounts of cash for the bills falling due must spread, causing a series of insolvencies in a chain reaction, as commodities cannot be sold at expected prices. The whole credit system becomes paralysed by the reciprocal collapse of the commodity market and the money market. While new commercial credit would hardly be given among industrial and commercial capitalists, banks would also most severely restrict the issue of credit in the form of discounting bills, in order to secure their own cash reserves as well as to avoid the danger of insolvency. The interest rate rises more sharply, to the highest level of the whole phase of the business cycle, as the demand for credit in order to obtain money as the necessary means of payment desperately increases in spite of the severe restriction or the supply of credit. So far as the process of reproduction through commodity transactions is carried on on the basis of the credit system, its repetition becomes not merely difficult, but also meaningless as the process of valorisation of capital. Its repetition would mostly make a loss by paying such expensive interest rates. The sale of commodities therefore, even at a sacrifice; is urged on by the pressure to clear off past debts among real capitals. A general fall in commodity prices with the extreme difficulty of selling them appears in reciprocal relation with the general collapse of credit transactions.

In sum, the inner difficulty of the over-accumulation of real capital is expressed contradictorily in an absolute shortage of money capital in the money market as well as in a correlated absolute excess of commodity capital in the commodity market. Alongside the reciprocal collapses of the money market and the commodity market, 'in crisis, the antithesis between commodities and their value-form, money, is raised to the level of an absolute contradiction' (I, p. 236).[21] Through 'the monetary famine' (ibid.) or the collapses of the money and the commodity market, all capitalist business is generally paralysed and contracted. Values accumulated in the process of reproduction, e.g. in the form of raw materials and production equipment can no longer work as capital, and they are forcibly made idle and destroyed. A wave of bankruptcies hits many industrial and commercial capitals, and these do not exempt a number of bank capitals in the typical periodical crisis. At the same time a great number of workers have suddenly been made unemployed. Wages must be reduced as a reaction to the rises which took place towards the end of the phase of prosperity. The workers' effective consumers' demand is severely contracted, forming a vicious circle with the difficulty capitalists have to sell their commodities. A classic trinity of commercial crisis, credit crisis and industrial crisis is thus completed.

Marx attempted to analyse these three aspects of periodic crises in their mutual correlations for instance:

> Interest . . . reaches its maximum again as soon as the new crisis breaks out, credit suddenly dries up, payments congeal, the reproduction process is paralysed and, . . . there is an almost absolute lack of loan capital alongside a surplus of unoccupied industrial capital. (III, p. 620).
>
> Since certain price relationships are assumed in the reproduction process, and govern it, this process is thrown into stagnation and confusion by the general fall in prices. This disturbance and stagnation paralyses the function of money as a means of payment, which is given along with the development of capital and depends on those presupposed price relationships. The chain of obligations to pay at specific dates is broken in a hundred places, and this is further intensified by an accompanying breakdown of the credit system, which have developed alongside capital. All this therefore leads to violent and acute crises, sudden forcible devaluation, an actual stagnation and disruption in the reproduction process, and hence to an actual decline in reproduction. (III, p. 363).

It clearly shows the self-contradictory character of capitalism as a historical social formation, that capital as a process of self-augmentating value has thus to destroy its relations of production as well as its own value through the growth of its own internal productive power. In contrast to the theoretical beliefs of the classical school and the neo-classical tradition, capitalism cannot be a natural harmonious socio-economic order which can increase the welfare of workers without causing any serious disturbance or crisis by itself. As we have seen in the basic principles of political economy, the logical inevitability of periodical crisis is thus shown on the basis of Marx's notion of the 'absolute overproduction of capital' in relation to the labouring population. Disequilibrium among industrial spheres and the severe restriction on the effective demand of workers, both of which have been much emphasised in the excess commodity theory of crisis, appear as important moments, if not fundamental causes, of the process as well as the results of crisis.[22] The excess capital theory of crisis, of a labour-shortage type, sees the root of the self-contradiction of the capitalist economy causing periodical crises, not in the superficial balance between the demand and the supply of commodity products, but in the very essential precondition of capitalism which is to treat human labour-power as a commodity. It should also be noted that the logical inevitability of an acute general crisis is presented by showing not merely the fundamental difficulty of the over-accumulation of capital, but also the manner in which through competition and credit among capitals the difficulty of over-accumulation intensifies resulting in the trinity of commercial, credit and industrial crises.

There is a problem as to where and why the vicious circle of reciprocal contractions between the commodity market, the effective demand of labour and the reproduction of capitals ends. It seems difficult to think of the point where the vicious circle looses its violence, so long as capitals are conceived abstractly as a homogeneous entity. Indeed, if real capitals are assumed to be homogeneous, the theoretical limit to the destruction of capitals would be quite hard to define. Where can a fall in commodity prices, the contraction of effective demand and the wave of bankruptcies theoretically come to an end? As an answer it might be argued that there must be some minimum consumer demand by workers to sustain their lives. However, workers under capitalism cannot create an effective demand for consumption goods without being employed at least as part-timers, excepting the very limited amounts of their savings from the previous prosperous phase. We can see that the limit to the destruction of capitals must be a priority for the problem to be solved. Another possible proposal for the problem is to see a decisive moment in the reversal of the downward vicious circle in the expansion of gold production which must become profitable in the process of a general fall in commodity prices.[23] This proposal may not be very persuasive, as the size of gold industry would not be sufficiently big enough to counterbalance the downward pressure in all the other industrial spheres. In order to reach a more satisfactory solution, we have to remove the assumption of the homogeneity of capitals and re-examine the concrete process of crisis.

The downward vicious circle in the phase of crisis is carried on and strengthened, as we have seen by the process of clearing away the credit relations. Commodities have to be sold at a sacrifice so as to obtain necessary money for means of payment for debts in the form of due bills of exchange. Since commercial credit is mutually formed in order to finance circulating capital, and not for fixed capitals, the lives of the bills of exchange cannot be very long. Ordinarily they were typically three months, and at longest ten months in the British credit system of the mid-nineteenth century (cf. III, p. 536–7). Thus the intensive process of clearing away the previous debts generating an acute crisis would not last very long, since the additional formation of commercial credit by drawing new bills of exchange becomes so difficult in the phase of crisis. Actually the duration of an acute phase of the crisis in the classical business cycle was less than a year, and mostly about half a year. After the period of the intense clearing away of the preceding debt in the form of bills of exchange, the strong pressure to sell commodities even at a loss would be much reduced. The pressure of massive commodity stocks would also eventually be decreased through bargain sales, abandonment by bankrupted capitals, or loss of use-value and so value during the prolonged time of storage.

In the meanwhile the destruction of capitals in the acute phase of the crisis cannot be at all balanced and even. Corresponding to the speculative and uneven development of the last phase of prosperity and the anarchical nature of the process of crisis, the destruction of values of capitals in a crisis must also proceed anarchically and very unevenly. For example, the prices of commodities which have been artificially much elevated by speculative stockpiling towards the end of prosperity must fall sharply over a wide range as a reaction. In contrast there may well be other commodities whose prices do not fall so wildly as a result of the different conditions in the process of the preceding speculative development. The destruction of capital values in the industrial spheres producing the latter commodities must generally be milder. The degree of destruction of values of capitals would also vary according to the different conditions of production or to the different extent of the utilisation of credit even within the same sphere of production. In the process of clearing up complicated relations of debt and credit among capitals, while a number of capitalists would be bankrupted with huge amounts of debt often several times their net assets, other capitals may conserve at least a part of their value by getting back their own credits, if not from the direct debtors, then from the sureties as endorsers of the bills of exchange.

There must be similar unevenness in the destruction or conservation of bank capitals and their cash reserves as well. Although there is no guarantee for banks not to be bankrupted, the banks in a central money market and the central bank in particular are apt to be exempted from direct shocks and insolvensies which occur intensively in certain industries or areas. Their positions are in a sense neutralised by their wider business concerns. This is a reason why central bank notes are most likely to maintain their circulation and credibility throughout an acute crisis, in addition to the large size of capital forming the central bank (actually related also to its role as a monopolistic cashier to the government).

Since the destruction of capital values proceeds very unevenly in a crisis, not all the existing capitals are driven into bankruptcy. There can be a number of capitals whose difficulties are mitigated, neutralised or watered down even by the deepening difficulties of others. More or less of their values are conserved. When those capital values resume, one by one, their process of valorisation after the stormy procedure of clearing up both the preceding debt relations and excessive commodity stocks, the phase of an acute crisis passes and turns into the phase of depression. The crisis reveals the self-destructive and contradictory nature of a capitalist economy, but a crisis can never be a final breakdown of capitalism as a social order in the basic principle of its economic motion. The crisis in principle forms a phase in a whole business cycle, turning by its own process into the next phase of depression.

**Depression**

In the phase of depression the difficulty of capital accumulation in the production process, the commodity market and the money market continues for a certain period of time. Excessive real capitals, abundant money capitals and a relative surplus-population do coexist, and cannot easily be combined into the process of an extended and positive reproduction. In the typical business cycles of the mid-nineteenth century the phases of depression used to last for a period of between about three and five years. It is an important phase to be clarified theoretically, especially since it can serve as an important frame of reference for the current economic circumstances of our own age.

Why is it so difficult for capital to resume a positive process of expanded reproduction from a depression? After the destructive process of an acute crisis the difficulties of over-accumulation of capital expressed in the rise of wages and interest rate are already removed. As a great number of workers are thrown out of jobs in that phase of crisis their wage-rates would be cut as a reaction to its previous rise at the end of prosperity. In the very process of an acute crisis its fall *might* be more than compensated by a wild collapse of the prices of consumer goods so as actually to raise the real wage-rate, intensifying the difficulty for capitals, although the total real income for workers must surely be reduced. However, when the sharp collapse of the preceding credit relations and commodity stocks is finished, the prices of commodity products can to a certain degree be restored as a result of the reduction in their production and supply. In contrast the price of the commodity labour-power would not be subject to such a process of adjustment in supply, and must remain continuously under pressure of insufficient demand. A lower real wage-rate than the rate in the previous period of prosperity must thus prevail in depression. Such a fall in wages and the real wage-rate 'has exactly the same effect for capital as if relative or absolute surplus-value had been increased while wages remained at the average' (III, p. 363). In the meantime the rate of interest must also be reduced, once the intensive process of clearing up the existing debt relations is past. Money capitals, so far as they were retrieved by industrial and commercial capitalists and by banks tend to lie idle without being of positive use. In spite of these favourable conditions, real capital accumulation will remain stagnant for a considerable period.

A basic reason for this stagnation can no longer directly result from labour shortage, or in the high rate of interest, but in the difficulty of restructuring the balanced conditions for a new accumulation of real capitals. Actually, after the speculative and uneven development towards the end of prosperity and the following anarchical and uneven destruction of capitals, the balance among industrial spheres of production will certainly be broken and far from the best for smooth economic growth. In the distorted balance among the spheres of production, there will be a number of industries whose product prices tend to be pressed down due to unusually excessive idle capacity within them, while coexisting with industries with more favourable conditions for reproduction. Excessive productive capacity is most likely to appear and continue in many industries producing means of consumption and their raw materials, as the effective demand of workers is much reduced with a fall in both employment and wage-rates.

In this regard the excess commodity theory of crisis of both the disequilibrium and under-consumptionist types may have a certain relevancy as a direct explanation of the difficulty of capitals in a depression. Such a difficulties in this phase however, must not be confused with the fundamental difficulty which causes crisis in the basic theory of typical business cycles. It should be defined as a result of the over-accumulation of capital in relation to the labouring population, and also as an inevitable appearance of the inner difficulty of capital to cope with excessive fixed capitals in the production processes.

If it were not for the restriction of existing fixed capitals, industrial capitalists might fairly easily shift their capitals into more profitable spheres or technologies, and thus might escape the difficulty of the oversupply of their commodity products in many industries. But industrial capitalists cannot easily sacrifice or completely abandon the values remaining in their fixed capitals. They have to depreciate much of the value in fixed capitals before scrapping them, and have to accumulate sufficient amounts of money capital including depreciation funds, in order to build up new fixed equipment either in other industrial spheres or upon different technical bases. Commercial credit, and bank credit based on short-term commercial credit are unsuitable for long-term loans for constructing fixed capitals, as we have seen.

When the capitalist process of reproduction resumes its extension, if slowly in depression, the forms of commercial credit and bank credit are reconstructed and begin to work again. However, the reconstructed credit system can not yet be actively utilised, so far as the accumulation of industrial capitals still remains inactive or stagnant under the constraint of existing fixed capitals. The quantitative expansion of both commercial credit and bank credit is small and slow whereas a relative plenty of money capital tends to lie idle, as a sort of unemployed capital. Therefore, a low rate of interest and a loose link between demand and supply in the money market prevail on the credit system during depression. Marx points to the appearance of such a loose credit condition as follows:

> Not every increase in money capital for loan is an index of genuine capital accumulation or an expansion of the reproduction process. This is shown clearly in the phase of the industrial cycle immediately after the crisis, when loan capital lies idle on a massive scale. At these moments, when the production process has undergone a contraction (and after the crisis of 1847, production in the English industrial districts was cut by a third), when commodity prices stand at their lowest point, and when the entrepreneurial spirit is crippled, there is a low rate of interest, which in this case simply indicates an increase in loanable capital presisely as a result of the contraction and paralysis of industrial capital. (III, p. 616).

This situation in the money market is not limited to the moments immediately after crises, but rather continues during most of the depression. Industrial capitalists consciously pile up money capital, such as depreciation funds and accumulation funds, in order to prepare the necessary funds for investing in new methods of production or in other industrial spheres. Therefore, the supply of loanable money capital would continue to increase, and tends to command a low rate of interest, counterbalancing the gradual increase of demand for credit with the extension of reproduction. The low rate of interest, though it may possibly be a favourable condition for economic growth, cannot by itself activate the accumulation of industrial capitals, in so far as the root of their difficulties is not in circulating capital but in fixed capital. As a whole, the credit system and the rate of interest cannot play a positive role in reactivating the capitalist economy in the process of depression, or in removing the root of stagnation.[24]

The constraint of existing fixed capitals upon the rate of profit and accumulation acts as a fundamental basis for stagnation, not merely in the money market, but throughout the whole economy. The tendency to an excessive supply of commodity products, making their prices unprofitable during the depression, arises from the excessive idle capacity which is linked to the much decreased effective demand of workers, as well as with the broken balance among industrial spheres, as is often underlined in the excess commodity theories of crisis. At the same time, a heavy reduction in functioning living labour, due to the decrease of both employment and working hours for the individual worker, may be combined with much idle fixed capital and an inactive money capital so as to cause an unfavourable effect on the profit rate in a similar fashion as that emphasised by the excess capital theory of crisis of a rising composition of capital type; a fall in the rate of profit is effected by a rise in the composition of capital, although the elevated composition of capital, or the lowered capital-output ratio in this phase of depression, expresses the difficulty of unused capacity, and not a rise in the organic composition of capital based on the technological changes. Thus, various types of Marx's crisis theory can have a certain relevancy in understanding the continuous difficulty of capital accumulation in relation to the constraint of existing fixed capitals in a depression. Among the four types of crisis theory, the labour shortage type of excess capital theory can establish the logical necessity for capitalism to suffer periodical crises within the basic principle, whereas the other three would be relevant, if in a different context, in seeing the structural moments which form a stagnating current in a depression. The different aspects of Marx's crisis theory must thus be organically mobilised in this regard.

The constraint of existing fixed capital on the motion of individual capitals however, would no longer be the same as it used to be in the phase of prosperity. In the process of prosperity, existing fixed capitals tended to be used as long as physically possible, for they were generally profitable. In contrast, they become generally unprofitable in the phase of depression, and their replacement with new equipment is anxiously undertaken if economically possible. In Marx's words, after an acute crisis, 'the fall in prices and the competitive struggle, . . . impel each capitalist to reduce the individual value of his total product below its general value by employing new machinery, new and improved methods of labour and new forms of combination' (III, p. 363). Such impulses to new methods of production cannot be instantly realised, so long as remaining values in existing fixed capital are still to be depreciated. Lowered wage-costs or the reduced wage-rate would intensify this constraint, as it reduces the benefit of new labour-saving technology to some extent. While general capitals are still restricted by existing fixed capitals, exceptional capitals having adopted improved new machinery would obtain extra profit and can individually escape the general constraints on capital accumulation. This possibility of extra profit surely adds to the drive to improvement of methods of production among capitalists in severe competition. Unlike the phase of prosperity where capitals act as 'a practical freemasonry' in competition, equalising the rate of profit, here in the depression 'competition now becomes a struggle of enemy brothers' (III, pp. 361–2), and makes it a cardinal issue for capitals to improve their methods of production. Technological innovations and their generalisation are thus strongly sought after, and characterise the phase of depression.

Towards the end of a depression when most capitals in the leading industries have depreciated substantial portions of their old fixed capitals, they begin simultaneously to replace fixed capitals by rebuilding plant and equipment. They mobilise for this reconstruction various money funds of their own, not limited to the depreciation fund, but also the accumulation fund and idle-money capital, which have been intensively and consciously piled up throughout the depression. In such a process of the simultaneous replacement of fixed capitals, an intermediary boom may often appear in the spheres of production of machinery and equipment, whereas weaker capitals being unable to replace their fixed capitals may unevenly find their difficulties compounded and often driven to bankruptcy. While various money funds are mobilised into the reconstruction of plant and equipment, the money market is often tightened and the interest rate rises deepening the difficulty of the weakened capitals. Thus an intermediary boom and a further collapse as an intermediate crisis may appear at the turning-point from depression to prosperity.

Individual capitals, which contrive to replace fixed capitals, cannot merely adopt new profitable methods of production in the same industries where they have operated, but also move into other more promising industries. Competition among industrial capitals seeking a higher rate of profit across various methods and spheres of production is actually realised by their direct mobility particularly in this process, though such direct mobility is too generally assumed in conventional economic theories.

Anyway, through the process of replacing fixed capitals, various imbalances and disequilibriums, or discord between the existing relations of production and productive power are all fundamentally readjusted. New technical relations of production are formed to suit the new development of productive power so as to enable a positive quantitative expansion in the reproduction of capitals. The substantial effects of changes in the methods of production by replacing fixed capitals can further be broken down into four aspects as follows: (i) With the reduction of individual values of commodity products, capitals are able to valorise even below the prices which have been unprofitable in the depression on the basis of old technologies. (ii) With a fall in commodity values, the value of labour-power must also be cut. This enables the production of relative surplus-value, increasing the rate of surplus-value. (iii) The growth of labour productivity in new methods of production ordinarily brings with it a rise in the organic composition of capital as a whole. With this rise in the organic composition of capital the number of workers employed by a certain quantity of capital decreases, additionally forming the relative surplus-population. It shows the specific contradictory nature of capitalism as was pointed out in Section 8.2, to make more workers redundant and unemployed by a 'rationalization' of production when a great number of workers have already been thrown out of jobs through crisis and depression. (iv) A new general rate of profit with a set of prices of production is reconstructed together with a reformation of new value relations. On the basis of a more or less restored balance between industrial spheres of production, the competitive process of the equalisation of the rate of profit across different spheres will again work, anarchically swaying individual profit rates around this general profit rate, and promoting the positive expansion of reproduction.

Thus, when new relations of production are formed by most capitals in the main industrial spheres, corresponding to a new level of productive power, capitals can positively resume expanded reproduction with a restored rate of profit, turning the phase of the business cycle into prosperity again. Construction of fixed capitals continues mainly as a process of the generalisation of new methods of production already implemented and socially initiated towards the end of depression. The deepening accumulation of capital with radical changes in the productivity of labour is changed into the widening accumulation of capital once again characterising the phase of prosperity. With the positive process of capital accumulation by industrial capitals, the credit system is also effectively restored to its function with a relatively low rate of interest just as in the previous phase of prosperity. The process of prosperity will reach a higher level of accumulation of capital on the basis of the relative surplus population produced by a rise in the organic composition of capital in comparison with the previous level of prosperity.

The business cycle, composed of three phases of prosperity, crisis and depression, thus runs its course anew. Each phase becomes the cause of the successive phase in turn, and 'the same vicious circle is pursued once more with expanded conditions of production, a wider market and increased productivity' (III, p. 364). The 'life-cycle' of fixed capitals in the main spheres of industry 'is one of the material foundations for periodic cycle in which business passes through successive periods of stagnation, moderate activity, over-excitement and crisis' (II, p. 264), and it determines in particular the length of time of the circuit of business cycles, as the simultaneous renewal of fixed capitals in the main spheres serves as the starting-point for every new prosperity phase in typical periodical cycles. Marx noted that 'this life cycle is now on average a ten-year one' (ibid.). The inner contradiction of capitalist production, which arises from the difficulty of treating human labour-power as a commodity, and which bursts out in periodic crises through the working of capitalist competition and credit, thus finds an actual solution in the circular course of business cycles. Nevertheless it cannot be a fundamental solution, and so it must repeatedly appear in similar business cycles and crises.

## 9.4 BUSINESS CYCLES AND THE LAW OF VALUE

As business cycles and crises not only reveal the inner contradiction in capitalism, but also serve as an actual solution to the contradiction, they form a concrete mechanism for the law of value to carry itself through as the law of motion of a capitalist economy. The theoretical relations between the law of value and the dynamics of business cycles must be analysed in three co-related aspects; the relations between first the fluctuation of wages and the value of labour-power, second the fluctuation of relative prices among commodity products and their values, and third the fluctuation of the general price level and the value of the money commodity gold.

First, as Marx formulated, 'taking them as a whole, the general movements of wages are exclusively regulated by the expansion and contraction of the industrial reserve army, and this in turn corresponds to the periodic alternations of the industrial cycle' (I, p. 790), or 'the rate of accumulation is the independent, not the dependent variable; the rate of wages is the dependent, not the independent variable' (I, p. 770). However, the latter famous mathematical formulation should not be understood too mechanically. For the movements of the wage-rate, which is basically determined by the process of capital accumulation and the relative weight of the industrial reserve army, do react dialectically to the features of accumulation especially, as we have seen, in the process of causing periodical crises. Nevertheless, it is clear that the motion of wages is regulated as a whole basically by the process of capital accumulation through the changing phases of business cycles. Nominal wages in particular would never fail to rise towards the end of prosperity, fall sharply in the phase of crisis and remain stagnant and at a low level in the depression.

The movement of real wages is theoretically more complicated in relation to the motion of prices of commodity products. The degree of a rise of real wages towards the end of prosperity may be mitigated by a rise in prices of consumer goods. For the capitalists in certain industries a rise of wage costs may well be more than counterbalanced by a greater rise in the prices of their products. However, as we have argued against the Kalechi–Okishio type of business cycle theory in Section 8.3, the pressure of the over-accumulation of capital to push up real wages in response to a labour shortage in our basic theory cannot be stopped in the final instance in spite of a speculative rise in other commodity prices, because of the fundamental inelasticity of supply of labour-power. A favourable condition in the labour market for workers also easily strengthens the negotiating power of trade unions if they exist and tend to loosen labour discipline in the work place, adding to a substantial rise in wages. A fall in the nominal wage-rate may sometimes be more than counteracted in the phase of crisis by a sharp decline in the prices of the means of consumption, although the real income of workers must generally decline with the reduction of employment and working hours. However, the real wage-rate must definitely become lower in depression, when an acute collapse of the prices of commodity products, reinforced by the breakdown of credit relations and speculative stockpiling have passed by, reflecting a very unfavourable market condition for workers. Marx's formulation of the general movement of wages must thus be relevant for the motion of real wages too.[25] Anyway, the rigidity of wage-rates cannot be assumed here with a freely competitive market both for workers and capitalists.

The real income of workers families would increase first with the growing number of employees and then with a rise in the real wage-rate in the process of prosperity, whereas it must shrink in a depression as a reaction to it. Through a spiral motion of workers' real income along with periodical business cycles, changes in the contents of the average means of consumption for workers, which are socially necessary to reproduce their labour-power, will tendentially take place. In the initial definition of the substance of value of labour-power, we had to assume abstractly, certain quantities of means of consumption as necessary material for the social reproduction of labour-power. Theoretically we could define the labour-substance embodied in those means of consumption, once their range and quantity together with a social set of the technological conditions of the production processes are given. The contents of the necessary means of consumption form the material conditions of the standard of living for workers, and are theoretically assumed to be given including 'a historical and moral element' (I, p. 275). A plain neo-Ricardian theory would assert that the physical data of real wages are to be determined independently of the production system of capitalism. Though any level of real wages can determine a consistent system of prices with a corresponding profit rate as neo-Ricardians underline, this does not mean that real wages are really determined freely from the law of motion of capitalism. Now we see that the very process of periodic business cycles with its fluctuations in wages serves as a capitalistic mechanism to incorporate social changes in the substantial material contents of the value of labour-power, although it would not solely and wholely determine the full range of the necessary means of consumption and the 'historical and moral element' contained therein.[26] The fluctuation of nominal and real wages through the alternate phases of the business cycles gravitates, on the one hand, around the historically and socially given standard of living of an average ordinary wage-worker (in a certain period for any particular country), but it also works simultaneously as a means continuously to channel the changes in level of standard itself. In these regards the process of business cycles forms a social mechanism for the typical and concrete working of the law of value as regards labour-power, the central commodity in capitalism, through market fluctuations.

Second, fluctuations in relative prices among commodity products would proceed, gravitating around the market prices of production as a concrete form of the values of those products, on the basis of the fluctuation of wages in the process of business cycles. So far as wages remain relatively stable with an available relative surplus-population for the labour market during the widening process of the accumulation of capital in prosperity, the anarchical deviation of the prices of commodity products from their values or their market prices of production could be incessantly readjusted in a narrower range of fluctuation around a relatively stable set of prices of production, upon the basis of relatively stable conditions of production as well as a stable real wage-rate. Allocation of living and dead labour among the industrial spheres is realised relatively smoothly in this prosperous phase guided by the motion of profit rates which also fluctuate in a relatively narrow range corresponding to the motion of commodity prices. Though such a process tends to be regarded as the natural harmonious order of things in the classical and neo-classical theoretical views it cannot last indefinitely. When capital accumulation becomes excessive in relation to the existing labouring population, the relative prices of commodity products must be very much distorted in the process of speculative development, along with a rise in wages towards the end of prosperity. The relations between commodity prices are further broken in the following phase of crisis through the reversed and destructive functions of competition and the credit system among capitals. The working of the law of value which anarchically adjusts the allocation of social labour together with the fluctuations of commodity prices is paralysed and collapses in these phases. It cannot be fully restored throughout most of the depression with its stagnant reproduction of capital.

However, through such destructive and stagnant phases in business cycles, capitalism is driven to innovate in industrial technologies and the development of productive power. Especially as most capitals in the leading industries are mutually pressed and prepared simultaneously to replace fixed capitals towards the end of a depression, the basis for the balanced relations among relative commodity prices is reconstructed corresponding to the social system of newly introduced production technologies. The social allocation of labour is fundamentally readjusted in the same process. The working of the law of value to regulate the relative prices of commodity products in accord with the changing labour-substance of their values in the process of the development of productive power, is thus actually carried on throughout the whole process of business cycles. The equalisation of the profit rate between industrial spheres, along with the social process of the development of productive power, is also achieved concretely through business cycles, which repeatedly reproduces phases of overall prosperity based on renewed productive power introduced through the phases of crisis and depression. The process of the readjustment of the substance of values and the corresponding relative prices of commodity products in accord with development of productive power through the business cycles, simultaneously regulates the value of labour-power and thus the rate of surplus-value, in combination with the regulation of the material contents of the standard of living of wage labourers in the same course of business cycles.

Third, the working of the law of value in regulating the fluctuations of the general price-level in the process of business cycles must also be cleared up. Against the quantity theory of money in the tradition of the classical school, Marx asserted that the general price-level is determined not by the quantity of money, but basically by the substantial relation between the values of general commodities and the value of the money commodity gold. He pointed out that money is used not merely as a means of circulation, but also as hoard or as universal money kept outside of commodity circulation, as we saw in Chapter 4, Section 4.2. Recognition of the basic logic of the determination of the general price-level by the substance of values of ordinary commodities and gold, would not exclude the theoretical possibility of general price-level deviating from the substantial value-relations. Marx actually notices such movements in the general price-level – a rise in the phase of full employment, and a fall in the phase of crisis – as follows:

> In times of prosperity, of great expansion, when the reproduction process exhibits a great acceleration and energy, the workers are fully employed. In most cases there is even a rise in wages, which to some extent balances the fall in wages below the average level in the other phases of the commercial cycle. At the same time, the capitalists' revenues grow significantly. Consumption generally rises. Commodity prices rise just as regularly, at least in certain decisive branches of business. (III, p. 578).
>
> In periods of crisis, the opposite is the case. Circulation no. I [which refers to the commodity transactions by expenditure of revenue in distinction from circulation no. II referring to transactions by capitals – M. I.] contracts, prices fall, and so on wages. (III, p. 580).

Prices that fall in the phase of crisis will not fully recover and remain lower than in the previous period of prosperity, reflecting stagnation in reproduction and circulation (including circulation no. II). In sum, commodity prices would rise towards the end of prosperity from their standard level in mid-prosperity, fall sharply during crisis as a process of the breaking down of the whole market mechanism, and not fully recover from the very bottom of the crisis and will remain low or stagnate during depression before finally being restructured into a new standard level corresponding to a new technological basis for expanded reproduction.

Such fluctuations of prices in the course of a typical business cycle are clearly not caused by changes in the quantity of money. They occur even when the total quantity of hard money in a society remains unchanged, while the credit system expands, collapses, or stagnates. Towards the end of prosperity, for instance, the total sum of prices of transactions among capitals would increase with the speculative rise of commodity prices along with a general rise in wages. The necessary increase in the amount of the means of circulation and payment to satisfy those transactions is flexibly supplied by mobilising idle-money capitals through the credit mechanism. The increase in the quantity of credit money, however, cannot be an independent external factor to, or a cause of, a rise in prices. On the other hand, the existence of idle money kept outside of the commodity circulation does not always guarantee the regulation of the general price-level in accord with the substantial value-relations between the general commodities and gold. It serves rather as a basic condition of a capitalist social mechanism to enable the upward deviation of commodity prices from values through speculative developments in the process of the over-accumulation of capital towards the end of prosperity. As a reaction to such an upward deviation, the general price-level must fall sharply in crises and stay at a low and stagnant level during depression, reflecting the dynamism in capitalist mechanisms of accumulation as a whole in the process of business cycles, which cannot at all be limited or attributed to the quantitative movement of money.

So long as the general price-level regularly moves up and down in the changing phases of prosperity and depression, the profit rate in the gold industry must fluctuate counter-cyclically due to changing production costs. Therefore, production in the gold industry must be reduced towards the end of prosperity, and expanded in crisis and depression. Though the annual gold production forms just a marginal addition to the existing gold stock in its various interchangeable forms (not being confined to money in circulation or in reserves), its reduction can be an additional factor in narrowing the basis for credit expansion or in promoting a shortage of loanable money capital towards the end of prosperity. The reduction of effective demand by the gold industry would also act counter-cyclically in this phase, though the effect might not be very significant. The expansion of gold production in the phase of depression must contrarily add to the relative superabundance of loanable money capital, and must counter-cyclically increase effective demand to some extent. (These counter-cyclically movements and effects of gold production can be analogous to those of the balance of trade in the process of business cycles for a capitalist economy in the world market. Actually most capitalist countries used to obtain gold by making surpluses in their balances of trade, and not by their own gold production.)

The counter-cyclical unprofitableness and profitableness of the gold industry in the alternate phases of business cycles may not be perfectly counterbalanced within a single cycle. This is in a sense a part of impossibility of fully guaranteeing balanced profitability across various industrial spheres because of the anarchic fluctuation of exchange ratios among commodity products in the circuit of the business cycle. As for the relative prices of general commodity products in the process of mid-prosperity, however, the process of the equalisation of profit rates through competition between capitals will take place fairly smoothly in accordance with the law of value, without causing extreme and one-sided deviations from values or prices of production. A similar regulation by the law of value would work also in the exchange relations between the money commodity, gold, and other general commodities, in the phase of mid-prosperity more clearly than in other phases. With the given technological conditions, the capitalists in the gold industry must in principle obtain the general rate of profit, by deducting the cost-prices of wages and the necessary means of production from the amount of gold produced. A rise in the general price-level would then push down the profit rate in the gold industry by increasing its cost-prices, and vice versa. Capitalist competition forming a set of prices of production, must basically include the regulation of the general price-level so as to equalise the rate of profit of the gold industry with others.

However, there are certain complications in the working of the law of value in its regulation of the general price-level in relation to the purchasing power of the money commodity gold.[27] The adjustment of the quantity of gold production would be accompanied with a process of readjusting the differential and absolute ground-rent of gold mines, and the resultant changes in the representative conditions (and costs). Besides there must be a general difficulty in closing down or reopening the marginal mines with all the fixed capitals. The representative conditions of supplying gold would therefore change slowly. The social demand for gold also includes some uncertainties. The social need for gold is objectively certainly not unlimited, apart from the individual subjective desire for money in a commodity economy. However, some additional supply of gold can be absorbed flexibly in such forms as reserve funds or simple luxuries without causing over-supply of currency and a direct immediate downward pressure on the purchasing power of gold. On the contrary, some shortage of yearly gold production can also easily be adjusted to by readjustment among different interchangeable forms of gold, together with the elastic expansion of the credit system. Therefore, the social functions of money and capitalist reproduction will not immediately be disturbed, even when the gold industry is receiving a rate of profit either above or below the general rate in the phase of mid-prosperity. When the gold industry is getting extra profit its production would be expanded faster than the social average. But it will take a certain length of time by a complicated and roundabout way for the effects of the faster expansion of gold to cause, directly or indirectly (through the credit mechanism), a rise in the general level of prices and wages so that the extra profit in the gold industry as well as its faster rate of expansion will cease. The same must also be true for the case where the general price-level is too high for the gold industry to obtain the general rate of profit.

In this regard there is a difference in the features or the mechanisms by which the law of value regulates the purchasing power of the money commodity gold or the general price-level in comparison with that of the case of the relative exchange ratios between other commodity products. The working of the law of value in regulating and adjusting the levels of both general prices and gold production through the process of the equalisation of the rate of profit will thus not necessarily be fully achieved within a single process of prosperity. It will rather form a tendentially longer wave of fluctuations in the general price-level across the phases of mid-prosperity, including also the effect of changes in the relative productivity of the gold industry and others behind the market. The general price-level which basically reflects the trend of changes in the relative productivity of the gold industry, can either be rising or falling through consecutive business cycles. The trend has actually alternated in the shape of long waves through multiple business cycles. The general price-level as an aggregate form of value can thus deviate from, and be readjusted to, the substantial value-relations not merely through specific phases within each business cycle, but also through multiple cycles as longer waves. Even under the gold standard system, the general price-level could not remain statically stable and fixed. Its alternate long trends can possibly be regarded as a part of the logical basis for the long wave of capital accumulation, which should be properly discussed in a separate item.

## 9.5 THE METAMORPHOSES OF THE BUSINESS CYCLE AND THE LONG WAVES

Although the periodical business cycle is 'of such a nature that the same circuit must reproduce itself, once the first impulse has been given' (III, p. 620), it cannot continue to move for ever in the same circuit like the motion of 'the heavenly bodies' (I, p. 786).

As we noted in the first section of this chapter, capitalism used to repeat the regular periodical business cycle most typically about every ten years in the period of liberalism between the 1820s and 1860s. The basic theory of regular business cycles could be abstracted from the historical experience of Marx's age, assuming a certain range of size and type of fixed capitals, which were replaceable more or less concertedly in the leading industries within the period of the business cycle. It implies that regular business cycles were a historical phenomenon subject to metamorphoses with the development of capitalism. A shift in leading sector from the light (especially cotton) industries to the heavy industries actually induced the metamorphoses of business cycles, initiating the stage of imperialism. A full investigation of the transformation of business cycles, in relation to the socio-economic structural changes, in the course of the historical development of capitalism certainly requires upper levels of research as proposed in the stages theory, or more concrete empirical studies beyond the basic theory of capitalism. However, let us try in this section to theorise, at the level of the basic theory the logic of the metamorphoses of business cycles as far as possible. Then we will also examine what we can say about long-wave theories and the nature of long waves, considering the relevance of our basic theory of capitalism as a frame of reference for more concrete researches. The historical experiences must also be taken into consideration here, but they will presently be referred to just as illustrations of the basic logic.

Through the process of capital accumulation, which develops its inner contradiction between the relation of production and the growth of productive power, in regular business cycles, the growth of the productive power of capital eventually results in the uneven development of the size of fixed capitals among industrial spheres, and an increase of the weight of certain industries with huge fixed capitals. As we have argued in Chapter 8, the credit system based on commercial credit is insufficient, or rather unsuitable, for promoting the expansion of industries with huge fixed capitals. The role of joint-stock capital therefore must much increase. The construction of gigantic fixed capitals, which is impossible for individual capitalists, is often realised in the form of joint-stock capital by extending the range of joint investors. In the process of this uneven development the relative weight of the industries with smaller fixed capitals and extensive circulating capitals tends to decline, while that of industries with huge fixed capitals increases. The feature of the regular periodical business cycle must then be transformed, as the axis of the leading industries shifts from the former to the latter.

Expansion of the productive capacity of the industries which have gigantic fixed capitals, cannot be one of continuous linear change by every small unit. It is generally performed by constructing massive new plant and equipment on a giant scale. Construction of large plant takes a considerable time, extending over more than a year or two, absorbing large sums of capital and many workers. Once completed, the new plant with its huge fixed capital would add a considerable proportion to the existing industrial capacity as a whole, and must work for many years to come. Therefore, individual firms can no longer assume that the expansion of their productive capacity will be marginal to the total capacity of the industry. Each project expanding productive capacity would then involve much speculation as to the rate of growth of demand for the product for a fairly long while ahead. The role of the speculative expectations of capitalists gains importance in the very basic economic activity of construing new plant and equipment. The anarchical decisions on the planning and practice of investment among individual firms tends to intensify speculative expectations in the same direction. The effect of the gestation period, when the construction of fixed capital increases effective demand without increasing the supply of commodity products, particularly strengthens the speculative nature of real capital investment as well as the conformity of the direction of speculation among firms. This effect tends to promote a speculative boom especially among the capital goods industries, where investment increases mutual demand for their products. Thus, the process of prosperity led by the expansion of industries with huge fixed capitals tends to appear as a speculative and uneven development from the beginning.

Corresponding to this the end of prosperity also becomes uneven and irregular. The possibility of the over-accumulation of capital in relation to the labouring population cannot at all be excluded.[28] However, since the prosperity does not proceed universally, the collapse of speculative development in some industries may end the prosperity, often long before the process of capital accumulation becomes excessive enough to cause a general rise in wages. The moment for the downturn would be given, for instance, by the failure of a realisation of the speculative expectation among capitalists concerning the growth rate of the market for their products, or the growth rate of the productive capacity among rival firms, or the availability of cheap money and high prices of stocks which easily attract such money from a capital market, or their combination. The failure of speculative expectations for the profitability of fixed capital investments on a gigantic scale would become a central problem at all events. A collapse of stock prices in a capital market would occur often leading to a financial crisis. The money market would already have been tightened in the process of the speculative development of both fixed capital investment and the boom in stock markets. A rise in the interest rate appears in the tightening money market, and it must be further pushed up with a collapse in the capital market by clearing up the debt relations formed in the boom. Such a rise in the interest rate together with the failure of a real capital investment boom may often induce a commercial and an industrial crisis as well.

The possibility of a full-scale crisis combining total and acute collapses of the financial system, and commercial and industrial activities can again not at all be excluded. Such a crisis may occur even before full-scale over-accumulation of capital in relation to the labouring population appears, as we experienced in the great crisis following 1929. However, the collapse of a boom as a reaction to the speculative and uneven development of fixed capital investment may also often take the form of an indecisive and partial crisis. The collapse of a capital market might not involve the total collapse of the credit system, as the short-term credit system would not necessarily be extended for the speculative trading of circulating capitals. Thus, the acute total character of periodic crises in the course of regular classical business cycle is transformed into irregular forms of collapse of the prosperous process, often taking the form of milder indecisive crises.[29]

Such a metamorphosis of crises does not necessarily mean that the difficulty of capital accumulation in the next phase is easier to overcome. Rather, the contrary is the truth. Through a milder indecisive crisis, industrial capitals tend to carry over massive and excessive productive capacity, being mostly exempted from radical destruction such as business failures. Besides it is not uncommon that the construction of huge fixed capitals is completed through a long gestation period after the boom that promoted it and so in the phase of depression, adding much to excess capacity. Since gigantic plants and their equipment embody huge amounts of capital values, they cannot simply be abandoned, even in the case of business failures or in an acute destructive crisis. They are mostly conserved and taken over by other firms or the reorganised firms. It usually takes quite a long time to depreciate them before scrapping. Thus, in the industries with large fixed capitals, superabundant real capital in the form of excess capacity tends to persist, and prolong the difficulties of restructuring during the process of depression.

All the characteristics of the phase of depression in the regular periodical business cycles reappear, only on much extended scale and as a persistent tendency. The pressure of excess capital based upon superabundant productive capacity in the main industrial spheres tends continuously to depress the rate of profit and capital accumulation as a whole. Various imbalances such as those among industrial spheres, or between limited effective demand (especially of workers) and the capacity to supply the commodity products, or between the total value accumulated and the reduced number of workers producing surplus-value, prevail chronically, and it is difficult to restructure these under the pressure of excess capital as a whole. The equalisation of the rate of profit across industrial spheres, as well as the working of the law of value to readjust the imbalance in the social allocation of labour, must still basically operate, but with much retardation and hardship. Monopolistic organisations with monopolistic pricing tend to be formed in order partially to avoid and mitigate the total difficulty in accumulation and profitability. The form of joint-stock capital facilitates the formation of giant monopolistic capitals in the major industries with huge fixed capitals as we mentioned in Chapter 8. Needless to say, the formation of monopoly capitals cannot be a solution to the overall depression. On the contrary, they rather add to the difficulties in the non-monopolistic industries with smaller-sized firms and the imbalances of an economy in every aspect, making them harder to readjust.

Under the circumstances it has often been asserted that upon the basis of the under-consumptionist tendency in a capitalist economy, monopoly capital is the major cause of the prolongation of depressions.[30] It must be noted, however, that the depressive burden of excess capital, especially in the form of superabundant huge fixed capitals, is the more basic issue and also historically preceded the establishment of monopoly capitals in the great depression of the late nineteenth century, although monopoly capital can surely aggravate the depression as was experienced in 1930s. Anyway, as the difficulty of positive accumulation becomes chronic in the main industrial spheres, with their gigantic fixed capitals, the moment for the next upturn to prosperity cannot appear generally from within these existing industries. New and radical innovations in some industries, often outside of the existing major industries, are seriously sought for together with political and social policies and changes, in order to restore profitability in some economic areas or industries. The upturn to a new prosperity must thus often begin as a partial, uneven and speculative development again, on the basis of the chronic depressive burden of excess capacity which tends to remain in a number of major existing industries. The prosperity which follows must be of a speculative uneven character, and often short-lived.

Thus the transformed business cycle tends to proceed irregularly with complicated features. The time period of a business cycle can no longer be determined by concerted replacement of fixed capitals, and it must become more or less irregular. The process of uneven speculative prosperity often cannot wipe out the heavily depressive keynote in the major industries. As a result, business cycles are metamorphosed into complicated multiple cycles, being composed of smaller or medium cycles and greater ones, as we are now experiencing a combination of a great depression since 1973 and smaller cycles within it, just as in the previous great depressions. The inner contradiction of capitalism, or the clash between its relations of production and the growth of its productive power, is not necessarily revealed any longer in the outburst of the full-scale economic crisis, but often rather in the persistent depressive tendency of the major industries with their huge excess capacities. In practice this generates socio-political attempts to alleviate the chronic problem by oppressing workers though such forms as imperialist foreign policies, fascism, wars and austerity policies. Since the depressive keynote in the major industries tends to persist strongly, a series of exceptionally favourable conditions for profitability and capital accumulation are necessary to cause an upward turn in the greater cycles. It is not entirely impossible, though difficult, for capitalism to create the conditions for a long upswing, as in the periods between 1897 and 1913, and more recently between 1945 and 1973.

We have already come to discuss the long waves, which are generally assumed to last about fifty years each. The greater cycles including smaller cycles in them are virtually nothing but long waves, which have become a popular topic again among economists, and not confined to Marxians, in the process of the current great depression. It must be noted, however, that long waves have gained actual significance through the metamorphoses of the business cycle as we have seen. This is a reason why the long wave theories could only begin to be explored, initially among Marxians like Parvus and K. Kautsky,[31] since about the turn of the last century. It would be dogmatic and improper not to recognise the importance of the metamorphoses of business cycles and the resulting long waves, by adhering to the idea of a continuation of regular periodical business cycles and crises as a way of application of Marx's crisis theory.[32] Also it would be improper to treat long waves as if they were entirely parallel with, even if not replacing, regular business cycles in the basic theory of capitalism.

Nevertheless, in attempting to formulate a theory of long waves in one way or the other, major theorists in this area like N. D. Kondratieff, J. A. Schumpeter and recently E. Mandel among others are all apt to believe that long waves have always existed in parallel with regular periodical business cycles from the very beginning of industrial capitalism. Can we really believe in the existence of a long down-swing in the quarter-century until 1847 which is comparable with later great depressions? That was a distinct period when British capitalism could develop the central cotton industry quite rapidly on the achievements of the preceding Industrial Revolution. Even though the effects of a rise in prices due to the discovery of the Californian gold mines and the defeat of radical social movements, combined with some aggregate statistical data, may well be referred to as distinctions between the two quarter-centuries before and after 1847, historically it must be much more important to see that British capitalism with its central cotton industry was continuously developing as 'the workshop of the world', promoting a consistent period of liberalism in these two quarter-centuries.[33] At this stage of liberalism the inner contradiction of capitalism was clearly revealed in the repetition of periodical crises in regular business cycles, as Marx intended to show in the basic theory, and not yet in the great depression as with the downswing of long waves. Over-generalisation of a theory of long waves would not be a correct way to clarify the historical meaning and significance of the long waves themselves.

Over-generalisation of the causes of the upturns and the downturns in the long waves should also be avoided. A type of long-wave theory has been constructed, analogising with a theory of regular business cycles. N. D. Kondratieff, for instance, maintained that an upturn to a long period of prosperity appears on the precondition of the formation of abundant cheap loanable capital and low prices which stimulate long-term investment in large-scale plant and equipment, land improvement or the training of highly skilled workers; while the downswing of the long wave begins with a relative shortage of loanable capital and a rise of prices and costs.[34] According to him, other factors such as the development of industrial technologies, gold-mining, the incorporation of new markets into the world economy, wars and revolutions are not the causes of the long waves, though they often correspond to the rhythms of long waves. The causality of long waves is assumed within the economic order of capitalism itself, analogous to that of regular business cycles. However, this theory was not very persuasive. Can it just be a quantitative difference which determines whether similar causes lead to the upswing of the long wave or merely to that of the regular cycle? As a historical fact, abundant cheap loanable capital was virtually non-existent in most of the countries just after the Second World War as the precondition for the subsequent long upswing,[35] whereas it did play a role to some degree in the upturn from the great depression of the late nineteenth century.

Although Schumpeter called the long waves 'Kondratieff cycles', he did not follow Kondratieff as to their causality.[36] In his theory, major technological innovations invented in the preceding downswing prepare and cause the upswing of long waves in the process of their industrial diffusion, while smaller innovations generate regular business cycles inside them. Though technological innovations certainly play an important role in the whole dynamism of capitalism, Schumpeter's position seems to me *an* assumption for empirical historical research, rather than a complete theory by itself. It could not be logically established as to why major innovations are invented, diffused and then loose their effect in creating upswings and downswings of the long waves so regularly as about every fifty years. The concrete timing and the features of the upswing and the downswing of each long wave cannot be determined just by the rhythms of the major innovations, without taking into consideration a wider range of conditions of capital accumulation, such as changes in the forms of organising capitals including the financial system, the availability of cheap and quiesent workers, low prices of raw materials from abroad, and socio-political processes including the state policies and wars. The actual course and the effects of major technological innovations must develop closely and dialectically with these concrete conditions of capital accumulation, and the total relations are rather impossible to formulate as a general regular pattern.

By criticising Kondratieff's over-generalisation of the economic theory of long waves L. D. Trotsky maintained that the long waves should not be understood as waves analogous to regular business cycles.[37] In his view the major causes of long waves are not in the inner economic dynamism of capitalism, but in the changes of its external conditions such as the opening of new markets, the discovery of new natural resources, wars and revolutions. E. Mandel follows this view in one-half of his theory as to the upturn of long waves, whereas he asymmetrically explains the cumulative nature and the downturn of each long wave from the internal logic of a capitalist economy, especially underlining the role of Marx's law of tendential fall of the profit rate due to the rising organic composition of capital.[38] Excepting the role of the law of tendential fall of the profit rate, Mandel's explanation fits the course of long waves in the post-Second World War period fairly well. However, the upturn of a long upswing in about 1897 seems explicable not so much by the changes in the external socio-political conditions as by the internal dynamism of capital accumulation on a world scale, while the end of that upswing is clearly given directly by the political upheaval of the First World War. The whole economic process in the interwar period including the great crisis after 1929 cannot be understood as a mere continuous economic downswing of a long wave, since actually it was overwhelmingly conditioned and affected by stormy socio-political events in the forms of great wars, revolutions and fascism. Obviously it was the historical background for Trotsky's assertions about long waves.

Thus, the causes of turning-points as well as the processes of upswings and downswings in the long waves contain rich historical specificities. As a result, theoretical attempts to formulate a general theory of long waves in one way or another have had to involve unpersuasive over-generalisation. Neither the endogenous theories nor the exogenous theories of long waves, or the combination of both types of theory are successful, so far as they intend to present a uniform explanation for all long waves. The endogenous dynamism of the process of capital accumulation and its exogenous conditions must not be treated mechanically and one-sidedly, but more flexibly and concretely according to the historical specificities of each period. This caution applies also to 'the social structure of accumulation theory' of long waves recently presented by D. M. Gordon, R. Edwards and M. Reich among others.[39] It is their definite contribution to have pointed out anew the importance of the changes in the social structure of accumulation, especially in respect to the organisational structure of the labour process, for the course and nature of capitalist economic development. However, the changes in the social structure including that of the labour process may not always be a cause, but rather a result of the pressure of the process of the long wave, just as we are now keenly experiencing with the current great depression. In some other cases the social structure of accumulation would change as a result of further external political events like fascism, wars or the end of wars, and possibly also as a result of changes in the international political and economic order.

The indeterminate character of the causality of long waves represents the fundamental instability of the course and mechanism of capital accumulation after the transformation of regular business cycles, as we have argued. With the metamorphoses of the regular classical business cycles, the depressive keynote of the major industries, having excessive and huge fixed capitals, has become so persistent that capitalists are forced to make a variety of attempts to escape from the long downswing depression. Their attempts are not confined to the endogenous restructuring of the existing industries, but extend to explorations of fundamentally new technologies to create new types of commodities and industrial fields, as well as to the changes in the socio-political structures for capital accumulation. The decisive moments for a new upturn would vary and not be predetermined. These considerations must be relevant to the process of current global great depression. It is still highly questionable whether a new upswing to a long wave can ever be possible after this great depression. And if it is, how and when will the new upturn be ready? Can it be ready without actually experiencing further and more catastrophic economic and political disasters, especially on the part of working people even in the advanced capitalist countries? More concrete analyses at a level of research separate from the basic theory of capitalism are necessary precisely to clarify the major moments forming this great depression with all its socio-political impacts.

For such concrete analyses of the current situation of capitalism, thc whole of our basic theory of capitalism, which shows in particular the fundamental position of wage-workers under the law of motion of capital, including the logic of regular business cycles and their metamorphoses, must be fully mobilised as an indispensable frame of reference. At least one thing seems to me clear by now, however, from our discussion on the basic theory. We should not be fatalistic about the future course and the social effects of the current great depression in view of the indeterminate native of long waves, despite a strong tendency for capitalism to transfer the heavy burden of excess capitals on to the shoulders of working people and the weak in the world and domestic economic orders. At the same time we should not confuse the present impasse of capitalism, with a dead end for historical development itself particularly for working people. In order to conclude our considerations on the basic theory of capitalism in this respect, a final chapter on socialism would further be a necessary and desirable addendum.

# Part IV
# Socialism – an Addendum

As we have seen, the basic theory of capitalism enables us systematically to understand the historically specific character of a capitalist economy by clarifying its essential forms and its substance, together with its mechanisms of motion. With these contents the basic theory of capitalism serves as a fundamental frame of reference, not merely for the more concrete analyses of actual capitalist developments and the current situation, but also for the theoretical argument for socialism. Let us therefore try to deduce and summarise some possible implications for socialism from what we have discussed in this volume. Even though the final part VII of the third volume of *Capital* contains certain insights for socialism, Marx seems to have rather deliberately avoided describing a full design for a socialist (or communist – which was his usual wording) economic system, excepting some abstract basic ideas and pointers. In this respect his attitude on socialism was quite a contrast to that of Utopian socialists like F. M. C. Fourier.[1] He might have assumed that the socialist economic system could be simple, being consciously constructed upon some clear rules, and not as complicated as a capitalist economy. He might have as well believed that the basic theory of capitalism presented in *Capital* would simultaneously give a basic guide for a socialist economic order.

The actual process of constructing a socialist economy in post-revolutionary societies has now turned out to entail many more difficulties and complications than was ever expected. For one thing a basic general theory of socialism, which is comparable with the basic theory of capitalism, cannot logically be formulated. This is particularly because political and social decisions become so important for the whole course and structure of socialist economic development. This means that there is considerable freedom for strategic decision-making for the actual processes of socialist economic growth. Nevertheless its final and intermediary goals and main policies must always be discussed with reference to the basic theory of capitalism, even if the theory often only serves as a negative although solid sort of criteria.

It is worth trying here as far as possible to examine where such criteria can be established from our basic theory of capitalism by reviewing its implications. There are two reasons for this. First, Marx did not return to a systematic and positive discussion of socialism after writing *Capital*.[2] Therefore, a problem remains as to how his earlier views on socialism based rather directly upon historical materialism can be strengthened or widened by his theoretical achievements in *Capital*. Second, the possible implications of our own recent contributions to Marxian principles of political economy must also be examined in regard to the debates on socialism. In examining the basic criteria for socialism and for socialist movements in our age, the problems and complications of the Soviet types of societies, with all the serious debates about them, should certainly be taken into consideration. What concern me as problems of the Soviet types of societies can briefly be summarised as follows.

First, the working people do not seem to be fully liberated as the actual subject of a society which is under the strong control of the state and the Party bureaucracy from above to below, against Marx and Engels's idea of socialism, aiming at the extinction of the state with all its power apparatus. Second, the centrally planned socialist economy has become 'abraded' and inefficient both in adjusting the allocation of resources and labour for social needs and in improving productivity, as well as the quality of the products within each enterprise. The introduction of more flexible pricing in a market with the 'profit principle', is repeatedly proposed and tried with continuous and heated debates concerning the danger of revisionism far socialism. Third, the quality and the contents of the growth of productive power, as the human ability to control its own metabolic relation to nature, in Soviet-type societies have substantially followed technologies developed by capitalism with all their destructive effects on the ecological environment and on human abilities.

These problems are not at all simple and have to be investigated at various levels of research. Our task in this Part cannot be a full treatment of them, but is rather confined to some of essential points for socialism which can be discussed from our presentation in the preceding chapters, while the actual concerns and worries about these problems must be kept in mind. Our examination will remain at a basic abstract level, but may still actually be more or less relevant to these problems, since they are problems for societies theoretically and consciously founded upon the name of Marxism. At least some confusions in socialist movements and in the process of constructing societies after the socialist revolution seem to spring from simple and mechanical applications of Marx's historical materialism and economic theories without the careful re-examination of the remaining problems or the solution of the difficulties therein. Anyway, a brief single chapter will suffice for out present examinations in this Part.

# 10 On Socialism

## 10.1 HISTORICAL MATERIALISM AND THE NECESSITY FOR SOCIALISM

It is often believed among Marxians that Marx proved the logical inevitability of socialism. It is undeniable that Marx intended to show such an inevitability. The formula of historical materialism, which was presented prior to writing *Capital* as we saw in Chapter 3, Section 3.1 already contained a sort of consistent logic of the historical transformation of various societies which finally reach a classless socialist society driven by the growth of productive power. The dialectical conflict between the growth of productive power and the existing relations of production would inevitably cause a period of revolution, changing the existing social formation into another new form of society. This basic view of historical materialism is incorporated continuously in some parts of *Capital*. The problem is whether those parts are theoretically well founded and valid or central to the main theoretical contents of *Capital*.

For example, Marx formulated a theory of the progressive creation of a relative surplus-population due to the rising organic composition of capital in his presentation of the general law of capitalist accumulation in chapter 25 of the first volume of *Capital*. According to this argument the increasing misery of workers extends with the growth of productive power, making a capitalist society finally untenable. Corresponding to this, 'the historical tendency of capitalist accumulation' is summarised as follows in chapter 32 of the same volume. Capitalist production, which was born by 'the expropriation of the immediate producers, i.e. the dissolution of private property based on the labour of its owner' (I, p. 927), would increase 'the mass of misery, oppression, slavery, degradation and exploitation' of workers in the process of accumulation, centralisation and expropriation among capitals along with the development of productive power in the form of socialisation of labour and the means of production (I, pp. 928–9). Through such a process, there also grows the revolt of the organised working class, reaching a point where the centralisation of the means of production and the socialisation of labour 'become incompatible with their capitalist integument'. Then 'the expropriators are expropriated' as 'the negation of negation' (I, p. 929).

Apparently Marx's argument in these parts directly follows after the line of discussion already presented in the first section, 'Bourgeois and Proletarians', of *The Manifesto of the Communist Party*. The polarisation of a society into a fewer and richer capitalists and more and more degraded workers living in increasing misery, is regarded as the inevitable result of the development of productive forces in capitalism which prepare its own collapse and transformation into socialism. This view is easily combined with the underconsumptionist type of crisis theory, and has long been treated as the orthodox Marxist position. Orthodox Marxians are all expected to support or defend this view in one way or another. In this view the fundamental contradiction in capitalism must be in the increasing poverty and unemployment among workers in contrast with the growing productive forces, and it indicates the logical inevitability of socialism. This position has been a focus of attack and defence between non-Marxians and orthodox Marxians concerning the basis of Marxism. However, it seems to me doubtful whether Marx's theories along this line are well founded and consistent with his own more developed theoretical views in *Capital*.[1]

For instance, in his summary of 'the historical tendency of capitalist accumulation', in order to conclude with the expropriation of the expropriators as the dialectical negation of the negation. Marx starts with the expropriation of 'private property based on the labour of its owner' as the initial state of immediate producers, and emphasises the process of expropriation among capitalists substantially socialising labour and the means of production, which proceeds in parallel with the degree of poverty and the immiserisation of the mass of workers. However, as Marx more properly notices, 'the expropriation of the agricultural producer, of the peasant, from the soil is the basis of the whole process' (I, p. 876) of the 'primitive accumulation of capital' which initiates capitalist production, and soil, as the central object of expropriation in this process was not a product of labour or perfect private property in general. Further, once capitalism is established, the keynote of capitalist accumulation is not in the expropriation among capitals but rather in the exploitation of wage-workers and the transformation of surplus-value exploited into capital, as was shown in Marx's own theoretical treatment of capital accumulation. In such a process of accumulation, 'offshoots split off from the original capitals and start to function as new and independent capitals' (I, p. 776) especially through technical and product innovations. It would be difficult to save in view of the basic private character of capital to grow through any opportunity, that the number of independent capitals definitely decreases in the process of capital accumulation at the level of basic theory. Even the giant joint-stock monopoly capitals must essentially remain private firms seeking private profit, and never aim at organising social reproduction or even a single industrial sphere as a whole. In this regard the capitalist process of accumulation would not realise 'the socialization of labour and the means of production' to a degree worth calling 'socialisation'.

On the other side, the increasing misery of the mass of labour with the progressive production of a relative surplus-population, is also difficult to establish from the basic theory of capitalism. The degree of exploitation of wage-workers can be intensified by maintaining or even elevating the use values commanded by wages (i.e. the material contents of real wages) within the range of the increase in labour productivity, as shown in Marx's theory of production of relative surplus-value. In cases such as the long upswing of the post-Second World War period, raising real wages somewhat would even become a necessary condition for capital accumulation to extend the effective demand for new types of commodities. Besides, the creation of a relative surplus-population due to the rising organic composition of capital would not proceed so persistently and progressively. In the phase of prosperity in particular, capitals extend production rather quantitatively within the restrictions of existing fixed capitals, and increase employment in the process of accumulation even with a rising organic composition of capital. As we examined in the previous chapter, Marx himself did not present the capitalist law of population simply and one-sidedly as the logic of an incessant and progressive production of a relative surplus-population, and properly pointed out that the business cycle 'depends on the constant formation, the greater or less absorption, and the reformation of the industrial reserve army or surplus population' (I, p. 785). In the phase of the absorption from the reserve army, real wages would also be able to rise especially towards the end of prosperity.

Thus, Marx's summary of the historical tendency of capitalist accumulation, which emphasises the polarisation of society into smaller numbers of richer capitalists and the increasing mass of misery in the form of a reserve army, is not well founded and hardly consonant with his own more promising theoretical views. This reflection does not at all deny that capital accumulation, including the process of expropriation, actually brings about an increase in the extent of misery at certain historical conjunctures, which must be analysed at more concrete level of research. For example, even in the long upswing in the post-Second World War period, the economic misery of the great mass of people in most of the third-world countries was increasing under the pressure of capital accumulation on a world scale. In contrast, however, in the same long upswing, the real wages of workers in the advanced capitalist countries were steadily rising, with a high level of employment until 1973, and it is this historical experience that substantially eroded the prestige of the orthodox Marxian position. Moreover, the collapse of capitalism and its transformation into socialism are not theoretically guaranteed as a sort of mechanical automatic process, even if the polarisation of a capitalist society with its increasing immiserisation is given. The growth of an organised class-conscious workers' movement is an essential precondition for a socialist revolution. This precondition may not automatically be met through the increasing misery of the masses. Although Marx correctly referred to the role of the workers' revolt and their organisation in his summary of the historical tendency of capitalist accumulation, he seems to have too easily believed that this factor would be prepared 'by the very mechanism of the capitalist process of production' (I, p. 929). The formation and the growth of this crucial factor as a precondition for socialism are determined by various concrete historical and social conditions, as well as by the actual subjective ability of the leadership of the workers' movement, and cannot be deduced mechanically from the basic economic theory of capitalism, even when the so-called law of increasing misery is included.

The same problem is also presented to the other attempts to apply historical materialism more or less directly to the logical necessity for the collapse of capitalism. The typical breakdown theory of capitalism has been based upon Marx's law of the tendency of the rate of profit to fall, as an attempt to show that the growth of productive forces would become incompatible with the capitalist relations of production. As we argued in Chapter 9, section 9.1, Marx's law of the tendential fall of the profit rate, due to the rising organic composition of capital, can well contain a continuous increase in the absolute amount of surplus-value and capital in the process of accumulation even if at a reduced pace, and therefore it cannot logically, in itself show the inevitability of a dead end to capital accumulation. Thus, a representative breakdown theorist H. Grossmann attempted to show the disappearance of the portion of surplus-value consumed by capitalists, by combining with this law a mechanical assumption that the rate of yearly increase in constant capital is higher than that of variable capital with a constant rate of surplus-value[2]. Needless to say, this assumption is arbitrary and far from logically inevitable. Marx's law of tendential fall in the profit rate cannot thus be used as a theoretical basis to show the inevitability of either periodical crises as we have argued, or the collapse of capitalism. It cannot be a satisfactory theoretical ground for conceiving socialism, also since the law does not express a specific contradiction in capitalism. So far as it signifies a substantial reduction in the pace of accumulation in terms of labour, as a result of the relative reduction of living labour against dead labour in the process of rising productivity, a similar effect must remain with a socialist economy as well. The workers' movement for socialism is not only neglected as crucial for the ending of capitalism in the Grossmann type of mechanical breakdown theory, but would also be at a loss for a clear theoretical goal.

Another new type of attempt to apply historical materialism to the logical necessity of the collapse of capitalism is presented for example by N. Okishio in his assertion that the productive forces in our age are already out of the control of the system of private capitalist firms, and as a result threaten the continuing existence of human society, because of the progressive destruction of the ecological environment and human health or of the uncontrollable danger of nuclear war among other things.[3] In my view this assertion presents serious reasons for us to end capitalism and to transform it into socialism. The goals to be achieved by socialism are also clearly implied. However, these needs are still not identical with the logical inevitability of the collapse and the transformation of capitalism to socialism. Capitalism, with state policies, may continue to operate by attempting to curb the immediate dangers for human existence, or it may fail to do this and finally to destroy humanity itself in one way or the other, if the workers movement for socialism is not ready in time. Nevertheless, this subjective social factor, workers organisation, cannot be guaranteed theoretically even by the dangerous use of the productive forces in our age.

Thus, various attempts to show the logical inevitability of the collapse and the transformation of capitalism into socialism within the basic economic theory are more or less unpersuasive. A crucial point in my view is that the growth of workers organisations and their militating for socialism are not logically guaranteed or provable within the economic theory of capitalism. In contrast with the birth of capitalism, which was brought about basically through the anarchical growth of a commodity economy driven forward by the development of productive forces, the end of capitalism and the beginning of socialism cannot simply be a process of unintentional economic change, but requires conscious socio-political action by workers' movements. This is because capitalism forms a total socio-economic system, generating its own movement basically by itself through anarchical and unconciously individualistic transactions. The task of economic theory as a basic social science is to reveal such a historically specific character in a capitalist economy, including the mechanism of the exploitation of the working class with all its inner contradictions which result in business cycles and crises as we have seen. With this content the basic economic theory of capitalism surely presents a theoretical basis for the conscious workers movement for socialism by showing the possibility of abandoning capitalism and the desirable ultimate goals of their organized action.

Nevertheless, as we have argued in Chapter 3, Section 3.1 it must be the task of the socialist ideological world view, summarised in historical materialism, which is based on but remains outside of economic theory as an objective social science, to assert the necessity of socialism in the light of the long history of human societies up to capitalism. Furthermore, it must be the ultimate task of a practical workers' movement both actually to prove and realise socialism, on the grounds of the possibility and the necessity of socialism, presented by both Marxian economic theory and historical materialism. Marxian political economy clarifies both the object of, and the actual conditions for the workers struggle for socialism, guided by historical materialism. Still it is the role of conscious socialist practical activities based on the workers' movement to elevate the possibility of socialism established in political economy to actual historical necessity and inevitability. The attempts to show the logical inevitability of the collapse and the transformation of capitalism into socialism within the basic economic theory, more or less confuse these different roles and tasks of political economy, historical materialism and the practical socialistic workers' movement, and they must consequently weaken the scientific basis for socialism.

A simple and mechanical application of historical materialism, treating the growth of the productive forces by itself as the final driving force of the progress of human history, has thus not merely obstructed a correct understanding of the essential nature of the transformation from capitalism to socialism, but also distorted the course of the construction of socialism in post-revolutionary societies. In a Soviet type of society it has generally been believed that the growth of the productive forces in the form of large-scale industrialisation through fraternal co-operation between the working class, the peasant class and a section of the intelligentsia will harmoniously drive a socialist society on to the higher stage of a communist society. According to the orthodox Soviet view, Soviet society completed the transition to a socialist society twenty years after the October 1917 Revolution which expropriated the capitalists and landlords and pushed forward the nationalisation and the socialisation of the means of production.[4] However, a type of economism, the simple belief in the progressive effect of the growth of productive forces in the form of large-scale industrialisation, has brought about serious distortions in the course of Soviet types of societies. In particular, this view has tended to be used as a basis of statism without forming other alternative social initiatives but for the state in place of capital, in order to carry forward the growth of the productive forces. Under the control of the privileged state bureaucrats and the Party apparatus, not only were the peasants substantially exploited in the name of socialisation and with top priority going to large-scale industrialisation, but also the industrial workers themselves have been made inactive and oppressed. Marx's ideal of a socialism which liberates workers as the true subject of their society and finally to reduce the state itself to nothing seems hard to realise and far away. Despite this, the Soviet type of post-revolutionary societies with all their oppressive control of the workers tend to be legitimated ironically through the name of Marxism on the grounds of a simple and mechanical application of historical materialism in the form of a specific economism.

In addition, the ordinary interpretation of the formula of historical materialism conceives the path of the growth of productive forces as a linear, technically determined process, independent of the nature of the relations of production. Natural science and technologies developed under capitalism in pursuit of the production of relative surplus-value are regarded as neutral and separable from the capitalist relations of production, and therefore they are imitated as they stand, imported and incorporated into a Soviet type of society as rapidly as possible. In contrast, Marx pointed out that large-scale industry under capitalism separated intellectual work and physical labour, crippling the body and minds of workers generally, and further that by separating manufacturing and agriculture to towns and rural areas respectively 'it disturbs the metabolic interaction between man and the earth, i.e. it prevents the return to the soil of its constituent elements consumed by man in the form of food and clothing' (I, pp. 482–4, 636–7). These destructive effects on the human body and mind as well as on the ecological conditions of society, which have become more sophisticated and intensified since Marx's age, will not so easily be mended even when the capitalist relations of production are essentially abolished in a post-revolutionary society, in so far as the use of same technology or its development in a similar directions as in capitalism is continued.[5] The danger of such destructive effects might even become greater in some cases in a Soviet type of society, since the possible countervailing power of opposition movements against, for example, the construction of nuclear power stations or pollution by petrochemical industries cannot be strong if they ever existed.[6] The qualitative contents and the direction of the development of productive forces must be re-examined and re-oriented so as to suit a sounder economic life for the workers including the metabolic relation with nature. The workers should also be expected to use their own initiatives, and positive social participation, in such a re-orientation of the development of technologies, as a part of constructing a substantial economic democracy in a sounder socialist society.

## 10.2 THE IMPLICATIONS OF VALUE THEORY FOR SOCIALISM

In so far as both socialist ideology and movement should be grounded not merely in historical materialism but also on the theoretical achievements of political economy, we must always pay attention to the possible implications of economic theories for socialism. Though economic theories have developed as a self-recognition of a capitalist commodity economy, as we saw in the first part of this volume, they must serve as the theoretical basis for socialism, especially in the Marxian School. Improper understandings of economic theories will easily lead to confusions in the concept of feasible socialism, or the actual process of constructing a socialist economy, and further in the practical movements for socialism. Since value theory is the core basis of the economic theories of capitalism, as we discussed in the previous chapters, let us examine its implications for socialism at some length in this section.

### The Theory of Forms of Value for Socialism

Marx's creation of the theory of the forms of value, which was totally absent in the classical school, was a decisive innovation for the theoretical clarification of the historically specific character of the capitalist economy based upon a commodity economic order. However, prior to his presentation of the development of the forms of value, Marx, at the very beginning of *Capital*, defined commodity value as the crystalisation of abstract human labour, by abstracting from use-value in the exchange relations of commodities. As a result commodity value was conceived one-sidedly in its substance separated from the forms of transactions of commodities. In this respect we have to admit that there is a residue of Ricardo's ahistorical and abstract labour theory of value in Marx. Marx's own socialist views which emphasised the role of human labour, might also have been a psychological reason for him presenting the labour theory of value as the basis of his whole theories from the very beginning. Anyway, the potentiality of Marx's original theory of the forms of value was much restricted as a result. For instance, standard prices as a form of value tended to be narrowly defined as a formal intermediator of the equal exchange of labour, always expressing exchange relations in exact proportion to quantities of embodied labour as the social substance of reproduction. Conversely, Marx's own sharp theoretical recognition, that the forms of commodity economy originally spring from the exogenous inter-social economic relations and therefore continue to have the external quantitative form more or less independently of the endogenous quantitative relations of the social labour process, was not sufficiently incorporated in his value theory especially in the conception of the contents of the law of value. This has been an important source of the confusing and continuous controversy over value theory after Marx.

The attempt of K. Uno and his followers to purify the theory of the forms of value prior to presenting the labour theory of value in the analysis of the capitalist process of production, must be a relevant contribution in this context. As we examined in the previous chapters, such an attempt is significant and useful in solving the difficulties and confusions in the Marxian labour theory of value. In addition, the purification of the theory of the forms of value makes clear the exogenous historical character of the forms of value, as well as the endogenous general economic rule in the social labour process which is common to all the forms of societies. The three following theoretical implications for socialism can be deduced herefrom.

First, the forms of the commodity economy are basically separable and removable from economic reproduction in the process of a co-operative and consciously managed social labour process, as they are exogenous to the social labour process as the general economic norms of all human societies. In contrast, if these forms had originated from within the development of the social labour process, as in the growth of the division of labour as A. Smith suggested, then they can hardly be removed, especially from industrially advanced societies. Thus, it is decisive, in judging the basic direction of the development of a socialist society, how to understand the forms of a commodity economy in the basic theory of political economy. In my understanding the forms of a commodity economy are theoretically not merely removable, but should also have their social functions reduced and finally abolished in order to construct a fully socialist economy based upon conscious co-operation among workers freed from the unconscious anarchical forces of the market economy. Since the law of value works only through the forms of value in a commodity economy, its social functions must also be reduced and finally extinguished in a process of constructing a socialist economy.

This position is not at all identical with the negation of the social necessity for a socialist economy to take good care of the substantial quantitative relations of labour embodied in various goods which are to be reproduced. Conversely rather, as the role of the law of value is reduced, a socialist economy must so much move consciously maintain and adjust the relations of the amounts of labour necessary for the reproduction of industrial spheres through the distribution and the non-market exchange of products and services. The general norms of economic life common to all societies based upon human labouring activity, which become the social substance of value in a capitalist commodity economy, should be carefully carried out in a socialist society basically without depending upon the value relations in a market. As we saw in chapter 5, Section 5.1, Marx pointed out that 'economy of time, along with the planned distribution of labour-time among the various branches of production, remains the first economic law on the basis of communal production', although the 'economic law' of the general economy of time in communal production cannot be the law of value, but rather the general norm of economic life. In this respect, his statement that the relations between Robinson Crusoe and his labour products 'contain all the essential determinants of value' (I, p. 170) was theoretically confusing, as well as his following substantially similar proposition: 'Even after the capitalist mode of production is abolished, though social production remains, the determination of value still prevails in the sense that the regulation of labour-time and the distribution of social labour among various production groups becomes more essential than ever, as well as the keeping of accounts on this.'(III, p. 991).

Although 'the regulation of labour-time and the distribution of social labour among various production groups' must surely be performed in a socialist economy, this should be consciously achieved in socialism as far as possible by getting free from the determination and the regulation of the law of value, which is inseparable from the market system. Marx's confusion here apparently comes from an aspect of his concept of value defining value one-sidedly as the crystallisation of human labour, and abstracting from his other view of the value concept, that of the forms of value. J. V. Stalin, among others, succeeded to and much extended this confusion when he said that the law of value (unlike the law of surplus value) was not the basic law of capitalism and that it would continue to exist in a socialist society. He simply thought that the laws of political economy were utilisable in the interest of a socialist society, just like the laws of natural science, though inconsistently he also had to recognise that the law of value is a historical category and will disappear in the second phase of a communist society.[7] The law of value regulates commodity exchanges and production, with *social* necessity only in the fully developed commodity economy as a capitalist commodity economy, and serves as the basic economic law of capitalism with a wholly commoditised form of labour-power. It cannot be used in a socialist economy as if it were a law of natural science, but its abandonment must be intentionally aimed at.[8] The general economic norms, including the establishment of the socially necessary relations between the quantities of labour, which are theoretically recognisable in capitalism through the working of the law of value, must be carefully learned and socially fulfilled in a socialist society, but these norms are quite different from the law of value. In this respect A. Nove, as well as contemporary theorists in a similar position, cannot theoretically be justified in conceptualising 'the law of value 1' or 'LV1' relating to 'the allocation of labour in various proportions for various purposes, which must exist in any society', against 'LV2' manifesting itself only in the commodity economy.[9]

Second, apart from theoretical misconceptions of the law of value and the incorrect notions of the possibility of utilising it in a socialist economy, we should recognise that the forms of value, especially the price-form, would often actually remain and can be utilised in the process of constructing a socialist economy. Corresponding to the basic premises of capitalism a socialist economy must start with the liberation of the labour process from the control of capitals as the self-augmenting motion of money, by abolishing private ownership of the means of production and the commodity form of labour-power. The form of the motion of value in capital as a private property cannot be permitted in socialism. However, the price form or money can remain at least with two functions for quite a long period of time after capitalism.

One of them is to serve as a conventional unit or measure of account for the economic activities and for personal income as the dividend of the society to its members. There must be some common unit or measure between the various use-values produced and personal income in order to acquire goods for individual consumption, even though the physical quantities of use-values and actual labour-time in concrete forms would be given much more importance in a socialist economy and its planning than in a capitalist economy. The amounts of abstract human labour embodied in each product or expended in each form of service must be a desirable common unit in complete socialism. However, while the measurement and accounting for labour-time embodied in numerous kinds of goods would presently be practically and technically difficult, if theoretically possible, then the conventional accounting unit of money prices would continue to be used as a matter of convenience. The price-form would remain as a convenient accounting system especially in so far as the socialist economy must keep in touch with outside capitalist countries and needs common measure of comparison of economic activities with them. As an accounting unit, prices must be conceived also for stocks and products which are not actually sold in a market, just as in a statistical estimation of national wealth and income including the directly consumed products of farmers in capitalist countries. The portion of such estimated prices in the national income would increase when the communal consumption of goods and services or the non-market distribution of the necessary goods and services increases relatively with the development of a socialist economy.

In a centrally planned economy, officially fixed prices become generalised and are typically combined with the planned production quotas or norms and the rationing of products. Then prices become a means of formal accounting being deprived of their essential function in a commodity economy, anarchically to adjust social demand and supply. Such a centrally planned economy, with official prices was effective in the USSR in securing employment, equalising income among the working population, and industrialising a national economy for a certain period of time including a severe war period. The system, however, has become ineffecient in satisfying the varying and sophisticated needs of members of a society as consumers, there being a chronic shortage of sophisticated durable consumers' goods, while the quality of products are often unreliable. The enterprises or firms tend, bureaucratically, to dislike radical changes in norms, the sorts of products, or the methods of production, concentrating just quantitatively to keep up the norms. The system has failed to activate the workers' own subjective co-operation and efforts in the regular work places. The second economy, through black or grey markets, has increased its role in offering and obtaining various goods and services, thus much obstructing the efficiency of the regular economy. The cumulative effects of these factors, besides the unfavourable effects of the economic depression in the external capitalist countries, are probably the basis of 'the abrasion' of the soviet type of economy which has become conspicuous since the 1970s.[10]

In order to overcome these difficulties in the centralised planned economy, another function of the price-form as a flexible market mechanism has repeatedly been proposed as a possible solution. Although distribution of the basic means of consumption should be planned and performed outside of market fluctuations in socialism, the prices of some kinds of consumer goods in short supply, which must be personally selected outside of the goods given in common level of subsistence, can flexibly be elevated as in a sort of voting system where money serves as a more efficient and fairer way of distribution, in so far as money incomes among members of society are carefully equalised. The raised prices would stimulate the production processes of those goods and the series of means of production for them, by distributing some portions of increased monetary revenue or 'profit' even after increased 'taxes' among the members of the enterprises in those processes. Also from the view of reducing the bureaucratic state centralised control, the flexible price-form would be utilised as an alternative soft economic system to distribute and transfer various goods and services with the necessary information about them, among relatively independent communal enterprises and regions under workers self-control. Just as the forms of a commodity economy sprang up outside of the social labour process as the economic form of the inter-communal and interregional exchange of goods, indifferent of the particularity of the internal mode of production of the societies, the price-form might be utilisable for the time being in the process of constructing a socialist economy, even after abolishing the capitalist mode of production, as a possible economic form of interregional or inter-communal relations.

However, the utilisation of the flexible price system and the 'profit principle' should not be taken as a fundamental revision of the basic goals of socialism. It must be regarded as a device which may only partially solve the actual economic problems in soviet type societies. It is a sort of fetishism of the market principle to believe in it as a final and absolute solution to the current ineffectiveness and other related problems in existing socialist societies.[11] In considering the possibility of the use of the flexible market principle in socialism, we should keep in mind how the market economy in capitalism has resulted in various 'failures of market' such as the inequality of incomes, alienation of workers, economic crises and depressions, ecological destruction and the devastation of big towns. Just as the extention of the commodity economy was more or less destructive of the precapitalist economic order, it must work against the egalitarian and co-operative principles of a socialist economic order, if the socialist society does not consciously control the range and effects of market pricing, through practical social trial and error.

Third, in this respect, unlike capitalism the introduction of the flexible price system and the 'profit principle' cannot actually be thoroughgoing in a socialist society. Geared to a co-operative and egalitarian society, a certain range of the means of subsistence including extended public facilities and services such as child care, education, medical services and public transportation should not be supplied through competitive anarchical market. A portion of social labour-time and resources should be commonly pooled in order to supply sufficient of these basic means of subsistence by free distribution or low fixed official prices. It must be an important strategic item for an economic democracy that all members of the society, directly or indirectly, participate in deciding what range of goods and services should be included among these basic means of subsistence. The greater the range of them, the more equality and stability will be acquired by the members of the society, but the narrower the range of personally selective consumer goods, and subsequently there may be less incentives for dynamic change and improvement.

In case flexible pricing in a market is confined only to the 'non-basic products' of Sraffa's model,[12] which do not enter directly or indirectly into the reproduction of other products, the fluctuation in the prices of those goods would not affect the costs and prices of other goods. When the range of flexible market pricing is extended more generally, the priority of reproducing and supplying the basic means of subsistence, as well as their means of production, must be guaranteed in one way or the other. Even double pricing may be necessary for some raw materials differentiated according to different lines of reproduction.

Thus, the working of the law of value in readjusting the social allocation of labour and resources, guided by the motion of market prices, must be narrowed and cannot be at all thorough. Even in case where the enterprises behaved upon the basis of monetary costs and prices, 'the profit' rates need not necessarily be equalised. A higher rate of profit in the production of luxury goods due to a shortage of supply could be heavily taxed and would therefore not be easily reduced by a rapid increase of production, whereas the production of the basic means of subsistence and their means of production may often been subsidised. Moreover, the monetary wage-rate in socialism can be lower than that in capitalism while workers receive a similar material level of living, as the greater part of the basic means of subsistence become obtainable as public and free services or by low fixed official prices. Unlike under capitalism, wages would not fully represent the necessary means of subsistence or the socially necessary labour-time embodied in them. As a result the monetary costs of socialist firms, in so far as the costs are counted in monetary terms, actual prices of their factors of production cannot be an accurate indicator or measure of efficiency of production in terms of labour, since they no longer fully represent the equivalent labour-time of $(c + v)$. Together with the lack of competitive pressure to drive on firms to higher rates of profit, here is a basis for the strategic flexible operation of the price system in a socialist society, which enables low prices of the basic means of subsistence even without subsidy. However, in order that the price system acts as a consciously strategic tool for the democratic consensus of all members of a society, the exact relations between real labour productivity or embodied labour-time, and the prices of products should be accounted for and openly understood as accurately as possible. The possible gap here between prices and the labour-substance embodied in products must be much easier to understand in the light of our theory of the forms and the substance of value.

In contrast there seems to be a fundamental difficulty for orthodox or conventional Marxist value theory to analyse such a role for the price system and its significance in a socialist economy, so far as the value concept has been one-sidedly identified with the labour substance, more or less neglecting the theoretical potentiality of Marx's theory of the forms of value. When prices as a form of value are always conceived as the merely proportional formal expression of the labour-substance embodied in products, then the strategic operations of the price system in a socialist society will either become theoretically inconceivable, or the estimation of the labour-substance is assumed to be altered in accordance with market prices *à la* Rubin School, or the efficiency of pricing according to the marginal theory is rather off-handedly asserted by abandoning the labour theory of value, as the theoretical basis of the analysis of a socialist economy. While the 'normalisation' of the price structure is often and repeatedly argued in soviet type societies, the theoretical basis or the standard of the 'normal' price system is not then so clear-cut. It can neither be fully market determinable nor technologically determinable. An important basis of socialist economic democracy exists rather in strategic room for manipulation of the price system according to social decisions. This does not at all extinguish the crucial importance of the attempt to measure and account for the relations of labour-time embodied in each product on the basis of the objective technological conditions of reproduction, by mobilising the developing micro-electronics computer technologies, in order to confirm the social effects and possible rational range of pricing.

The development of the micro-electronics computer technologies would also possibly enable a new type of multi-terminal system of adjustment of economic relations including the necessary information system between socialist firms or regions on the basis of a more co-operative principle; the new system of economic transmission and communication being different from the previous centralised planning system or the free market mechanism.[13] A germ of such a possibility already seems present in the organisational growth of some types of consumers co-op movements or even in the inner organisation of giant capitalist corporations.

## The Concept of Labour-substance for Socialism

The clarification of the forms of value as the historically specific forms of a commodity economy was surely coupled in Marx with the clarification of the labour process as the endogenous common universal condition for all societies, being separable from the commodity economic order. In contrast, the labour theory of value in the classical school was still buried entirely in the commodity economic order, and lacked the concept of the labour process as such as well as the theory of the forms of value. Marx poses us a problem in his theory of the labour process as to what the exclusive characteristic of human labour is when differentiated from 'the first instinctive forms of labour which remain on the animal level' (I, p. 284). As Marx points out, the basis of characteristically human labour is that it has a conscious purpose and will steering the exertion of the working organs so as to cause appropriate changes in external materials as a part of metabolism with nature. This characteristic is shown first of all in the aspect of concrete useful labour as 'purposeful activity aimed at the production of use-values' (I, p. 290).

However, as we have argued in Chapter 5, Section 5.1, the human ability to work in each individual is not destined for each fixed form of useful labour. On the contrary, it can be expended in various forms of useful labour according to the differing purposes aimed at, which can themselves be flexibly altered and widened in scope of coverage on the grounds of human intellectual ability. In this qualification human labour appears not merely as concrete useful labour, but also simultaneously as abstract human labour being quantitatively comparable simply by the physical time of duration. Marx did not define abstract human labour in his analysis of the labour process, since he reduced commodity value to the crystallisation of abstract human labour at the very beginning of *Capital*, contrasting it with trans-historical use-values made by concrete useful labour. Rubin and similar value theorists in the Rubin School have thereupon deduced that abstract human labour is a result of commensuration through commodity exchange in a market, or that abstruct human labour cannot exist apart from a commodity economy.[14] This interpretation is not only inconsistent with Marx's view (for instance in the section on 'The Fetishism of the Commodity and Its Secret') that the appropriate distribution of labour-time to various necessary types of useful labour must be performed commonly in any societies, but also neglects the theoretical determinableness of the amount of abstract human labour-time embodied in each product upon the basis of technological conditions of production processes in a society, independently of the estimation by the market.

Rejection of the concept of abstract human labour outside of a commodity economic order would have three possible implications for socialism. First, reproduction and distribution in a socialist economy may be conceived just in physical terms, counting various heterogeneous use-values and useful labour as such, without any commensurability. An input–output–table type of analysis for social reproduction and the distribution of various goods and services in physical terms may be thinkable, when a socialist society need no longer care about 'economy of time', or if income need not be distributed in it by some commensurable unit *either* at a very low level of productivity barely maintaining as equal level of subsistence for its members, *or* at an extremely developed level of productivity hardly likely to be realised in the foreseeable future. Second, the commensurability of a commodity economy in terms of prices, or the resulting abstract human labour-time, would be expected to exist continuously, so far as socialist society needs some unit(s) to measure economic efficiency and income distribution among its members. Or, third, if the commodity economic order is not to be relied upon in socialism and yet some commensurable unit of accounting is necessary, then a third character of human labour, besides its useful concrete and abstract characters, must be introduced, such as Rubin's concept of 'socially equalised labour'.[15] However, there must be a great danger of arbitrariness in estimating various types of useful concrete labour as socially equalised labour-time, in comparison with the technically determinable abstract human labour-time.

The concept of abstract human labour-time therefore, should rather remain as a basic measurable unit of economic activity in the process of socialist economic construction.

In dealing with labour-time as a unit of measuring economic activity, there has been another controversial problem concerning how skilled or complex labour can be reduced to simple labour. As we discussed in Chapter 6, Section 6.1, this problem can be broken down into two aspects; one aspect relates to the labour-cost necessary to reproduce skilled labour-power, and the other to the estimation of labour expended by skilled workers. If the socially necessary sorts of skilled labour-power must be reproduced over generations through the personal income of skilled workers, then the costs of training or educating children to the same grade of skilled workers as their parents must be included in the personal income of skilled workers even in a socialist society, just as the higher wages of skilled workers in capitalism more or less has such a social function. This type of social system for reproducing skilled workers is not only conceivable but also apt actually to be effective, whenever the access to higher or better education or training is available by personal payment along with differentiated incomes according to the grades of skill. Although such a social situation is often reported to be evident in soviet types of societies, it is clearly against one of the socialist ideals – egalitarianism. In particular it would perpetuate the social stratification of the privileged bureaucrats and skilled workers, being economically separated from the general workers. Therefore it is quite important that socialism realises the egalitarian and co-operative principle for access to any type of education and training. Once educational and training costs for skilled or complex work are dealt with not on an individual basis but on a perfectly social communal basis, then the personal income of skilled workers need no longer be higher in order to meet these special costs.

As for the estimation of labour expended by the skilled workers, there have been three positions. The first position assumes that the educational and training labour-costs necessary to produce skilled labour-power is transferred into the products of the skilled worker on the average basis. This position basically contradicts our understanding that the labour-costs or the necessary labour-time to reproduce labour-power is determined independently from the labour-time expended as the realisation of the use-value of that labour-power. Especially as the educational and training costs for the socially necessary skill can be supplied by communal funds under socialism, these costs do not need to be individually restored by the estimation of skilled work as intensified labour, including the transfer of these costs. The second position assumes that the market prices or the exchange rates of the products or the services of skilled workers would determine the coefficients for reducing skilled labour to certain quantities of simple labour. This position contradicts the basic view of the labour theory of value that the labour-time embodied in the products is determined by the technical conditions of production, independently from the movement of market prices or the fluctuating balance between demand and supply in a market. Moreover, this position would become unreliable in a socialist economy as the role of market is controlled and reduced. The third position assumes some reduction coefficients to be determined socially for each sort of skilled labour as certain quantities of simple labour, as with Rubin's concept of 'socially equalized labour'. Although the social grading of workers more or less indifferently to both the technical costs of education and market conditions, is actually observable in existing socialist societies, and partly in one aspect of the segmentation of workers within a capitalist firms as well, there is no persuasive reason to explain why certain types of skilled labour in one period of time equals so many multiples of simple labour on any objective grounds.

Conventional explanations for the degree of intensity of skilled labour are often circular in relying upon the differentiated incomes of skilled workers, which in capitalism also tend to reflect educational costs and market conditions.

Marx did not give a sound theoretical solution to the problem of how to estimate skilled labour, though he regarded skilled labour as a sort of intensified labour. All the attempts after Marx to reach a more objective or satisfactory solution to determine the reduction coefficients for skilled labour against simple labour in either of the three positions above, might probably have been hunting for a false problem which has no correct solution. Being unconvinced of the preceding solutions, I reformulated the problem itself and asked if skilled or complex labour really does more intensive work containing certain multiples of simple labour in a period of time, or if it should necessarily be regarded as doing so in general economic life. On reflection, it becomes clear that even an unskilled simple grade of work must contain a variety of intensities, using different human physical and mental abilities according to the various sorts of useful labour. There cannot be an accurate objective measurement of the intensity of labour across different kinds of useful concrete labour. This can also be a basis for a (more or less arbitrary) managerial segmentation of workers. What convinces us theoretically of the commensurability of different kinds of useful concrete labour is, not in the same degree of intensity of labour, but in the fact that they are all commonly the forms of expenditure of fundamentally the same human ability to work. This human ability to perform a wide range of work flexibly, malleably and dynamically is the result of the long historical development of humanity itself starting from the instinctive animal level of labour, and it must be a final grounds on which to conceive simple abstract human labour common to all the different useful forms of labour. There cannot be any exceptions, even in case of skilled labour, in this regard. Also skilled or complex labour is nothing other than the expenditure of the general human ability to work in specific forms, though it requires some additional costs arising from the time of education and training. Skilled or complex labour can generally be performed after the necessary special education and training, without any additional intensity and possibly rather easily and with pleasure. Thus, I believe that skilled or complex labour need not be treated as intensified labour supplying more units of labour in the same time period than unskilled simple labour.[16]

In his *Critique of Gotha Programme* Marx proposed the unequal 'bourgeois right' to a quantity of products proportional to the labour that the workers provide in the lower phase of communist society. When this proposition is combined with the concept of skilled or complex labour as intensified labour or the concept of socially equalised labour across various sorts of useful labour, it could have been utilised so as to legitimise the hierarchical privileges of the state and party leaders and bureaucrats for material goods and services in soviet types of societies. Since the grade of intensity of labour across various kinds of useful and skilled labour cannot be objectively determined on solid theoretical grounds, the grading of works can be easily arbitrarily done in favour of the higher administrative positions and bureaucrats. Such treatment of skilled labour and the grading of works, assuming different amounts of labour expended in the same unit of time, is theoretically unfounded from what we have seen. By recognising that all the sorts of socially necessary work basically contain the same character as simple abstract human labour, based upon the common human ability to work, the more co-operative and egalitarian principles, such as 'from each according to his ability, to each according to his need!', must consciously be pursued from the very beginning of socialist economic construction, and not put aside as a goal so far away as actually to be achieved for generations to come.

Though our position favours the co-operative and egalitarian way of income distribution, personal incomes need not be rigorously and mechanically equalised. The different needs of workers, for instance, by the size and age structure of the family, or by the site of house and work-place must be taken into consideration. Some bonus would be added for work which tends to bear a heavy responsibility, or has a hazarous or disagreeable content, or requires a longer period of education and training, etc. If given in money form this additional wage may amount of a considerable addition to the general money wage, as the basic means of subsistence are distributed at low controlled prices or freely. However, its substantial proportion compared to the total means of subsistence or to the necessary labour-time to reproduce labour-power should remain relatively small so just compensating the unpopular specific effort of the work in question and securing the necessary numbers of persons to do it. It must clearly be understood that the amount of such incentive wages is not based on the different quantity of labour supplied in the same period of time, but simply an operational device to induce the necessary number of people to do certain sorts of work. Therefore the work with incentive wages need not be fixed, but can be flexibly altered in the process of changes of technologies and preferences of the people. The social educational and training system should be freely open to all members of society on equal footing, if with some competition, and should not function to consolidate a privileged social class or stratum which has an easier access to higher education on an individual family basis. At the same time it should continuously raise the general human ability to work more freely in wider range of fields, developing further more the common individual capacity of being able to perform abstract human labour in various concrete forms.

## 10.3 ACCUMULATION AND THE STATE IN SOCIALISM

Socialism aims at the abolishment of the exploitation of the surplus-labour in capitalism, through the self-liberation of workers from the commodity form of labour-power under the control of capital. The abolition of *exploitation* of surplus-labour is however not identical with the abolition of the surplus-labour performed beyond the necessary labour-time. Certainly the antagonistic relation between surplus-labour and necessary labour as the economic basis common to all the class societies should be abolished in socialism. But the portion of the surplus-labour time beyond the labour-time necessary to sustain and reproduce labour-power of workers must exist also in a socialist society for the sake of the expansion of reproduction, or as insurance against accidents, etc. This was pointed out by Marx as follows:

> Surplus-labour in some form must always remain, as labour beyond the extent of given needs. It is just that in the capitalist, as in the slave system, etc., it has an antagonistic form and its obverse side is pure idleness on the part of one section of society. A certain quantum of surplus-labour is required as insurance against accidents and for the progressive extension of the reproduction process that is needed to keep pace with the development of needs and the progress of population, which is called accumulation from the viewpoint of the capitalist.[17] (III, p. 958).

As the exploitation and appropriation of surplus-labour by the ruling class no longer exists in a socialist economic order; the total labour-time including surplus-labour must be used either directly or indirectly for the working people as a whole. The relation between the portion of surplus-labour and that of necessary labour is no longer an opposition or contradictory. The social function of surplus-labour when serving as insurance or for accumulation is no longer antagonistic, but complementary to that of directly necessary labour.[18] In a sense the portion of surplus-labour beyond the given direct needs can also be regarded as a portion of necessary labour to sustain working people for the future. Nevertheless, the concept of surplus-labour is analytically useful in examining the working of a socialist economic system, upon the ground of the basic theory of capitalism, though its different social character should not be neglected.

The dynamic process of capitalist accumulation is full of lessons for possible socialism. They are not limited to the defective contradictory character of capitalism which must be overcome in socialism. For instance, in the capitalist process of extended reproduction, the flexible distribution of surplus-labour in the form of fluctuating market prices and profit rates serves as a social buffer or a pool to allow the readjustment of imbalances among industrial spheres caused by dynamic changes in production technologies, and to meet the needs of readjusting industrial structures in the face of changing consumers' preferences. In the phase of prosperity especially, such readjustment can proceed relatively smoothly and positively, also utilising the credit system and the form of interest as a mechanism of redistributing surplus-labour. If the content of the law of value is conceived simply as the equal exchange of the labour embodied in commodities, the fundamental ability of capitalism flexibly to cope with surplus-labour and its social functions in the process of a dynamically changing balance among industrial branches tends to be neglected as the working of the law of value. If a socialist economy is designed to carry out what capitalism has done as the substantial content of the law of value in maintaining social relations in quantities of labour-time, just as is summarised in the conventional reproduction schemes, by using an understanding of the law of value simply as the equal exchange of labour-time, then socialist economic planning would inevitably become inflexible and inefficient in readjusting social reproduction to meet dynamic changes in technologies and social needs.[19]

Socialism should indeed consciously realise what capitalism performed unconsciously through the working of the law of value, while removing the anarchical waste and inhuman devastation in capitalism. The conceivable devices for social allocation of labour products in the process of constructing a socialist economy appear to be: officially fixed pricing, partial utilisation of flexible market pricing, centrally planned distribution or rationing of products and co-operative direct exchanges outside of the price system. Actually these devices must be utilised in combination, and it would long continue to remain a complicated issue, to be decided socially, as to how to combine these devices in the development of a socialist economy. Whatever the combination may be, operational flexibility given by surplus-labour-time should clearly be borne in mind, being separated in the management of socialist firms as well as of the whole economy, from the necessity of supplementing the portion of labour-time transferred from the means of production and that of necessary labour-time defined to sustain the workers in each process of production. This consideration, which is a corollary of our re-examination of the substantial content of the law of value in this volume, cannot provide an instant and complete key to the current inefficiency of soviet type societies, but would probably serve as a theoretical basis for its solution.

The relatively smooth process of capitalist accumulation in the phase of prosperity is also based upon an elastic availability of additional workers from the industrial reserve army, along with the flexible redistribution of surplus-labour. From the view of wage-workers this aspect of capitalist accumulation holds the constant menace of unemployment or an irrational loss of the means of subsistence, not only confined to the phase of economic crisis and depression. Socialism aims, above all, at the removal of this menace to workers, and must guarantee work for all workers as an essential part of their liberation from the commodity form of labour-power – wage-labour – under capitalism.[20] Full employment cannot be a stable economic phenomena under capitalism. When it appears towards the end of periods of prosperity, there must be an unstable excessive accumulation of capital in relation to the labouring population, and a resultant fall in the profit rate due to a rise in wages, leading to a destructive phase of crisis in a typical case, as we have seen in the theory of periodic business cycles. In this regard, socialism must solve two problems.

First, how can it control the range of the necessary means of subsistence so as not to impede the portion of economic surplus for accumulation, etc.? If left open to determination by the balance of demand and supply in a free market, wages can rise easily, without the pressure of an industrial reserve army in the process of extended reproduction. A centrally planned economy would be able, relatively easily, to control the material standard of workers and retain an appropriate proportion of surplus-labour in relation to productivity. Clearly, workers' co-operative self-management concerning their own material standard of living becomes essential as a part of economic democracy, if centralised authoritative planning is to be relaxed. Socialist arguments for workers control and regional autonomy must then be prepared to accept a democratic process of decision-making about living standards so as to leave room for the social need for growth, insurance and so forth, according to a basically egalitarian principle.

Second, how can socialism maintain a flexible adjustability of the economy comparable to that in capitalism? Capitalism secured its basis for dynamic adjustment in the industrial reserve army, and therefore becomes inflexible and increasingly maladjusted when most of industrial reserve army is absorbed through the over-accumulation of capital at the end of prosperity. The very success of socialism in removing the threat of unemployment would, ironically, pose the structural difficulty of an inflexible labour-supply in its economy. It would be desirable in this respect for a socialist economy to incorporate in its planning a positive socialist form of an industrial reserve army, which is surely different from unemployment but some sort of arranged leave, or sabbatical, with a sufficient guarantee of income and possibly learning or training as well as of certain employment in the near future. Even with such a socialist industrial 'reserve army', the workers' own positive social attitude towards their own mobility would be imperative for a flexible and dynamic socialist economy.[21]

The importance of promoting the workers' own positive social co-operation and self-management has not been sufficiently emphasised in soviet types of societies, with a contrary tendency towards hypertrophy of state authority. Theoretically this is most probably due to an improper understanding of the fundamental contradiction in capitalism. It is a task of Marxian crisis theory to reveal the fundamental contradiction in capitalism and its concrete appearances in the process of accumulation. While the orthodox Marxians have believed in the excess-commodity theory of crisis, they tend to see the basic restriction in a capitalist economy as the conditions for the realisation of surplus-value, rather than in the condition for the production of it. They generally depend on Marx's propositions that 'The conditions for immediate exploitation and for the realization of that exploitation are not indentical. . . . The former is restricted only by the society's productive forces, the latter by the proportionality between the different branches of production and by the society's power of consumption.' (III, p. 352). The formula of historical materialism naturally overlaps with this view. The anarchical relations between the branches of production, and the narrowly restricted power of consumption of the masses are interpreted as corollaries of capitalistic relations of production based upon the capitalist mode of appropriation, while its productive power is already developing with its social character. Thus Engels typically argued that 'In these crises, the contradiction between social production and capitalist appropriation ends in a violent explosion',[22] and Lenin echoed this by defining the capitalist 'contradiction between the social character of production and the private character of appropriation'.[23]

Socialism which is designed upon these theoretical views would expect the nationalisation of the means of production with central planning to be a powerful way out of the roots of social contradictions in capitalism. If the fundamental contradictions of capitalism are indeed between the social character of production and the private character of appropriation, and in the resulting disproportionality, or the under-consumption of workers, they could surely be removed by nationalisation of the means of production. As nationalisation would be the surest device of eliminating private capitalistic appropriation, central planning with nationalised work-places would end capitalism's anarchic disproportionality, and the extinction of unemployment, with rising real incomes of workers under the planned economy, would remove the difficulty of under-consumption faced by capitalism. It has also been emphasised that Marxism, unlike anarchism, assumes a revolution in the native of the state, i.e. from a capitalistic to a proletarian state, so that the state can be used as a central organiser of economic planning, especially in the first and lower stage of communism, rather than the instant abolition of the state. Thus, consolidation of the state apparatus with a strong leadership for central planning of the national economy in post-revolutionary societies has been regarded as a certain guarantee of constructing sound socialism by eliminating both the bourgeois right of appropriation as well as anarchic disproportionality and unequal income distribution. This conception is reinforced by assuming that Marx's ideal socialism where the state itself is abolished will be realisable only in at a higher stage of communism, not easily achieved in the foreseeable future.

We have to acknowledge that the soviet economy has actually worked and shown certain achievements upon the basis of this way of understanding. It has overcome the great economic difficulties of the initial period of its construction, and those of the Second World War period, and achieved conspicuous industrialisation free from capitalistic economic crises. Nevertheless, as we have argued, there remain a number of serious problems too. On top of the simplified application of the formula of historical materialism, the technologies and methods of production developed by capitalism tend to be uncritically approved, accepted and followed up on quantitatively extended scales in nationalised work-places. The economic and social interests of the peasant class were sacrificed in the process of large-scale socialisation and industrialisation.[24] As a result there remains the difficult problem of how to secure and increase agricultural production in parallel with industrial development. With the consolidation of the state apparatus the positions of the state and party bureaucrats have been strengthened through authoritative managerial power and economic and social privileges, in contrast with the still weak social position of the general workers who are displaced from various levels of decisions. We have to recall here that the fundamental human ability to labour on the basis of conceptual thought has also served as a potential basis for the subordinate position of workers, by the social separation of the conception of work and its actual execution in class societies, as we saw in Chapter 5, Section 5.1.

There has been a hot debate about how to understand the historical character of the soviet type of societies, including the difficult position of workers in particular. Diverse notions have been presented. For instance, the notions of early socialism in an infant or formation period,[25] the Stalinisation phenomena,[26] or the bureaucrats' agent-state[27] would admit the distortions of the soviet type of society but do not accept that antagonistic class relations exist in a proletarian socialist state. The notions of state capitalism[28] or the new post-revolutionary class society[29] would more radically criticise the 'oppressive character' of the 'class relation' in such states.

As P. Sweezy has sharply criticised in *Post-Revolutionary Society*, it would not be very persuasive to explain the present problems, particularly hypertrophied state power and the weak position of workers in the soviet type of industrialised society, from the mere personal faults of Stalin, or from the initial shortage of professional specialists who were placed as the bureaucratic agents of the workers, as emphasised by L. Trotsky and E. Mandel, or from the revival of the law of motion of capitalism as stressed by C. Bettelheim. Thus, I am sympathetic to Sweezy's suggestion that we should think of a concept of the new type of post-revolutionary class society with its critical implication for soviet types of societies. However, I am not yet confident of this conception for three reasons: (i) Theoretically, the definition of the senior bureaucrats in those societies as a privileged ruling class still relies upon more or less a sociological view of a social class. There remains a problem of how this definition, or the concept of 'the state class', can be consistent with Marxian theory which has underlined the economic basis of social classes in the ownership of the means of production. To be consistent we might have to re-examine the concept of class in Marxian theories of political economy and the state, as well as in historical materialism, probably emphasising more the role of social decision-making at various levels, and the means of coping with social surplus-labour. The roots of the weaknesses in Marxian theories which have allowed the hypertrophy of the state must also be reflected upon further. (ii) Actually the hypertrophy of state power is in a sense a phenomenon which is not confined to the second world, but a global feature of our age including both first- and the third-world countries. We have to notice that this feature seems internationally to reinforce itself especially through cold-war structures, and therefore its historical necessity and meaning cannot be totally explicable from internal social factors alone.[30] (iii) Practically, it would require further social revolution(s) in Soviet types of societies to define it as a class society. I do not yet despair of expectating or hope that the USSR and similar types of societies may progress internally and develop into fully socialist societies. The economic reforms proposed and attempted in the East European countries, China and the USSR, and international opinion about them among Marxians as well as their prospects in the various revolutionary movements in the first and the third worlds, may be effective in widening the possibility of such expectations. At least without such expectations I am honestly worried that the friendly co-operation and solidarity among so many Marxians and working people in the world tend continuously to be too heavily and often obstructed by this issue, both domestically and internationally.

Coming back to our theoretical concern here, in contrast to the orthodox excess-commodity theory of crisis, the excess-capital theory of crisis of a labour-shortage variant, which has been endorsed in Chapter 9, defines the root of the contradiction of a capitalist economy in the commodity-form of labour-power, or in the fundamental difficulty capital has in treating the human ability to labour as a commodity, just like other producible commodity goods. Socialism, to overcome the fundamental contradiction in capitalism in the light of this crisis theory, cannot be achieved merely by the abolition of the private ownership of the means of production and the nationalisation of them. Though the nationalisation of the major means of production must be an essential initial step in a socialist revolution, the subjective self-liberation of working people from their subordinate social position subject to the commodity-form of labour-power must surely continue. The real concern of socialism to liberate workers from the commodity-form of labour-power, must be clarified on the basis of the logic and the mechanism of the oppression and alienation of wage-workers by capitalism. The solution of the one-sided separation between alienated manual labour and mental work, as well as the devastating capitalistic division of labour between agriculture and manufacturing industries, is certainly contained therein.

Even though the apparatus and the functions of the socialist state would have to be extended in the initial step of nationalisation, they must be reducted as soon as possible, so that they be socialised communally by the increase in workers' initiatives from below. The argument for the decentralisation of power and workers' self-management becoming popular in various quarters in both Eastern and Western Europe, as well as in other parts of the world, appears to indicate the necessary direction and some of the contents of socialist societies following the abolition of the commodity-form of labour-power. These reflections on a more desirable socialism are actually indispensable also for the appropriate assessment of both the achievements and limitations of social democracy in capitalist countries too. The basic theory of capitalism presented in this volume must hopefully be consistent with and supportive of such further arguments for a sounder socialism.

# Notes

## PART I ECONOMIC SCHOOLS AND IDEOLOGIES

1. M. Dobb, *Theories of Value and Distribution since Adam Smith* (Cambridge: Cambridge University Press, 1973) p. 1.
2. M. Weber, 'Die "Objektivität" sozialwissenschaftlicher und sozialpolitischer Erkenntnis', *Archiv für Sozialwissenschaft und Sozialpolitik*, XIX (1904).

### 1 The Birth of the Theoretical System of Capitalism.

1. A. Smith, *An Inquiry into the Nature and Causes of Wealth of Nations* (1776), ed. R. H. Campbell, A. S. Skinner and W. B. Todd, vol. 1 (Oxford: Clarendon Press, 1976) pp. 434–5.
2. K. Marx, *Theories of Surplus-Value*, part I (London: Lawrence & Wishart, 1969) p. 43.
3. J. D. Steuart, *An Inquiry into the Principles of Political Economy*, vol. I (London: Millar & Cadell, 1767) p. 206.
4. Marx, op. cit. p. 41.
5. K. Marx, *Capital*, vol. I (Harmondsworth, Middx: Penguin Books, 1976), p. 876. Throughout this volume references to *Capital* includes volume and page of the Penguin Edition only in parentheses.
6. In the Marxian School the tendency to neglect the contributions of mercantilism used to be legitimised by K. Kautsky's method of editing Marx's manuscripts of the *Theories of Surplus Value*. Instead of Marx's original order beginning from J. Steuart, as we see in the recent revised edition by the Marxism-Leninism Institute, Kautsky began his edition of *Theorien uber den Mehrwert*, vol. I (Friedenau, 1905), from Marx's treatment of the growth of the labour theory of value since W. Petty. Marx would probably have discussed mercantilist theories more extensively if he had intentionally written a full historical review of the development of economic theories as a whole, not merely those of surplus-value.
7. R. L. Meek, *The Economics of Physiocracy, Essays and Translations* (London: George Allen & Unwin, 1962) pp. 150–67.
8. To quote Marx's definition, 'by classical political economy I mean all the economists who, since the time of W. Petty, have investigated the real internal framework [*Zusammenghang*] of bourgeois relations of production, as opposed to the vulgar economists who only flounder around within the apparent framework of those relations' (I, pp. 174–5). In the broadest range of the definition, Marx indicated both the British genealogy from Petty to Ricardo, and the French from Boisguillebert to Sismondi (*A Contribution to the Critique of Political Economy*, Moscow: Progress Publishers, p. 52). This range seems too wide for us to confirm a

common theoretical basis. To be strict in this regard the British genealogy was decisively the main body of the classical school.

9. W. Petty, *A Treatise of Taxes and Contributions*, (1662), in *The Economic Writings of Sir William Petty*, ed. by C. H. Hull (Cambridge: Cambridge University Press, 1899) p. 68.
10. Petty, op. cit. p. 44.
11. Smith, op. cit. p. 48.
12. Smith, op. cit. p. 50.
13. Smith, op. cit. p. 47.
14. Smith, op. cit. p. 51.
15. Smith, op. cit. p. 65.
16. Smith, op. cit. p. 65.
17. D. Ricardo, 'An Essay on the Influence of a Law Price of Corn on the Profit of Stock' (1815), in *The Works and Correspondence of David Ricardo*, vol. IV, ed. P. Sraffa (Cambridge: Cambridge University Press, 1951).
18. D. Ricardo, *On the Principles of Political Economy and Taxation* (1817), in *The Works and Correspondence of David Ricardo*, vol. 1. ed. P. Sraffa (Cambridge: Cambridge University Press, 1951) pp. 21–2. (This book is hereafter abridged as *Principles*.)
19. Ricardo could not distinguish the basic problem of transforming the embodied labour values into prices of production through the equalisation of the rates of profit *and* the comparatively secondary problem, of analysing the effect of a rise or a fall of wages on the exchange values. This is because he always identified the embodied labour values with natural prices. As a result he tended to believe that the effectual revisions in his value theory were insignificant and exceptional; so he stated that 'The reader, however, should remark, that this cause of the variation of commodities is comparatively slight in its effect. . . . Not so with the other great cause of the variation in the value of commodities, namely, the increase or diminution in the quantity of labour necessary to produce them.' (*Principles*, p. 36.)
20. 'This definition of an equal rate of profit. . . yielded by capitals of different organic compositions, contradicts the law of value or, as Ricardo says, constitutes an exception to it, whereupon Malthus rightly remarks that in the progress of industry, the rule becomes the exception and the exception the rule'. K. Marx, *Theories of Surplus Value*, part III (London: Lawrence & Wishart, 1972) p. 72. See also p. 31 of the same volume.
21. D. Ricardo, 'Absolute Value and Exchange' (1823), in *The Works and Correspondence of David Ricardo*, vol. 4, ed. P. Sraffa (Cambridge: Cambridge University Press, 1951).

## 2 The Dissolution of the Classical School and Diversification

1. K. Marx, *Theories of Surplus Value*, part III (London: Lawrence & Wishart, 1972) p. 61.

2. T. R. Malthus, *The Principles of Political Economy*, 2nd ed. (London: William Pickering) p. 60.
3. Malthus, op. cit. p. 326.
4. Malthus, op. cit. pp. 398–413.
5. Malthus, op. cit. p. 140.
6. J.-B. Say, *Letters to Thomas Robert Malthus on Political Economy and Stagnation of Commerce* (1820), translated 1821, with an historical preface by H. J. Laski (London: Harding, 1936).
7. J. C. L. Simonde de Sismondi, *Nouveaux Principes d'Économie Politique* (Paris: Delaunay, 1819) pp. 335–8.
8. In so far as romanticism in economics is a tendency to idealise past precapitalist social life-styles by criticising the capitalist economic order, it reappears from time to time in various expressions. For instance, such a tendency is recognisable in some ecologist's arguments as well as I. Illich's position as in his *Shadow Work*, (London: Marion Boyars, 1981).
9. C.-H. de R. Saint-Simon, *Catéchisme Politique des Industriels* (1823–4. in *Oeuvre de Saint-Simon et d'Enfantin* (Paris: Ed. Dentu, 1865–76, t. 37–9).
10. F. M. C. Fourier, *Le Nouveau Monde Industriel et Sociétaire ou Invention du Procédé d'Industrie Attrayante et Naturelle Distribuée en Série Passionnées* (1822, in *Oeuvres complètes de Ch. Fourier* (Paris: La Librairie Sociétaire, 1845) t. 6.
11. e.g. R. Owen, *A New View of Society* (1813–14) in *The Life of Robert Owen Written by Himself*, vol. I (New York: A. M. Kelley, 1976).
12. T. Hodgskin, *Labour defended against the Claims of Capital; or the Unproductiveness of Capital proved* (1825) (New York: A. M. Kelly, 1963).
13. W. Thompson, *An Inquiry into the Principles of the Distribution of Wealth most conducive to Human Happiness* (1824) (New York: A. M. Kelly, 1963).
14. F. Engels, *Socialism: Utopian and Scientific* (1892) (Peking: Foreign Languages Press, 1975).
15. James Mill, *Elements of Political Economy* (London: Baldwin, 1821).
16. J. R. McCullock, *The Principles of Political Economy* (1825) (Edinburgh: A & C. Black, 1864).
17. John Stuart Mill, *Principles of Political Economy* (1848), ed. by W. J. Ashley, (London: Longmans, Green, 1921) pp. 199–200.
18. Ibid. pp. 457–8.
19. R. Jones, *An Essay on the Distribution of Wealth, and on the Sources of Taxation* (London, 1831); *Text-book of Lectures on the Political Economy* (Hertford, 1852); *Literary Remains*, ed. W. Whewell (London: Murray, 1859).
20. F. List, *The National System of Political Economy* (1841), translated by S. S. Lloyd (London: Longmans, 1885) p. 177.
21. e.g. W. Roscher, *Grundriss zu Verlesungen über die Staatwirtschaft* (Göttingen: Dieterichschen Buchhandlung, 1843). *System der Volkswirtschaft*, 5 vols (Stuttgart: Cotta, 1882–94). B. Hildebrand, *Die gegenwärtige Aufgabe der Wissenschaft der Nationalökonomie* (1863). K. Knies, *Die politische Ökonomie vom Standpunkte der geschichtlichen Methode* (Braunschweig: Schwetsche, 1853).

22. G. Schmoller, *Grundriss der allgemeinen Volkswirtschaftslehre* (Leipzig: Duncker & Humbolt, t. 1–2. 1908–9).
23. L. Brentano, *Das Arbeitiverhältniss gemäss dem heutigen Recht* (Leipzig: Duncker & Humbolt, 1877).
24. A. Wagner, *Lehrbuch der politischen Ökonomie* (Leipzig: Winter, 1879).
25. K. Menger, *Untersuchungen über die Methode der Sozialwissenschaften, und der politischen Ökonomie insbesondere* (Leipzig: Duncker & Humbolt, 1883).
26. M. Weber, *Die protestantische Ethik und der 'Geist' des Kapitalismus*, in *Archiv fur Sozialwissenschaft*, Bd 20–1, 1904–5.
27. W. Bagehot, *Lombard Street* (London: John Murray, 1915).
28. J. A. Hobson, *Imperialism* (New York: Pott, 1902).
29. T. B. Veblen, *The Theory of Leisure Class* (New York: The Macmillan Co., 1899); *The Theory of Business Enterprise* (New York, 1904).
30. J. K. Galbraith, *American Capitalism* (Boston: Houghton Mifflin, 1952); *The New Industrial State* (Boston: Houghton Mifflin, 1978).
31. K. Polanyi, *The Great Transformation* (Boston: Beacon Press, 1944).
32. M. Itoh, *Value and Crisis* (London: Pluto Press; New York: Monthly Review Press, 1980) ch. 1.
33. As for the history and characterisation of the neo-classical school see, for example, E. Sugimoto (1901–52) [*Elucidation of Modern Economics*] 2 vols (Tokyo: Riron-sha, 1950). Reprinted by Iwanami Shoten, 1981), E. K. Hunt and J. G. Schwartz, *A Critique of Economic Theory* (Harmondsworth Middx: Penguin Books, 1972), and B. Rowthorn, *Capitalism, Conflict and Inflation*, (London: Lawrence & Wishart, 1980) ch. 1.
34. Their main works are C. Menger, *Grundsätze der Volkswirtschaftslehre* (Wien: Braumüller, 1871), M. E. L. Walras, *Elements of Pure Economics* (1874), translated by W. Jaffé (London: Allen & Unwin, 1954), W. S. Jevons, *The Theory of Political Economy* (London: Macmillan, 1871).
35. E. von Böhm-Bawerk, *Capital and Interest* (1884–89) translated by W. Smart (New York: Brentano, 1922).
36. V. Pareto, *Manuale d'économia politica* (Paris: Giard, 1906).
37. J. A. Schumpeter, *Das Wesen und der Hauptinhalt der theoretischen Nationalökonomie* (Leipzig: Duncker & Humbolt, 1908).
38. J. R. Hicks, *Value and Capital* (Oxford: Clarendon Press, 1939).
39. A. Marshall, *Principles of Economics* (London: Macmillan, 1890).
40. A. C. Pigou, *Economics of Welfare* (London: Macmillan, 1920).
41. J. M. Keynes, *The General Theory of Employment, Interest and Money* (London: Macmillan, 1936).
42. M. Kalecki, *Essays in the Theory of Economic Fluctuations* (London: Allen & Unwin, 1939), *Theory of Economic Dynamics* (London: Allen & Unwin, 1954).
43. B. Rowthorn, op. cit. p. 16.
44. K. Marx, *Theories of Surplus-Value*, Addenda in part III.
45. P. Sraffa, *Production of Commodities by Means of Commodities* (Cambridge: Cambridge University Press, 1960) ch. XII.

## 3 The Marxist Theory of Capitalism

1. G. W. F. Hegel, *Grundlinien der Philosophie des Rechts* (1821) (Frankfurt am Main: Suhrkamp, 1970) S. 24.
2. L. A. Feuerbach, *Das Wesen des Christentums* (Leipzig: Otto Wigand, 1841).
3. Marx later in 1845 formulated such insufficiencies in Feuerbach's materialism briefly in the 'Theses on Feuerbach', in *K. Marx, F. Engels Collected Works* (Moscow; Progress Publishers, 1975– , This *Collected Works* is abbreviated to *MECW* hereafter), vol 5. pp. 3ff. The thesis eleven 'The philosophers have only interpreted the world, in various ways; the point is to change it' is particularly famous.
4. K. Marx, *A Contribution to the Critique of Political Economy* translated by W. Ryazanskaya (Moscow; Progress Publishers, 1970) p. 20. English translation 'the guiding principle' from German original 'Leitfaden' in this edition seems too strong and may be misleading. I follow here the wording in *K. Marx Selected Writings*, ed. by D. McLellan (Oxford: Oxford University Press, 1977) p. 389.
5. The following paragraph is a summary of Marx's formulation in the Preface to *A Contribution to the Critique of Political Economy*.
6. F. Engels, *Dialectics of Nature* (Moscow: Foreign Languages Publishing House, 1954).
7. F. Engels, *Landmarks of Scientific Socialism (Anti-Dühring)* translated and edited by A. Lewis (Chicago: Charles H. Kerr, 1907).
8. F. Engels, *Socialism, Utopian and Scientific* (1880) (Chicago: Charles H. Kerr, 1918) p. 93.
9. K. Uno, [*The Methodology of Political Economy*] (Tokyo: University of Tokyo Press, 1962) p. 107.
10. P. M. Sweezy, *Post-Revolutionary Society* (New York: Monthly Review Press, 1980), contains a sharp critique of such a tendency in Soviet society. We shall return to this issue in Part IV.
11. K. Marx and F. Engels, *Manifesto of the Communist Party* (1848, in *MECW*, vol. 6) pp. 477–519.
12. K. Marx, *Grundrisse, Foundations of the Critique of Political Economy* (rough draft), translated by M. Nicolaus (Harmondsworth, Middx: Penguin Books, 1973).
13. K. Marx, *Zur Kritik der Politischen Okonomie (Manuscript 1861–1863)*, in *Marx–Engels Gesamtausgabe*, 2. Abteilung, Band 3, 6 vols. (Berlin: Dietz Verlag, 1976–82).
14. T. Kuhn, *The Structure of the Scientific Revolution* (Chicago: University of Chicago Press, 1970).
15. See, for example, K. Marx, *Grundrisse*, op. cit. p. 108, pp. 264, 275–6; *A Contribution to the Critique of Political Economy*, op. cit. p. 19, Marx's letter to Engels on 2 April 1858, and also the editor's preface to *Theories of Surplus Value*, part 1 (London: Lawrence & Wishart, 1969) p. 14. It would be interesting to examine the substantial similarity of the range of topics in these plans to those of the classical school, as in D. Ricardo's *Principles*, and to contemplate how and why Marx's *Capital* was completed, covering only the basic theoretical portions at most.

16. The quotation from p. 482 of vol. III. is not literal. The English translation in the Moscow, and Lawrence & Wishart edition lacks the important nuance of 'the further' analysis in the German original here.
17. R. Wilbrandt, *Karl Marx* (Leipzig and Berlin: B. G. Teubner, 4. Aufl. 1920) s. 97.
18. K. Kuruma ['For Confirmation of Marx's Theory of Crisis' (1930) in his *Studies in the Crisis Theory*] (Tokyo: Otsuki-Shoten, 1965).
19. V. S. Vygodski, *The Story of a Great Discovery*, translated by C. S. V. Salt (1973) p. 118. An editorial note to the vol. 23 (*Das Kapital*, vol 1) of *Marx-Engels Werke* (Berlin: Dietz Verlag, 1962) s. 844. The editor's preface to *Theories of Surplus Value*, part 1, ibid. p. 16. See also A. M. Kogan, [*The Plan of the Critique of Political Economy and 'Capital'*], translated from Russian by Y. Nakano (Tokyo: Otsuki-Shoten, 1979).
20. H. Grossmann, 'Die Änderung des ursprünglishen Aufbauplans des Marxschen "Kapital" und ihre Ursachen', *Archiv für die Geschichte des Sozialismus und der Arbeiterbewegung*, XIV – 2 (1929) 305 ff.
21. K. Tribe, 'Remarks on the theoretical significance of Marx's Grundisse', *Economy and Society* (May 1974) highly appreciates Grossmann's argument on this point in a survey of the debates on the plan problem in the appx I, while it does not refer to weaknesses in Grossmann's standpoint.
22. F. Behrens, *Zur Methode der politischen Ökonomie* (Berlin: Akademie-Verlag, 1952) s. 31–48.
23. R. Rosdolsky, *The Making of Marx's 'Capital'*, translated by P. Burgess (London: Pluto Press, 1977) p. 54.
24. Ibid. p. 56.
25. M. Itoh, book review: 'The Making of Marx's *Capital*, *Science and Society*, XLII–3 (Fall 1979) p. 362.
26. K. Uno, [*The Theory of Crisis*], (Tokyo: Iwanami-Shoten, 1953.), appx 1.
27. Cf. K. Uno, *Principles of Political Economy* (Brighton: Harvester Press; Atlantic Highlands, N. J. Humanities Press, 1980) pp. xxi–xxiii. M. Itoh, *Value and Crisis* (London: Pluto Press; New York: Monthly Review Press, 1980) pp. 39–42.
28. K. Uno's methodology is presented in more detail with favourable assessments from different angles in T. Sekine, 'Uno-Riron: a Japanese Contribution to Marxian Political Economy', *Journal of Economic Literature*, 13–3 (September 1975); R. Albritton, *A Japanese Reconstruction of Marxist Theory* (London: Macmillan, 1986), and M. Itoh, *Value and Crisis*, ch. 1.
29. e.g. K. Suzuki ed., [*Principles of Political Economy*], 2 vols (Tokyo: University of Tokyo Press, 1960, 1962), H. Iwata, [*World Capitalism*] (Tokyo: Mirai-Sha, 1964).
30. E. Bernstein, *Die Voraussetzungen des Sozialismus und die Aufgabe der Sozialdemokratie* (Stuttgart: Dietz, 1899).
31. K. Kautsky, *Bernstein und das Sozialdemokratische Programm* (Stuttgart: Dietz, 1899).
32. K. Kautsky, *Die Agrarfrage* (Hannover: J. H. W. Dietz, 1899).
33. V. I. Lenin, 'The Proletarian Revolution and a Renegade Kautsky' (1918), in vol. 28 of *The Collected Works of Lenin*, vol. 28, (Moscow: Foreign Languages Publishing House, 1965).

34. R. Luxemburg, *The Accumulation of Capital* (1913), translated by A. Schwarzschild (New York and London: Monthly Review Press, 1968).
35. R. Hilferding, *Finance Capital* (1910), translated by M. Watnick and S. Gordon (London, Boston and Henley: Routledge & Kegan Paul, 1981).
36. Ibid. p. 225.
37. V. I. Lenin, *Imperialism, The Highest Stage of Capitalism* (1917) (Peking: Foreign Languages Press, 1965).
38. Ibid. p. 3.
39. Ibid. p. 14.
40. As for some more details about this controversy, see Itoh, *Value and Crisis*, ch. 1.
41. Cf. e.g. Ch. 1 of P. Baran and P. Sweezy, *Monopoly Capital* (New York and London: Monthly Review Press, 1966).

## PART II VALUE, LABOUR AND CAPITAL

1. P. A. Samuelson, 'Understanding the Marxian Notion of Exploitation: A Summary of the So-called Transformation Problem between Marxian Values and Competitive Prices', *Journal of Economic Literature*, 9–2 (June 1971); also in his *Collected Scientific Papers*, vol. 3. I. Steedman, *Marx after Sraffa* (London: New Left Books, 1977).
2. Another interesting linguistic analogy is in the similarity between the syntax or the grammatical form of expression and the forms of value as the surface structure, being relatively independent from semantics or the substantial labour relations of a society. cf. A. Lipietz, *The Enchanted World*, translated by I. Patterson (London: Verso, 1985) appx IV.

### 4 The Forms of Value – Commodity, Money and Capital

1. As Marx notes, 'it is one of the chief failings of classical political economy that it has never succeeded, by means of its analysis of commodities, and in particular of their value, in discovering the form of value which in fact turns value into exchange-value. . . . The explanation of this is not simply that their attention is entirely absorbed by the analysis of the magnitude of value. It lies deeper. The value-form of the product of labour is the most abstract, but also the most universal form of the bourgeois mode of production; by that fact it stamps the bourgeois mode of production as a particular kind of social production of a historical and transitory character. If then we make the mistake of treating it as the eternal natural form of social production we necessarily overlook the specificity of the value-form, and consequently of the commodity-form together with its further developments, the money-form, the capital-form, etc.' (I, p. 174). The failing criticised here is clearly not confined to the classical school.
2. K. Uno, *Principles of Political Economy* (1964), translated by T. Sekine (Brighton: Harvester Press; Atlantic Highlands, N.J. Humanities Press, 1980), part I: The Doctrine of Circulation. This is a condensed revised

version of [*Principles of Political Economy*] (2 vols, Tokyo: Iwanami-Shoten, 1950, 52), which systematically presented Uno's discovery on this point for the first time, initiating many debates in Japan.

3. In the context of the value controversy, an orthodox Marxian position maintained that the relation between values and prices of production should be understood as a historical-logical sequence following the development from a society of simple commodity producers up to capitalist society. This interpretation of Marx's value theory was suggested originally by Engels in the supplement to the third volume of *Capital*. Engels criticised C. Schmidt's view of the law of value as a 'scientific *hypothesis*', and emphasised its historical and material basis in a precapitalist period of simple commodity producers (III, p. 1037). Though this position has been followed and amplified by not a few Marxians, beginning from R. Hilferding's anti-critique of Böhm-Bawerk in P. Sweezy, ed., *Karl Marx and the Close of His System by E. von Böhm-Bawerk and Böhm-Bawerk's Criticism of Marx by R. Hilferding* (New York: A. M. Kelley, 1966), it contradicts the initial intention by assuming an imaginary or hypothetical classless society. As for a little more detail see also M. Itoh, *Value and Crisis* (London: Pluto; New York: Monthly Review Press, 1980) pp. 18–19, with its notes in pp. 168–9.
4. K. Uno defines the concept of value at the beginning of 'The Doctrine of Circulation' as follows: 'Although commodities are heterogeneous as use-values when they serve specific purpose of consumption, they possess the property of being qualitatively uniform, i.e. independent of their material characteristics, and distinct only quantitatively. . . . The value of a commodity refers to its quality to homogeneity to other commodities and the use-value to its quality of heterogeneity from others.' (*Principles of Political Economy*, op. cit. 1980, p. 5). This definition seems to me too abstract to be clear, though it may be prudently comprehensive to cover the notion of both the substance and the form of value. Then Uno concretises the subject of the form of value, saying, 'This quality of homogeneity stems from the fact that every commodity must be exchanged by its owner for a definite quantity of other commodities that he might choose. It is this requirement of exchange that endows the commodity with its value.' (ibid. p. 5). In my understanding the commodities requirement for exchange must accompany a general request also for quantitative comparability and standard exchange ratios as an essential property of value.
5. At the beginning of the second chapter, 'The Process of Exchange', Marx says: 'Commodities cannot themselves go to market and perform exchanges in their own right. We must, therefore have recourse to their guardians, who are the possessors of commodities.' (I, p. 178). Marx seems to treat the logical necessity of the money-form from the view of the possessors of commodities in the second chapter, whereas he abstracts the possessors from the analysis of the value-form in the third section of the first chapter. The separation of analytical views in these chapters concerning the same subject is not proper, since the exchange relations of commodities cannot be conceivable from the beginning without their possessors. A reason for the somewhat mechanical separa-

tion in *Capital* is probably to be found in the fact that the third section of the first chapter was formulated and inserted in its place later, from the second German edition (1872), leaving the contents of the second chapter unaltered.

Uno avoided the separation of views and the overlapping of the subject of analysis in these places of *Capital*, by introducing the role of possessors of commodities as well as the essential contents of the second chapter into the theory of value-form. I believe that Uno's revision here is proper to make the theory of value-form easier and clearcut. The possessors of commodities, however, must be conceived here not as human beings in general, but as specifically those regulated by commodities which they own. Their will and behaviour are not free from commodities. Here is a basic distinction between the marginal utility theory of value which pretends to rest on the general psychological preference in human beings and the Marxian position.

6. G. Pilling, *Marx's Capital* (London, Boston and Henley: Routledge & Kegan Paul, 1980) is one of the recent Western works which emphasises the importance of Marx's theory of the value-form. Its explanation, however, that the elementary value-form (20 yards of linen = 1 coat) is 'the exchange of two commodities' (p. 147) as well as its emphasis of Marx's analyses of the labour-substance through the value-form, does not seem to sharpen either Marx's originality or his essential points in the theory of value-form, although it may not be inappropriate as an interpretation of the third section in the opening chapter of *Capital*. U. Krause, *Money and Abstract Labour*, translated by P.Burgess (London: NLB and Verso, 1982) is another conspicuous work underlining Marx's theory of the value-form. In ch. 2 of this book, Krause discusses the value-form without reference to labour just like Japanese Uno School. However, he also treats the value-form as the exchange relation, unlike us, and concentrates rather on the quantitative problem to solve the possible inconsistency in the exchange ratios between commodities without money.
7. Though Marx titles this second value-form 'the total or expanded form of value', the expansion of the equivalent commodities can not really be so 'total' as to embrace all kinds of commodities from the view of the possessor(s) of linen in the relative form of value.
8. This situation is formulated by Marx at the beginning of 'Form IV' in the first chapter of the first edition of *Capital* (K. Marx, *Value: Studies by Karl Marx*, translated and edited by A. Gragstedt, London: New Park Publication, 1976, pp. 33–4). The 'Form IV' is there placed after the general form of value in the 'Form III' and the form is further reversed to turn every commodity into the universal equivalent-form, which is actually and theoretially impossible in making every commodity directly exchangeable with others. Therefore, this form is omitted from the appendix on the form of value to the first edition of *Capital* and thereafter. Marx's idea contained in the 'Form IV', however, can be utilised in the transformation from the second to the third value-form of commodities.
9. Marx later refers to the substitutability of gold (hard) money as the

means of circulation by inconvertible paper money issued by the state, and also to the possibility of appearance of credit money such as bank notes or bills of exchange on the basis of the function of money as the means of payment (I, p. 224, p. 238). In my view such *possibilities* reside more basically already in the money-form itself, and hence can extend to other functions of money as well.

10. Uno, *Principles of Political Economy*, op. cit. pp. 9–10.
11. D. Ricardo, *On the Principles of Poliltical Economy and Taxation*, ed. P. Sraffa (Cambridge: Cambridge University Press, 1951.) p. 12.
12. K. Marx, *Grundrisse*, translated by M. Nicolaus (Hamondsworth, Middx: Penguin Books, 1973) p. 71, pp. 215–18.
13. An acute attention to such a phase of crises, where the credit system was suddenly turned into a monetary system, causing theoretical dismay, was probably an actual basis for inducing Marx to analyse a whole range of functions of money in comparison with the classical school.
14. Although Marx says that 'in the case if interest-bearing capital, the circulation $M - C - M'$ presents itself in abridges form, in its final result and without any intermediate stage, in a concise style, so to speak, as $M - M'$, i.e. money which is worth more money, value which is greater than itself' (I, p. 257), interest-bearing capital $M–M'$ cannot be made simply by condensing the form of merchants' capital $M - C - M'$. The form of interest-bearing capital historically originates generally in the development of commodity economy along with merchants' capital from very ancient ages, as a different type of proliferation of money as capital.
15. See also ch. 20, 'Historical Material on Merchant's Capital', and ch. 36, 'Pre-Capitalist Relations' of interest-bearing capital in the third volume of *Capital*.
16. K. Uno, [On 'The Transformation of Money into Capital'] (1964) in his [*Problems in Marxian Economics*] (Tokyo: Iwanami-Shoten, 1969). See also his *Principles of Political Economy*, op. cit. pp. 14–18.
17. A. Emmanuel, *Unequal Exchange*, translated by B. Pearce (New York and London: Monthly Review Press, 1972) defines international 'unequal exchange in the strict sense' on the basis of lower wages in the peripheral countries (pp. 60–4). Though the commodity products from the peripheral countries may not always be the products of capital, or may not bring about the international equalisation of profit rates unlike in Emmanuel's model, there seems to be still plenty of room for the international unequal exchange of labour or the transfer of surplus-labour from the peripheral to the central capitalist countries on the basis of the lower wages and living standards of the workers and peasants in the peripheral countries with lower costs of production. Especially the prices of the commodity products of more or less self-sufficient non-capitalist modes of production, such as a peasant economy, can be cut down often irrationally from a capitalist standard to a level regardless of reproduction costs. The form of merchants' capital would not miss the chance to utilise these circumstances, although the basic theory of the forms of value cannot directly analyse or refer to them behind the sphere of circulation.
18. Uno, *Principles of Political Economy*, op. cit. p. xxii.

19. Among others H. Ouchi, [*The Formation of the Theory of Value*] (Tokyo: Tokyo University Press, 1964), H. Hidaka, [*Principles of Political Economy*], revised ed. (Tokyo: Jichosha, 1974), F. Tokinaga, [*The 'Transformation' Problem in 'Capital',*] (Tokyo: Ochanomizu-shobo, 1981), T. Ouchi, [*Principles of Political Economy*], 2 vols (Tokyo: Tokyo University Press, 1981–82) are some representative works in this group of the theorists of pure capitalism.
20. K. Suzuki ed., [*Principles of Political Economy*], 2 vols. (Tokyo: Tokyo University Press, 1960, 1962), H. Iwata, [*World Capitalism*] (Tokyo: Mirai-sha, 1964), M. Itoh, [*The Theory of Value and Capital*], (Tokyo: Iwanami-shoten, 1981) are in this line of works by the theorists of world capitalism. M. Takumi, [*World Capitalism*] (Tokyo: Nihon-hyoron-sha, 1980) reviews the extensive methodological implications in the controversy between these two groups in the Uno School in favour of the theory of world capitalism.
21. Marx comes very close to such a recognition in saying: 'Within its circulation process, in which industrial capital functions either as money or as commodity, the circuit of capital, whether in the form of money capital or commodity capital, cuts across the commodity circulation of the most varied modes of social production, in so far as this commodity circulation simultaneously reflects commodity production. Whether the commodities are the product of production based on slavery, the products of peasants (Chinese, Indian ryots), of a community (Dutch East India), of state production (such as existed in earlier epochs of Russian history, based upon serfdom) or of half-savage hunting peoples, etc. – as commodities and money they confront the money and commodities in which industrial capital presents itself, and enter both into the latter's own circuit and into that of the surplus-value borne by the commodity capital . . .' (II, p. 189). 'Capitalist production never exists without foreign trade. If normal annual reproduction on a given scale is presupposed, then it is also supposed together with this that foreign trade replaces domestic articles only by those of other use or natural forms, without affecting value ratios, and therefore without affecting either the value ratios in which the two categories, means of production and means of consumption, mutually exchange for one another.' (II, p. 546). If we compare such an actual situation with the case in which all the articles are domestically produced by capital, we see an additional effect similar to the increase of productivity by means of the international exchange replacing domestic by foreign articles.

## 5 Capitalist Production and the Law of Value

1. A. Smith, *An Inquiry into the Nature and Causes of Wealth of Nations*, vol. 1 (Oxford: Clarendon Press, 1976) p. 48.
2. H. Braverman, *Labour and Monopoly Capital* (New York and London: Monthly Review Press, 1974) p. 48.
3. Ibid. p. 51.
4. Obviously the workers who have to do simple work in a subordinate position cannot dispense with mental endeavour. The case is often to the

contrary. As Marx points out, 'The less he is attracted by the nature of work and the way in which it has to be accomplished, and the less therefore he enjoys it as the free play of his own physical and mental powers, the closer his attention is forced to be.' (I, p. 284).

5. Marx continues to say that instruments of labour 'also indicate the social relations within which men work' (I, p. 286). As a rough indicator, instruments of labour have represented the degree of development of productive power and thus tended to define the corresponding relations of production in a long historical process. However, in view of the recent radical critiques of modern natural sciences and technologies, as well as the actual tasks for socialist movements in our age, we must notice that the path of development of instruments of labour and its productive power *can* be diverse and chosen from alternatives for the future. Furthermore, the character of the relations of production may not strictly be determined by the sorts of instrument of labour or the path of the development of productive power. The formula of historical materialism, as we have seen in Chapter 3, Sec. 3.1, must now be applied more elastically than Marx suggests here.
6. I. I. Rubin, *Essays on Marx's Theory of Value* (1928), translated by M. Samardzija and F. Perlman (Detroit: Black & Red, 1972) p. 97.
7. D. Gleicher, 'A Historical Approach to the Question of Abstract Labour', *Capital and Class*, 21 (1983), and his 'Note: A Rejoinder to Eldred', *Capital and Class*, 24 (1985). I am uncertain whether all the theorists listed by Gleicher in these papers can correctly be called the Rubin School in this regard, since their positions are various. Whereas, U. Krause, in *Money and Abstract Labour*, translated by P. Burgess (London: Verso, 1982), must be added to Gleicher's list, in addition to S. Himmelweit and S. Mohun, 'The Anomalies of Capital', *Capital and Class*, 7 (1978), M. Eldred and M. Hanlon, 'Reconstructing Value-form Analysis', *Capital and Class*, 13 (1981), D. Foley, 'The Value of Money, the Value of Labour Power and the Marxian Transformation Problem', *Review of Radical Political Economy*, 2 (1982) as some representative examples. Although, Lipietz, op. cit., appx 'The Value Controversy', also highly appreciates Rubin's approach, his treatment of the forms and the substance of value, such as his view of labour-time spent by Robinson Crusoe (p. 161) or in his analogy with linguistic structure (pp. 172–7), seem rather closer to our understanding in its spirit.
8. For instance, Marx states in the section on fetishism in the first chapter of *Capital*: 'Men do not bring the products of their labour into relation with each other as values because they see these objects merely as the material integuments of homogeneous human labour. The reverse is true: by equating their different products to each other in exchange as values, they equate their different kinds of labour as human labour.' (I, p. 166).
9. K. Marx, *Grundrisse*, translated by M. Nicolaus (Harmondsworth, Middlx: Penguin Books, 1973) pp. 172–3.
10. Though Marx uses the term 'economic law' in the quotation above, the general norms of economic life for all social formations must be distinguished conceptually from economic laws in a strict sense like the law of value which presents itself automatically through the anarchical ac-

tions of individuals in a commodity economy, so unconsciously realising always *post factum* the general economic norms. See also K. Uno, *Principles of Political Economy* (Brighton: Harvester Press; Atlantic Highlands, N.J.: Humanities Press, 1980) pp. 21–2, p. 32, P. 171.

11. Rubin, op. cit. p. 99.
12. Marx notes the interrelation of the production process in the section on the labour process and says: 'If we look at the whole process from the point of view of its result, the product, it is plain that both the instruments and the object of labour are means of production and that the labour itself is productive labour. Although a use-value emerges from the labour process, in the form of a product, other use-values, products of previous labour, enter into it as means of production. The same use-value is both the product of a previous process, and a means of production in a later process. Products are therefore not only results of labour, but also its essential conditions.' (I, p. 287). Uno defined the production process by emphasising this point of view when he states: 'The end-result of a labour-process is its product, and from the point of view of the product the same process can be viewed as a production-process.' (*Principles of Political Economy*, op. cit. p. 23). While treating such a labour-and-production process, Uno clarified that the dual character of labour is definitely a content of the general norms of economic life common to all societies. However, he did not show how the quantities of abstract labour-time are theoretically determinable on the basis of socially interrelated conditions of production.
13. N. Okishio, ['Value and Prices', *Research in Economics* (University of Kobe)], (Mar. 1955) would be one of the earliest papers which substantially clarified this solution. However, it was not proper that Okishio defined there the labour quantities thus determined as directly being values. It is because his solution can also be fully applicable to the forms of economy without commodity relations acting as the basis of the production processes.
14. P. Sraffa, *Production of Commodities by Means of Commodities* (Cambridge: Cambridge University Press, 1960) p. 89. We can get (5.4) from (5.1) by solving the simultaneous equations as follows, where $q_1$ times, and $q_2$ times of the scale of production of coal and iron compared with 5.1 are assumed to maintain 1 lb. of cotton as net product, leaving no net product in the form of coal and iron.

$$\begin{aligned} \tfrac{1}{4}q_1 + \tfrac{1}{2}q_2 + \tfrac{3}{4} &= q_1 \\ \tfrac{1}{6}q_1 + \tfrac{1}{3}q_2 + \tfrac{1}{2} &= q_2 \end{aligned} \qquad (5.5)$$

15. When labour-power is continuously obtained from outside, enforced labour until death with insufficient means of subsistence has been historically repeated in some forms of slave economy especially in the production of gold or silver, or in the early stages of the capitalist factory system. However, such economic systems must remain partial and cannot be a case for general economic norms.
16. The final clause after 'which' is somehow missed in the Penguin Books edition.

17. Marx, *Grundrisse*, op. cit. p. 708. Along with such development, the burden of domestic labour which has been so much on the shoulders of women in class societies, especially in capitalism, must be reduced and shared with men. The extension of communal social life and its facilities will be helpful for it, and in economic life it will further reduce the relative role of the portion of private means of consumption and the labour-time embodied in them. Then, the necessary labour-time embodied in the necessary means of subsistence essentially comprises two different portions. The portion to be consumed in a communal form in particular will be closely related and mutually supplementary to the social function of surplus-labour, though theoretically those are still distinct.
18. Within these 54 hours, 6 hours of necessary labour-time must be a more flexible portion than the other even on the basis of fixed conditions of production, so far as the necessary means of subsistence include historical and social elements independent of technological conditions of production.
19. A contrary procedure is assumed in a traditional Marxian interpretation of values and prices of production, presented in a historical-logical sequence, following the development from a precapitalist commodity economy to a capitalist. Besides the fact that there are certain weaknesses in this type of theory (as we have already examined in Chapter 4, Section 4.1) it is also inappropriate as an interpretation of the theoretical system in *Capital*. This is because the contents of capitalist production are analysed by means of the theory of value in *Capital*, and not directly using the theory of prices of production. Our critique of this type of value theory from the view of the Uno School however, does not imply a negation of the relevancy of the law of value in a precapitalist commodity economy. D. Gleicher, 'A Historical Approach to the Question of Abstract Labour', op. cit. seems to misunderstand this point. although its position is quite close to ours.
20. P. Samuelson, 'Wages and Interest: A Modern Discussion of Marxian Economic Models', *American Economic Review*, XLVII (Dec 1957) pp. 891–2. 'Understanding the Marxian Notion of Exploitation', *Journal of Economic Literature*, 9–2 (June 1972) p. 415. M. Morishima, *Marx's Economics* (Cambridge: Cambridge University Press, 1973) ch. 7.
21. This position is first presented briefly in chapter 2 of M. Itoh, *Value and Crisis* (London: Pluto Press; New York: Monthly Review Press, 1980). Even when standard prices as the form of value are assumed to be in direct proportion to the labour-substance of commodities, according to the conventional notion of the law of value in the analyses of the capitalist process of production prior to the theory of prices of production, the possibility and the general scope of deviation of prices from such a direct proportionality had better be noted. The hypothetical character of, say, the third position above would be clarified and theoretically supplemented by noting these points as being examined below.
22. Cf. Braverman, op. cit. ch. 13, 'The Universal Market', I. Illich, *Shadow Work* (London: Marion Boyars, 1981).
23. Although excessive overwork in domestic labour of housewives is

actually enforced, often by wages insufficient to purchase necessary goods and services in a market, it does not enhance the substance of value of labour-power. It tends to act even to the contrary by restricting the social average of the necessary means of subsistence to be purchased in a market, and thus indirectly increasing the efficiency of the capitalist production of surplus-value. However, the substance of surplus-value is formed by the surplus-labour of wage-workers in the capitalist production process and does not include any domestic labour.

24. Marx's notion of the production of absolute surplus-value is dual. First, it refers to the general basic method of capital to produce surplus-value by aquiring the surplus-labour-time beyond the necessary labour-time. Second, it also refers to the method of increasing surplus-value by extending surplus-labour-time beyond the necessary labour-time. With social conditions of production being given, the method is realised either by lengthening a working day or by intensifying labour. In either case the result is relative increase of surplus-value against the value of labour-power. Whereas, as we shall soon see, the production of relative surplus-value on the basis of increasing productivity reducing the value of labour-power can also be regarded as the production of absolute surplus-value in a broadest first sense, for it also extends the surplus labour-time beyond the necessary labour-time. Thus, 'from one standpoint the distinction between absolute and relative surplus-value appears to be illusory. . . . But if we keep in mind the movement of surplus-value, this semblance of identity vanishes.' (I, p. 646).
25. Sraffa, op. cit. p. 8.
26. In contrast, the portion of social surplus-labour in the form of extra profit redistributed to landowners as differential rent does not have such a positive social function from the viewpoint of general economic norms common to all societies, as we shall see in Chapter 7, Section 7.3. See also ch. 3 of Itoh, *Value and Crisis* (op. cit.).

## 6 The Extension of the Theory of the Substance of Value

1. P. M. Sweezy ed., *Karl Marx and the Close of his System by Eugen von Böhm-Bawerk and Böhm-Bawerk's Criticism of Marx by Rudolf Hilferding* (New York: A. M. Kelly, 1949) p. 86.
2. E. Bernstein, 'Zur Theorie des Arbeitswerts', *Die Neue Zeit*, XVIII (1899–1900) part I.
3. Sweezy ed., op. cit. pp. 136–46.
4. N. Okishio, 'A Mathematical Note on Marxian Theories', *Weltwirtschaftliches Archiv*, Heft 2 (1963).
5. B. Rowthorn, *Capitalism, Conflict & Inflation* (London: Lawrence & Wishart, 1980) ch. 8. In his more recent 'Notes on Skilled Labour' (mimeo, 1985) Rowthorn has deepened his theoretical view of this problem, and basically come closer to my position in this section. Therefore, my treatment and criticisms of his argument here cannot be applicable to his recent view, although his previous argument would remain as a typical case for the technological approach to this issue.

6. M. Morishima, *Marx's Economics* (Cambridge: Cambridge University Press, 1973) p. 181.
7. S. Bowles and H. Gintis, 'The Marxian Theory of Value and Heterogeneous Labour', *Cambridge Journal of Economics*, vols. 1–2 (1977).
8. I. Steedman, *Marx after Sraffa* (London: NLB, 1977) ch. 7.
9. S. Bowles and H. Gintis, 'Labour Heterogeneity and the Labour Theory of Value: A Reply', *Cambridge Journal of Economics*, vol. 5–3 (1981). See also E. McKenna, 'A Comment on Bowles and Gintis' Marxian Theory of Value', in the same issue.
10. K. Uno, *Principles of Political Economy* translated by T. Sekine, (Brighton: Harvester Press; Atlantic Highlands, N.J.: Humanities Press, 1980) pp. 33–4.
11. H. Braverman, *Labour and Monopoly Capital: The Degradation of Work in the Twentieth Century* (New York: Monthly Review Press, 1974).
12. Cf. R. Edwards, 'System of Control in the Labour Process', in R. Edwards *et al.* (ed.) *The Capitalist System* (Englewood Cliffs, N.J.: Prentice-Hall, 1978); R. Edwards, *Contested Terrain* (London: Heinemann, 1979); D. Gordon, R. Edwards, and M. Reich, *Segmented Work, Divided Workers* (Cambridge: Cambridge University Press, 1982).
13. S. Himmelweit, 'Value Relations and Divisions within the Working Class', *Science and Society* (Fall 1984) p. 334. Although I disagree with the treatment of the skilled-labour problem in this paper, the extension of theoretical implication of the problem to the international exchanges and the female workers' problem in the paper is both suggestive and interesting.
14. The effects of financial arrangements in this regard, however, should not be exaggerated. The value of skilled labour-power cannot substantially be reduced, as the borrowed educational costs must be paid back later from a part of the wages of skilled workers. Social mobility over generations would not be very much enhanced by this device, since the children of common workers would not have easy access to a loan for expensive educational costs usually requiring guarantees of sufficient earnings and assets among parents or relatives.
15. K. Marx, 'Critique of the Gotha Programme', in D. McLellan (ed.), *Karl Marx: Selected Writings* (Oxford: Oxford University Press, 1977) p. 567.
16. Marx, op. cit. pp. 568–9.
17. P. Sraffa, *Production of Commodities by Means of Commodities* (Cambridge: Cambridge University Press, 1960) p. 43.
18. Steedman, op. cit. p. 202.
19. Ibid. p. 202.
20. Ibid. pp. 151–4.
21. P. Sweezy, 'Marxian Value Theory and Crisis', in I. Steedman *et al.*, *The Value Controversy* (London: Verso and NLB, 1981) p. 26.
22. N. Okishio, [*Marxian Economics*] (Tokyo: Chikuma-shobo, 1977) p. 169.
23. P. Armstrong, A. Glyn and J. Harrison, 'In Defence of Value – A Reply to Ian Steedman', *Capital and Class*, 5 (Summer 1978) p. 8.
24. Ibid. p. 9.
25. S. Himmelweit and S. Mohun, 'Real Abstractions and Anomalous

Assumptions', in Steedman *et al.*, *The Value Controversy*, op. cit. p. 262.

26. In this regard Himmelweit and Mohun show a Rubinite tendency which we have criticised in the previous chapter and section, although in this paper they also basically accept a technical approach to defining the quantities of labour-value by the physical data of production.
27. Uno, op. cit. part I. See also M. Itoh, *Value and Crisis* (London: Pluto Press; New York: Monthly Review Press, 1980) ch. 2.
28. See also Itoh, op. cit. ch. 3.
29. The similarity and difference between Quesnay's *Tableau* and Marx's reproduction scheme, as well as comparison between Marx's scheme and Keynes's notions of aggregate, are analysed by S. Tsuru in his Supplement 'On the Reproduction Scheme' to P. Sweezy, *The Theory of Capitalist Development* (1942) (New York: Monthly Review Press, 1956).
30. For instance, as for I 4000c, the A group of capitalists in department I expends 2000 million pounds to purchase the means of production from the B group of capitalists in the same department, and then the money goes back to the A group through purchase of means of production by the B group from A. As for the transaction between the department I and II (I 1000$v$ + 1000$s$ = II$c$), let us assume that the capitalists in II initially expend 2000 million pounds to buy the means of production from the capitalists in I. Then, 1000 million pounds out of this 2000 million flows back directly from the capitalists in I to those in II through their purchase of the means of consumption. The rest of it, 1000 million pounds, is paid as wages to the workers in I, and thus indirectly goes back to the capitalists in II through purchase of the means of consumption on the part of those workers. Since money as the means of circulation for these transactions certainly runs faster than once a year, not so much as 2000 million pounds is necessary for exchange of I 4000$c$ and so forth. However, rapidity of the circulation of money does not affect the basic character or the route of its motion presented here.
31. The same points on the theoretical tasks and limits of the reproduction scheme are discussed in Uno, *Principles of Political Economy* (op. cit. p. 69.), and also in E. Mandel, *Late Capitalism*, translated by J. De Bres (London: NLB, 1975, p. 25).

## PART III THE MOTION OF CAPITALS AS A CONCRETE MECHANISM

### 7 Competition among Capitals

1. L. von Bortkiewicz, 'On the Correction of Marx's Fundamental Theoretical Construction in the Third Volume of Capital', in P. Sweezy (ed.), *Karl Marx and the Close of His System by E. von Böhm-Bawerk and Böhm-Bawerk's Criticism of Marx by Rudolf Hilferding* (New York: A. M. Kelley, 1966).
2. P. Sweezy, *The Theory of Capitalist Development* (1942) (New York: Monthly Review Press, 1956) p. 117.

3. Sweezy, ibid. p. 124.
4. Sweezy, ibid. pp. 122–3.
5. J. Winternitz, 'Values and Prices: A Solution of the So-called Transformation Problem', *The Economic Journal* (June 1948). The notation in *B–S* is maintained hereafter to express the main points of the various disputants.
6. K. May, 'Value and Price of Production: A Note on Winternitz's Solution', *The Economic Journal* (Dec 1948) pp. 596–9.
7. R. L. Meek, *Economics and Ideology and Other Essays* (London: Chapman & Hall, 1967) p. 153. Meek also maintains that the rate between total value and total variable capital must be equal to the rate between total price and total wages, by assuming the organic composition of capital in the wage-goods industry to be the social average. This point follows M. Dobb's position in his *Political Economy and Capitalism* (London: Routledge & Kegan Paul, 1937) pp. 72–3.
8. F. Seton, 'The "Transformation Problem"', *The Review of Economic Studies* (June 1957).
9. H. D. Dickinson, 'A Comment on Meek's "Note on the Transformation Problem"', *Economic Journal* (Dec 1956).
10. P. A. Samuelson, 'Understanding the Marxian Notion of Exploitation: A Summary of the So-called Transformation Problem between Marxian Values and Competitive Prices', *Journal of Economic Literature*, 9–2 (June 1971).
11. M. Morishima, *Marx's Economics* (Cambridge: Cambridge University Press, 1973) ch. 7.
12. Ibid. ch. 14.
13. I. Steedman, *Marx after Sraffa* (London: NLB, 1977) p. 202.
14. M. Desai, *Marxian Economic Theory* (London: Basil Blackwell & Mott, 1974) chs 8–12.
15. For instance, S. Himmelweit and S. Mohun, 'The Anomalies of Capital', *Capital and Class*, 7 (1978) among others referred to in note 7 of Chapter 5, can be interpreted in this way.
16. D. Yaffe, 'Value and Price in Marx's Capital', *Revolutionary Communist*, 1 (Jan 1975).
17. D. Laibman, 'Values and Prices of Production: The Political Economy of the Transformation Problem', *Science and Society*, XXXVII–4 (Winter 1973–4).
18. A. Shaikh, 'Marx's Theory of Value and the "Transformation Problem"', in J. Schwartz (ed.), *The Subtle Anatomy of Capitalism* (Santa Monica: Goodyear, 1977).
19. N. Okishio, [Convergence of Marx's "Transformation" Procedure] [*Riron-Keizaigaku*] (Aug 1973).
20. The essence of the analysis below, together with a review of the transformation controversy above, was originally presented in my essay 'A Study of Marx's Theory of Value', *Science and Society* (Fall 1976), which was later reprinted in my book *Value and Crisis* (London: Pluto Press; New York: Monthly Review Press, 1980).
21. In the theory of reproduction schemes Marx's division of two departments is fundamental in order to show how a basic economic rule

common to all the societies can be satisfied within capitalistic commodity economy. Marx's model of five spheres of production in the theory of prices of production has a different purpose and meaning. It is an illustration showing the principles of capitalist competition across many industrial spheres. The *complementary social relations* between the quantities of products from each industry (conceivable as a horizontal link) and the total quantities of means of production and final consumption goods socially wanted (conceivable as a vertical link) were beyond Marx's concern in the theory of prices of production. However, there must be a certain quantitative structure to be balanced, between outputs and inputs plus consumption, just as suggested in social input–output analysis, corresponding to a given technological system of production processes and a system of social needs. In this regard, a *B–S* type three-sector model can be regarded as illustrating such a social balance in all of the *n* kinds of products. Certainly, such a balance between outputs and inputs cannot be maintained without disturbance, but is tendentially realised through the incessant oversupply and shortages of goods and the resulting fluctuation of prices in a capitalist economy.

22. This applies to the marginal least-fertile condition of land as a gold mine, if gold production actually depends on the different fertility of mines. In other words, the quantity of labour embodied in a unit of gold to define *z* must be counted on the basis of the least-fertile kind of gold mine which is socially necessary. The magnitude of socially necessary gold contains a sort of elasticity, as it includes various luxurious uses, and gold bars to be hoarded besides direct monetary use. The amount of the supply of gold money can also be flexible, depending on the existing stock of gold outside the money-form in addition to newly produced gold. As a result, the relative purchasing power of gold money in a market would be relatively stable, in comparison with the case where it directly reflects the fluctuating relations between annual production and socially necessary gold as money. Nevertheless, the law of value would also eventually regulate the purchasing power of the money commodity gold in the long run on the basis of the conditions of production.
23. The socially necessary labour allocation among spheres of industry cannot be totally determined just by the physical data of technical processes of production and the material contents of real wages. Another condition determining the allocation of social labour would be the quantitative composition of goods socially necessary for final consumption, or what Marx called a system of 'social needs' (e.g. III, p. 774). The quantitative composition of social needs for various goods is certainly affected, but not totally determined by the level of the substantial value of labour-power and the technological conditions of production or the level of productive power. When a type of commodity is overproduced beyond the social need for it, the labour-substance of value embodied in it cannot fully be realised for its producers. Thus, a system of social needs serves as a constraint in allocating social labour, and as a passive framework or condition for the working of the law of value. Its role is not positive but passive, because capital can adjust its scale of production so as to suit social needs, whatever composition those needs may become,

on the basis of objective conditions of production and the level of real wages, being relatively independent at least for a certain period of time from the motion of social needs. Such a relatively hard structure of conditions of production, being comparatively independent of social needs, must be a basis for the labour theory of value as well as for the Sraffian theory, and must be borne in mind also in the analysis of market value below.

24. Marx did not write the content of ch. 4, 'The Effect of the Turnover on the Rate of Profit' in the third volume of *Capital*, except its title. Engels provided the content, although in a somewhat mechanical way, by calculating the effect of different periods of the turnover of capital on the rate of profit in terms of value-prices. As a result, the effect of possible fluctuations or differences in the circulation period and the cost of circulation upon the rate of profit has not much been investigated. K. Uno suggested the problem, but emphasized onesidedly, in my view, the difficulty for industrial capitals to treat the circulation period and cost as a part of the objective basis for the equalisation of the rate of profit, when he wrote as follows:

    'The inequalities of the rate of profit in different branches of industry caused by the differences in the length of the production-period can be settled by the conversion of values into production-prices, . . . The circulation-period, in contrast, must in general be expected to differ with every individual capital, although there may be a few instances in which the length of circulation-period is determined by the quality of the product itself. The inequalities of profit-rates due to the individual differences in the circulation-period cannot be eliminated by the conversion of values into production-prices. The equalisation of profit must be completed, as will be explained later, by the formation of commercial capital which relieves industrial capital of the unproductive costs of circulation by specialising in the operation of buying and selling commodities.' K. Uno, *Principles of Political Economy*, translated by T. Sekine (Brighton: Harvester Press; Atlantic Heights, N. J.: Humanities Press, 1980) p. 79.

25. Conversely, correction of the imbalance in the labour-allocation among industrial spheres and the resulting anomaly in the circulation-period and its costs would surely be slowed down and hampered, when fluctuations of market prices are avoided by monopoly capitals. This effect would also be connected with the role of increased scale of fixed capital in the process of production.
26. Uno, op. cit. p. 83. See also my essay 'Marx's Theory of Market Value', in *Value and Crisis* (op. cit.), which was originally written in collaboration with N. Yokokawa.
27. Marx's *Capital*, vol. III, locates the theory of ground-rent in part 6, which is the last part theoretically to develop the forms of distribution of surplus-value. It clarifies the secondary position of the landed property, and ground-rent as a basis of a social class in a capitalist economy, especially in comparison with D. Ricardo's *On the Principles of Political Economy and Taxation*, which devoted the second chapter to rent, prior

to the chapters on wages and profit to be analysed very much in view of the tendential increase of rent due to the law of decreasing return of land. Ricardo's theoretical composition reflects his political opposition to the corn laws and the power of landed interests. In contrast, Marx's theoretical treatment of rent as well as its location in *Capital* shows that the law of motion of capital itself determines the passive and secondary position of landed property under capitalism. This implies that the central socio-economic problem is not in the relation of distribution of annual products between the landed interests and the industrial capitalists, but in the capitalist relation of production based upon exploitation of wage-workers. The subjugation of landed property to the law of motion of capital would become clearer if we located the theory of rent just after the theory of market price of production in accord with the main contents as its application.

28. There must be a conceptual gap between modern landed property and capitalistic landed property, although we cannot concretely deal with various forms of modern landed property other than the capitalistic in the basic theory of capitalism. Marx seems to identify modern and capitalistic landed property, and not a few Marxians follow him in this regard. For example, among four 'principal features of modern landed property' summarised by R. Murray, we read: 'a) property rights could be bought and sold', and 'c) the landlord's payment in rent was no longer directly appropriated from agricultural labour, but received as a residual payment in cash from a capitalist farmer' (R. Murray, 'Value and Theory of Rent, part I', *Capital and Class*, 3, Autumn 1977, p. 113). In my view, feature a) is essential for modern landed property in general, but it is often not combined with the specifically capitalistic feature c). As a historical precondition for the development of capitalist production in urban industries, dissolution of the feudal ownership of land and establishment of modern private ownership were generally essential, but establishment of fully capitalistic farming based upon wage-workers in rural areas was not a requisite, and was actually dispensed with as in the case of Japanese capitalist development from the Meiji Restoration in 1868. Fully capitalistic farms with the feature c) were not totally dominant even in England. According to statistics, small farm holdings operating on less than 100 acres which could be maintained mainly with work-forces within a family occupied 75.4 per cent of the number of farms, and 28.9 per cent of the cultivated land reported in England and Wales agriculture in 1885 (J. Clapham, *An Economic History of Modern Britain*, book II (1933) pp. 264–5).

In T. Ouchi, [*Ground-Rent and Landed Property*] (Tokyo: Tokyo University Press, 1958) and H. Hidaka, [*Studies in the Theory of Ground-Rent*] Tokyo: Jichoscha, 1962), the authors asserted that the logical necessity of formation of landed property must be shown through the theory of ground-rent starting from non-existence of landed property. This was to emphasise that the logical contents of capitalistic landed property should be given only through the theory of capitalistic ground-rent. In my opinion, however, this position obscures the conceptual distinction between modern landed property in general and specifically capitalistic landed property, and tends to neglect the important historical fact that the formation of modern private ownership of land was an essential precondition for the birth and the development of capitalist production.

29. To quote Marx, 'as far as land for building is concerned, Adam Smith has discussed how the basis of its rent, as with all non-agricultural land, is governed by agricultural rent proper (book I, Chapter XI, 2 and 3)' (III, p. 908). Though the logic of determining the amount of rent is quite similar to agricultural rent, non-agricultural rent in urban areas cannot be governed by agricultural rent proper as Smith has defined. For one thing, the rent of land for buildings in urban area 'is characterized by the predominant influence that location exerts here on the differential rent'. It is characterised also 'by the prevalence of a monopoly price in many cases, and particularly the most shameless exploitation of poverty' (III, p. 908).

30. This position was represented by L. Y. Lyubimof, [*Theoretical Outline of Ground Rent*] (1930), translated by S. Matsumura (Tokyo: Nauka, 1934). The position was regarded as orthodox, and was followed up by Japanese Koza-ha theorists like K. Yamada in his [*A Critique of Controversy on the Theory of Rent*] (Tokyo: Doyusha, 1948) among others. Against this it has also been asserted by other Japanese Marxian theorists in the Rono-ha and then the Uno Schools, like I. Sakisaka in his [*Studies in the Theory of Rent*] (Tokyo: Kaizo-sha, 1930) and K. Susuki in his [*Controversy on the Theory of Rent*] (Tokyo: Keiso-shobo, 1952) that the source of differential rent must be a part of total redistributed social surplus-value. See ch. 1 of my *Value and Crisis* (op. cit.) as for Koza-ha, Rono-ha and Uno Schools, as well as a brief outline of Japanese controversy on the theory of rent. R. Murray coincides rather with the orthodox Russian and Koza-ha line in this regard when he states: 'The increase in [differential – M. I.] rent therefore represented the appropriation of increased surplus value produced by agricultural labour, rather than a deduction from a given quantum of surplus value in the economy as a whole.' ('Value and Theory of Rent, part I'. op. cit. p. 103). To my regret I cannot agree with this, while I certainly agree with Murray's general proposition that 'in all cases rent is a deduction from total social value, and is limited by the total value produced by labour' (ibid. p. 102).

31. The conceptual distinction between real wages, nominal wages as the form of value of labour-power, and the substance of value of labour-power must clearly be kept in mind here. It is important especially for the study of the motion of differential rent and the value of labour-power. Suppose, for example, that the worst type *A* land is pushed out of cultivation in a reduced scale of reproduction (historically, say in a former period). Then the type *B* land in Table 7.7 would become the regulative condition for the market price of production. The governing price of wheat would decline to 30 sh. a quarter so as to make differential rent 0 on the land *B*, just 30 sh. on *C*, and 60 sh. on *D*. 9 qrs. of wheat production now yields only 90 sh. of differential rent, whereas 10 qrs. of wheat production yielded in Table 7.7 360 sh. of rent. In maintaining the

same level of real wages to give the same quantity of wheat per hour of labour, the nominal wages as the form of labour power are to be halved as for the portion of wheat. The substance of value of labour-power obtainable through its form of value, however, is not reduced so much, since 'the real production price' would decline from 24 sh. a quarter to just 20 sh. a quarter (180 sh / 9 qrs.). Thus, the quantitative changes in this case can be ordered from smaller to larger upon the same level of real wages; the substance of value of labour-power, nominal wages as the form of value of labour-power, and the amount of differential rent in its substance and form.

32. However, Uno did not thoroughly clarify the substantial source of differential rent, and remained just to quote Marx's notion of 'false social value' which was paid by society considered as a consumer (Uno, *Principles of Political Economy*, op. cit. p. 98, p. 104). He distinguished extra profit as 'false social value' to be converted into differential rent from extra surplus-value obtained in the process of improvement in productive methods, on the ground that the latter, unlike the former, could be recognised as the cost of innovation common to all societies as a part of general economic rule. Although this distinction is suggestive and relevant to a clarification of different social functions and characters of two sorts of extra profit, it would not establish that either of them has some special source outside of the total surplus-labour as the substance of social surplus-value. My position is thus *different from Uno's* on this point.
33. Uno also followed Marx here in defining absolute rent within a gap between the value and the price of production of agricultural product (ibid. p. 102). It coincides with Uno's treatment of the transformation problem mostly following Marx. It was contribution of T. Ouchi and H. Hidaka (in op. cit.) among Uno theorists that initiated the theoretical critique and solution of the problem here left over since Marx.

## 8 The Mobilisation of Capitals

1. When monopolistic capitals become dominant the competitive motion of market prices of their products tend to be avoided. As a result, the informational function of market in readjusting the misallocation of social labour would be reduced, and the effect of the prolongation of selling time together with the degree of idle capacity in factories would become so much more important in determining both the individual rate of profit and the necessary direction of the adjustment of the labour-allocation.
2. Marx states at the beginning of part IV of the third volume of *Capital* the following: 'Merchant's or trading capital is divided into two forms of species, commercial capital and money-dealing capital, which we shall go on to distinguish in such detail as is needed in order to analyse capital in its basic inner structure. And this is all the more necessary in so far as modern economics, and even in its best representatives, lump trading capital and industrial capital directly together and in fact completely

overlook trading capital's characteristic peculiarities.' (III, p. 379). Even though money dealing concerning the technical movement of money in the process of circulation, such as storage, sending or collection, and in particular international exchange business, was an important aspect of activities of merchants' capital as well as of money-lending capital in the precapitalist periods, it cannot form an independent species of capital in most cases. In a capitalist society money-dealing becomes mostly absorbed as an aspect of banking business, which must be separable theoretically from commercial capital. Therefore, it would be too formalistic to assume that two forms of capital in circulation, commodity and money, would become separate objects of two different species of trading capital. Although bank capital is also a sort of trading capital its main business is not concerned with the mere technical movement of money, as we shall see in Section 8.2.

3. In his analyses of the costs of circulation in ch. 6 of the second volume of *Capital*, Marx defines the costs arising 'from the peculiar nature of commodity production' or of 'capitalist commodity production' as unproductive, not entering into the values of the commodities but constituting deductions, losses of value, in distinction from the costs which are common to all social production. (II, pp. 217, 225). Although workers are exploited in a sense that they perform, say, 8 hours of labour in a working day and receive say, 4 hours of labour as the substance of value of their labour-power, the workers employed for such unproductive costs of circulation cannot add to the values of the commodities in this regard. On the other hand, workers employed by commercial capitals as well as those in other spheres of the tertiary sector would add to value and surplus-value in the aspect of their labour which is common to all social production such as some parts of storage, transportation or repair. The relative growth of the tertiary sector in the advanced capitalist countries, therefore, would not actually mean a directly proportional growth of unproductive labour.
4. Investment of commercial capital into pure expenses of circulation, as *faux frais* (II, p. 214) with regards to value-formation, would thus contrariwise produce the positive effect of reducing idle or negative portions of capital and costs overall. This is a point theoretically emphasised by S. Yamaguchi, [*Competition and Commercial Capital*] (Tokyo: Iwanami-Shateu, 1983).
5. For instance, the high rate of saving of Japanese households has structurally not changed much in the last three decades and still remains above 17 per cent in 1983 in comparison with 5.2 per cent in US and 7 per cent in UK, despite the increased weight of the tertiary sector, conspicuous urbanisation, and a stagnating workers' income since the middle of 1970s.
6. C. Panico, 'Marx's Analysis of the Relationship between the Rate of Interest and the Rate of Profit', *Cambridge Journal of Economics*, vol. 4–4 (Dec 1980) p. 373.
7. B. Fine, 'Banking Capital and the Theory of Interest', *Science and Society*, XLIX–4 (Winter 1985–6) p. 391. Although Fine does not and probably cannot refer to it, the same point of correcting Marx's numerical

example was already presented by D. I. Rozenberg, [*Commentary for Capital*] (Russian first edition, 1931, second edition, 1961. Japanese second edition translated by M. Udaka and T. Soejima, Tokyo: Aoki-Shoten, 1962) vol. 4, p. 239.

8. K. Uno, *Principles of Political Economy*, translated by T. Sekine (Brighton: Harvester Press; Atlantic Heights, N.J.: Humanities Press, 1980.) p. 114.
9. Giant joint-stock banks with national networks of branches were formed in England through the merger movement in the last quarter of nineteenth century. 'Until the last quarter of the century the English banking system remained what is known as a "unit" banking system. At a time when the financial needs of different districts differed even more widely than they do now, a localised banking system could function efficiently only through a sort of central pool by means of which the credit surpluses of one type of district (the agricultural areas) and the credit deficiencies of the other type of district (the industrial areas) could find their level. The Discount Market (and its ultimate corollary, the short-loan market) proved such a pool, as well as the conduit-pipes by which it was tapped and fed.' (W. T. C. King, *History of the London Discount Market*, London: George Routledge & Sons, 1936, pp. xii–xiii). Unlike the later branch-banking system, banks in a unit-banking system were relatively small in size and were more competitive with industrial and commercial capitals. And their major form of credit was discounting commercial bills of exchange, not yet so much dealing with cheques.
10. The qualitative division of profit into interest and profit of enterprise means that the division of profit into these two parts becomes universal, and not confined to the profit earned by borrowed capital. As a result, even 'the capitalist who works with his own capital, as well as the one working with borrowed capital, divides his gross profit into interest that accrues to him as owner, as lender of his own capital to himself, and profit of enterprise, which accrues to him as an active, functioning capitalist' (III, p. 498). This line of theory did not exist in the tradition of British classical school. It was G. Ramsay, *An Essay on the Distribution of Wealth* (Edinburgh, 1836, e.g. pp. 193, 210), who, after Ricardo, developed this type of theory, following J.-B. Say or H. Storch and influenced Marx on this point. However, the amount of profit remaining after deducting interest for his own capital would generally be more or less in proportion to the amount of his own capital, and cannot totally be attributed to capitalistic activity as entrepreneurship even from a common-sense view.
11. K. Uno reordered the structure of Marx's theory of interest in part V of the third volume of *Capital*, and began his theory of interest as a form of surplus-value directly from the theory of credit system in his *Principles of Political Economy* (op. cit.). However, Uno attempts to maintain Marx's theory of the qualitative division of profit, by emphasising the special character of commercial capital representing capitalistic activity in circulation. In Uno's *Principles*, given a general rate of interest in the money market, the qualitative division of profit into interest and profit of enterprise is initiated in commercial capital and then universalised as the

highest form of fetishism of capital as automatically interest-bearing capital. Although a fetish belief in automatically interest-bearing capital would surely appear among capitalists, it may not be linked with the notion of the qualitative division of profit, and it seems rather difficult to show as an essential form of appearance of the basic mechanisms of the law of motion of capital. Thus I am sceptical of the theoretical possibility and relevance of presenting the qualitative division of profit into interest and profit of enterprise despite of Uno's attempt.

12. Marx quotes W. Leatham to show the actual size of the total amount of commercial credit. The amount of the bills of exchange 'for the whole of the year of 1839 . . . to be £528,493,842'. The bills of exchange make up 'one component part greater in amount than all the rest put together' (III, p. 526). This £528 millions is even greater than the estimated total gross national income of £452 in 1841 (cf. B. R. Mitchell, *Abstract of British Historical Statistics*, Cambridge: Cambridge University Press, 1962, p. 366). According to the evidence of W. Newmarch to the Bank Act Committee in 1857, 'The total circulation of banknotes in the United Kingdom, including these £1 notes, is £39 million.' 'The gold circulation is £70 million.' (III p. 656). When the currency school, an antecedent of the recent monetarists, following the quantity theory of money, asserted the need to control the quantity of bank notes in accordance with the motion of the amount of gold in a country, in order to remove strong fluctuations of prices and crises, they clearly failed to take into consideration the possibility of an elastic increase in demand so as to cause fluctuations in prices by means of commercial credit from below. While the banking school criticised this weakness of the currency school, they tended to assume one-sidedly the soundness of all commercial bills, neglecting the actual possibility of utilising commercial credit in speculative and fictitious trading.
13. Loanable-money capital gathered into banks must be conceived, in our basic theory, also as springing from idle-money capital in the turnover of industrial and commercial capitals, such as depreciation funds, accumulation funds or reserves for price fluctuations. In other words, monetary funds which are utilizable for industrial and commercial capitals to earn profits would not be used for loans, or mobilised for credit, especially as the rate of interest obtained by loans would generally be lower than the rate of profit earned by actual investment. Marx's position at the beginning of his abstract formal theory of interest-bearing capital, as follows is not agreeable in this regard. 'On the basis of capitalist production, money – can be transformed into capital. . . . In this way the money receives, besides the use-value which it possesses as money, an additional use-value, namely the ability to function as capital. Its use-value here consists precisely in the profit that it produces when transformed into capital. In this capacity of potential capital, as a means to the production of profit, it becomes a commodity, but a commodity of a special kind. Or what comes to the same thing, capital becomes a commodity.' (III, pp. 459–60). From the view of the owner, only money which he *cannot* transform into real capital would be mobilisable for credit. And what is lent out, even through banks in the form of interest-

bearing capital, is still money, a special commodity as money-fund, and is not yet a commodity form of capital itself in its capacity to gain profit through a real process. We have to distinguish the commodity form of capital realised in joint-stock capital in a capital market, from the commodity form of money in the form of interest-bearing capital in the credit system, in spite of Marx's proposition above.

14. According to Engels, 'there is no advance [of capital – M.I.] at all, but simply an ordinary purchase and sale' in the case of discounting a bill of exchange at a bank, whereas there is 'a genuine capital advance' in a case where a capitalist 'obtains the sum advanced by the bank on his personal credit.' (III, pp. 587–8). It must be stressed, however, that the discount of commercial bills is the basic form of bank credit and by far more important than the case of advances on personal credit, and further that it is a part of a total mechanism of the credit system where idle capitals can be mobilised to accelerate the motion of the valorisation of capitals even in the form of the transactions between commercial bills and money funds as a special commodity. Besides, the sale of a commercial bill to a bank leaves the capitalist the responsibility 'to the bank in default of payment' as the last endorser of the bill (III, p. 588), unlike an ordinary sale of a commodity.

    R. Hilferding, *Finance Capital*, (translated by M. Watnick and S. Gordon, London, Boston and Henley: Routledge & Kegan Paul, 1981) introduced a new conceptual distinction between circulation credit and capital (investment) credit to the basic theory of credit in his ch. 5. The distinction comes at least partly from Engels's formulation above. The notion of circulation credit is in 'a substitute for money' by facilitating the transfer of commodities without the use of money (p. 83), and in this regard includes bank credit in the form of the discounting the commercial bills. In contrast, 'credit which converts idle money of whatever kind – into active money capital is called capital (or investment) credit' (p. 87). Though *Finance Capital* contains first important contributions to the Marxian study of the credit system, the conceptual distinction here is confusing, as bank credit in the form of discounting also substantially converts idle money into active money capital in the hands of capitalists seeking discount. Therefore, Hilferding's distinction must not be substituted for Marx's distinction between commercial and bank credit. The actual background for Hilferding's new conception of capital credit was the way in which German banks gave huge amounts of long-term credit to industrial capitalists in their construction of fixed capitals, eventually so as to make up the German type of finance capital under the control of the banks. This is a case of how carelessness about the historical basis of theoretical abstraction can cause confusion in parts of the basic theory of capitalism.

15. The relative independence in the creation of various forms of private and individual bank debt and credit continues to exist through the historically changing organisations of the credit system. It is a source of difficulty defining and measuring the quantity of money even under the system of 'managed' currency, with an even greater difficulty for the state to effectively control total demand by means of manipulation of the quan-

tity of money supplied, as we see in the recent renewed experiments of monetarist policies.

16. In 1844 when Peel's Bank Act was passed there were £8.63 million country bank notes in circulation besides £21 million Bank of England notes inside England and Wales. There were also important banks of issue beside these in Scotland and Ireland. The British credit system in the period of liberalism was developed very similarly to the international forms of credit transaction, in accordance with the fundamental character of capitalism which converted the originally external forms of economic interactions into the internal social order.
17. Actually the Bank of England did not then issue bank notes smaller than £5, even with their right to issue their notes as legal tender. A £5 bank note was definitely useless in paying and receiving weekly wages of say 12 shillings (£0.6) at most for women spinners.
18. For instance, increasing opportunities for lending abroad seem to have exceeded the tendential increase of the rentier class and their loanable assets in the UK from the last quarter of nineteenth century, so as to keep the rate of interest higher than the level favourable for domestic industrial investment. In contrast, in Japan in the post-Second World War period, rapid industrial accumulation was promoted by the relatively low rate of interest maintained by a high rate of saving by the general population despite of lower numbers in the rentier class.
19. Panico, op. cit. p. 377.
20. There is a methodological controversy as to whether the functions of joint-stock capital can or cannot be presented in the basic principles of political economy among Japanese Uno theorists. Uno himself referred to the form of the industrial joint-stock corporation as just a factual example of capital as automatically interest-bearing capital, which arose as a result of the qualitative division of profit into interest and profit of enterprise. In his words, 'The diffusion of the joint-stock-company (corporate) system in industry, promoted by the employment of increasingly heavier fixed-capital equipment, ushers in the epoch of the so-called 'finance capital' and entails a host of new phenomena quite beyond the scope of the theory of pure capitalism.' (Uno, op. cit. p. 125). This accords with his basic methodology of deducing the theory of pure capitalism as the set of basic principles from the historical experience of British capitalism which developed increasingly toward a perfect capitalist society with three major classes up until the middle of the nineteenth century. Among his followers, K. Suzuki in his ed. [*Principles of Political Economy*], 2 vols (Tokyo: University of Tokyo Press, 1960–2), H. Iwata in [*World Capitalism*] (Tokyo: Miraisha, 1964) and myself in [*The Theory of Value and Capital*] (Tokyo: Iwanami-Shoten, 1981) insisted on broadening the historical basis of abstraction of the basic principles for one thing so as to enable a more complete basic theory of joint-stock capital and its substantial social functions. This position, however, does not negate the need for more concrete studies of different features and types of development of giant joint-stock companies which make up finance capital in various countries at higher levels of research. In respect to the stages theory of capitalist development, the

special development of German finance capital including the specifically close relations with banks must be carefully emphasised in contrast to other types of finance capital in the UK and US. However, the form and the functions of joint-stock capital are still common to these different types of finance capitals and enable us to analyse them, in my view, on the basic principles only if we do *not* adhere to UK capitalist development up until the middle of the nineteenth century as our basis of abstraction.

21. Marx did not clarify the limitations to the centralisation of capitals when he said, referring to the role of joint-stock companies in facilitating the fusion of capitals: 'In any given branch of industry centralization would reach its extreme limit if all the individual capitals invested there were fused into a single capital. In a given society this limit would be reached only when the entire social capital was united in the hands of either a single capitalist or a single company.' (II, p. 779). The primitive stage of large-scale enterprise in the form of joint-stock capital as with railways might have enabled him abstractly to speculate on such extreme cases. In contrast, on the basis of the mature stage of giant corporations, V. I. Lenin sharply pointed out that 'not in every branch of industry are there large-scale enterprises' (V. I. Lenin, *Imperialism, the Highest Stage of Capitalism*, 1917, Peking: Foreign Languages Press, 1973, p. 14). Even in heavy industries where large-scale enterprises dominate, perfect monopoly by a single company has not been achieved. I believe that this is not a mere accidental or immatured fact but logically related to the fundamental restrictions on capitalism, based as it is upon the individualistic profit-seeking motive. Even giant joint-stock capitals cannot escape such a restriction.
22. The monopolistic behaviour of large-scale joint-stock capitals is certainly implied here. Unlike the prices of production, however, the determination of monopoly prices cannot be presented in the basic principles. All the concrete conditions such as the range of the major market, the nature or the elasticity of demand, the structure of monopolistic organisations and their strength among corporations, competition with foreign rivals, etc., which should be analysed at more concrete levels of researches, beyond those basic principles, must effect the levels of monopoly prices. Excepting the vague definition that monopoly prices enable companies to obtain higher rates of profit than the general rate of profit or the rate available in free competition, by shifting either a portion of surplus-value from other capitals or a part of the value of the income of workers and the middle class, we cannot have much to say about monopoly prices at our present level of discussion. Similarly, monopoly capital, which must be analysed in its all concrete forms of organisation, and the effect on social economic processes as well as on state policies, cannot be explicitly discussed here.
23. Hilferding, *Finance Capital*, op. cit. pp. 118–19.
24. Ibid. p. 119.
25. Ibid. pp. 115–16.
26. Ibid. p. 112. *Gründergewinn* might better be translated into English as 'founder's gain' rather than 'promoter's profit'. Actually it can be ob-

tained by the founders of an enterprise when it is converted into a joint-stock company, not merely by the promoters pushing forward such conversion and sale of stocks. However, Hilferding assumes a bank which promotes the conversion of individual firms into joint-stock companies, initially accepting and getting hold of the whole stock to be sold eventually in the capital market. In such a case a large portion of *Gründergewinn* often actually flew to the bank as a promoter. At the same time the initial investment obtaining the whole stock of the enterprise is conceived, not as the actual amount of investment of the founders, but as the *estimated* price of the annual yield of the enterprise ($Y$) in comparison with the average rate of profit ($p$); thus in Hilferding's formula 'promoter's profit' ($P$) is defined as follows:

$$P = \frac{100Y}{d} - \frac{100Y}{P}$$

where the dividend (yield) ($d$) is conceived as identical to the rate of interest (ibid. p. 114). The item deduced can be nearer to the actual amount of investment if the founders of a firm can manage to convert their own firm into joint-stock company and sell the stocks themselves or through a stockbroker paying a smaller amount of commission and costs.

27. Ibid. pp. 111–12.
28. Ibid. p. 129.
29. Historically the commodity form of land and its pricing through the capitalisation of ground-rent, is much older than the growth of joint-stock industrial companies. The formation of a capital market initially mainly to trade state bonds at prices determined by the capitalised sum of the annual interest payment from the government, estimated at the current rate of interest, also long preceded it. Even the form of the joint-stock company itself was seen already in the stage of mercantilism as a form of organisation combining merchants' capitals for joint ventures. Thus industrial capitals did not here create those forms through which they organise themselves either, as in many other cases that we have seen. It must be noted, however, that the form of joint-stock capital and the way of capitalising their annual profit rates did not become popular with industrial firms throughout the whole stage of liberalism, and that such forms spread throughout the central industries later, in the stage of imperialism, and thus completed commoditisation of the whole economy.
30. Since Hilferding's concept of finance capital was based too exclusively upon the experience of Germany, especially concerning the role of the banks, P. Sweezy in *The Theory of Capitalist Development* (New York: Monthly Review Press, 1956, pp. 267–9) proposed among others a more appropriate term to define the dominant capitals in the latest stage of capitalism, 'monopoly capital' rather than 'finance capital'. The term 'finance capital' can be maintained as a key concept for the dominant capital of our age and not confined to the German type, if we can establish a basic theory of joint-stock capital within the basic principles,

as a common logical standard for the analyses of the dominant corporations with their national differences. In such analyses of finance capital, monopolistic organisations and their workings must certainly be one of the most important aspects to be clarified. An advantage of the term 'finance capital' over 'monopoly capital' is in its wider implications, in seeing the importance of the financial form and organisation for the motion of capital. The basic theory of joint-stock capital would serve as the frame of reference for such a concept of finance capital which emphatically includes monopolistic elements in its actual process.

## 9 Business Cycles and Crises

1. G. Haberler, *Prosperity and Depression* (London: George Allen & Unwin, 1937, 4th ed., 1964) p. 7.
2. R. Hilferding, *Finance Capital*, translated by M. Watnick and S. Gordon (London, Boston and Henley: Routledge & Kegan Paul, 1981) p. 261.
3. Further documentation from Marx's writings is presented in M. Itoh, *Value and Crisis* (London: Pluto Press; New York: Monthly Review Press, 1980) ch. 4, with an analysis of the formation of Marx's theory of crisis from *Grundrisse* via *Theories of Surplus Value* to *Capital*. It is noteworthy that the labour-power-shortage variant of the excess capital theory was formulated for the first time in *Capital*.
4. Such an attitude has been dominant in the so-called 'orthodox Marxian' position, underwriting the under-consumptionist variant of crisis theory against other variants. A similar attitude is still seen among contemporary Marxian theorists who sometimes have different positions. For instance, J. Weeks denounces my labour-power-shortage type of crisis theory as 'a great leap backwards . . . in favour of Ricardo's [contribution]', suggesting 'better marks' for 'the more sophisticated brands of under-consumptionism' in his article 'The Process of Accumulation and the "Profit Squeeze" Hypothesis' (*Science and Society*, Fall 1979, pp. 259, 279), and B. Fine and L. Harris define my analysis as 'a neo-Ricardian view' in their *Rereading 'Capital'* (London: Macmillan Press, 1979, p. 80) vaguely favouring the rising organic composition variant of excess-capital theory. In my paper 'On Marx's Theory of Accumulation: A Reply to Weeks' (*Science and Society*, Spring 1981, p. 76), I have already criticised these denunciations as unfair and confusing, since one important aspect of Marx's formulation of crisis theory found rather finally and uniquely in *Capital*, must then also be called 'Ricardian' or 'neo-Ricardian', while Ricardo and neo-Ricardians have never attempted to build up a crisis theory.
5. M. Tugan-Baranowsky, *Les Crises Industrielles en Angleterre* (translated by J. Schapiro, Paris: M. Giarde & É. Brière, 1913), and Hilferding, *Finance Capital*, op. cit. part 4, among others, was a representative example of the disequilibrium type of excess commodity theory of crisis. Against these, K. Kautsky, 'Krisentheorien' and 'Finanzkapital und Krisen', in *Neue Zeit* (20, no. 2, 1901–2, 29, no. 2, 1911), or N. Bukharin, *Imperialism and the Accumulation of Capital*, translated by R. Wichmann, (New

York and London: Monthly Review Press, 1972), asserted the under-consumptionist variant of crisis theory as an orthodox Marxian position. In these classical arguments initiated by Tugan-Baranowsky, Marx's theory of the reproduction schemes was much utilised in order to show the difficulties in maintaining the balance between various items in the schemes, although essentially it was an unsuitable theory for proving the logical inevitability, and not merely the possibility, of periodical crises, as we saw in Chapter 6, Section 6.3. More recently, P. Sweezy, *The Theory of Capitalist Development* (1942, New York: Monthly Review Press, 1956), ch. 10, and his other writings follow the orthodox Marxian position of the under-consumptionist type.

6. N. Okishio, [*The Theory of Accumulation*] (Tokyo: Chikuma-Shobo, 1976) for instance, presents a sort of sophisticated type of under-consumptionism in a model of the cumulative process of disequilibrium between the effective demand of wage-workers and the increasing productive power of society. In his model, incessant shortage of effective demand due to restricted real wages can be balanced more than sufficiently by investment demand so as to cause a rise in commodity prices or inflation in the phase of prosperity. With this rise in prices, real wages must fall more and more so that reproduction of labour-power becomes impossible to maintain. A reversal of such a process of accumulation through crises is necessary for capitalism to survive as a social system. Though Okishio sees the operation of the law of value in the reversal of the cumulative upward and downward process of disequilibrium in turn, he tends to negate the working of the law of value in readjusting the disequilibrium between demand and supply with relative stability in the process of prosperity. It is also difficult for me to agree with his recognition that real wages must fall in the actual process of prosperity when in fact expanding employment creates a shortage of labour-power.
7. H. Grossmann, *Das Akkumulations und Zusammenbrucksgesetz des kapitalistischen Systems* (Leipzig: Hirschfeld, 1929), assumes an increase of variable capital of 5 per cent a year and of constant capital of 10 per cent with a constant rate of surplus-value of 100 per cent in order to show the breakdown of a capitalist system due to the disappearance of the portion of surplus-value for consumption by capitalists. E. Preiser, 'Das Wesen der Marxschen Krisentheorie', in *Festschrift für Franz Oppenheimer – Wirtschaft und Gesellschaft* (Frankfurt: Frankfurter Societats-Druckerei, 1924) assumes a fall in the rate of surplus-value, as in the labour-power-shortage theory, in his example of the sudden decline of the rate of profit. M. Dobb, *Political Economy and Capitalism* (London: Routledge & Kegan Paul, 1937) ch. 4, and E. Mandel, *Late Capitalism*, translated by J. De Bres (London: New Left Books, 1975) combines this variant of crisis theory with varying circumstances in a multicausal approach. D. Yaffe, 'The Marxian Theory of Crisis, Capital and the State', in *Bulletin of the Conference of Socialist Economists*' (Winter 1972), P. Bullock and D. Yaffe, 'Inflation, the Crisis, and the Postwar Boom', in *Revolutionary Communist*, no. 3/4 (Nov 1975) stand purely upon the law of tendential fall of profit rate as the causal basis for crisis. A. Shaikh, 'An Introduction to the History of Crisis Theories', in URPE

*U.S. Capitalism in Crisis* (New York: Monthly Review, Press, 1978) assesses this latter type of approach favourably.

8. Outside of Japanese Uno School, O. Bauer, 'Die Akkumulation des Kapitals', in *Neue Zeit* (31, no. 1, 1913), and P. Sweezy, ch. 9 of *The Theory of Capitalist Development*, have attempted to deduce this variant of crisis theory from Marx, though with less sophistication in relation to the theories of accumulation and credit. As representative works in the Uno School, K. Uno, [*Theory of Crisis*] (Tokyo: Iwanami-Shoten, 1953) followed up by M. Itoh, [*Credit and Crisis*] (Tokyo: University of Tokyo Press, 1973), and *Value and Crisis* (op. cit.) can be mentioned.
9. For example, Weeks, op. cit. in note 4, p. 268.
10. I shall much utilise my paper 'On Marx's Theory of Accumulation', cited in note 4 in this section. The following summary is mostly extracted from this paper.
11. Sometimes Marx's theory of capital accumulation, assuming a constant composition of capital, is interpreted as being concerned with only the primitive stage of capitalism, prior to the Industrial Revolution. But this interpretation cannot be satisfactory, since Marx clearly refers to the complete cyclical motion of wages and the labour market precisely in reference to the established business cycles which were absent in such a primitive stage. Nevertheless, it is theoretically premature to construct a complete theory of business cycles without taking into consideration a rise in the organic composition of capital in the process of capital accumulation.
12. Sweezy, op. cit. p. 149.
13. K. Marx, *Grundrisse*, translated by M. Nicolaus, (Harmondsworth, Middx: Penguin Books, 1973) p. 766.
14. For instance in the period of the high rate of economic growth by post-war Japanese capitalism, while the organic composition of capital considerably rose, the employment of wage-workers did not at all decrease but absolutely and continuously increased. In the period from 1955 to 1970, for example, despite a more than threefold rise in Japanese business capital per worker in 1970 US dollars, the ratio of the active working population in agriculture and forestry fell from 36.1 per cent to 16.5 per cent as a result of its continuous absorption into the urban work-force. The over-accumulation of capital, of a labour-shortage type, with a rise in wages had to occur as a result. Thus, in so far as the existing fixed capitals are fully utilised and unwillingly abandoned, the sustained and profitable accumulation of capital, even with a rising organic composition would sooner or later cause an over-accumulation in relation to the labouring-population. In the basic theory of regular business cycles, such over-accumulation is more strongly demonstrated as inevitable in the process of capital accumulation with a relatively constant organic composition.
15. In the analysis of the dynamic relation between the accumulation of money capital and that of real capital through the working of the credit system, Marx begins by defining real capital as 'commodity capital and productive capital' (III, p. 607). However, in his analysis of the dynamic relation of real capital with the accumulation of loanable money capital

in the money market, real capital is actually treated as commercial capital and industrial capital. I am following this use of the words, since the whole process of the business cycle must be analysed by taking up the relation between the accumulation of industrial capital plus commercial capital, not merely productive capital and commodity capital as specific forms in their circuit, and that of loanable money capital in the money market.

16. This ability of trade-union bargaining-power to squeeze the profit rate is underlined in A. Glyn and B. Sutcliffe, *British Capitalism, Workers and the Profit Squeeze* (Harmondsworth, Middx: Penguin Books, 1972), and P. Armstrong, A. Glyn, G. Harrison, *Capitalism since World War II* (London: Fontana, 1984).
17. D. Ricardo was already aware of this effect, and Marx treated it more systematically in ch. 11, 'The Effects of General Fluctuations in Wages on the Prices of Production' in the third volume of *Capital*.
18. Although I fundamentally rely upon K. Uno's crisis theory, I disagree with his position that the speculative developments towards the end of prosperity should be referred to simply as factual phenomena without being logically necessary. In his treatment, the role of commercial capital and speculative trading are mentioned only as superficial features, often obscuring the basic difficulties of capital accumulation which cause crises. In such a treatment, I am afraid that the logical necessity of a sharp rise in the interest rate and the process of the collapse of trading causing an acute crisis would not be shown in its actuality.
19. It is one of Uno and his followers' contribution to Marxian theory to have underlined this aspect of Marx's theory and to have attempted to show the logical necessity of periodical crisis through the working of the credit system and the interest rate. This corresponds to their position which emphasises the importance of the forms and the mechanisms of a capitalist economy besides its internal substantive relations of production.

    P. Bullock and D. Yaffe, 'Inflation, the Crisis, and the Postwar Boom', *Revolutionary Communist*, 3/4 (Nov 1975), contains one of the rare attempts among Western Marxians to examine how the credit mechanism operates up to the crisis, although it is based upon the rising organic composition variant of the excess-capital theory of crisis and so is different from the Uno School.
20. In the actual process of business cycles in the mid-nineteenth century, the outflow of gold reserves from the Bank of England heralded the outbreak of periodical crises, by tightening the money market. It often appeared alternately as a drain to foreign countries and then an internal drain to domestic circulation. Although 'with the possible exception of 1837, the real crisis has always broken out only after the exchange rates have moved, i.e. once the import of precious metal has the upper hand again over the export' (III, p. 702), the internal drain, often to Scotland and Ireland, has usually followed this movement and basically had a similar nature, actually often involving a hidden continuous drain to abroad. The basic theory must reflect the nature and the working of the credit system of that period, which organised both domestic and foreign

transactions in a homogeneous fashion and in the same forms.

21. This is the moment when money appears as the sole incarnation of wealth, as was believed by the bullionists, and thus the 'sudden transformation of the credit system into a monetary system adds theoretical dismay to the actually existing panic' (K. Marx, *A Contribution to the Critique of Political Economy*, Moscow: Progress Publishers, 1970, p. 146).
22. In this respect the aspects of those difficulties in capitalism which have been underlined by the excess-commodity theories of crisis must not be disregarded. The excess-capital thoery of a labour-shortage type would not be complete without locating those aspects theoretically and properly clarifying their relevancy.
23. Following up Uno's crisis theory, M. Yoshitomi, '[Credit and Business Cycles]', in K. Suzuki, ed., [*Studies in Credit Theory*] (Tokyo: Hosei University Press, 1961) and K. Baba, [*The World Economy, Its Centre and Periphery*] (Tokyo: University of Tokyo Press, 1973) raised this problem and presented a solution in this direction.
24. This would be a reason why monetary policy, in operating the official rate of interest tends to be ineffective in promoting recovery from depression. The basic difference between the determination of the profit rate and that of the interest rate, as we have discussed in Chapter 8, Section 8.2, must be remembered, in understanding why the lowered rate of interest cannot serve very effectively in reactivating real capital investment.
25. This implies that countervailing social factors including the power of trade unions are quite necessary in order to maintain the real-wage rate under the pressure of actual depression.
26. K. Uno, [The Tasks of the Crisis Theory]', in his [*Problems in Marxian Economics*] (Tokyo: Iwanami-Shoten, 1969), argued that the contents of the necessary means of consumption for wage-workers are determined through the capitalist process of business cycles. A linkage between value theory and crisis theory is thus being sought out, together with a critique of a misconception that the real wage is determined entirely outside of the law of motion of capitalism. However, I cannot totally agree with him where he seems to neglect the 'historical and moral element', possibly including social forces in the determination of real wages, even in the basic theory.
27. There was an interesting controversy over this problem in relation to the actual rising price-level at that time, by a series of Marxians such as E. S. Varga, R. Hilferding, K. Kautsky and O. Bauer among others, in *Neue Zeit*, 30, Bd 1–7–31, Bd 1–16 (Nov 1911–Jan 1913). The articles in the controversy were collected and translated in S. Ryu, [*Gold and Pices*] (Tokyo: Dojin-Sha, 1932).
28. For instance, P. Armstrong, A. Glyn, J. Harrison, *Capitalism since World War II* (London: Fontana, 1984) among others, show empirically that over-accumulation in this regard was the major cause for the beginning of the recent great depression.
29. In a letter of 12 September 1880 to N. F. Danielson, Marx notices the absence in the present crisis of the collapse of the market in bills of

exchange in London, which used to form the peak of the periodical crises in England. The same was also true for the crisis in 1873, and in 1890. And Engels wrote in a note to the third volume of *Capital* that 'the acute form of the periodic process with its former ten-year cycle seems to have given way to a more chronic and drawn-out alternation, affecting the various industrial countries at different times, between a relatively short and weak improvement in trade and a relatively long and indecisive depression' (III, p. 620). Although various factors, such as the expansion of the means of transportation and communication, the formation of competing industrial countries, as well as cartels and trusts, or the growing investment of surplus European capitals in all parts of the world, are suggested by Engels as the causes of such metamorphoses of business cycles, a fundamental moment would be in the difficulty of coping with excessive large-scale fixed capital. In this respect R. Hilferding's treatment of the problem in ch. 20 of *Finance Capital* is neither sufficient and thorough. Hilferding stresses there that the formation of cartels in particular mitigates the acuteness of crises while intensifying the difficulties in the non-cartelised industries.

30. A representative work from this viewpoint is P. A. Baran and P. Sweezy, *Monopoly Capital* (New York and London: Monthly Review Press, 1966).
31. Parvus (alias A. Helphand), *Die Handelskrisen und die Gewerkschaften* (München: M. Ernst, 1901). K. Kautsky, 'Die Wandlungen der Goldproduktion und der wechselnde Charakter der Teuerung', in *Die Neue Zeit*, supplement to no. 16 (Jan 1913).
32. Russian orthodox studies of the theories and the history of business cycles and crises have not been entirely immune from such a tendency. See for instance L. A. Mendelison, [*The Theory and History of Economic Crises*], translated into Japanese by K. Iida *et al.*, (Tokyo: Otsuki-Shoten, 4 vols, 1960–1), and I. A. Trakhatenberg, [*The Money Crises*], translated into Japanese by A. Oikawea, (Tokyo: Iwasaki-Gakujitsu, 3 vols, 1967–8). Their prestige was effectively weakened by the historical experience of the sustained long upswing in the post-Second World War period.
33. The overall index of prices also seems strikingly stable during this period in comparison with the preceding or the following periods, though a slight uprise is discernible in the second quarter-century as a result of the discovery of Californian gold mines, especially taking into account a generally rising productivity in other commodity products (cf. B. R. Mitchell, *Abstract of British Historical Statistics* (Cambridge: Cambridge University Press, 1962, pp. 471–2).
34. N. D. Kondratieff, 'Die Langen Wellen der Konjunktur', in *Archiv für Sozialwissenschaften und Sozialpolitik*, Bd 56 (1926), 'The Long Waves in Economic Life', in *Review of Economic Statistics*, 60 (1935).
35. This coincides with a point among Bob Rowthorn's critical comments on E. Mandel's *Late Capitalism*. Bob Rowthorn, *Capitalism, Conflict and Inflation* (London: Lawrence & Wishart, 1980) pp. 101–2. In general the existence of abundant cheap loanable capital is neither a sufficient nor an indispensable precondition for the upturn, though it can serve as *a*

favourable initial condition for the upturn of capital accumulation when combined with other conditions such as renewed international economic relations, the upturn in the trend of prices, and concerted waves of technological innovations. Conversely, when the real rate of interest is high a new upturn of real capital investment is generally obstructed as we have experienced in the first half of 1980s.

36. J. A. Schumpeter, *Business Cycles* 2 vols, (New York: McGraw-Hill, 1939). As is well known, Schumpeter called the regular business cycles of between about eight and ten years duration 'Juglar cycles', and the shortest business cycles mainly due to fluctuations in inventory investment 'Kitchin cycles'.
37. L. P. Trotsky, 'On the Curve of Capitalist Development', in *Fourth International* (May 1941).
38. E. Mandel, *Long Waves of Capitalist Development* (Cambridge: Cambridge University Press, 1980) pp. 21, 55. See also his *Late Capitalism* (op. cit.) ch. 4.
39. D. M. Gordon, R. Edwards and M. Reich, *Segmented Work, Divided Workers* (Cambridge: Cambridge University Press, 1982) ch. 2.

## PART IV SOCIALISM – AN ADDENDUM

1. Cf. F. M. C. Fourier, *Le Nouveau Monde Industriel et Sociétaire ou Invention du Procédé d'Industrie Attrayante et Naturelle Distribuée en Serie Passionnées* (1822, in *Oeuvres complètes de Ch. Fourier* (Paris: La Librairie Societarie, 1845, t. 6).
2. In the preface to the second German edition of the *Manifesto of the Communist Party* (1872), Marx and Engels confirm that 'the general principles laid down in this *Manifesto* are, on the whole, as correct today as ever', though they admit that 'the practical application of the principles will depend . . . on the historical conditions for the time being existing, and for that reason, no special stress is laid on the revolutionary measures proposed as the need of Section II' concerning the possible concrete reforms. Their major modification stated in that preface is on the role of the state after the experience of Paris Commune, saying: 'One thing especially was proved by the Commune, viz. that "the working class cannot simply lay hold of the ready-made State machinery, and wield it for its own purposes" ' (K. Marx, *Selected Writings*, ed. D. McLellan, Oxford: *Oxford University* Press, 1977, p. 559). Marx's most important statement on the possible future communist society after writing *Capital* was presented rather fragmentarily in the form of *Critique of the Gotha Programme* in 1875. In my view his presentation of the lower phase of communist society, being distinct from a higher phase, based upon 'the right of the producers' to claim income proportional to the labour they supply to the society, after deducting various commonly necessary portions of labour products, contains the theoretical insights obtained through his studies on the social functions and historical character of the substance of value and surplus-value in *Capital*. However, we also have to examine the limitations of Marx and his orthodox followers'

concept of the substance of value in the Chapter 10 below, in relation to the possible understanding of the nature of socialism.

## 10 On Socialism

1. K. Uno presented this problem openly, by analysing in detail Marx's summary of 'The Historical Tendency of Capitalist Accumulation' in ch. 32 (in the English version, or the seventh section of ch. 24 in the German version) of the first volume of *Capital*, in his article ['Socialism and Political Economy'] (in his [*The Fundamental Problems in a Social Science*], Tokyo: Aoki-Shoten, 1966).
2. H. Grossmann, *Das Akkumulations-und Zusammenbruchsgesetz des kapitalistishen Systems* (Leipzig: Hirschfeld, 1929) pp. 121–2. cf. also note 7 for Chapter 9.
3. This assertion of N. Okishio is shown for instance in his [*Contemporary Capitalism and Political Economy*] (Tokyo: Iwanami-Shoten, 1986). I have discussed this point with him and other related problems in a dialogue for a journal [*Shiso*], (Apr 1986).
4. This has been the officially declared position since Stalin's Constitutional Law of 1936.
5. Since the close correlation between the development of modern industrial technologies and the development of the 'scientific' management of labour in the forms of Taylorism, Fordism and segmentation of workers (with their artificial gradings) is so obvious, the possibility of their separation would have to be tested practically and established according to each type of technology, along with the attempts to alter the nature of technologies itself. We cannot expect that the separation will be easy.
6. While I wrote this paragraph the worrying news of the Chernobyl nuclear reactor accident came on the air.
7. J. V. Stalin, *Economic Problems of Socialism in the U.S.S.R.* (1952, Peking: Foreign Languages Press, 1972) pp. 3–4, p. 22, pp. 38–9.
8. In 1953, three years earlier than de-Stalinisation in the Soviet Union and its influence in Japan, K. Uno, ['The Law of Value and Socialism'], (in [*Shiso*], Oct 1953, also in his ['*Capital*' *and Socialism*], (Tokyo: Iwanami-Shoten, 1958), criticised Stalin's problematic notion of the law of value and of its useability under socialism.
9. A. Nove, *The Economics of Feasible Socialism* (London: George Allen & Unwin, 1983) pp. 12–13.
10. In this respect I am not persuaded by the view which conceives of a single global economic crisis in our age resulting from the impact of the crisis in the advanced capitalist countries, as the centre of a unified world system including the second world. Certainly, I do not deny the importance of the negative influence of the capitalist world crisis on Soviet types of societies. The burden of cumulative international debt combined with the depressed export market is surely serious for many countries in the second world as well as in the third world. However, a problem with the view of a single global crisis, presented for instance in A. G. Frank, *Reflections on the World Economic Crisis* (New York and London:

Monthly Review Press, 1981), and *Crisis in the World Economy* (New York: Holmes & Meier. 1981), is that the indedependent cause(s) of the economic difficulties inside Soviet types of societies themselves cannot properly be underlined.

11. For example, L. von Mises, 'Economic Calculation in the Socialist Commonwealth', (1920, in A. Nove and D. M. Nuti, eds, *Socialist Economics*, Harmondsworth, Middx: Peguin Books, 1972), typically asserts that socialism without market pricing lacks a rational measurement of efficiency and therefore cannot be a rational economy. Von Mises points to the difficulty of reducing the products of skilled labour to units of simple labour as an important reason. Hence, we also see in this example how essential is our search for a sounder labour theory of value in oder to examine and clarify the basis of the argument for socialism.
12. P. Sraffa, *Production of Commodities by Means of Commodities* (Cambridge: Cambridge University Press, 1960) ch. II.
13. O. Lange, 'The Computer and the Market' (1967, in A. Nove and D. M. Nuti, eds, op. cit.), suggested that 'Mathematical programming assisted by electronic computers becomes the fundamental instrument of long-term economic planning, as well as of solving dynamic economic problems of a more limited scope. Here, the electronic computer does not replace the market. It fulfils a function the market never was able to perform.' (pp. 404–5). The more recent development of information technologies seems to widen the possibility of the more flexible application of electronic computers as a means for a multi-terminal system of adjusting economic relations, and useable not merely for long-term centralised economic planning. The social decision on how to use and apply newly growing technological possibilities will become quite important in this respect being related to the desirable socio-economic order being realised in socialism.
14. I. I. Rubin, *Essays on Marx's Theory of Value* (1982, translated by M. Samrdzija and F. Perlman, Detroit: Black & Red, 1972). See note 7 of Chapter 5 for the recent representative value theorists in the Rubin School. The theoretical similarity does not necessarily mean that all these recent theorists I call the Rubin School have studied and depended upon Rubin's work to form their views. Since their position can be deducible rather directly from a part of Marx's conception as well as from a certain type of attempt logically to formulate the relation between the form and substance of value.
15. Rubin, ibid. pp. 139 ff.
16. If one adheres to a rigorous measurement of the intensity of labour across different concrete forms and grades of work, a completely objective way to define the measurement would not be available. In this regard we have to admit the basic human ability to work in various forms as a basis for our conception of human labour equally forming the social substance of economic life, being indifferent to the concrete forms or the grades of skill, specially in a really socialist society. This reflection on the basis of the measurability of abstract human labour under socialism, basically relies upon our understanding of value theory, but it may

reciprocally serve to clarify how to conceive abstract human labour as the substance of value.

17. In his *Critique of the Gotha Programme* Marx points to the necessary portions of the social product to be deduced by society before determining the distribution of the means of consumption to individual members of it , as follows: 'cover for replacement of the means of production used up', 'additional portion for expansion of production', 'reserve or insurance funds against accidents, dislocations caused by natural calamities, etc.', and a further three items as follows to be deduced from the means of consumption: 'the general costs of administration not directly belonging to production' to be restricted and diminished in a new society, the portion 'intended for the common satisfaction of needs, such as schools, health services, etc.' to grow in proportion as the development of the new society, and 'funds for those unable to work, etc.' (K. Marx, *Critique of the Gotha Programme*, 1875, Peking: Foreign Languages Press, 1976, pp. 13–14). These items include not merely the result of surplus-labour, but also embodied deed labour and a part of necessary labour to reproduce labour-power. Although we can easily discern among them the funds or costs relying upon the surplus labour of the workers, such as those for the expansion of production, insurance, administration and for people unable to work, the social meaning of the distinction between surplus and necessary labour will obviously become different in a co-operative socialist society in comparison with in class societies.
18. Upon the basis of social consensus the length of a working day, as well as the proportion between the surplus and the necessary labour within it, must become flexibly determinable in socialism. As Marx suggests: 'The real wealth of society and the possibility of a constant expansion of its reproduction process does not depend on the length of surplus labour but rather on its productivity and on the more or less plentiful conditions of production in which it is performed. The realm of freedom really begins only where labour determined by necessity and external expediency ends; it lies by its very nature beyond the sphere of material production proper.' (III, pp. 958–9).
19. Such an understanding of the usability of the law of value in the process of socialist economic construction is seen in some recent Chinese Marxian views following the position of J. V. Stalin, despite their very practical position of reintroducing market mechanism, e.g. Chiao-mu, Hu, 'Observe Economic Laws, Speed Up the Four Modernizations', *Peking Review*, 45–47 (10–24 Nov 1978).
20. This aspect has been achieved fairly well in soviet types of societies along with the industrialisation policies. The participation rate of women in the work-place, for instance, has been clearly higher than that in capitalist countries, although it may not yet be a full solution of the problems of women.
21. In order to induce workers to volunteer for the position, membership of the socialist reserve army should not be an unpleasant position but rather a fortunate opportunity. However, the position should not be regarded

as an equally distributed and established private right. Otherwise, the flexible mobilisation of such a socialist industrial reserve army in accord with the dynamic changes in social needs would remain difficult.

22. F. Engels, *Socialism: Utopian and Scientific* (1892, Peking: Foreign Languages Press, 1975) p. 87.
23. V. I. Lenin, *A Characterization of Economic Romanticism* (1897, in his *Collected Works*, vol. 2 (Moscow: Foreign Languages Publishing House, 1963) p. 167.
24. Among others, C. Bettelheim, *Class Struggles in the USSR: Second Period, 1923–1930* (translated by B. Pearce, New York: Monthly Review Press, 1978) extensively re-examines this process at that time.
25. This notion is comparatively nearer to the orthodox Soviet conception even with some criticisms.
26. See, e.g., R. A. Medvedev, [*Let History Judge: The Origins and Consequences of Stalinism*] (1968) translated by S. Ishido, Tokyo: Sanichi-Shobo, 2 vols, 1973–4), and J. Elleinstein, *The Stalin Phenomenon*, translated by P. Lantham (London: Lawrence & Wishart, 1976).
27. This notion defines the hypertrophy of soviet state power as a result of the historical necessity of placing specialists in the position of bureaucratic agents of workers due to the lack of managerial and technological skills among the labourers in the initial phase of Soviet history after the revolution. L. Trotsky, *The Revolution Betrayed*, translated by M. Eastman (London: Faber & Faber, 1937), initially and typically formulated this view and E. Mandel follows this lead for instance in his article, 'On the Nature of the Soviet State', in *New Left Review* (Mar–Apr 1978).
28. This position was shown in *Mao Tse-tung* and his followers' critiques of the USSR during the Cultural Revolution. Bettelheim, op. cit., for example, maintains this notion in his works.
29. This notion is presented in P. Sweezy, *Post-Revolutionary Society* (New York and London: Monthly Review Press, 1980) and also in S. Amin *et al.*, *Dynamics of Global Crisis* (London and Basingstoke: Macmillan Press, 1982) p. 201.
30. This reflection implies that we not only need the basic theory of capitalism, but also studies in the historical changes in the roles of the capitalist state and nationalism, in the stages theory of capitalist development, or the more concrete analyses, in order to secure our frame of reference for the critical considerations of the problems of the soviet types of societies. The reciprocal intensification of state power between the first and the second world especially, with the structural order of international political and economic relations under the leadership of the super-powers, must be analysed, criticised and solved from both sides for a more hopeful human future.

# Bibliography

I have mainly listed the literature directly referred to in this volume. (For books and papers published in Japanese, I have translated the titles into English and put them in square brackets throughout this volume.)

AGLIETTA, M. *A Theory of Capitalist Regulation: US Experience*, translated by D. Fernbach (London: New Left Books, 1981).

ALBRITTON, R. *A Japanese Reconstruction of Marxist Theory* (London: Macmillan, 1986).

AMIN, S. *The Law of Value and Historical Materialism*, translated by B. Pearce (New York and London: Monthly Review Press, 1978).

___ ARRIGHI, G., FRANK, A. G. *Dynamics of Global Crisis* (London and Basingstoke: Macmillan Press, 1982).

ARMSTRONG, P., GLYN, A., HARRISON, J. 'In Defence of Value – A Reply to Ian Steedman', *Capital and Class*, 5 (Summer 1978).

___ ___ ___ *Capitalism since World War II* (London: Fontana, 1984).

BABA, K. [*The World Economy: Its Center and Periphery*] (Tokyo: University of Tokyo Press, 1973).

BAGEHOT, W. *Lombard Street* (London: John Murray, 1915).

BARAN, P., SWEEZY, P. *Monopoly Capital* (New York and London: Monthly Review Press, 1966).

BAUER, O. 'Die Akkumulation des Kapitals', *Neue Zeit*, XXXI–1 (1913).

BECKER, J. F. *Marxian Political Economy* (Cambridge: Cambridge University Press, 1977).

BEHRENS, F. *Zur Methode der Politischen Ökonomie* (Berlin: Akademie-Verlag, 1952).

BERNSTEIN, E. *Die Voraussetzungen des Sozialismus und die Aufgabe der Sozialdemokratie* (Stuttgart: Dietz, 1899).

___ 'Zur Theorie des Arbeitswerts', *Die Neue Zeit*, XVIII–1 (1899–1900).

BETTELHEIM, C. *Class Struggles in the USSR: Second Period, 1923–1930*, translated by B. Pearce (New York and London: Monthly Review Press, 1978).

BLEANEY, M. *Underconsumption Theories: A History and Critical Analysis* (London: Lawrence & Wishart, 1976).

BÖHM-BAWERK, E. VON *Capital and Interest* (1884–1889), translated by W. Smart (New York: Brentano, 1922).

BORTKIEWICZ, L. VON 'On the Correction of Marx's Fundamental Theoretical Construction in the third Volume of Capital', in P. Sweezy (ed.), *Karl Marx and the Close of His System by E. von Böhm-Bawerk and Böhm-Bawerk's Criticism of Marx by Rudolf Hilferding* (New York: A. M. Kelley, 1966).

BOWLES, S., EDWARDS, R. *Understanding Capitalism* (New York: Harper & Row, 1985).

___ GINTIS, H. 'The Marxian Theory of Value and Heterogeneous Labour', *Cambridge Journal of Economics*, vol. 1–2 (1977).

—— —— 'Labour Heterogeneity and the Labour Theory of Value: A Reply', *Cambridge Journal of Economics*, vol. 5–3 (1981).

BRAVERMAN, H. *Labour and Monopoly Capital: The Degradation of Work in the Twentieth Century* (New York and London: Monthly Review Press, 1974).

BRENTANO, L. *Das Arbeitsverhältniss Gemäss dem Heutigen Recht* (Leipzig: Duncker & Humbolt, 1877).

BRUNHOFF, S. DE, *Marx on Money*, translated by M. G. Goldbloom (New York: Urizen Books, 1973).

BUKHARIN, N. *Imperialism and the Accumulation of Capital*, translated by R. Wichmann (New York and London: Monthly Review Press, 1972).

BULLOCK, P., YAFFE, D. 'Inflation, the Crisis, and the Postwar Boom', *Revolutionary Communist*, 3/4 (Nov 1975).

CLAPHAM, J. *An Economic History of Modern Britain*, 3 vols (Cambridge: Cambridge University Press, 1926–38).

COLLETTI, L. *From Rousseau to Lenin*, translated by J. Merrington and F. White (New York and London: Monthly Review Press, 1972).

DESAI, M. *Marxian Economic Theory* (London: Basil Blackwell & Mott Publisher, 1974).

DICKINSON, H. D. 'A Comment on Meek's "Note on the Transformation Problem"', *The Economic Journal* (Dec 1956).

DOBB, M. *Political Economy and Capitalism* (London: Routledge & Kegan Paul, 1937).

—— *Theories of Value and Distribution since Adam Smith* (Cambridge: Cambridge University Press, 1973).

EDWARDS, R. C. *Contested Terrain* (London: Heinemann, 1979).

—— REICH, M., WEISSKOPF, T. E. *The Capitalist System* (Englewood Cliffs, N. J.: Prentice-Hall, 1978).

ELDRED, M., HANLON, M. 'Reconstructing Value – From Analysis', *Capital and Class*, 13 (1981).

ELSON, D. ed., *Value: The Representation of Labour in Capitalism* (London: CSE Books, 1979).

ELLEINSTEIN, J. *The Stalin Phenomenon*, translated by P. Lantham (London: Lawrence & Wishart, 1976).

EMMANUEL, E. *Unequal Exchange*, translated by B. Pearce (New York and London: Monthly Review Press, 1972).

ENGELS, F. *Socialism: Utopian and Scientific* (1892) (Peking: Foreign Language Press, 1975).

—— *Landmarks of Scientific Socialism (Anti-Dühring)*, translated and edited by A. Lewis (Chicago: Charles H. Keer, 1907).

—— *Dialectics of Nature* (Moscow: Foreign Languages Publishing House, 1954).

FEUERBACH, L. A. *Das Wesen des Christentums* (Leipzig: Otto Wigand, 1841).

FINE, B. *Marx's 'Capital'* (London: Macmillan, 1975).

—— 'Banking Capital and the Theory of Interest', *Science and Society*, XLIX–4 (Winter 1985–6).

—— and HARRIS, L. *Rereading 'Capital'* (London: Macmillan, 1979).

FOLEY, D. 'The Value of Money, the Value of Labour, Power and the

Marxian Transformation Problem', *Review of Radical Political Economy*, 2 (1982).
FOURIER, F. M. C. *Le Nouveau Monde Industriel et Sociétaire ou Invention du Procédé d'Industrie Attrayante et Naturelle Distribuéeen Série Passionnées* (1822), in *Œuvres Complètes de Ch. Fourier* (Paris: La Librairie Societaire, 1845, t. 6).
FRANK, A. G. *Crisis in the World Economy* (New York: Holmes & Meier, 1980).
___ *Reflections on the World Economic Crisis* (New York and London: Monthly Review Press, 1981).
GALBRAITH, J. K. *American Capitalism* (Boston: Houghton Mifflin, 1952).
___ *The New Industrial State* (Boston: Houghton Mifflin, 1978).
GLEICHER, D. 'A Historical Approach to the Question of Abstract Labour', *Capital and Class*, 21 (1983).
___ 'A Rejoinder to Eldred', *Capital and Class*, 24 (1985).
GLYN, A., SUTCLIFFE, B. *British Capitalism, Workers and the Profit Squeeze* (Harmondsworth, Middx: Penguin Books, 1972).
GORDON, D., EDWARDS, R., REICH, M. *Segmented Work, Divided Workers* (Cambridge: Cambridge University Press, 1982).
GREEN, F., NOVE, P. *Economics: An Anti-Text* (London and Basingstoke: Macmillan, 1977).
GROSSMANN, H. *Das Akkumulations-und Zusammenbruchsgesetz des Kapitalistischen Systems* (Leipzig: Hirschfeld, 1929).
___ 'Die Änderung des ursprünglichen Aufbauplans des Marxschen "Kapital" und ihre Ursachen', *Archiv für die Geschichte des Sozialismus und der Arbeiterbewegung*, XIV–2 (1929).
HABERLER, G. *Prosperity and Depression* (London: George Allen & Unwin, 1937).
HEGEL, G. W. F. *Grundlinien der Philosophie des Rechts* (1821) (Frankfurt am Main: Suhrkamp, 1970).
HELPHAND, A. *Die Handelskrisen und die Gewerskschaften* (München: M. Ernst, 1901).
HICKS, J. R. *Value and Capital* (Oxford: Clarendon Press, 1939).
HIDAKA, H. [*Studies in the Theory of Ground Rent*] (Tokyo: Jichosha, 1962).
HILDEBRAND, B. *Die Gegenwärtige Aufgabe der Wissenschaft der Nationalökonomie* (1863).
HILFERDING, R. *Finance Capital* (1910), translated by M. Watnick and S. Gordon (London, Boston and Henley: Routledge & Kegan Paul, 1981).
HIMMELWEIT, S., MOHUN, S. 'The Anomalies of Capital', *Capital and Class*, 7 (1978).
___ ___ 'Real Abstractions and Anomalous Assumptions', in I. Steedman *et al.*, *The Value Controversy* (London: Verso and NLB, 1981).
HOBSON, J. A. *Imperialism* (New York: Pott, 1902).
HODGSKIN, T. *Labour Defended against the Claims of Capital; or the Unproductiveness of Capital Proved* (1825) (New York: A. M. Kelly, 1963).
HU, CHIAO-MU. 'Observe Economic Laws, Speed up the Four Modernizations', *Peking Review*, 45–47 (10–24 Nov 1978).

HUNT, E. K., SCHWARTZ, J. G. *A Critique of Economic Theory* (Harmondsworth, Middx: Penguin Books, 1972).
ILLICH, I. *Shadow Work* (London: Mariou Boyars, 1981).
ITOH, M. [*Credit and Crisis*] (Tokyo: University of Tokyo Press, 1973).
—— Book Review: 'The Making of Marx's "Capital"', *Science and Society*, XLIII–3 (Fall 1979).
—— *Value and Crisis* (London: Pluto Press; New York: Monthly Review Press, 1980).
—— [*Contemporary Capitalism*] (Tokyo: Shinchi-Shobo, 1981).
—— [*The Theory of Value and Capital*] (Tokyo: Iwanami-Shoten, 1981).
—— 'On Marx's Theory of Accumulation', *Science and Society*, XLV–L (Spring 1981).
—— [*Marxian Economics Today*] (Tokyo: TBS Britanica, 1982).
IWATA, H. [*The World Capitalism*] (Tokyo: Mirai-Sha, 1964).
JEVONS, W. S. *The Theory of Political Economy* (London: Macmillan, 1871).
JONES, R. *An Essay on the Distribution of Wealth, and on the Sources of Taxation* (London: 1831).
—— *Text-book of Lectures on the Political Economy* (Hertford, 1852).
—— *Literary Remains*, edited by W. Whewell (London: Murray, 1859).
KALECKI, M. *Essays in the Theory of Economic Fluctuations* (London: Allen & Unwin, 1939).
—— *Theory of Economic Dynamics: An Essay on Cyclical and Long-run Changes in Capitalist Economy* (London: George Allen & Unwin, 1954).
KAUTSKY, K. *Die Agrarfrage* (1899) (Hannover: J. H. W. Dietz, 1966).
—— *Bernstein und das Sozialdemokratische Programme* (Stuttgart: Dietz, 1899).
—— 'Krisentheorien', *Neue Zeit*, XX–2 (1901–2).
—— 'Finanzkapital und Krisen', *Neue Zeit*, XXIX–2 (1911).
—— 'Die Wandlungen der Goldproduktion und der Wechselnde Charakter der Teuerung', *Neue Zeit*, XVI–Supplement (Jan 1913).
KEYNES, J. M. *The General Theory of Employment, Interest and Money* (London: Macmillan, 1936).
KING, W. T. C. *History of the London Discount Market* (London: George Routledge & Sons, 1936).
KNIES, K. *Die Politische Ökonomie vom Standpunkte der Geschichtlichen Methode* (Braunschweig: Schwetschke, 1853).
KOGAN, A. M. [*The plan of the Critique of Political Economy and 'Capital'*, translated by Y. Nakano (Tokyo: Otsuki-Shoten, 1979).
KONDRATIEFF, N. D. 'Die Langen Wellen der Konjunktur', *Archiv für Sozialwissenschaften und Sozialpolitik*, 56 (1926).
—— 'The Long Waves in Economic Life', *Review of Economic Statistics*, 60 (1935).
KRAUSE, U. *Money and Abstract Labour*, translated by P. Burgess (London: NLB and Verso, 1982).
KUHN, T. *The Structure of the Scientific Revolution* (Chicago: University of Chicago Press, 1970).
KURUMA, K. [*Studies in the Crisis Theory*] (Tokyo: Otsuki-Shoten, 1965).
LAIBMAN, D. 'Value and Prices of Production: The Political Economy of

the Transformation Problem', *Science and Society*, XXXVII–4 (Winter 1973–4).

LANGE, O. 'The Computer and the Market' (1967), in A. Nove and D. M. Nuti, eds, *Socialist Economics* (Harmondsworth, Middx: Penguin Books, 1972).

LENIN, V. I. 'A Characterization of Economic Romanticism' (1897), in *The Collected Works of Lenin*, vol. 2 (Moscow: Foreign Languages Publishing House, 1963).

____ *Imperialism; the Highest Stage of Capitalism* (1917) (Peking: Foreign Languages Press, 1965).

____ 'The Proletarian Revolution and a Renegade Kautsky' (1918), in *The Collected Works of Lenin*, vol. 28 (Moscow: Foreign Languages Publishing House, 1965).

LIPIETZ, A. *The Enchanted World*, translated by I. Patterson (London: Verso, 1985).

LIPPI, M. *Value and Naturalism in Marx*, translated by H. Steedman (London: NLB, 1979).

LIST, F. *The National System of Political Economy* (1841), translated by S. S. Lloyd (London: Longmans, 1885).

LUXEMBURG, R. *The Accumulation of Capital* (1913), translated by A. Schwarzschild (New York and London: Monthly Review Press, 1968).

LYUBIMOF, L. Y. [*Theoretical Outline of Ground Rent*] (1930), translated by S. Matsumura (Tokyo: Nauka, 1934).

McCULLOCH, J. R. *The Principles of Political Economy* (1825) (Edinburgh: A. & C. Black, 1864).

MACKENNA, E. 'A Comment on Bowles and Gintis' Marxian Theory of Value', *Cambridge Journal of Economics*, vol. 5–3 (1981).

MALTHUS, T. R. *The Principles of Political Economy* (1820), 2nd ed. (London: William Pickering, 1836).

MANDEL, E. *Late Capitalism*, translated by J. De Bres (London: NLB 1975).

____ 'On the Nature of the Soviet State', *New Left Review* (Mar–Apr 1978).

____ *Long Waves of Capitalist Development* (Cambridge: Cambridge University Press, 1980).

MANIFESTO Il, *Power and Opposition in Post-Revolutionary Societies*, translated by P. Camiller and J. Rotschild (London: Ink Links, 1979).

MARSHALL, A. *Principles of Economics* (London: Macmillan, 1890).

MARX, K., ENGELS, F. *Manifesto of the Communist Party* (1848), in *K. Marx, F. Engels Collected Works*, 6 (Moscow: Progress Publishers, 1976).

____ *Grundrisse: Foundations of the Critique of Political Economy* (rough draft), translated by M. Nicolaus (Harmondsworth, Middx: Penguin Books, 1973).

____ *A Contribution to the Critique of Political Economy* (1859), translated by S. W. Ryazanskaya (Moscow: Progress Publishers, 1970).

____ *Zur Kritik der Politischen Ökonomie (Manuscript 1861–1863)*, in *Marx–Engels Gesamtausgabe*, 2. Abteilung, Band 3, 6 vols (Berlin: Dietz Verlag, 1976–82).

____ *Theories of Surplus-Value* (1861–3), translated by E. Burus, R. Simpson and J. Cohen, 3 vols (London: Lawrence & Wishart, 1969).

____ *Value: Studies by Karl Marx*, translated and edited by A. Dragstedt (London: New Park Publications, 1976).

—— *Capital* translated by B. Fowes and D. Fernbach, 3 vols (Harmondsworth, Middx: Penguin Books, 1976, 1978, 1981).
—— *Critique of the Gotha Programme* (1875) (Peking: Foreign Languages Press, 1976).
—— *Selected Writings*, edited by D. McLellan (Oxford: *Oxford University Press*, 1977).
MAY, K. 'Value and Price of Production: A Note on Winternitz's Solution', *Economic Journal* (Dec 1948).
MEDVEDEV, R. A. [*Let History Judge: The Origins and Consequences of Stalinism*], 2 vols, translated by S. Ishido (Tokyo: Sanichi-Shobo, 1973–4).
MEEK, R. L. *Studies in the Labour Theory of Value* (New York and London: Monthly Review Press, 1956).
—— *The Economics of Physiocracy, Essays and Translations* (London: George Allen & Unwin, 1962).
—— *Economics and Ideology and Other Essays* (London: Chapman & Hall, 1967).
—— *Smith, Marx and After* (London: Chapman & Hall, 1977).
MENDELISON, L. A. [*The Theory and History of Economic Crises*], translated by K. Iida *et al.*, 4 vols (Tokyo: Otsuki-Shoten, 1960–1).
MENGER, C. *Grundsätze der Volkswirtschaftslehre* (Wien: Braumüller, 1871).
—— *Untersuchungen über die Methode der Sozialwissenschaften, und der Politischen Ökonomie Insbesondere* (Leipzig: Duncker & Humbolt, 1883).
MILL, J. *Elements of Political Economy* (London: Baldwin, 1821).
MILL, J. S. *Principles of Political Economy* (1848), edited by W. J. Ashley, (London: Longmans, Green, 1921).
MISES, L. VON 'Economic Calculation in the Socialist Commonwealth' (1920), in A. Nove and D. M. Nuti, ed., *Socialist Economics* (Harmondsworth, Middx: Penguin Books, 1972).
MITCHELL, B. R. *Abstract of British Historical Statistics* (Cambridge: Cambridge University Press, 1962).
MORISHIMA, M. *Marx's Economics* (Cambridge: Cambridge University Press, 1973).
—— CATEPHORES, G. *Value, Exploitation and Growth* (Maidenhead, Berks.: McGraw-Hill, 1978)
MURRAY, R. 'Value and Theory of Rent', Part I, II, *Capital and Class*, 3, 4 (Autumn 1977, Spring, 1978).
NAPOLEONI, C. *Smith, Ricardo and Marx*, translated by J. M. Gee (Oxford: Basil Blackwell, 1975).
NOVE, A. *The Economics of Feasible Socialism* (London: George Allen & Unwin, 1983).
—— NUTI, D. M. eds, *Socialist Economics* (Harmondsworth, Middx: Penguin Books, 1972).
OKISHIO, N. ['Value and Prices'], [*Research in Economics*] (University of Kobe) (Mar 1955).
—— 'A Mathematical Note on Marxian Theories', *Weltwirtschaftliches Archiv*, Heft 2 (1963).
—— ['Convergence of Marx's "Transformation" Procedure'], *Riron-Keizaigakul* (Aug 1973).

____ [*The Theory of Accumulation*] (Tokyo: Chikuma-Shobo, 1976).
____ [*Marxian Economics*] (Tokyo: Chikuma-Shobo, 1977).
____ [*Contemporary Capitalism and Political Economy*] (Tokyo: Iwanami-Shoten, 1986).
OUCHI, T. [*Ground-Rent and Landed Property*] (Tokyo: University of Tokyo Press, 1958).
OWEN, R. *A New View of Society* (1813–14), in *The Life of Robert Owen Written by Himself*, vol. I (New York: A. M. Kelley, 1976).
PANICO, C. 'Marx's Analysis of the Relationship between the Rate of Interest and the Rate of Profit', *Cambridge Journal of Economics*, vol. 4–4 (Dec 1980).
PARETO, V. *Manuale d'Économie Politique* (Paris: Giard, 1906).
PETTY, W. *A Treatise of Taxes and Contributions* (1662), in *The Economic Writings of Sir William Petty*, edited by C. H. Hull (Cambridge: Cambridge University Press, 1899).
PIGOU, A. C. *Economics of Welfare* (London: Macmillan, 1920).
PILLING, G. *Marx's Capital* (London, Boston and Henley: Routledge & Kegan Paul, 1980).
POLANYI, K. *The Great Transformation* (Boston: Beacon Press, 1944).
PREISER, E. E. 'Das Wesen der Marxschen Krisentheorie', in *Festschrift für Franz Oppenheimer – Wirtschaft und Gesellschaft* (Frankfurt: Frankfurter Societats-Druckerei, 1924).
RATTANSI, A. *Marx and the Division of Labour* (London: Macmillan, 1982).
RICARDO, D. 'An Essay on the Influence of a Law Price of Corn on the Profit of Stock' (1815), in *The Works and Correspondence of David Ricardo*, edited by P. Sraffa, vol. IV (Cambridge: Cambridge University Press, 1951).
RICARDO, D. *On the Principles of Political Economy and Taxation* (1817), in *The Works and Correspondence of David Ricardo*, edited by P. Sraffa, vol. 1 (Cambridge: Cambridge University Press, 1951).
ROLL, E. *A History of Economic Thought* (London: Faber & Faber, 1938).
ROSCHER, W. *Grundriss zu Verlesungen über die Staatwirtschaft* (Göttingen: Dieterischschen, 1843).
____ *System der Volkswirtschaft*, 5 vols (Stuttgart: Cotta, 1882–94).
ROSDOLSKY, R. *The Making of Marx's 'Capital'*, translated by P. Burgess (London: Pluto Press, 1977).
ROWTHORN, B. *Capitalism, Conflict and Inflation* (London: Lawrence & Wishart, 1980).
ROZENBERG, D. I. [*Commentary for 'Capital'*] (1961), translated by M. Udaka and T. Soejima, 5 vols (Tokyo: Aoki-Shoten, 1962–4).
RUBIN, I. I. *Essays on Marx's Theory of Value* (1928), translated by M. Samardzija and F. PERLMAN (Detroit: Black & Red, 1972).
RUBIN, I. I. *A History of Economic Thought* (1929), translated by D. Filtzer (London: Ink Links, 1979).
SAINT-SIMON, C-H. DE R. *Catéchisme Politique des Industriels* (1823–4), in *Œuvre de Saint-Simon et d'Enfantin* (Paris: Éd. Dentu, 1865–76).
SAKISAKA, I. [*Studies in the Theory of Rent*] (Tokyo: Kaizo-sha, 1930).
SAKURAI, T. [*The Theory of Prices of Production*] (Tokyo: University of Tokyo Press, 1968).

SAMUELSON, P. 'Wages and Interest: A Modern Discussion of Marxian Economic Models', *American Economic Review*, XLVII (Dec 1957).
SAMUELSON, P. 'Understanding the Marxian Nation of Exploitation: A Summary of the So-called Transformation Problem between Marxian Values and Competitive Prices', *Journal of Economic Literature*, 9–2 (June 1971).
SAY, J.-B. *Letters to Thomas Robert Malthus on Political Economy and Stagnation of Commerce* (1820), translated by H. J. Laski (London: Harding, 1936).
SCHMOLLER, G. *Grundriss der Allgemeinen Volkswirtschaftslehre*, t. 1–2 (Leipzig: Duncker & Humbolt, 1908–19).
SCHUMPETER, J. A. *Das Wesen und der Hauptinhalt der Theoretischen Nationalökonomie* (Leipzig: Duncker & Humbolt, 1908).
SCHUMPETER, J. A. *Business Cycles*, 2 vols (New York: McGraw-Hill, 1939).
SCHWARTZ, J. G., ed., *The Subtle Anatomy of Capitalism* (Santa Monica: Goodyear, 1977).
SEKINE, T. T. *The Dialectic of Capital: A Study of the Inner Logic of Capitalism*, 2 vols (Tokyo: Yushodo, 1984, 1986).
SEMMLER, W. *Competition, Monopoly, and Differential Profit Rate* (New York: Columbia University Press, 1984).
SETON, F. 'Transformation Problem', *The Review of Economic Studies* (June 1957).
SHAIKH, A. 'Marx's Theory of Value and the Transformation Problem', *The Subtle Anatomy of Capitalism* (Santa Monica: Goodyear, 1977).
—— 'An Introduction to the History of Crisis Theories', in *URPE, U.S. Capitalism in Crisis* (New York: Monthly Review Press, 1978).
SIMONDE DE SISMONDI, J. C. L. *Nouveaux Principes d'Économie Politique* (Paris: Delaunay, 1819).
SMITH, A. *An Inquiry into the Nature and Causes of Wealth of Nations* (1776), edited by R. H. Campbell, A. S. Skinner and W. B. Todd, 2 vols (Oxford: Clarendon Press, 1976).
SRAFFA, P. *Production of Commodities by Means of Commodities* (Cambridge: Cambridge University Press, 1960).
STALIN, J. V. *Economic Problems of Socialism in the U.S.S.R.* (1952) (Peking: Foreign Languages Press, 1972).
STEEDMAN, I. *Marx After Sraffa* (London: New Left Books, 1977).
—— *et al.*, *The Value Controversy* (London: Verso and NLB, 1981).
STEUART, J. D. *An Inquiry into the Principles of Political Economy*, 2 vols (London: A. Millar & T. Cadell, 1767).
SUGIMOTO, E. [*Elucidation of Modern Economics*], 2 vols (1950) (Tokyo: Iwanami-Shoten, 1981).
SUZUKI, K. [*Controversy on the Theory of Rent*] (Tokyo: Keiso-shobo, 1952).
—— (ed.), *Principles of Political Economy*, 2 vols (Tokyo: University of Tokyo Press, 1960, 1962).
—— (ed.), *Studies in the Credit Theory* (Tokyo: Hosei University Press, 1961).
SWEEZY, P. *The Theory of Capitalist Development* (1942) (New York: Monthly Review Press, 1956).

___ (ed.), *Karl Marx and the Close of His System by E. von Böhm-Bawerk and Böhm-Bawerk's Criticism of Marx by R. Hilferding* (New York: M. Kelley, 1966).

___ *Post-Revolutionary Society* (New York and London: Monthly Review Press, 1980).

___ 'Marxian Value Theory and Crisis', in I. Steedman *et al.*, *The Value Controversy* (London: Verso and NLB, 1981).

TAKUMI, M. [*World Capitalism*] (Tokyo: Nihonhyoron-Sha, 1980).

THOMPSON, P. *The Nature of Work* (London: Macmillan, 1983).

THOMPSON, W. *An Inquiry into the Principles of the Distribution of Wealth most Conducive to Human Happiness* (1824) (New York: A. M. Kelley, 1963).

TRAKHATENBERG, I. A. [*The Money Crises*], translated by A. Oikawa, 3 vols (Tokyo: Iwasaki-Gakujitsu, 1967–8).

TRIBE, K. 'Remarks on the Theoretical Significance of Marx's Grundrisse', *Economy and Society* (May 1974).

TROTSKY, L. *The Revolution Betrayed*, translated by M. Eastman (London: Faber & Faber, 1937).

___ 'On the Curve of Capitalist Development', *Fourth International* (May 1941).

TSURU, S. 'On the Reproduction Scheme', in P. Sweezy, *The Theory of Capitalist Development* (1942) (New York: Monthly Review Press, 1956).

TUGAN-BARANOWSKY, M. *Les Crises Industrielles en Angleterre*, translated by J. Schapiro (Paris: M. Jiard & E. Brieve, 1913).

UNO, K. [*The Theory of Crisis*] (Tokyo: Iwanami-Shoten, 1953).

___ ['The Law of Value and Socialism'] (1953), in his ['*Capital*' *and Socialism*] (Tokyo: Iwanami-Shoten, 1958).

___ ['*Capital*' *and Socialism*] (Tokyo: Iwanami-Shoten, 1958).

___ [*The Methodology of Political Economy*] (Tokyo: University of Tokyo Press, 1962).

___ [*The Fundamental Problems in a Social Science*] (Tokyo: Aoki-Shoten, 1966).

___ 'The Tasks of Crisis Theory', in his [*Problems in Marxian Economics*] (Tokyo: Iwanami-Shoten, 1969).

___ *Principles of Political Economy*, translated by T. Sekine (Brighton: Harvester Press; Atlantic Highlands, N.J.: Humanities Press, 1980).

VEBLEN, T. B. *The Theory of Leisure Class* (New York: The Macmillan Co., 1899).

___ *The Theory of Business Enterprise* (New York, 1904).

VYGODSKI, V. S. *The Story of a Great Discovery*, translated by C. S. V. Salt (Berlin: Verlag die Wirtschaft, 1973).

WAGNER, A. *Lehrbuch der Politischen Ökonomie* (Leipzig: Winter, 1879).

WALRAS, M. E. L. *Elements of Pure Economics* (1874), translated by W. Jaffé (London: Allen & Unwin, 1954).

WEBER, M. *The Protestant Ethic and the Spirit of Capitalism* (1904–5), translated by T. Parsons (London: George Allen & Unwin, 1930).

___ 'Die "Objektivität" Sozialwissenschaftlicher und Sozial Politischer Erkenntnis', *Archiv fur Sozialwissenschaft und Sozialpolitik* XIX (1904).

WEEKS, J. 'The Process of Accumulation and the "Profit Squeeze" Hypothesis', *Science and Society*, XLII–3 (Fall 1979).

WILBRANDT, R. *Karl Marx: Versuch einer Würdigung* (Leipzig and Berlin: B. G. Teubner, 4 Aufl., 1920).
WINTERNITZ, J. 'Values and Prices: A Solution of the So-called Transformation Problem', *Economic Journal* (June 1948).
YAFFE, D. 'The Marxian Theory of Crisis, Capital and the State', *Bulletin of the Conference of Socialist Economists* (Winter 1972).
—— 'Value and Price in Marx's *Capital*, *Revolutionary Communist*, 1 (Jan 1975).
YAMADA, K. [*A Critique of Controversy on the Theory of Rent*] (Tokyo: Doyu-Sha, 1948).
YAMAGUCHI, S. [*Competition and Commercial Capital*] (Tokyo: Iwanami-Shoten, 1983).

# Index

*Note*: Even where there is a grouped series of references to the item, only the initial page is indicated.